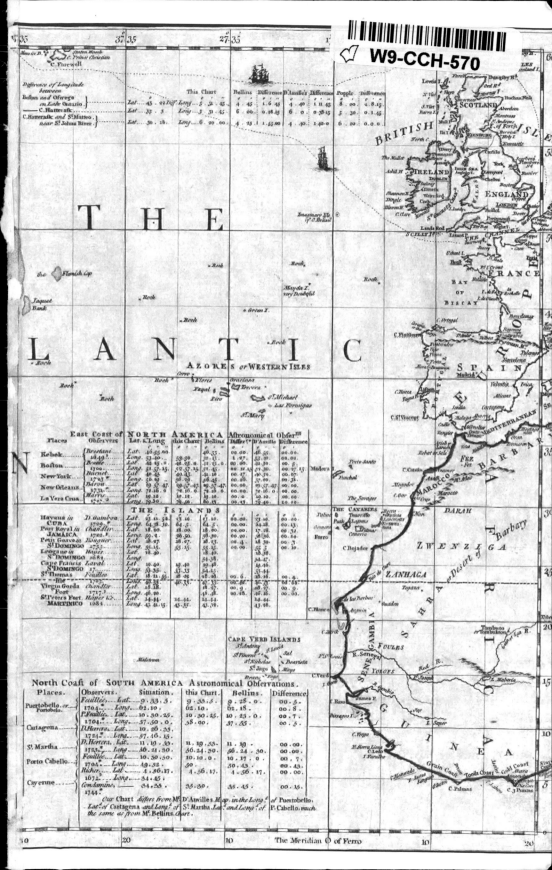

Revolutions without Borders

Revolutions without Borders

The Call to Liberty in the Atlantic World

JANET POLASKY

Yale UNIVERSITY PRESS

New Haven & London

Published with assistance from the foundation established in memory of Amasa Stone Mather of the Class of 1907, Yale College.

Published with assistance from the Annie Burr Lewis Fund.

Endpapers map courtesy of Yale Sterling Memorial Library Map Collection.

Yale University Press books may be purchased in quantity for educational, business, or promotional use. For information, please e-mail sales.press@ yale.edu (U.S. office) or sales@yaleup.co.uk (U.K. office).

Designed by James J. Johnson.
Set in Garamond type by IDS Infotech, Ltd.
Printed in the United States of America.

Library of Congress Control Number: 2014030322
ISBN 978-0-300-20894-8 (cloth : alk. paper)

A catalogue record for this book is available from the British Library.

This paper meets the requirements of ANSI/NISO Z39.48-1992 (Permanence of Paper).

10 9 8 7 6 5 4 3 2 1

FOR MY ADVISERS,

Professors Carl Weiner,
Carleton College,

and the late

Gordon Wright,
Stanford University,

border crossers who challenged their students to
venture forth in new directions

Contents

Illustrations

Dramatis Personae

ADAMS, JOHN. American revolutionary and founding father who spent time engaged in diplomatic service in Europe.

AELDERS, ETTA PALM D'. Born in the United Provinces, she traveled to the center of revolutionary politics in Paris, where she established the first women's club.

BARBÉ-MARBOIS, FRANÇOIS, MARQUIS DE. French consul in Philadelphia who did not fare well in the Caribbean.

BARLOW, JOEL AND RUTH. Connecticut poet–turned–European businessman, and his wife, who shared his correspondence.

BARTHÉLEMY, FRANÇOIS. French diplomat with experience in Stockholm, Vienna, and London, who accepted a post as minister plenipotentiary to the Swiss cantons.

BELLEY, JEAN-BAPTISTE. Former slave who sailed with the tricolor delegation from Saint-Domingue to France by way of the United States.

BICKER, JAN. Dutch banker who fled the United Provinces with his family when the Prussians invaded.

BRISSOT, JACQUES-PIERRE. French lawyer, pamphleteer, journalist, outspoken abolitionist, and revolutionary. Author of *The Philadelphian in Geneva*, he witnessed three revolutions.

CAPELLEN TOT DEN POL, JOAN DERK VAN DER. Dutch aristocrat, revolutionary, and author of the 1782 pamphlet *An Address to the People of the Netherlands*.

CARTWRIGHT, JOHN. Prominent British supporter of the American revolutionaries who led the Society for Constitutional Information.

CÉRISIER, ANTOINE. French-born Dutch journalist whose "pen erected a monument to the American cause more glorious and more durable than brass or marble," in the words of John Adams.

CLARKSON, JOHN. Recruited from the navy to accompany black loyalists from Nova Scotia to Sierra Leone, where he served as their governor.

CLARKSON, THOMAS. Leading British abolitionist, who traveled to Paris on mission to invigorate the sparsely attended Society of the Friends of Blacks.

CLAVIÈRE, ÉTIENNE. Wealthy banker and senior statesman of the Genevan Revolution who joined Mirabeau's workshop and collaborated with Brissot in Paris.

CLOOTS, [JEAN-BAPTISTE] ANARCHARSIS. Prussian-born Dutch aristocrat and self-proclaimed orator of humanity who died by the guillotine in France.

COBBETT, WILLIAM. Federalist editor of *Porcupine's Gazette*, which condemned the Jacobins in France and the Republicans in America.

CONDORCET, NICOLAS DE. French philosopher and author of *Letters of a Citizen of the United States to a Frenchman*.

CRÈVECOEUR [OTTO], AMÉRICA FRANCÈS DE. Daughter of Saint John de Crèvecoeur, she married Louis Otto and moved to Europe.

CRÈVECOEUR, SAINT JOHN DE. Son of a French nobleman who fought for the British in Canada and defined his identity during the American Revolution as a New York farmer in the widely read *Letters from an American Farmer*.

CUGOANO, QUOBNA OTTOBAH. Abducted from a Fante village, he published a blistering attack on the slave trade.

DAWES, WILLIAM. Former governor of penal colony of Botany Bay, who replaced John Clarkson in command of Sierra Leone.

DEKEN, AAGJE. Dutch writer and Betje Wolff's partner and collaborator.

DESMOULINS, CAMILLE. Editor of *Révolutions de France et de Brabant*, who was sent to the guillotine by his friend Robespierre.

DUMAS, CHARLES. Frenchman born in a German principality who yearned to represent the newly independent Americans in the United (Dutch) Provinces.

DUMONT, ÉTIENNE. Genevan revolutionary who took exile in Saint Petersburg and London before settling outside of Paris and joining Mirabeau's circle.

DUMOURIEZ, CHARLES. Girondin general and French foreign minister who led troops into the Austrian Netherlands and the United Provinces before falling from favor.

EQUIANO, OLAUDAH. Former slave who purchased his freedom and led the "poor blacks" of London. He wrote the influential *Interesting Narrative of the Life of Olaudah Equiano or Gustavus Vassa the African*, recounting his travels back and forth across the Atlantic.

FALCONBRIDGE ANNA MARIA. Traveled to Sierra Leone with her new husband as the first European woman to chronicle her adventures among the settlers of West Africa.

FÖRSTER, GEORG. Chronicled voyage with Captain Cook and subsequent travels through revolutionary Europe. He founded the Jacobin Club in Mainz.

FRANKLIN, BENJAMIN. American printer, diplomat, and inventor, he came to represent America to the French.

GEORGE, DAVID. Escaped his Virginia master and founded the first black Baptist church in America before emigrating to Nova Scotia and Sierra Leone.

HARDY, THOMAS. Scottish cobbler who gathered together tradesmen in the London Corresponding Society, an association that supported the French Revolution.

HARPE, FRÉDÉRIC-CÉSAR DE LA. Lausanne lawyer and tutor to grandsons of Catherine the Great of Russia who advised French Directory on Swiss policies.

HAYS, MARY. English novelist befriended by William Godwin and Mary Wollstonecraft, and author of *Memoirs of Emma Courtney*, a semiautobiographical tale of unrequited love.

HOCHE, LAZARE. French general and Bonaparte's rival who sailed from France in 1796 aboard the *Indomitable* to foment revolution in Ireland.

HORNE TOOKE, JOHN. Leader of the London Society for Constitutional Information, which met in his solicitor's quarters in Chancery Lane.

HUGUES, VICTOR. Son of a Marseille baker who sailed and traded in the Caribbean and served as judge in revolutionary France before arriving in Saint-Domingue to retake the island for the French.

HUMBERT, JEAN-JOSEPH. French general who invaded Ireland unsuccessfully.

IVERNOIS, FRANÇOIS. Genevan revolutionary who attempted to negotiate with the French in 1782 and 1792.

JACKSON, WILLIAM. Anglican clergyman who published American state constitutions in Britain, traveling to Ireland on a French mission to stir up revolution.

JOHN FREDERICK. Son of Prince Naimbana who was sent to London to be educated and died on his return to Sierra Leone.

KING, BOSTON. Raised as a slave on a South Carolina plantation, he emigrated as a Methodist preacher with black loyalists first to Nova Scotia and then to Sierra Leone.

KOŚCIUSZKO, THADDEUS. Polish hero of the American Revolution who led an uprising in Poland in 1791. Imprisoned in Russia, he tried to retire in Philadelphia, but ended up in Europe.

LAFAYETTE, MARIE-JOSEPH PAUL YVES ROCH GILBERT DU MOTIER, MARQUIS DE. Fought in the American and French revolutions. Gave Thomas Paine the key to the Bastille to present to George Washington.

LEBRUN, PIERRE. Editor in Liège of the *Journal général d'Europe*, he served as French foreign minister from 1792 to 1793.

LIVINGSTON, HENRY BEEKMAN. Son of a prominent New York family and husband of Nancy Shippen.

MACAULAY, ZACHARY. Governor of Sierra Leone settlement.

MALLET DU PAN, JACQUES. Genevan journalist whose work inspired Brissot to write a history of the Genevan Revolution of 1782.

MARAT, JEAN-PAUL. Jacobin editor of *L'Ami du Peuple* who dubbed himself "father of the clubs."

MAZZEI, FILIPPO. Tuscan merchant who lived for a time next door to Thomas Jefferson in Virginia before accepting a post as the Polish king's emissary in Paris during the French Revolution.

MERCIER, LOUIS-SÉBASTIEN. Author of the prophetic utopian novel *L'An 2440*, which foretold the rise of the slaves' avenger.

MIRABEAU, HONORÉ GABRIEL RIQUETI, COMTE DE. French revolutionary writer, journalist, and statesman who supported a constitutional monarchy and was an avid abolitionist.

MIRANDA, FRANCISCO. Venezuelan general who fought for Spain, assisted George Washington in the American Revolution, and led two campaigns for independence in South America.

MOREAU DE SAINT-MÉRY, LOUIS ELIE. Lawyer born in Martinique who practiced at Cap Français and in Paris before being elected president of the Electors of Paris.

NAPOLÉON BONAPARTE. French military leader whose success on the battlefields of the Italian peninsula propelled him onto the political stage.

NOOT, HENRI VAN DER. Lawyer to the Brabant Estates who led the Belgian revolutionaries in reestablishing the power of the traditional orders after expelling the Austrians in December 1789.

OCHS, PETER. Swiss president under the Directory who told Bonaparte, "The Revolution is done."

OGÉ, VINCENT. Free man of color who was denied seating by the National Assembly in Paris in 1789 and returned to lead an armed revolt in Saint-Domingue in 1790.

OTTO, LOUIS. German-born French diplomat who courted Nancy Shippen and married América Francès de Crèvecoeur.

PAAPE, GERRIT. Dutch revolutionary and self-proclaimed "human book factory" who fled to France after the Prussians crushed the Dutch Patriot Revolution.

PAINE, THOMAS. British emigrant whose pamphlet *Common Sense* contributed to the American Revolution. He joined the French Revolution, too, before returning to America after writing *The Rights of Man*.

PETERS, THOMAS. Freed slave and leader of the black loyalists in Sierra Leone.

POLVEREL, ÉTIENNE. French commissioner to Saint-Domingue.

PRICE, RICHARD. Welsh philosopher and Unitarian minister whose pamphlet *Observations on the Nature of Civil Liberty* was addressed to British and American readers.

RAIMOND, JULIEN. Grandson of indigo planters in Saint-Domingue who represented the interests of the free people of color in Paris before the French Revolution.

RAYNAL, ABBÉ GUILLAUME-THOMAS. His *Histoire philosophique des deux Indes* was one of the most widely read travel journals written by someone who did not travel.

ROCHEFOUCAULD, ALEXANDRINE CHARLOTTE SOPHIE DE ROHAN-CHABOT, DUCHESSE DE LA. Wife of a member of the liberal nobility who lived outside of Paris and corresponded with William Short.

ROUSSEAU, JEAN-JACQUES. Genevan philosopher whose novels defined roles for women within the family. Known today more for his *Second Discourse on Inequality* and *Social Contract*.

ROWAN, ARCHIBALD HAMILTON. Founding member of the United Irishmen, he aided Wolfe Tone in preparing for an Irish revolution before escaping from prison, bound first for France and then the United States.

SECRÉTAN, PHILIPPE. Genevan tutor arrested in 1789 in Brussels by the Austrians as a Brabant Revolutionary. He was named president of the Helvetic Republic in 1798.

SHARP, GRANVILLE. Early British abolitionist and one of the founders of the colony of free blacks, Sierra Leone.

SHIPPEN, NANCY. Daughter of a prominent Philadelphia family who was courted by Louis Otto but married the more eligible bachelor Henry Livingston.

SHORT, WILLIAM. "Adopted son" and secretary to Thomas Jefferson in Paris, who was torn between a career in America and romantic interest in Europe.

SONTHONAX, LEGER FELICITÉ. French commissioner to Saint-Domingue who in August 1793 in the Northern Province proclaimed: "Men are born free and equal in rights."

STANISLAS AUGUST PONIATOWSKI. Last king of Poland, who oversaw the writing of the Polish Constitution of 1791.

TONE, THEOBOLD WOLFE. Anglican lawyer who led the United Irishmen and lobbied the French to support an uprising in Ireland.

TOUSSAINT LOUVERTURE. Free man of color who abandoned the Spanish to fight for the French in Saint-Domingue.

WATSON, ELKANAH. American entrepreneur whose journals documented his travels through prerevolutionary Europe.

WILLIAMS, HELEN MARIA. English poet who sympathetically described the French Revolution for readers in her multivolume *Letters Written in France*.

WOLFF, BETJE. Dutch novelist, author of *Sara Burgerhart*, who sought exile in provincial France before returning to the newly established Dutch republic.

WOLLSTONECRAFT, MARY. English author of the *Vindication of the Rights of Woman* and of the novels *Maria* and *Mary*, who took up residence in Paris during the French Revolution.

Revolutions without Borders

MAP I

The Atlantic World, 1776. Map by Bill Nelson

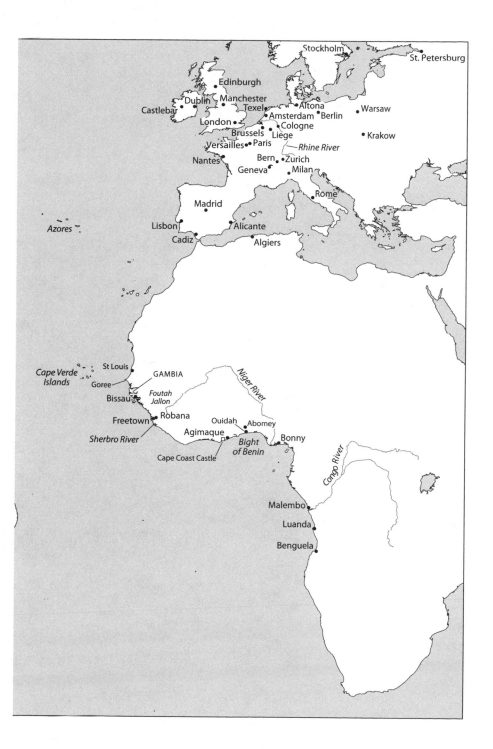

Introduction:
Revolution without Borders

In 1779, a young American apprentice named Elkanah Watson set off from Boston for Paris to deliver funds and correspondence to Benjamin Franklin, who was serving the American Revolution as ambassador to France. Watson was no stranger to revolution. Since the beginning of the War for Independence, he had carried letters to George Washington, armed and sailed an old fishing schooner to rescue American patriots held captive in Boston by the British, and smuggled money, sewn into his quilted jacket, to provision the army in South Carolina. After his rendezvous with Franklin in Paris, Watson remained in Europe until 1784, long enough to witness the stirring of revolution across the continent. He learned that the Dutch revolutionaries, like the Americans a decade earlier, considered themselves God's chosen people. Watson's travels abroad put national pride in perspective. Unlike his compatriots who "only vegetated beneath the smoke of their native land," he had discovered "new faces, new objects, strange customs and languages."[1] He returned to his home in America a believer in the promise of revolution on the other side of the Atlantic, as in the Americas.

In the decades after the American Revolution, freed slaves, poets, and philosophers took to the roads of America, Europe, and Africa and the sea lanes of the Atlantic and the Mediterranean in search of liberty. Some of these transatlantic travelers sought to spread the American Revolution, others to escape its consequences in the new republic that permitted slavery. Many of these revolutionary travelers were chased into exile by invading armies that crushed their rebellions. Dutch bankers, Polish generals, British poets, and American merchants all were drawn to Paris by the initial salvos of the French Revolution in 1789. Black Americans such as David George and Boston King traveled farther. After escaping their victorious masters, they migrated to Nova Scotia and then journeyed on to Sierra Leone in search of "the Priviledges of Freeman," their quest supported by philanthropic abolitionists and enterprising colonialists.[2] Revolutions made for unexpected allies. They made for more enemies.

One revolutionary traveler, the self-described human "book factory" Gerrit Paape, was forced, disguised under wig and hat, to flee his home in Amsterdam when Prussian armies crushed the Dutch Patriot Revolution in 1787. With just a sleep sack and two false passports, Paape crossed the border into the Austrian Netherlands, where another revolution for liberty was brewing. "For me, the world was completely transformed today," he reflected en route.[3] What could be more enticing, he asked his wife, than to join revolutions that promised to humble aristocrats and to dethrone emperors? Watson, Paape, and countless other revolutionary itinerants were convinced, as Thomas Paine reminded George Washington in October 1789, that "a share in two revolutions is living to some purpose."[4] Paape found a share in four.

"The universal cry of liberty"

Between 1776 and 1804, the possibility of revolution loomed large over four continents. Revolutions were erupting everywhere. "Over half of the globe, all men utter but one cry, they share but one desire," a pamphleteer proclaimed from Brussels. He witnessed "humanity, united in action" all around him, people "rising up to reclaim a majestic and powerful liberty."[5] The call to liberty, he reported, could be heard wherever tyrants oppressed their subjects. It was not just in America and France that revolutions were overturning governments. Revolutions cascaded through all of the continents bordering the Atlantic. From the Americas to Geneva, the Netherlands, Ireland, the Belgian provinces, France, Saint-Domingue, Guadeloupe, Poland, Martinique, Sierra Leone, Italy, Hungary, and Haiti, revolutionaries challenged the privileges of aristocrats, clerics, and monarchs to claim their sovereignty. Sometimes their insurrections founded independent nation-states that endured. Those we remember. More often, revolutionary movements fizzled out and have been largely forgotten. Empires threatened by change also intervened to snuff out the flames of revolution before they spread, engulfing neighbors. They scattered revolutionaries. Defiant, determined refugees carried latent revolutions into exile in the form of pamphlets and other documents.

The founding fathers of the small set of revolutions we commemorate did not conceive of freedom in isolation. The Atlantic world had never been as tightly interconnected as at the end of the eighteenth century, when Tuscan merchant Filippo Mazzei, Thomas Jefferson's Virginia neighbor, served as the Polish king's liaison in Paris, or when Anna Falconbridge, the wife of a British abolitionist who founded Freetown in Sierra Leone, recounted her encounters among the Temne people. Fifty years before red flags above the barricades announced the revolutions of 1848 and almost a century before the Socialists of the Second International assembled in Paris to debate a common strategy, revolutionaries throughout the Atlantic world staked their claim to the rights of man. Two centuries before the Arab Spring, without social media or even an international postal system, revolutionaries shared ideals of liberty and equality across entire continents. Theirs, too, was an international movement connected by ideas that traveled.

No single all-encompassing vision united all of the eighteenth-century revolutionaries from four continents into a common party. They were not all democrats, nor even all supporters of republics. In a time of upheaval so turbulent that anything seemed possible, no simple dichotomies divided revolutionaries from counterrevolutionaries, or even radicals from conservatives. Modern divisions based on twentieth-century categories do not capture the full range of compelling plans for a new world to be built on the ruins of an old order.[6] A Dutch pastor's wife writing a novel in a thatched garden shed will have defined liberty differently than did a free man of color storming Grand-Rivière at the head of a hastily mustered militia. They never met at a formally convened congress and rarely signed the same petition. Some of the paths of traveling revolutionaries that did cross were no less unlikely. Ideas entangled, connecting seemingly contradictory movements.[7]

Most of these eighteenth-century revolutionaries would have understood what French lawyer-turned-philosopher Jacques-Pierre Brissot meant when he alluded to "le cri universel de la liberté"—the universal cry of liberty.[8] More than contemporary historians of national revolutions, Brissot saw the continuity that linked one movement to another. In the French campaign to abolish slavery and overturn the race-based hierarchy of their Caribbean colony, Saint-Domingue, Brissot heard echoes of the revolutions he had personally witnessed in Geneva, America, and France. Another French philosopher, Nicolas de Condorcet, not so widely traveled himself, traced the progress of this universal cry across the Atlantic as it was relayed among "men whom the reading of books of philosophy had secretly converted to the love of liberty." From the center of Europe to the periphery of the Atlantic world, one people after another "became enthusiastic over liberty abroad while they waited for the moment when they could recover their own."[9] Theirs was an Atlantic Revolution broadly cast.

Revolutionaries from small states, more freely than the large, long-lived revolutions in America and France that bookmark the era, borrowed and incorporated rhetoric, strategy, and political theory from their revolutionary neighbors. In the shadows cast by their larger neighbors, these insurrections functioned as veritable political laboratories. At the crossroads of travel routes in Brussels, as in Warsaw, Amsterdam, and Le Cap, lively debates raged, unencumbered by an Alien and Sedition Act and not restrained by a guillotine. The author of a pamphlet, the *Mercure Flandrico-Latino-Gallico-Belgique*, in the newly independent United States of Belgium, explained, "What might pass elsewhere in any other nation as a ridiculous, mixed-up piece of colored cloth, with the BELGIANS constitutes a useful and amusing variety."[10] Local historical traditions informed an idealistic cosmopolitanism in this now largely forgotten revolution at the center of Europe.

On the periphery of the eighteenth-century Atlantic world, too, revolutionaries incorporated and blended together others' ideas from near and far. A vibrant universalism stoked by disparate experiences often undergirded their ideal of liberty. Traditions of insurgency stoked the rumors that coursed inland from Caribbean harbors. Across the Atlantic, on the west coast of Africa, black loyalists who revolted in Sierra Leone for self-rule claimed a liberty they had witnessed widely in the Americas but never enjoyed. These settlers turned for aid to the indigenous Temne and Mori-Kanu peoples, who had been rebelling over the previous decade against the increasingly harsh terms of enslavement. Labeled thoroughgoing Jacobins by the British, the black loyalists were defeated on the western shore of Sierra Leone by Maroons, former slaves from Jamaica seeking liberty and property themselves.

All of these revolutionaries evoked the ideal of freedom, even if the call to liberty resonated with different accents across the Atlantic world as it evolved from 1776 to 1804. In its most general sense derived from the Enlightenment, in the words of French philosopher Denis Diderot, liberty meant the freedom to enjoy the "true inalienable *natural rights*" of humanity.[11] More often, to revolutionaries and their critics, liberty meant freedom from oppression. In the midst of a transatlantic crossing from a France he found oppressive, the marquis de Lafayette explained his dramatic decision to leave for America in a letter to his wife. "Having to choose between the slavery that everyone believes he has the right to impose upon me, and liberty, which called me to glory, I departed."[12] At the time, slavery meant just the boredom of aristocratic obligations to him, and liberty his reputation. At Washington's side in America, he learned new meanings for both terms. It is in these variations that the sense of possibility in the midst of a rowdy revolutionary era can be discovered.

Utopian dramas written in the midst of the revolutions played out the shared and ever-changing ideals of liberty, equality, and peace for all to see. Tales of time travel reverberated across continents in the years before the revolutions. In one of the most influential utopias, the prolific French philosopher and author Louis Sebastien Mercier, writing in 1770, dispatched a time traveler into a fictional future. His traveler fell asleep after an argument with a philosopher about the old order and woke up, still in Paris, in the year 2440. Guided by a citizen of the new world, the time traveler encountered a towering statue of a black man, "the Avenger of the New World." Around the pedestal of the monument lay twenty shattered scepters of deposed rulers, testimony to the revolution that the traveler's guide said had transformed the world at the end of the eighteenth century, freeing the slaves and restoring natural rights to all citizens. In Mercier's vivid portrait of a postrevolutionary future, set against the backdrop of "the climate, the soil, the water" that all remained the same, eighteenth-century readers glimpsed a world where "the laws have changed, and men with them."[13] Sheer reason had accomplished the utopian transformation.

J'ai sept cent ans .

FIGURE I

Louis Sebastien Mercier, *L'an deux mille quatre cent-quarante: rêve s'il en fût jamais*, 1786. In the frontispiece to Mercier's utopia, the eighteenth-century time traveler to the year 2440 gazes in wonder at the ordinances posted on the wall of an urban center. Courtesy of Houghton Library, Harvard University, 40516.50.10

Taking up Mercier's vision in 1776, Dutch novelist Betje Wolff identified the printing press as her instrument of change that would bring women and men together for revolution. In her version of the year 2440, citizens deliberated in assembly halls, surrounded not by sword-carrying aristocrats but by sailors sauntering on the piers of a prosperous republic at peace.[14] Instead of listening to lengthy sermons on Sundays, presumably delivered by self-righteous pastors like Wolff's own husband, families strolled through vibrant villages. Children studied this New World through their own microscopes and telescopes. Each house had its own library, while the state maintained a massive collection of specialized books on every possible subject. How sublime, Wolff's time traveler exclaimed, to know that mankind had finally discovered universal laws, and that humanity had awakened from its centuries of slumber.

At the end of more than two decades of revolution, Gerrit Paape, who had fled the Netherlands in 1787, published *De Bataafsche Republiek, zo als zij behoord te zijn, en zo als zij weezen kan: of revolutionaire droom in 1798* (The Batavian Republic: A Revolutionary Dream in 1798) to suggest that indeed anything was possible in revolution. The host to his post-revolutionary world reassured his amazed time traveler, "It took much less commotion than you might imagine."[15] Mercier described the process of writing utopias as "*fictionner*," roughly translated as to make fiction, or less literally, to imagine virtuous characters who would populate societies transformed for the better.[16] Philosopher-turned-revolutionary, the marquis de Condorcet explained, "If men could confidently predict what would follow from given principles," then they would act on their dreams.[17] And act they did. Liberty as depicted by the utopias motivated freed American slaves to seek shelter on the rocky coast of Nova Scotia, haunted governors of Caribbean colonies, informed English novelists, and was proclaimed by revolutionary armies marching down the Italian peninsula.

On the eve of his death, former American president and seasoned European traveler John Adams reflected in a letter addressed to his sometime rival and frequent Parisian dinner guest Thomas Jefferson on the revolutions that had completely transformed the world during their lifetime. The real "revolution was in the minds of the people," not on the battlefields of America and Europe.[18] At the end of all of these debates and discussions, some conducted within the confines of the nation-state, but others across borders, people on both sides of the Atlantic understood the world and their place in it totally differently.

"A world in motion"

Today, no one would dispute the obvious fact that ideas travel, revolutionary ideas above all. Protesters in a city park in Istanbul proclaim themselves global citizens, those in Rio de Janeiro declare: "We are the social network." A banner quotes Bertolt Brecht, "Nothing should seem impossible to change." The interconnections of a global society are inescapable. So why assume that founding fathers building new nations out of old worlds lived in isolation through a quarter of a century when revolution loomed, ever present on the horizon?

How, though, did revolutions travel in the eighteenth century before computers or even typewriters, and without planes or even railways? Documents left behind by travelers—evangelical abolitionists, cosmopolitan sons of Temne chiefs, novelists espousing companionate marriage, and politician-defying generals—provide an answer. Their pamphlets, letters, novels, and journals reveal a contentious interconnected struggle for universal human rights that spanned the Atlantic and stretched across continents at the end of the eighteenth century. From small city-states located in the heart of Europe to islands off the coast of West Africa, revolutionaries shared their dreams of a new world, filling in the arc of the Atlantic Revolution between the American and the French revolutions.

Then, as now, revolutionaries and their ideas ignored the national borders that figure so prominently on maps and in history books. From Boston to Le Havre, from Paris to Geneva, from Stockholm to Granville Town in Sierra Leone, from Pisa to Warsaw, and from Malembo to Port au Prince, for twenty-five years, men and women, black and white, charted journeys following the revolutionary currents that felled monarchs and drowned the privileged. Amid shifting empires, in pursuit of unprecedented opportunities, revolutionaries set out on journeys, crossing mountains and seas.[19] Adventurers pursued economic or political ends, most often both. Exiles were chased from home by the armies that crushed their incipient insurrections. Many travelers relied on preexisting networks established by family and commercial connections. Others explored what loomed for them as uncharted territories, bringing their hopes and expectations as luggage with them. Theirs was "a world in motion" not contained within the boundaries of nation-states or empires.[20]

In the second half of the eighteenth century, for the first time in world history, travel was no longer the exclusive domain of the wealthy and titled for whom the Grand Tour completed their claim to culture. It was now open to men and women of at least modest means, even if it was sometimes dangerous and often uncomfortable. That made for disconcerting encounters, especially for Europeans visiting the reportedly egalitarian American middle Atlantic. French diplomats in the years immediately following the American Revolution were unnerved to find themselves sharing tavern benches with stable hands who had just tended to their horses. Journeying in the other direction in the years before the French Revolution, Elkanah Watson was alarmed by the beggars and ruffians who accosted travelers on the highways of rural France. They almost all shared what the freed slave who explored the North Pole, Equiano, called a "roving disposition."[21]

Something set them apart from their friends and family who stayed at home. Travelers saw the world differently, with new eyes as a result of their experiences. Lying awake in their hammocks slung across the deck of the *Sensible*, a young John Quincy Adams and François, marquis de Barbé-Marbois, secretary to the French legation in Philadelphia and future intendant of Saint-Domingue, replayed the keelhauling of a slave on a passing corsair. In her Paris salon, English poet Helen Maria Williams discussed the Festival of the Federation with French Jacobin Maximilien Robespierre, American poet Joel Barlow, German chronicler Georg Forster, Venezuelan revolutionary General Francisco Miranda, and Polish general Thaddeus Kościuszko. Williams explained: "It required but the common feelings of humanity to become in that moment a citizen of the world."[22]

These itinerant revolutionaries, like the Enlightenment philosophers of the "Republic of Letters," aspired to be "strangers nowhere in the world," to quote the philosopher Denis Diderot.[23] They did not deny their attachment to a particular birthplace. Instead, their multiple and ever-shifting allegiances transcended the boundaries of the nation-state. Librarian and chronicler Georg Förster, accused of treason in Prussia, acknowledged that although born in Danzig, he left the then-Polish city before it became Prussian to travel around the world. "Wherever I was, I strove to be a good citizen," he wrote. "I am a good Prussian, in the same way I was a good Turk, Russian, Chinese, and Moroccan."[24] Essential to this cosmopolitanism was a refusal to exclude others.[25]

Many of these revolutionary travelers saw themselves as part of a revolutionary movement cascading from one place to another and leading toward the creation of a world at peace.[26] They recognized that the Americans, French, and Haitians could not stand alone as revolutionary peoples in their interdependent world still dominated by empires in conflict.

Of course, not all itinerants at the end of the eighteenth century were cosmopolitan revolutionaries, nor did experience abroad always radicalize revolutionaries. A case in point is William Cobbett, the British editor of the widely read American newspaper *Porcupine's Gazette*. Cobbett had sought discharge from the British army after service in Nova Scotia. He fled England after lodging accusations of military corruption against his superiors, arrived in France to witness the massacre of the Swiss Guard at the Tuileries in August 1792, and sailed to America later that year as a refugee in search of liberty. He returned to England in 1800 a loyal patriot and a conservative. He wanted nothing more to do with the "*liberty*, of which, out of its infinite variety of sorts, yours unfortunately happens to be precisely that sort which I do not like," he wrote upon departure from America.[27] The liberty "tainted with democracy" that he had witnessed in revolution alarmed him because it threatened to "flatter and inflame the lower orders of the people."[28]

Alternative Political Sphere

French Jacobin Jean-Paul Marat, a more avid democrat when he returned in 1776 from London than when he left Paris several years earlier, celebrated the dissemination of ideals beyond the political elite, reaching down to the common people. If the tradesmen and artisans "know their rights, they owe this advantage to Philosophy." Marat believed that widely circulated pamphlets and newspapers proclaiming liberty and equality "had removed the blindfold of error imposed by despotism."[29] This alternative political sphere inhabited by the so-called popular classes was a rowdy world full of revolutionary possibilities.[30] Some schemes advanced by political outsiders appear today as far-fetched as Don Quixote tilting at windmills or as futile as Sisyphus rolling his rock up the hill. Others would be adopted decades later as eminently sensible.

Returning from his European travels, Yale graduate Abraham Bishop demanded to know why his fellow Americans would not intervene in Saint-Domingue in 1791 to win "the rights of black men" and were instead among "the first to assist in riveting their chains."[31] The English abolitionist Thomas Clarkson, dining with delegates from Saint-Domingue at the marquis de Lafayette's hotel in Paris, reminded his French hosts that their revolutionary rhetoric would ring hollow if they failed to extend the rights of man to citizens of color in their colonies. Bishop and Clarkson were just two of the travelers who challenged more settled revolutionary leaders to confront questions that might more conveniently have been buried in expedient compromises.

Itinerants viewed "objects comparatively with a foreign eye," in Elkanah Watson's terms.[32] In their confrontations in shifting spaces between new societies, they were exposed to ideas and customs previously foreign to them. As a result, traveling revolutionaries often grasped contradictions inherent in the implementation of the ideals of liberty and equality, both abroad where they alighted and at home when they returned. Their compatriots who stayed at home assumed the choices made by their governments to be natural. They did not see the alternatives. Traveling revolutionaries, exposed to other possibilities, returned home to challenge the perpetuation of slavery in an era of freedom, to probe the limitations of private domesticity in a society where virtue was publicly defined, and to question the national and racial limitations on citizenship imposed by self-proclaimed universal republics.

Grudging though the welcome extended to newcomers was, politics was no longer the exclusive province of the privileged. In March 1793, "the new citizens of Guadeloupe" blamed the "odious faction, enemy of the French Revolution, that misled us about the extent of our rights" as they helped the newly arrived French troops plant trees of liberty.[33] The mix of access to travel and the opening of an alternative political sphere rendered itinerancy revolutionary. Few common travelers would have ventured so far from home earlier in the eighteenth century, nor would they have expected any say within parliaments or the counsel of monarchs. By the age of revolutions, they could make their voices heard, sometimes more readily abroad than at home. They dropped into Jacobin clubs, wrote their own pamphlets and translated others for the press, and sent letters to be read aloud to assembled friends and family. Their ideals reverberated throughout the Atlantic basin.

Revolutions without Borders not only recovers the idealism of these eighteenth-century revolutionaries, but also probes the uncertainty and disappointments they experienced in the search for liberty. Their short-comings, contradictions, and inconsistencies not only were constituent of the transnational revolutions that upended the Atlantic world at the end of the eighteenth century, they endure as testimony to the daring of its vision. This is a history of the variety of visions from an era when anything seemed possible. Ignored by historians focusing on the big two or three national revolutionaries, America, France, and Haiti, ideals and schemes spun at the crossroads or on the periphery of the Atlantic Revolution also changed our world, even if they did not establish a nation-state that has endured to the present.

History doesn't repeat itself, but historians do. Having privileged successful revolutions, we look for our founding fathers' plans for democracies everywhere in every subsequent upheaval, from Romania to Egypt. We are then inevitably frustrated. Without an understanding of the rich variety of revolutionary possibility in the past, we are condemned to judge the present through the blinders of a limited set of national narratives. Searching for new exceptional national revolutions, we neglect the men, women, and children of the Arab Spring who struggled, but who will not be cast as the heroes of a new democracy. *Revolutions without Borders* reminds us that revolutions travel easily across national borders and that many roads have led in different directions, not straight to the present.

At the end of the eighteenth century, only the rare revolutionary defining citizenship could imagine extending the vote to women, but some philosophers such as the marquis de Condorcet did.[34] A few more lent their voices to the campaign for the abolition of slavery. Although most of the revolutionaries demanding their rights on both sides of the

Atlantic advocated the gradual emancipation of those in chains, others owned slaves themselves. Many revolutionaries in central and eastern Europe settled for compromises with the nobility; the Polish hero of the American revolutionary war, Thaddeus Kościuszko, for example, preserved serfdom in revolutionary Poland. Some revolutionaries looked to kings to restore rights, while others brazenly denounced monarchy. Some looked to Christianity for salvation, while others denounced all religious practice as fanaticism.

Absent in *Revolutions without Borders* are the deeds and writings of most of the now famous but stationary figures from the American and French revolutions. Many of the revolutionaries who are included, conversely, could not make a convincing claim for their lasting fame. Lots of them were previously disenfranchised, newcomers venturing into politics for the first time. Their ideas often appear to us to be full of contradictions, neither traditional nor progressive. From out-of-the-way places or uprooted in the midst of their struggles, these travelers defined paths not always taken into the present. Overturning an old world is inevitably messy. That their ideas for moving forward were not always echoed in subsequent eras, however, made them no less significant in their own time.

Documents with Legs

Revolution traveled at the end of the eighteenth century because pamphlets and newspapers, novels and letters, and even rumors had legs. Revolutionaries, from founding fathers to insurgents, invested the printed word with unprecedented powers of persuasion; written documents carried weight. They were also portable. Some could be carried in a pocket, others posted on a wall or read in a coffee shop. Long after the revolutions have passed, they survive as evidence of public discussions of revolutionary liberty that crossed borders. They convey the magic of a past that would otherwise be unknowable. These documents form the foundation of *Revolutions without Borders*.

A few of the revolutionaries whose posted letters and widely disseminated pamphlets are included in this book stayed in one place themselves. Nancy Shippen, the duchesse de Rochefoucauld, the marquis de Condorcet, and Joan Derk van der Capellen served as conduits, often literally translating the work they received from others abroad, sometimes trying to cope with conflicting customs imposed by itinerants, and other times purposefully speeding along the transfer of ideas to new places. Translation was an important skill, as few men and fewer women had mastered all of the languages spoken around the Atlantic basin. Most of these "static" revolutionaries operated outside of formal institutions, and all helped transplant transnational ideas.

In following trails left by the itinerants ranging over four continents, *Revolutions without Borders* brings to the fore the archival work of the historian. Besides telling a good story, it demonstrates how historians use sources. On exhibit in the following chapters are pamphlets that were originally written in Dutch and collected for John Adams and newspapers translated from Polish for Jacobins in Paris. Many of the documents on which this history is based have never been published. The remnants of many of the protests had been relegated to the realm of rumors, now to be read only between the lines of official correspondence.

In each of the nine chapters in *Revolutions without Borders*, I pursue a different set of documents, most generated in the alternative political sphere beyond the official institutions of government. Pamphlets are the subject of the first chapter, memoirs and narratives of the second and third, newspapers and clubs of the fourth, rumors of the fifth, novels of the sixth, family correspondence of the seventh, and diplomatic correspondence of the eighth chapter. The chapters make transparent the use of sources for asking questions and deploying evidence as it was understood in the eighteenth century. In the second and third chapters I ask what distinguishes the perspective of journals written on the spot from narratives compiled for publication years later. In the fifth chapter I show how historians read rumors "against the grain," in the seventh chapter how seemingly sentimental letters can be read "between the lines."[35] How, I ask, do historians read novels, the subject of the sixth chapter? Do they reflect or recast families during revolutions? Can it be both simultaneously?

Although not a chronological survey of all of the revolutions constituent of the Atlantic Revolution, the narrative of *Revolutions without Borders* moves forward chronologically in its exploration of geographically dispersed revolutions, small and short-lived as well as large. The first chapter begins with the American Revolution in 1776 and the last chapter ends with the Haitian Revolution in 1804. The pamphlets of the first chapter are American, Genevan, Dutch, and Belgian; the rumors of the fifth chapter from the Caribbean; and finally the diplomatic correspondence of the eighth chapter is French, German, Italian, Irish, and Haitian. The history begins in 1776 with the American Revolution, and ends in 1804 with Haitian independence. That is not to suggest the insignificance of debates leading up to the American War for Independence. Ideas have roots and revolutionaries are influenced by their forebears. Nor does it mark an end to revolutions in the Atlantic world. The leaders of juntas and movements for independence in the two decades after 1804 traced connections back to earlier revolutionary decades. A second revolutionary period began in 1808 and extended, once again, on both sides of the Atlantic to 1848.[36]

A few of the sources for *Revolutions without Borders* are as familiar as Thomas Paine's *Common Sense* or Abigail Adams's letters to her husband, John. Other revolutionary remnants have collected dust in ancestors' attics or in municipal archives.[37] Finding them has been its own story. For example, in contrast to her well-known father's letters, collected in official depositories including the Library of Congress, and her husband's diplomatic correspondence, carefully catalogued in the archives of the French Ministry of Foreign Affairs, América Francès de Crèvecoeur Otto had all but disappeared from the historical record, other than the certificates of her birth and her marriage. The family of the Boston merchant who rescued her as a child from snow drifts in upstate New York apparently once possessed letters sent to them from Paris and Vienna by América Francès, the new wife of Louis Otto. They had gone missing.[38] Queries sent to local archives in New England retrieved several letters in Connecticut referring to her convalescence from a mysterious accident or illness, after the rescue and before her marriage.

In contrast to the voluminous and partially published correspondence from Louis Otto's earlier but unsuccessful courtship of Nancy Shippen, no letters between América Francès and Louis Otto, who was often dispatched on diplomatic missions, were to be found in any of the obvious repositories on either side of the Atlantic. The only trace led to a great-great-nephew who was reported to have showed a set of letters to the editor of Otto's diplomatic correspondence. They then disappeared without a trace. Finally, at the Library of Congress, an incredibly helpful librarian adopted my cause as her own and found a note in her files suggesting that Crèvecoeur family papers had been put up for sale in 1976, but at a price too high for archives on either side of the Atlantic, so they were sold off at private auction. Eventually, an Internet search revealed that the French Ministry of Foreign Affairs had recently acquired a few letters.

Once located, these letters between América Francès de Crèvecoeur Otto and Louis Otto testify to the expectations and disillusionment in what they imagined as a revolution without borders. In their world, as in those that followed, revolutions of all sizes had varied, unpredicted outcomes. The documents that crossed borders are evidence of the Atlantic Revolution, dead ends, unrealized dreams of liberty, and forays into a new world where "the laws have changed, and men [and women] with them."

Some of the revolutionary travelers venturing out into this rowdy world are well known. None is as venerated as that irascible son of an English corset maker who called on Americans to use their common sense. Thomas Paine's best-selling pamphlet guaranteed his place in American history. The other subjects of *Revolutions without Borders* were adventurers, too, who fortunately left us documents that tell those stories well.

ONE

"The cause of all mankind" in Revolutionary Pamphlets

A traveler returning home to Geneva a few years after the battles of Lexington and Concord was amazed by the veritable "brochure mania" that had seized his small city-state.[1] Within days of an armed skirmish, printing presses had churned out hundreds of pamphlets assaulting the governing councils of Geneva, many of the handbills framed in terms of individual sovereignty secured in Philadelphia. A few years later, first in the United Provinces of the Netherlands in 1787 and then in the Belgian provinces, lawyers, clerics, and the occasional philosopher launched another barrage of brochures denouncing the rule of tyrants and asserting the sovereign rights of independent peoples. The American War for Independence of 1776 was but the first of the cascading Atlantic revolutions.

Pamphlets, not muskets, ignited the revolutions that swept through America and Europe at the end of the eighteenth century. Written in Philadelphia coffeehouses, hawked on the streets of Geneva, and reprinted by Amsterdam booksellers, these documents defined the transgressions of tyrants as they called the people to rebellion. The rhetoric of freedom traveled on folded sheaves, often small enough to hide in a pocket. Transported, read, and debated in North America, Geneva, the United Provinces of the Netherlands, and the Belgian provinces, few were as bold and none were as widely read as Thomas Paine's, but like *Common Sense*, they roused their readers to revolution.

In 1776, Paine, like the pamphleteers he inspired on both sides of the Atlantic over the next two decades, deployed "language as plain as the alphabet . . . to make those that can scarcely read understand."[2] His was a readership largely unaccustomed to the world of politics. In uncompromising prose, Paine made his argument for American independence to farmers and merchants as well as members of Congress, caricaturing

British King George as "a worm, who in the midst of his splendor is crumbling into dust."[3] The forty-six pages of *Common Sense*, written, rewritten, and written again in Paine's rooms above Robert Aitken's bookshop on Front Street in Philadelphia and in noisy coffeehouses nearby, found their way into the hands of readers, some in positions of power, but more not. This network extended not only up and down the East Coast, it crossed the Atlantic. William Carmichael, aspiring to diplomatic service, pocketed *Common Sense* to give to Charles Dumas, a French immigrant born in the German principality of Ansbach and living in The Hague. From there, Paine's call to revolution resonated among small republics and monarchies from Edinburgh to Warsaw, challenging the reigns of foreign emperors and the privileges of aristocratic orders. "In this century when sovereigns force their subjects to submit to the yoke of despotism," the call for liberty could be read everywhere," a countess, Anne Thérèse Philippine d'Yve, proclaimed in her pamphlet published in Brussels, the capital of the Austrian Netherlands.[4]

For more than a hundred years, pamphlets had proved an ideal medium for disseminating messages of protest. These unbound booklets of printers' sheets, folded and stitched together without a cover, were published cheaply wherever there was a printing press and a cause. In the last decades of the eighteenth century, pamphlets, running the gamut from short poems in rhyming verse to theoretical treatises, some eight pages, others fifty-two, carried ideas across the Atlantic. Their crossings, like the revolutionaries who transported them, extended in both directions. In the 1770s, American pamphleteers quoted liberally from the philosophers of the European Enlightenment—Locke, Rousseau, Voltaire, Montesquieu, and Hume, among others—who had viewed the American wilderness as a blank slate on which to sketch the natural rights of man. American revolutionaries eagerly embraced this European vision of the exceptional promise of their primeval wilderness. A decade later, Genevan, Dutch, and Belgian insurgents, in turn, modeled their calls to arms on those of the victorious American patriots. They cast their struggles for sovereignty in the 1780s in the language of American liberty.

Monarchs and their ministers were as frightened by the discovery of a stack of new pamphlets as by the unearthing of a cache of arms. These small documents with their inflammatory rhetoric could be concealed in a closed hand and readily passed along. In 1787, an informant alerted Austrian spies to the identity of Brussels pamphleteers whose words incited villagers to revolt against their Austrian rulers. Austrian soldiers raided the house of a wine merchant in the center of Brussels, seized stacks of pamphlets, and, on the emperor's orders, set them ablaze in the Grand Place. Before they went up in smoke, these revolutionary pamphlets drew readers, some literate, others not, into debates and discussions that resonated in the streets and cafés far beyond the benches of parliament and the seats of government.

Annotations scribbled in the margins of the revolutionary pamphlets that survive today in libraries and archives reveal a chain of engaged readers on both sides of the Atlantic. This alternative political sphere entangled ideas of liberty ranging from grievances against hereditary despots living far away to visions of a new world of individual sovereignty. The French journalist Camille Desmoulins, later dispatched to the guillotine by his friend the Jacobin Maximilien Robespierre, marveled at the free exchange of revolutionary ideas in the small states at the center of Europe. Opposing ideas battled openly in the Belgian provinces, he wrote, truly "the land of the pamphlet."[5] That would not be as true in revolutionary France, where the concentrated political power and ever-present guillotine inhibited debate.

These pamphlets that readily crossed borders, oceans, and mountains linked the revolutions, small and large, short-lived and enduring. Wherever they alighted, the pamphlets forged constituencies of like-minded though often far-flung revolutionaries. The readers of *Common Sense* from Philadelphia to The Hague discovered an abstract liberty that called them to a shared revolutionary cause. At the beginning of the revolutionary era, John Adams, happy that he "had been sent into life at a time when the greatest lawgivers of antiquity would have wished to live," worried about the effect "so popular a pamphlet [as *Common Sense*] might have among the people."[6] He understood that it was in this alternative sphere of politics, the international network of individuals traveling outside the national institutions where Adams governed, that pamphlets resonated.

Paine's *Common Sense*: "We have it in our power to begin the world over again"

In 1775, the outspoken Philadelphia physician, philanthropist, and abolitionist Benjamin Rush envisioned a pamphlet that ventured far "beyond the ordinary short and cold addresses of newspaper publications" in its uncompromising proclamation of American rights and its resounding condemnation of British rule.[7] Rush would have written the argument for American independence himself, but many patients had left his care after the publication of his abolitionist tract a few years earlier. Instead he gave the assignment to an audacious young itinerant and part-time journalist, Thomas Paine, whom he had met at Robert Aitken's bookshop. Thirty-eight years old, Paine had weathered two short-lived marriages, two stints at sea, an apprenticeship in corset making, the bankruptcy of a tobacco goods store, and dismissal from positions as a government tax collector and a teacher.

Paine had come to America from England in search of employment, a letter of introduction from Benjamin Franklin in hand. He landed in Philadelphia, sick with what was probably typhus. Nevertheless, the English radical exulted: "Those who are conversant with Europe would be tempted to believe that even the air of the Atlantic disagrees with the constitution of foreign vices. There is a happy something in the climate of America which disarms them of all their power of infection and attraction."[8] In his optimism, he echoed any number of European exiles who had already arrived in American harbors and armchair philosophers like the widely read Abbé Guillaume-Thomas Raynal, who could only imagine this virgin land of forests and rocky coasts peopled by self-sufficient farmers and their families.

Writing did not come easily to Paine. Franklin furnished Paine copies of British treatises on liberty to consider. Paine cast aside these polite but often abstruse philosophical arguments. Instead, he chose to write in a clear, straightforward prose for all to read. No long sentences or classical references would get in the way of his argument for American independence. Rush struggled to find a publisher willing to take on the incendiary pamphlet. Philadelphia bookseller Robert Bell finally agreed to print the pamphlet intended for a wide audience in 1776, but only on the following

FIGURE I.I

Portrait of Thomas Paine, author of *Common Sense*. Portrait by James Watson,
copied from the original by Charles Wilson Peale. Henry Laurens commissioned
the portrait in 1779 to take with him to the United Provinces to raise money for
the Continental Congress. The portrait was seized by the British when they
captured Laurens at sea and has disappeared. It was acquired by a Paine admirer
who engraved it in 1783, and made it available to other admirers of *Common
Sense*, though labeled with the name "Edward Payne" instead of Thomas Paine.
By permission of the National Portrait Gallery, Smithsonian Institution,
Washington, D.C.

terms: if *Common Sense* lost money, Paine would pay publication costs himself; if it made a profit, half would go to Bell and the other half to buy mittens for American troops stationed in Canada.

Published anonymously, *Common Sense* fulfilled its author's expectations. Paine, never one to underplay his own achievements, estimated that 120,000 pamphlets were sold between February and May 1776.[9] Some readers speculated that the author, known only as "the Englishman," was Benjamin Rush; others suspected Benjamin Franklin, Thomas Jefferson, or perhaps John Adams, the author of *Novanglus* and no friend of the king. The first thousand copies sold out in a week. Without pausing to consult Paine, Bell printed a second edition. After arguing over profits and production costs, Paine engaged a new publisher for a third edition, which he signed and expanded. These six thousand copies sold for a shilling (a little over five dollars in current value), half the cost of the original edition. Before long, sixteen editions had been published in Philadelphia alone. Each copy sold typically had more than one reader, as it passed from hand to hand in households and on the streets. Whether one-fifth of all colonists read it, as many historians have claimed, no other pamphlet was as instrumental in fomenting revolution.

Benjamin Rush proudly observed that *Common Sense* had "an effect which has rarely been produced by type and paper in any age or country."[10] Delegates lodged in Philadelphia for the Continental Congress sent copies of the pamphlet home to be "lent round" to those still "afraid of the ideas conveyed by the frightful word Independence."[11] By February 1776, Samuel Ward wrote to his brother, "I am told by good judges that two-thirds of this City & Colony are now full in his Sentiments; in the Jerseys & Maryland &c they gain ground daily."[12] From North Carolina, John Penn told the other delegates to the Continental Congress that everyone was talking about "Common Sense and Independence."[13] Travelers carried it from one locale to another throughout the colonies, while other copies arrived by post. Where the pamphlet landed, booksellers set type to reprint it. Paine was particularly pleased that he had reached his intended audience, not just the literary elite with their substantial personal libraries and comfortable reading clubs but "those that can scarcely read." That was what set his pamphlet apart from what had come before.

A resolute republican, Paine set out to persuade Americans to "reject the usurpation" of both king and parliament with his scathing attacks on the powerful and his uncompromising argument for independence. "There is something exceedingly ridiculous in the composition of monarchy," Paine explained, casting the hero of the legendary Battle of Hastings as "a French bastard landing with an armed banditti, and establishing himself king of England against the consent of the natives."[14] The Americans needed no king, he argued; their liberty was their natural right. Press reports that King George had branded the Americans as rebels in his opening address to Parliament gave Paine's characterization credibility.

" 'TIS TIME TO PART." It was just "common sense," Paine told the colonists who drilled on their town commons, but still expected to resolve their grievances peacefully with the mother country. Independence, Paine insisted, a full six months before the Declaration of Independence, "is in reality a self-evident proposition." It was not reasonable that the vast American continent should be ruled by a "small island" on the other side of the Atlantic. Paine was calling for more than a break with England. "We have it in our power to begin the world over again," he assured his new compatriots in what he pictured as "Free and Independent States of America."[15] In this radically different republic, the world would find peace, civilization, and commerce.

Loyalists were quick in their retort. James Chalmers of Charlestown, Maryland, answered Paine's devastating critique of the English monarchy with *Plain Truth*, a forthright defense of the balanced constitution dependent on the crown. Criticizing Paine's "intemperate zeal . . . as injurious to liberty," Chalmers called for "a manly discussion of facts."[16] For him as for Edmund Burke, there was no such thing as abstract liberty. Instead, their liberty was anchored in traditional English principles. The readers of *Plain Truth* looked not to win American independence but instead to secure a British promise to respect individual civil liberties in America as in England.

Readers in England not only followed the discussion of rights in the colonies but jumped into the fray, even when their best interests might have counseled against it. Major John Cartwright published his defense of American natural rights in 1775, *American Independence*. He resigned his naval commission in 1777, acknowledging that his public support of the

American rebels might "possibly be displeasing to Government."[17] In his pamphlet, Cartwright did not envision the actual separation of the colonies from England, but sought reforms that would build the foundation for a "lasting union between our colonies and the mother country." Striving to write in "a plainer and indeed a coarser language . . . for the unrefined, though sensible bulk of the people," he proclaimed in terms less bold than Paine: "The Americans, in common with the whole race of man, have indisputably an inherent right to liberty."[18] Renowned Welsh philosopher and Unitarian minister Richard Price went farther, advancing an even more unapologetic justification of the American rebels in his pamphlet *Observations on the Nature of Civil Liberty* (1776). He blamed Parliament for letting loose "the spirit of despotism and avarice" in the colonies in the form of onerous duties. Their liberty threatened, Price explained, "the people fled immediately to arms and repelled the attack."[19] That was only natural.

Written for readers on both sides of the Atlantic, Price's pamphlet sold sixty thousand copies in just days. In gratitude, the Continental Congress offered Price citizenship if he and his family would emigrate to America. Price replied that although his ideas readily crossed the Atlantic, he could not travel. He regretted that he was too ill to visit "the future asylum for the friends of liberty."[20] So Thomas Paine and a number of Americans, including Benjamin Franklin, Thomas Jefferson, and John Adams, came to visit the English champion of American liberty at his home just north of London.

An aristocrat living in the northeastern reaches of the United Provinces of the Netherlands, Joan Derk van der Capellen translated Price's pamphlet into Dutch.[21] Van der Capellen had already published his own pamphlet asserting that if the American colonies rose up to claim their liberty, European revolution would follow. "The flame that burns in America will spread quickly," he wrote, "engulfing all of Europe, littered as the continent is with flammable material." The tyrannical blunders of despotic emperors, kings, and especially the Dutch stadtholders would provide ample fuel for the insurrections.[22] The Europeans had long suffered under their rulers. The Enlightenment ideals that sparked the rebellion in America would inspire them, especially the seasoned revolutionaries in the United Provinces, to claim their natural rights and to set the old order of

Europe aflame. Van der Capellen's stirring defense of the American revolutionaries and blistering attack on both the British king and Dutch stadtholder found its way into bookshops throughout the United Provinces.

Americans applauded their Dutch defender. Gosuinus Erkelen, a Dutch merchant living in Philadelphia, wrote van der Capellen in July 1777 to announce that he had distributed the pamphlet throughout the war-torn colonies. Erkelen conveyed greetings from the governors of Connecticut and New Jersey, Jonathan Trumbull and William Livingston. Trumbull thanked van der Capellen for his defense of liberty, which the American defined as "ancient and indubitable Rights, immunities & privileges . . . founded upon natural Liberty" and affirmed by royal charter and parliament. "The Cause of Liberty is not peculiar to our free State: it is a common cause," Trumbull asserted. He wrote van der Capellen from his conviction that the "the few other free States which God in his Providence hath preserved from being Swallowed up by Tyranny," could not rest "indifferent" to the destruction of American liberty.[23]

Van der Capellen suggested to his American correspondents that a diplomatic appointment might be fitting compensation for his pamphleteering. "My forefathers have, since time immemorial had a seat in the Corps and Estates of the Nobles," he boasted, "but the trust of the American people means more to me."[24] Van der Capellen hoped, he wrote Livingston, that their extensive transatlantic correspondence would "lead to friendship based on the mutual love of liberty for all the human race."[25] The appointment was not forthcoming. Instead, the colonial governors acknowledged van der Capellen's role in drawing the attention of readers on both sides of the Atlantic to "their common cause . . . the cause of liberty" and asked him to translate their pamphlets advocating the American position into Dutch.[26] Erkelen's mother would pay for the printing of the pamphlets, they promised van der Capellen, but would he please personally distribute them throughout his country. In letters to Price, van der Capellen had confided his dreams of emigrating to Maryland, where friends were launching a commercial venture. When he could not convince his wife that their daughter, who would inherit substantial lands in the United Provinces, would find suitable marriage prospects in America, van der Capellen returned to pamphleteering and translating, lecturing his compatriots "on the parallels between the American Revolution and the seventeenth-century Batavian Revolution."[27] He was often joined by John Adams, who was residing in The Hague trying to get the Dutch to be the first to acknowledge him as an official ambassador from the new republic.

The conservative English political philosopher Edmund Burke hailed that recognition of American independence as the beginning of "a great revolution." It had launched something new, unprecedented, and exceptional. His analysis, which would be echoed by generations of American historians, portrayed this new nation as "a new species, in a new part of the globe." For Burke, the American Revolution had altered politics as much "as the appearance of a new planet would in the system of the solar world."[28] The founding fathers of America had stunned the world with their declaration that all men were "created equal" and "created by their Creator with certain unalienable rights," including "life, liberty, and the pursuit of happiness." What was more, they had proclaimed those truths to be "self-evident."

Dutch, Genevan, and Belgian pamphleteers saw the American Revolution not as exceptional, but as a beacon foreshadowing what was to come in Europe. Was this first revolution fought on the farms and in the forests in the New World really so far removed from the despots of the old world and their mercenary armies, Dutch revolutionaries asked, echoing van der Capellen. They recognized the American ideas of insurrection that traveled freely in pamphlets eastward across the ocean and then from port cities around the European continent. In the smaller states of Europe where grievances had rumbled for decades, discussions of revolutionary commonality clearly overshadowed Burke's allusions to American exceptionalism, beginning in Geneva while the Americans were still fighting for their independence.

Brissot, or "Le Philadelphien" in Geneva: How Liberty Lost Its Only Asylum in Europe

Inspired by all that he read of liberty in America, a restless French lawyer–turned–journalist and aspiring philosopher, Jacques-Pierre Brissot, longed to cross the Atlantic to visit the newly independent republic for himself. As a young man, the thirteenth child of a Chartres tavern keeper,

Brissot had taken up residence in Paris, "the center of science and a stage worthy of his efforts."[29] Threatened there with a lettre de cachet for libel, he fled to England. In 1782, after he failed to raise the funds necessary for a transatlantic voyage, Brissot settled for a shorter journey, to Geneva.

Geneva lay just across the border from France. "I could not have chosen a more favorable time for understanding the energy of the republican spirit," Brissot mused. The disenfranchised poor of the independent city-state with its long republican traditions were demanding the rights of citizenship. Brissot arrived one year into the Genevan Revolution. In this, the first European revolution since the American War for Independence, Brissot expected to observe "man in all his force and dignity as nature made him."[30] Brissot narrated a pamphlet, *Le Philadelphien à Genève ou Lettres d'un Américain sur la dernière révolution de Genève* (The Philadelphian in Geneva, or Letters from an American on the recent revolution in Geneva), from the perspective of an American because, he wrote, America had many "lessons to share with an old continent."[31] If the Americans were "a people whom nature, education, and tradition had endowed with that equality of rights which is everywhere else considered a chimerical dream," the Genevans, independent heirs of William Tell, were worthy revolutionary followers.[32] The American Revolution was meant to be imitated, and where better than in the prosperous Genevan republic?

Brissot wrote to challenge stories told by the Paris-based Genevan journalist Jacques Mallet du Pan of crowds rampaging and blood flowing through the streets of a ravaged city-state. To discredit the first European challenge to the aristocracy, Mallet du Pan had substituted "romantic scenes for the truth," Brissot charged.[33] Determined to set the record straight, Brissot based his 231-page pamphlet not only on eyewitness observations but, he claimed, on research in Genevan libraries. He detailed the political disputes that had rumbled through Geneva over the course of the eighteenth century. The Genevan constitution as it had evolved limited the franchise to fifteen hundred wealthy Genevan burghers, excluding both the five thousand *natives*, artisans mostly employed in watchmaking, and the yet more numerous *habitants*, the newest immigrants. The Act of Mediation of 1738 had named France and the neighboring Swiss cantons of Bern and Zurich as responsible for maintaining peace in the prosperous city-state. In the 1760s, in a flurry of pamphlets, the party of

Représentants called for enlarging the franchise to include the natives. They denounced their opponents, the Négatives, as luxury-loving aristocrats determined to preserve the power of the oligarchic elite at all costs, even if that meant inviting foreign rulers to intervene in the affairs of the proudly independent Genevan republic. In the winter of 1780–81 Représentants warned the French, "in a century as enlightened as ours," not to interfere as they reached out to the natives.[34]

On 5 February 1781, a contingent of Geneva's natives and habitants stormed the municipal arsenal. In one of the many pamphlets printed in response, a fictional "Genevan citizen" explained to "a French philosopher" that disenfranchised Genevans had "armed themselves to secure their rights." Five days later, the largest of Geneva's governing bodies, the General Council of Geneva, voted to grant citizenship rights to one hundred of the natives and twenty habitants, hoping "to attach them permanently to the public interest" and thereby to defuse the unrest.[35]

The more elite Small Council refused to ratify the decision of the General Council. It stalled for more than a year, until April 1782, when it finally voted to overturn the reform. Within hours, armed natives took the Négatives hostage, occupied City Hall, closed the gates to the city, and persuaded the Représentants to support their insurrection.

The triumphant Genevan revolutionaries, including twenty-five-year-old François Ivernois, the wealthy financier and senior statesman Étienne Clavière, and Jacques Antoine du Roveray, the attorney general, welcomed Brissot to their city in June 1782. Brissot sensed the excitement of a people building their society anew without the constraints of the Old Regime. "Wherever a government does not respect property and crushes individuals, the people have the right to object and then to break their social contract and reclaim their liberty," he asserted. Genevans, like the Americans, had claimed the right to resistance as "a natural right."[36] Meeting in their *cercles* or neighborhood clubs, the revolutionary Genevans impressed Brissot with their talk of reconstituting their republic to redistribute rights and to break the aristocratic hold on the governing councils. Brissot was especially taken with the women of Geneva, who discussed politics with intelligence. Their political engagement would serve them well as republican wives and mothers, he predicted, not at all like the courtly French ladies with their affairs and idle gossip. Brissot would later compare the modest American women in their demure calicoes to his friends' wives in the Genevan republic.

Moderation was the badge of honor claimed by both sides in the Genevan Revolution of 1782. Pamphleteers espousing the cause of the Représentants, like Brissot, took on the identity of Bostonians or Philadelphians to emphasize the connection between the first two revolutions. They quoted liberally from Jean-Jacques Rousseau, a native son whose relations with Geneva and the natives were complicated. The Négatives' pamphlets alleged a determining foreign influence on the Genevan revolutionaries, charging that "most of the leaders of the faction are hardly Genevan," one of them even born in America.[37] They painted Genevan revolutionaries as wild democrats impetuously leading the once-prosperous city-state into anarchy.

"A pamphlet mania took possession of the excited townsmen," Mallet du Pan, born a Genevan *natif* himself, observed of the steady stream of brochures that issued forth from Geneva printing presses between February 1781 and August 1782.[38] Responding to events, usually within a day or two, pamphleteers often elicited an equally timely rejoinder. One anonymous pamphleteer claimed in verse, after the storming of the arsenal, that at least two thousand natives were ready to shed their last drop of blood to preserve the independence of the republic and the liberty enjoyed by citizens. Banned and censored by the Small Council before the revolt in April, these pamphlets were "for the government of our century, what light is for birds of the night," in the words of one pamphleteer.[39] Peddlers hid pamphlets inside the official calendars they sold and distributed them door to door. Although often addressed to the councils of Geneva, these pamphlets, whether legalistic letters or broad satirical dialogues, were clearly intended for a wider audience inside Geneva and beyond.

Like the Americans before them, the Genevans were convinced that "the universe" was watching them. They, too, assumed peoples from abroad would come to their aid in their struggle against a "monstrous government" imposed by violence and maintained by the force of foreigners, as they had for the Americans.[40] In a barrage of desperate pamphlets filled with dire descriptions of their besieged state, Genevan revolutionaries appealed to their potential foreign allies, including the British, for military support in the battle against their powerful neighbors. They tried to assure these neighbors that their intention was only to restore the rights formerly enjoyed by their ancestors, denying any claim to innovation. No foreign aid was forthcoming.

Instead, summoned by the Genevan Négatives, troops from France, Sardinia, and Bern approached the embattled city-state and encamped, ironically, at the chateau Ferney, which had formerly been occupied by the philosopher Voltaire. These foreign "war-making machines" were armed with an ultimatum for the revolutionary republic: restore the prerevolutionary aristocratic order or be slaughtered. Pamphlets circulated by the Négatives predicted the success of these well-drilled troops in "pacifying" Geneva.

Brissot described Genevan "women, children, men of every age" defiantly taking to the streets to fight for their city. "The enthusiasm for the defense of liberty was universal," he reported before he fled to safety in the mountains.[41] Others suggested that after years of governmental deliberation and reams of legislation, the Genevans themselves in one instant had become a people with one cause.[42]

Unlike the American revolutionaries, though, the Genevans found themselves surrounded by hostile forces intent on restoring the prerevolutionary governmental structure. After debating their options, Genevan revolutionaries fled across the lake. In a final pamphlet addressed to their fellow citizens left to the mercy of the French troops, the departing leaders pledged to seek recourse "under another sky, a land where it was possible to breathe the pure air of liberty."[43]

French troops marched through the city gates, disarmed the city's militia, overturned all the revolutionary decrees passed in the spring, and levied new taxes to support their occupation. Ivernois noted that many of these same French soldiers had fought sixteen years earlier in America to establish the new republic. His own king had dispatched them to lay siege to the Genevans, Brissot lamented. "Liberty has lost one of its rare places of asylum," Brissot wrote as he joined Genevan revolutionaries Clavière and Du Roveray in exile in Neuchâtel. They discussed the "what ifs" of the first European revolution in the company of the comte de Mirabeau and the printers of most of the revolutionary pamphlets who had also been forced to seek exile. If only the Genevan revolutionaries, "like the Americans, had had enough force to convince others to respect their struggle and to support their principles with arms."[44] If only they had had an ocean to protect them.

Americans were surprised to read about the defeat of the Genevan Revolution at the hands of the French, whose foreign minister had lent them his troops and wealth. In her history of the American Revolution, published in 1805, Mercy Otis Warren denounced the coalition of European aristocrats who had crushed the first hints of democracy on the other side of the ocean. She pronounced the French occupation of the Genevan republic as "inconsistent with the liberties of the people or the independence of their republic."[45]

An anonymous Genevan pamphleteer reflected on the irony that in this era "of justice and humanity," Geneva, the very symbol of liberty in Europe, had lost "its quality as a free state, independent, and sovereign."[46] Would the Genevans be ignored by history, they asked, their short-lived revolutionary triumph forgotten just because the city-state was "extremely small?"[47] Or was the problem their bad neighborhood?

Van der Capellen's Call to Arms in "A Republic such as ours": The Dutch Patriot Revolution of 1787

Upon hearing of the defeat of the Genevan revolutionaries at the hands of French troops, van der Capellen advised the Genevans not only to abandon their fallen city but also to poison its atmosphere, leaving it barren, "inhabitable only by screech-owls and bats." That warning would rouse "the remaining free commonwealths" to the defense of liberty, especially the Dutch republic that was straining under the rule of its hereditary stadtholder, Willem V.[48]

The irrepressible van der Capellen was convinced that the United Provinces of the Netherlands, which had itself originated in a revolution, would be the next stage on which eighteenth-century revolution would play. One hundred years earlier, Dutch nobles, merchants, and sailors had revolted against their tyrannical ruler, Philip II of Spain. Ever since, Dutch pamphlets had celebrated the courage of the revolutionary forefathers who established one of the most prosperous commercial republics in Europe. Van der Capellen saw the current stadtholder, Willem V, as but a faint reflection of the revolutionary leader chosen as the first stadtholder, William the Silent.

FIGURE 1.2

Portrait of Joan Derk van der Capellen, Patriot pamphleteer who roused the
Dutch to revolution. Portrait by Louis Jacques Cathelin, 1788. Courtesy of the
Atlas van Stolk Foundation, Rotterdam

European and American pamphleteers alike, including Thomas Paine, paid tribute to the heroic Dutch revolutionaries of centuries past. Few of them, however, expected the Dutch to rise up against their stadtholder in the 1780s, even though they had many grievances to lodge against the inept Willem V. On a visit to the United Provinces, Benjamin Franklin had scoffed at the mercantile practicality of his Dutch hosts. Commercial interests so dominated conversation, he reported, that a visitor could mistake the United Provinces for an immense spice shop.[49] These merchants were no more revolutionaries than their stadtholder was a leader. Another traveler, the future revolutionary leader Peter Ochs from Basel, visiting his Dutch relatives in the midst of the American Revolution, had dismissed the political debates he overheard as mere factional squabbles, not the enlightened political theory that emanated from the French philosophes and inspired the Americans. Ochs speculated derisively that the flatness of the Netherlands simply did not inspire grand thoughts.[50] Van der Capellen, however, was convinced that the Dutch just needed a signal to rally them to revolt.

In 1779, John Paul Jones sailed into the Dutch harbor of Texel trailing two captured English ships, all three flying the American flag. Striding ashore, Jones, the American naval hero and sometime pirate, challenged the standing Dutch foreign policy of neutrality. While he repaired his weather-beaten and battle-tested ships, Jones cast himself in verse to Anna Jacoba, Dumas's thirteen-year-old daughter, as the friend of liberty "who tyrant power pursues!"[51] Willem V, a pronounced Anglophile, called in vain for his arrest. Jones slipped safely out of Texel harbor past the storm-tossed British ships waiting to intercept him.

Jones's visit fanned popular enthusiasm for revolutionary America, especially in Amsterdam, where he had been publicly applauded, but it exacerbated diplomatic tensions. Even as the Dutch government officially pursued a policy of neutrality and the stadtholder openly favored the British, Amsterdam merchants brazenly explored the promise of trade with the Americans.[52] In December 1780, the revelation of secret negotiations between the city of Amsterdam and the Americans provoked the British to declare war on their former commercial ally. Humiliating losses in the Fourth Anglo-Dutch War shattered Dutch pretensions to status as a world power and proved the stadtholder, who would rather have allied with the British, an incompetent naval commander.

Van der Capellen seized the crisis to rally the Dutch people to form militias, drill on village greens, and free their republic from the rule of Willem V. "Arm yourselves; chuse your leaders, follow the example of the people of America," he urged readers of a new pamphlet, *Aan het volk van Nederlanden* (To the people of the Netherlands), which he published anonymously and distributed through the streets of cities and villages under cover of darkness in September 1781. He called on his countrymen— aristocratic regents, merchants, and farmers—to rise up against the stadt- holder who treated them, "the descendants of free Batavians," as "heredi- tary vassals." Van der Capellen proclaimed in a forthright assertion of nat- ural rights that echoed the Americans', "All men are born free." He promised that "Jehovah, the God of Liberty" would favor the Dutch with his protection as he had his first chosen people, the Israelites, and more recently, the Americans.[53]

Although not as widely read today in the Netherlands as *Common Sense* is in the United States, at the time *Aan het volk* caused a sensation, resonating among van der Capellen's aristocratic peers as well as with the bourgeoisie and the popular classes. While its rhetoric seems refined next to Paine's, a conservative professor from Leiden complained that its "grue- some language would raise the hair of the most savage barbarians."[54] The government banned it after one month, but *Aan het Volk* was reprinted in three Dutch editions in the first year and immediately translated into French, German, and English. John Adams wrote from The Hague to friends in America that the "large pamphlet" had everyone talking.

Van der Capellen's pamphlet soon was circulating in America, too. Abigail Adams wrote John of her hope that the spirit of the Dutch that led them "to repel the Tyranny of Philip administered by the cruel Alva" a century earlier would "cement an indissoluble bond of union between the United States of America and the United Provinces who, from a simi- larity of circumstances have each arrived at Independence, disdaining the Bondage and oppression of a Philip and a Gorge [*sic*]."[55] John judged "the originals of the two Republics . . . so much alike that the history of the one seems but a transcript of the other."[56] They balanced their definition of liberty differently, the Dutch emphasizing tradition over the natural rights that the Americans asserted, but the parallels between the Dutch and the Americans, both relying on citizen militias to defend their freedom, were obvious to revolutionaries on the two sides of the Atlantic.

A virtual pamphlet war ensued in the United Provinces between the Patriot Party (de Patriotten), the alliance of local and provincial regents, artisans, and merchants who opposed the stadtholder, and the Orangists (de Oranjepartij), the stadtholder's supporters, drawn from the popular classes as well as the aristocrats. Political allegiance did not necessarily follow socioeconomic divisions. As in Geneva, where the Négatives attracted support from the natives, Orangist crowds came from what the Dutch called *het grauw*, the mob. Ideology did not divide along the lines of an expected dichotomy, either. Patriot pamphlets like van der Capellen's drew lessons from both the seventeenth-century Netherlands and revolutionary America. They ran together appeals to universal natural rights and a liberty based solidly in Dutch history. This union of Enlightenment rhetoric and claims founded in tradition did not set the Dutch apart from other eighteenth-century revolutionaries. The Dutch Patriots, like the Genevan Représentants before them, saw no contradiction in their multifaceted argument for liberty.

Militias organized on village greens throughout the United Provinces while the Holland Free Corps endorsed the revolutionary *Leidse Ontwerp* (Leiden Draft), which proclaimed liberty "an inalienable right, adhering to all the burghers of the Netherlands commonwealth." The authors challenged the authority of the stadtholder or any other "power on earth" who would presume "to obstruct the enjoyment of this liberty."[57] Worried by the turn toward democracy, Willem V retreated to his country estate in the eastern province of Gelderland, beyond the reach of the armed Patriots.

The Patriot Revolution of 1787 was a decidedly diffuse affair, as decentralized as the Dutch republic itself. While Patriots controlled the provincial estates in Overijssel, Friesland, Holland, and Groningen, the Orangists held Zeeland and Gelderland. In Utrecht, rival estates, one Orangist and one Patriot, contended with each other for power. To break the deadlock, Princess Wilhelmina set out for The Hague. Her entourage was stopped by Patriot militias as it crossed into the province of Holland. The stadtholder was not alarmed that his wife, sister of Frederick William of Prussia, had fallen into enemy hands. Her detention would serve to justify an invasion by the Prussians led by the Duke of Brunswick. The Prussian army decisively overwhelmed the Patriot militias and crushed the

Dutch Patriot Revolution, allowing Willem V triumphantly to reenter Amsterdam in September 1787.

Based on the experience of the American war and secret promises from Paris, the Dutch Patriots expected assistance from the French. They appealed to Mirabeau, who had once lived in the United Provinces, to make their case to the French foreign minister. They reminded the French philosopher that ever since their revolution more than a century earlier, the Dutch had enjoyed more sovereign rights than any other republic in Europe.[58] Mirabeau, author of the influential *Essai sur le despotisme* (Essay on despotism), hesitated, torn between his personal friendship with the Prussian emperor and his commitment to the cause of liberty. Finally, in 1788, in collaboration with Genevan revolutionaries and Brissot, Mirabeau published *Aux Bataves* (To the Batavians), an ode to "the oldest of free peoples" in Europe. The pamphlet proclaimed the Dutch Patriot Revolution, like the American War for Independence, "the cause of all men," worthy of attention. However, it chided the Dutch Patriots that they should not expect foreigners to fight their battles for them. "It is up to free nations to save themselves."[59]

That was harsh advice to dispense in northern Europe, where small republics were at the mercy of the politics of their powerful imperial neighbors. Van der Capellen reminded his compatriots of the dangers for "a Republic such as ours that finds itself in the midst of European affairs."[60] At least the Americans had an ocean to protect them from what John Adams called the "Confederation" of "Crowned skulls, and numbskulls of Europe" who had allied "against Human Nature."[61] The Dutch Orangists, who supported the stadtholder much as the American Loyalists had the king, could call up imperial armies stationed in the neighborhood to maintain the privileges of the Old Regime. The Prussians had no interest in tolerating revolution just across their border in what was becoming an age of revolution.

The Revolt of the Belgians, 1787–1789:
"God's faithful servants"

"Everywhere you look, you see a continual struggle between a throne propped up by force and liberty supported by the voice of nature and law," Brussels lawyer Charles Lambert d'Outrepont observed in his 1787 pamphlet. The renowned legal theorist, whose earlier attack on the tithes had been translated into German and English, was convinced, as van der Capellen had been, that the ideal of liberty, shared from one continent to another, seemed destined in an enlightened age to triumph over the forces of despotism. "Never have enlightened peoples better understood the dignity of men and the worth of civil liberty," d'Outrepont explained, casting the growing Belgian resistance against their Austrian ruler's reforms as part of the chain of revolutions that began in America and spread to Geneva and the United Provinces.[62] D'Outrepont was not discouraged by the defeat of the first two European revolutions.

Just a year earlier, d'Outrepont had been one of the Austrian emperor's most vocal supporters in the Belgian provinces. He had praised the governance of the Austrian Netherlands that Joseph II had inherited from his mother, Empress Maria Theresa, as enlightened. That was before Joseph II forced reforms from above on the Belgians, who had historically vested sovereign authority in the three estates of each of the provinces. They had assumed the emperor governed, as his mother had done, to protect them from foreign invasion, not to interfere in domestic affairs. By 1787, d'Outrepont was ready to lead the next revolution.

In their precociously industrializing society, a Belgian pamphleteer explained, "everyone lives happily in the midst of prosperity. The farmer, the artisan, the clergy, the nobility are all just one family attached to the Estates."[63] The centuries-old constitutions of the nine Belgian provinces defined the mutual obligations of the sovereign, the Austrian emperor, and the people represented by the provincial estates. Joseph II ignored the constitution, presuming to "rule above the law," and the estates responded by threatening to withhold their taxes.[64] The Austrian ruler's proposed reforms of the church and the administration of his Belgian provinces, celebrated in pamphlets and newspapers abroad as enlightened, were denounced in a round of Belgian pamphlets as violations of their sovereignty.

Genevan and Dutch revolutionaries who had been offered shelter and freedom to worship in Brussels and Antwerp by Joseph II were caught in the middle of the battle of words. Why, the newly arrived refugees from the United Provinces asked, would the Belgians resist such an enlightened emperor? One Dutch Patriot, banker Jan Bicker, who arrived in Brussels with his family, wondered why the Belgians who had taken up arms against the Austrians claimed inspiration from the Dutch revolutionaries. "I found it a different patriotism," Bicker commented. After a stray bullet fired by a Belgian volunteer just missed him, the Dutch revolutionary swore "to God, it was not my affair," packed up his nine children and household help, and headed for France.[65] Other Dutch Patriots followed. The entanglements of European diplomacy made for strange revolutionary alliances. The French, who had helped the Americans, had disappointed the revolutionary aspirations of both the Genevans and the Dutch, while their Austrian hosts turned out to be their revolutionary allies' enemies.

The Belgians saw no ambiguity in their situation. They claimed, as had the Americans and Dutch before them, to be God's chosen people. "All of Europe will be our witness," an anonymous pamphleteer reassured his compatriots.[66] Bicker may have seen their handbills appealing openly to God to descend to earth to save the Belgians, his "faithful servants" from Joseph II and his Austrian infidels as he had rescued the Israelites.[67] Other Dutch Patriots would have noted the depictions of the ferocious Belgian lion, roaring, with claws extended, giving chase to the evil Austrian eagle that had ransacked churches, killed nuns, and carted off treasures.[68] Belgian pamphlets deliberately echoed Dutch ones comparing Joseph II to the Spanish monarch Philip II, felled in the sixteenth century for his refusal to honor the rights of the Low Countries.

François Xavier de Feller, an ex-Jesuit and newspaper editor, published many of the attacks on the Austrian imperial reforms from Liège, a city on the verge of its own revolution against its prince-bishop, beyond the reach of Austrian censors.[69] There, Jean-Jacques Tutot operated thirty-three printing presses. Other pamphlets were printed at Sint-Truiden, under the jurisdiction of Liège and controlled by the abbot of Saint Trudo, who sympathized with the revolutionaries. Brussels printer Joseph Michel, who had published many of the revolutionary pamphlets before one of his workmen denounced him to the Austrians in April 1788, moved his operations to Sint-Truiden. Michel and Tutot used an extensive network of shopkeepers, mail coaches, and friends to distribute the seditious literature through the Belgian provinces.

Many of these pamphlets likened the Belgians to the Americans, who had resisted a foreign ruler out of touch with the interests of his distant

FIGURE I.3

"Les Biens d'autruy ne disiras pour les avoir injustement," a satirical print from the Brabant Revolution. The Austrian eagle is attempting to escape with the treasures of the General Seminary, Leuven University, and other Belgian institutions. The Belgian lion, claws extended, roars back. J. J. Van den Elsken, 1789. By permission of the Bibliothèque Royale de Belgique/Koninklijke Bibliotheek België, Cabinet des Estampes, E 12.890 c

subjects. A naturally endowed, industrious people who had long enjoyed their liberty far from the interference of rulers, the Belgians had struggled mightily, as the pamphlets told it, to maintain the protection of a just and proven constitution against a foreign ruler. Like the Genevans and the Dutch before them, the Belgians were defending their historical rights as a traditionally free people. That meant the Belgians were "one hundred times more likely to succeed" than the neighboring French, who were also complaining about Louis XVI.[70] The Belgians, unlike the French, already had a written constitution that guaranteed their rights.

In 1788, the lawyer of the Estates of the Brabant province at the center of the Austrian Netherlands, Henri van der Noot, called on "the people who had vigilantly conserved their privileges" to rise up to resist "the most absolute despotism."[71] The emperor responded by ordering the arrest of all suspected revolutionary leaders. After van der Noot fled to exile in England, his mistress, Madame de Bellem, took up her pen in his absence to urge the Belgians to imitate the Americans. Together with her daughter Marianne, she distributed her own three-line poetic pamphlet, as well as other pamphlets, through the streets of Brussels.[72] They apparently escaped arrest because the Austrian spies did not suspect women of pamphleteering.

The Comtesse Anne Philippine d'Yve asked rhetorically in a pamphlet dedicated *À la nation* (To the nation), "If this nation that was once so important, the model of the universe whose ancient glory has been inherited by the present generation would be allowed to sink into oblivion?" She answered with assurance that even though their leaders had been forced to flee, the Third Estate, the "voice of the people," would soon rise up to remind the enlightened emperor of his duties to the sovereign people of these prosperous provinces.[73] She adroitly blended two strains of liberty, one based in local tradition and the other in transatlantic ideals. While she argued that the medieval constitutions of the Belgian provinces should be preserved as the foundation of the new state, she appealed to the Belgians to fight for their natural rights and to secure their sovereignty.

An anonymous pamphlet dedicated to the Comtesse d'Yve heralded the centuries-old tradition of feminine involvement in public life in the Belgian provinces. "If the Belgians, the oldest of free peoples, have never lost their liberty," the pamphleteer asserted, "it is because women no less than men have always worked to conserve it."[74] They were doing that still in 1789, hosting salons, but also writing, editing, and distributing pamphlets to an extensive network of correspondents from Vienna to Paris. After the countess left for Paris in 1789, she continued to send pamphlets to revolutionaries in Brussels, adding comments in the margins before she dispatched them across existing political borders. Her notations make clear the network of revolutionary writings reaching across Europe in 1789.

Working a very different set of connections, the exiled van der Noot asked the Dutch, the English, and the Prussian governments to lend military assistance to the Belgians. As recompense for driving out the

Austrians, van der Noot offered to install the second son of the prince of Orange as Belgian stadtholder. The three powers scoffed, refusing to commit troops to what they viewed as a hopeless cause. His shuttle diplomacy alarmed the Dutch Patriots. Why, they asked, would the Brabant revolutionaries seek aid from the leading counterrevolutionary empire, which had just defeated the Dutch Patriots? Van der Noot's appeal to foreign troops also unsettled many of the Belgian revolutionaries.

A secret committee, Pro Aris et Focis (For hearth and home), led by lawyer Jan Vonck, rejecting van der Noot's diplomacy, called on the Belgian people to arm themselves. They conceived of their revolt as part of a larger Atlantic revolution fought by locally recruited militia. "The end of the XVIIIth century seems predestined to witness revolutions blazing forth all over the surface of the globe," Vonck and his allies wrote, recounting the succession of cascading revolutions they expected to join. "The vast continent of colonial America was the first to erect the standard of liberty. . . . Supported by France, they broke forever the yoke of the cabinet of Saint James." The United Provinces of the Netherlands, which had also counted on the Court of Versailles, "the sometime haven of unhappy kings and occasional supporter of oppressed peoples, tried to recover its rights and thought the happy moment had arrived when it could break stadtholderian despotism." But, they continued, the French had abandoned the Dutch to their own means and the Patriots had been unable "to resist the force of twenty thousand Prussian bayonets."[75] The Belgians had learned their lessons from previous revolutions. They would look to their own forces and not count on foreign alliances. People made revolutions; imperial armies crushed them. Pro Aris et Focis printed thousands of pamphlets "to enlighten, awaken, and spark the genius of the Belgian people," urging them to gather just over the border to drill.[76] That was the other lesson they had learned: the force of militias recruited and sustained by widely distributed, plainspoken pamphlets.

Austrian troops swooped down on the militia's training grounds in Liège, but Pro Aris et Focis had been forewarned and fled. The Austrians dubbed the elusive force "the army of the moon." In September 1789, the Austrians raided a house in Brussels where, spies informed Minister Trauttmansdorff, popular revolutionaries gathered. They seized a stock of cartridges, three members of Pro Aris et Focis, and stacks of pamphlets.

One of the three pamphleteers was Philippe Secrétan, a Genevan who had come to Brussels five years earlier as a tutor. When he was taken into custody, Secrétan had in his pockets three manuscripts that laid out plans for an insurrection. Based on that evidence, Trauttmansdorff believed he had found the source of the Belgian revolutionary conspiracy: a Genevan refugee and Secrétan's lover, his employer, the Duchesse d'Ursel. Secrétan was arrested. In the pamphlet that he published in January 1790 to clear his name, Secrétan claimed the Austrians threatened to break him unless he gave them the names of the other leaders of Pro Aris et Focis. He named the duchess.[77]

On 24 October 1789, the feast day of the Archangel Raphael, the leaders of Pro Aris et Focis joined the provincial Belgian estates in the Dutch city of Breda to declare war against the Austrians. Their joint *Manifeste du peuple brabançon* (Manifesto of the Brabant people) borrowed language from the American Declaration of Independence as it enumerated the Belgian rights violated by Austrian tyranny. Joseph II "had tyrannized the Belgian People & reduced them to a Slavery contradictory to the Inaugural Pact," they declared as they pledged "to defend and maintain our Liberty, our Religion, our Rights, our Privileges, and our customs to transmit them intact to our descendants as they were transmitted by our forefathers."[78] Like the Dutch, the Belgian revolutionaries united their defense of traditional privilege with an appeal to liberty framed in the terms of the American Revolution.

In less than two months, Belgian volunteers drove the Austrian dragoons from their provinces. They took advantage of a ceasefire in November to regroup and attack the Austrians. European commentators called the victory of the shoeless, untrained Belgian militia over the army of one of the most powerful nations of Europe miraculous. Many of these international gazettes had previously dismissed the Brabant Revolution as a "civil war" rather than a struggle for independence. We are all "BELGIANS," the author of *Mercure Flandrico-Latino-Gallico-Belgique* replied indignantly, echoing Brissot's response to similar charges leveled against the Genevans by Mallet du Pan.[79] "Here we are all agreed," the Abbé de Feller added.[80] Pamphlets depicted van der Noot as the Belgian George Washington. The editor of the *Journal général de l'Europe*, originally a committed supporter of Joseph II's reforms, celebrated the Brabant

Revolution as the first stage of the "total overthrow of the political system of Europe."[81]

"All of Europe is watching with great curiosity to see how the Belgians will use their newly secured liberty," a pamphleteer advised van der Noot, who triumphantly returned to Brussels with his mistress, Madame de Bellem, the "Belgian Martha Washington" in December 1789.[82] Van der Noot ignored the warning. Rather than electing a new assembly, the United States of Belgium consolidated power in the existing provincial estates.[83] The rift between the Estates, dedicated to preserving traditional privileges, and Pro Aris et Focis, in league with the Genevan Représentants, Dutch Patriots, and American rebels, was soon apparent.

An allegorical pamphlet told the story of a band of revolutionaries who drove a despotic ruler from his throne and pursued him as he fled the palace of his forefathers. In his retreat, the prince's crown slipped off his head and fell at the feet of the band of revolutionaries. The narrator, "a deputy from the Committee of the Moon," asked the victorious revolutionaries what they would do with the crown.[84] Their answer: they would break it into tiny pieces and distribute individual liberties to every citizen in the land. First, exhausted, they fell asleep. A cabal of monks and nobles then crept in and seized the crown, squeezing all of their privileged heads into it before running off. The moral of the pamphlet: an independent people must remain ever vigilant to secure its liberty from the grasp of the powerful and privileged, even after revolutionary victory.

"Sleep in a state, as Montesquieu says, is always followed by slavery," Richard Price had warned in his pamphlet, *Observations on the Nature of Civil Liberty*. "There is nothing that requires more to be watched than power."[85] Pro Aris et Focis concurred; concentrated in the hands of the few, aristocratic power tended to tyranny. D'Outrepont, celebrating the "virtue and courage that severed the chains . . . of despotism," worried in his 1790 pamphlet about the fate of the United States of Belgium if the Estates "clung to their old constitution" and "failed to imitate the example of the Americans who united their provinces into a common association . . . a social contract."[86] His answer was not long in coming. The Austrians reconquered the feuding Belgian provinces in November 1790. The third of three revolutions to burst upon the European stage between 1776 and 1789 was extinguished within a year.

"A general fermentation": Independence and Liberty

America belonged to an interlinked Atlantic world where political ideas encapsulated in pamphlets traversed national borders as readily as the traveling revolutionaries who carried them. "Philosophy encouraged by the spectacle of America cannot be stopped in its progress," future French revolutionary Jean-Baptiste Mailhe exclaimed in his pamphlet *Discours sur la Grandeur et l'importance de la révolution dans l'Amérique septentrional* (Speech on the greatness and the importance of the American Revolution), published in Toulouse in 1784.[87] The American revolutionaries shared their revolutionary dreams, importing and exporting ideas as eagerly as they exchanged agricultural and manufactured products and traded slaves across the Atlantic. Benjamin Franklin wrote a friend that Europeans were convinced "that our Cause is *the cause of all* Mankind, and that we are fighting for their Liberty in defending our Own."[88] The American Revolution was no longer an exceptional event in the eyes of the revolutionaries themselves, even if Americans were surrounded by nature and their vast continent was separated from European corruption and despotism by an ocean.

"A general fermentation seems to be taking place thro' Europe," Richard Price, one of the conduits of that fermentation, observed in a letter addressed to Benjamin Franklin in 1787. "In consequence of the attention created by the American War, and the dissemination of writings explaining the nature and end of civil government, the minds of men are becoming more enlighten'd and the silly despots of the world are likely to be forced to respect human rights and to take care not to govern too much, lest they should not govern at all."[89] Europeans seeking "a reasoned and reasonable liberty," a "cosmopolite" wrote from Brussels, had adapted American rhetoric to their struggles for rights, both natural and historic.[90] The Genevans, the Dutch, and the Belgians discovered that overcoming entrenched privilege in Europe where monarchs lurked posed challenges not faced by Americans, an ocean removed from British rule. Even though they were defeated, the first three European revolutions shook the Old Regime. In the words of Thomas Paine, these first revolutionaries had begun, however haltingly, "the business of a world." In Europe, as in America, "the Rubicon" had been crossed.[91]

One of the few French philosophes who lived to witness these revolutions, Nicolas de Caritat, the marquis de Condorcet, applauded the American insurrection for "providing the first example" of revolution. For revolutions to radiate outward beyond the minds of the few, the ideals of the Enlightenment had to be enacted, he suggested. "It is not enough that the rights of man be written in the books of philosophers and inscribed in the hearts of virtuous men."[92] The Americans, "a great people," had built the philosophes' new world for all to see and to emulate. Pamphlets had inspired the Americans to begin; then they broadcast the momentous news of the American Revolution, causing revolutions to pile up, one upon another. "The more free peoples that exist in the world, the more the liberty of each individual is assured," Condorcet explained.[93] Condorcet, like Brissot, narrated from an American perspective, although he would never cross the ocean.

The French philosopher Abbé Guillaume-Thomas-François Raynal, another armchair traveler whose ideas journeyed farther than he did, wrote one of the most widely read European descriptions of America. He realized that he would die "without having seen the asylum of tolerance, of customs, of laws, of virtue and of liberty" as he imagined Americans living "among the rocks, the mountains, the vast plains and their open spaces on the edges of the forests where everything is still wild and nothing calls to mind the servitude and tyranny imposed by men." Nature itself had taught them to crave independence. The enlightened Americans recognized that "nature did not create the world so that the inhabitants of an island could force the whole world into submission."[94]

Hired by George Washington and encouraged by the French minister to the United States, the chevalier de la Luzerne, Thomas Paine replied to the Abbé Raynal with a new pamphlet. Paine was determined to convince European readers, as *Common Sense* had the Americans, that the American War for Independence was a struggle for liberty, rooted locally, but envisioned in global terms. Paine, who had read a pirated, abridged translation of Raynal's pamphlet, argued against what he characterized as Raynal's reduction of the American Revolution to a battle over "a slight tax." He did not acknowledge that Raynal had practically echoed *Common Sense*, and would have agreed with Paine that "our style and manner of thinking have undergone a revolution, more extraordinary than the political revolution."[95] The Americans had become a new people in revolution; for the first time in the history of the world, truly free to enjoy their natural rights. Theirs was a lesson for the world.

Dutch journalist Antoine Cérisier translated Paine's pamphlet into French.[96] Liberty was exportable. Like Paine, who signed his pamphlet as "a universal citizen," revolutionary ideas traveled well. An American traveler wrote home from Europe in 1783 to report that everyone was reading Paine's letter to the Abbé Raynal. "The point of his pen has been as formidable in politics as the point of the sword in the field."[97] Paine sent hundreds of copies of his pamphlet to George Washington and his friends who had financed it, but its influence may have been greater in Europe.

A decade after the American Revolution began, Paine the pamphleteer was more convinced than ever that revolutionary ideas traveling the seas would knit the Atlantic world together, bringing an end to conflict. No longer divided by the threat of war fomented by imperial ambitions, republics would come together in an international federation. Science and commerce would link the peoples of the world, extending civilization. Richard Price, whose pamphlets crossed the Atlantic in the other direction, predicted in a letter to Benjamin Franklin that all of the revolutions together would yield "a state of society more favourable to peace, virtue, science and liberty, (and consequently to human happiness and dignity) than has ever yet been known."[98] Camille Desmoulins concurred. Soon, he predicted, "the English, the French, the Americans, and the Brabançons would unite as brothers" to secure their liberty.[99] This revolution of the mind was more than a change in politics for Paine. In a postrevolutionary world, he predicted, "We see with other eyes: we hear with other ears; and think with other thoughts, than those formerly used."[100] Everything would change.

The French foreign minister, the comte de Vergennes, gave Paine fifty guineas to cover the costs of printing his pamphlet. It seemed a small price to pay in France's campaign against England at the time of peace negotiations. Little did Louis XVI's minister realize the greater threat posed to his monarch by "the contagion of liberty." He assumed France with its legendary history of centralized absolutism was safely protected from the contagion by troops strategically deployed to suppress insurrection.

He did not realize that Europe was on the cusp of another revolutionary explosion that would eclipse the first struggles for liberty. Within a year, Peter Ochs of Basel, who retired to his reading rooms after observing the crushing defeats of the first European revolutionaries, forecast that a "French Revolution would awaken slumbering people and send a chill up the backs of aristocrats and despots throughout Europe."[101] It in turn would lend new life to the short-lived revolutions whose leaders would congregate in the new revolutionary capital, Paris.

TWO

Journals Relating "A share in two revolutions"

Travel journals presented a more personal perspective than did the pamphlets. Like their travels between revolutions, the tales itinerants recounted in journals were often circuitous. So too were their loyalties. Many journal writers began their journeys to Philadelphia and Paris as revolutionaries. A few discovered revolution en route. Others, especially visitors to France frightened by the violence they witnessed after 1791, renounced revolution altogether. Their reflective journal entries betrayed their individual expectations, hopes, and disappointments as they compared the fate of their shared ideals from one revolution to another.

E verything remains to be done and everything is possible," Étienne Dumont, a Genevan revolutionary refugee who arrived in Paris via Saint Petersburg and Wiltshire, wrote, urging his friends to join the cosmopolitan coterie of revolutionaries in Paris. "All that was rock solid is now as malleable as wax," he added, calling them to come witness the Old Regime crumbling apart at its very core.[1] Americans, Genevans, Dutch Patriots, and Belgian refugees were all gathering in the salons and cafés of revolutionary France, the center of the Enlightenment. Their Atlantic world was not constrained by rigid national borders. Its permeable boundaries were readily crossed by travelers and their publications, as pamphleteers had discovered.

At the end of the eighteenth century, transatlantic travel was no longer the preserve of the privileged but was within the reach of individuals of at least middling means. Increasingly, European merchants came to America after the War for Independence looking for economic opportunities, while sons of American settlers sailed the Atlantic in the other direction seeking a European education. In the 1780s, Americans and Europeans crossing paths on the Atlantic compared the luxuries that ostentatiously accompanied privilege in Old Regime Europe with the practical frugality of their revolutionary American republic. A few years later, during the French Revolution, a number of itinerants from all over Europe joined American diplomats, poets, and merchants as witnesses to the unprecedented exuberance of the Parisian crowds in the new capital of Atlantic revolution.

To chronicle their journeys, these travelers kept journals, understood in the eighteenth century to mean daily, weekly, or monthly accounts of notable events.[2] The conventions of travel writing were well defined by the end of the eighteenth century. Manuals such as *An Essay to Direct and Extend the Inquiries of Patriotic Travellers* advised journal-keeping travelers to be meticulous observers, to take notes on the spot in shorthand, and to transfer their accounts to journals each evening.[3] Immediacy would render their accounts more convincing, transporting their readers to new worlds, in this case into the midst of revolution. The author of *A Tour in Holland in 1784 by an American*, Elkanah Watson strove to write regularly, "to seize the chain" of events as it was occurring. He edited his entries later, making sure they ran "along from link to link, in some regular order to the end of the sheet."[4] Often, travelers published their journals as collections of letters written to friends, one entry following from another, describing their journey.

"Of all the various productions in the press," an eighteenth-century editor commented, "none are so eagerly received by us Reviewers, and other people who stay at home and mind our business, as the writing of travelers."[5] Instead of focusing on tales of extraordinary individuals, as had earlier travelogues, these journals systematically recorded the details of foreign societies for their curious readers. The *Philosophical and Political History of the Settlements and Trade of the Europeans in the East and West Indies* published by the Abbé Raynal in 1770 helped to define the genre of travel journals as treatises on natural, civil, and political liberty, even though neither he nor the other philosophes who contributed to the six massive volumes had traveled to either the East or the West Indies.[6]

Georg Förster, whose descriptions of the flora and fauna on his first voyage with his father and Captain Cook around the world from 1772 to 1775 earned him a position as a professor at the University of Vilna in Poland, was one of the most accomplished of the so-called philosophical travelers who published their journals. In 1790, Förster, then the university librarian at Mainz, set off in the direction of England to buy books.

He planned his journey as the frame for a new travelogue and stopped at the numerous revolutionary sites of northern Europe en route. In letters addressed to his wife and friends, he recounted his conversations along the way with "free people who loved to discuss politics more than their private interests." That was just what he needed for his journal. Upon his return home, he collected his letters, supplemented these observations with historical research, and published the two-volume *Ansichten vom Niederrheim* (Views of the lower Rhine River) to substantiate his optimistic political conviction that "Europe has made an immense step forward."[7] The signs of revolution could seemingly be found wherever one looked.

If less overtly political than pamphleteers, many late-eighteenth-century travelers published their journals to argue a cause. They staked out strong positions on the French Revolution, which had felled the entrenched foundations of the Old Regime many of them despised. Unlike some pamphlets, the accounts of journal writers typically reflected their own immediate experiences in the towns of the newly independent American republic or surrounded by the crowds of the fast-moving French Revolution.

Personally, these travelers fostered transatlantic connections between the American and the French revolutions. In the friendships nurtured by their travels, they connected the two revolutions that continued to gather momentum after 1789. Published in Paris and Philadelphia, their journals often had just the opposite effect. Written for readers who had stayed behind, travel journals inadvertently reinforced the distinctions that would separate the Americans from the French in the 1790s. European travelers to the American Revolution perpetuated views of a primitive, unsullied American wilderness out of which the first revolutionaries had carved their republic, lending support to the notion of American exceptionalism. At the same time, French convictions that their liberty reached beyond both the political independence secured by the Americans and the failed revolutions of their neighbors were bolstered by the fearful reaction of the droves of visitors to their revolutionary capital. Travelers embracing bold new visions of liberty and equality as universal revolutionary principles could bring people together, while their own journals divided readers along national lines in a revolutionary era with so much at risk.

"Good living": An American Apprenticeship in Europe

Traveling transformed the revolutionary perspective of a young American in the years after the American War for Independence. Propelled by "my anxiety for change and desire of seeing the new world," Elkanah Watson developed the habit of daily journal writing. During the American War, he had smuggled more than fifty thousand dollars sewn into his clothes from Providence to the army in Charleston. He believed his uncommon adventures delivering letters to General George Washington, riding to Plymouth with a musket on his back to rouse the Committee of Safety, and sailing an old fishing schooner to set a British captive free warranted recording. That was even more true of his trip across the Atlantic, throughout which he "exulted in the comparative view of Europe and America."[8] He would correct, revise, and edit his journal entries multiple times.

Watson sailed in 1779 with funds and letters to be delivered to Benjamin Franklin, stationed in Paris on diplomatic mission. Without steady work in America, Watson had decided to hazard "the fate of the tortuous waves or some gloomy [British] prison" for the "alluring prospect of accumulating wealth." He expected, "after acquainting myself with the customs, manners, Religions & superstitions of other countrys" and after accumulating some wealth, "to return to the land which gave me existence."[9]

Watson's ship dropped anchor at Île au Rhé on the French coast in September, after twenty-nine days at sea. Ashore, he initially noted, "we stood to be gaz'd at, like so many stout piggs."[10] He revised his journal entry for publication, expanding his description of his first encounter with the Old World. "In a few moments, I was surrounded by a crowd, gazing at me with great interest. So strong and universal was the feeling in France, excited by our Revolution."[11] Although a vast sea separated the continents, he mused, "it is only a month since I was cantering thro' the streets of Boston. A short period Indeed to gain upward of three thousand miles East."[12] Other eighteenth-century travelers' descriptions of the ocean crossing, "the rolling, the pitching, the broken tables" resulting in "the disorder of a dinner seasoned with salt water" or the seasickness endured day after day in an airless, cramped cabin, suggest that few of them found

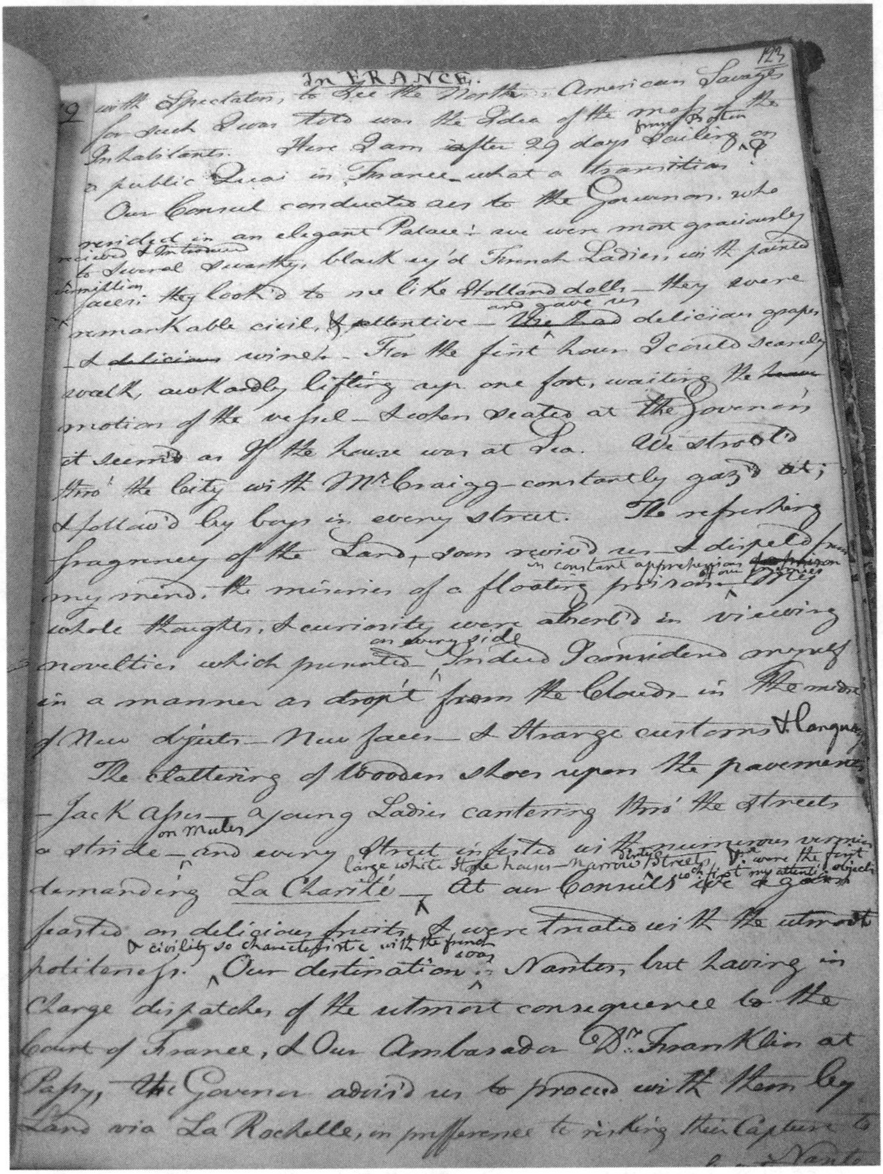

FIGURE 2.1
A page from Elkanah Watson's journal describing his arrival in France in
September 1779 after twenty-nine days at sea. He was met by spectators
expecting to see "North American Savages." From *Travels in France 1779 &
1780*, GB 12579, box 1, volume 3, New York State Archives. Courtesy New
York State Library, Manuscripts and Special Collections, Albany, N.Y.

the transatlantic crossing short.[13] Ocean crossings still separated the continents for all but the adventurous.

Watson may have survived the journey with little discomfort, but he was not prepared for the starkly different culture that confronted him in prerevolutionary France. After a visit to the court at Versailles to present his papers to the king, Watson was invited by Benjamin Franklin to dine with him at the home of his noble neighbor and landlord. "Having never as yet been introduc'd in France into the polite circles & intirely rusty in their polish'd manners," Watson was "determined to make the best of it." His first step, though, "betray'd" him as an American rustic. Following Franklin from the garden into his neighbor's lavishly decorated salon, where "a number of gentlemen elegantly dress'd were huddl'd in a body," Watson bowed deeply to them. Franklin did not. Only when the other guests laughed did he realize the two "gentlemen" were "domesticks" and meant to be ignored.[14]

Not long after, Watson hired a servant of his own. He also procured his own carriage to convey him around the city, now convinced that the French understood better than the Americans "the secret of making the most of life, and of good living." Watson was, in his own words, "enraptured." He quickly put aside the prejudice against the French he had harbored "since the cradle."[15] He began to learn French; his "whole thoughts and curiosity were absorbed by the novelties around me."[16] In his notebooks intended to be read, after revision, by Americans, Watson described in detail what native residents took for granted, down to "the clattering of wooden shoes upon the pavement," the "young ladies cantering thro' the streets astride mules," and the beggars who "infested" the highways, making travel unsafe.[17] For Watson, as for other revolutionary itinerants, everything seemed new and noteworthy.

Watson took advantage of his transatlantic connections and the "funds which had been intrusted to me" to launch a "mercantile house" in Nantes. He documented the progress of his business as a lesson to future generations on the uniquely American work ethic and ambition. In contrast to the lazy French aristocrats of the Old Regime, he noted, revolutionary Americans worked hard to make their own way in the world. Only in America had young men like himself learned "to seek resources in their own minds,—to rely on their own hands,—to earn their bread by the sweat of their brow, and to spurn the props of wealth earned by others."[18]

Watson struck up correspondence with other Americans engaged in "the busy theatre of Commerce" in Europe. John Adams, many years his senior, counseled the newly arrived Watson "to cultivate the manners of your own country, not those of Europe." That did not mean putting "on a long face" or avoiding dances, theater, and cards, he added. "But you may depend on this," Adams advised, "that the more decisively you adhere to a manly simplicity in your dress, equipage & behavior, the more you devote yourself to business & study, & the less to dissipation & pleasure, the more you will recommend yourself to every man & woman in this country whose friendship & acquaintance is worth your having or wishing." Watson replied, assuring Adams that "the pursuit of mony is my profession indeed sir."[19] In that, he would remain a good American.

Years later, as he edited his journal for publication, Watson reassured his readers that even if his young head had been temporarily turned by "the splendour, elegance, and taste" of French dinners where "at least forty different dishes were served in successive courses, and all on silver utensils," and even if he partook eagerly of the privileges of prerevolutionary France, he remained at heart an American egalitarian. Watson was determined to hold close the "cordiality and simplicity" of his native land because its liberty promised entrepreneurial success.[20]

When Thomas Paine arrived in Nantes in March 1781, Watson, now proficient in French, was pressed into service as his translator. By then, Watson had adapted to life in France and was appalled at the behavior of the American hero. He acknowledged that Paine's *Common Sense* had passed through Europe as an "electric spark." Everyone knew the name of Thomas Paine and associated it with American independence, he granted. However, Paine, who spoke no French and lodged in a common boarding house, appeared to Watson to be "coarse and uncouth in his manners, loathsome in his appearance, and a disgusting egoist."[21] His odor filled the room and sent the French fleeing for air. As Watson told the story in his journal, he persuaded Paine to bathe by promising him English newspapers and instructing servants in French to turn up the heat of the water until the American hero was "well boiled." Paine appeared not to notice, asked Watson for a clean shirt, and commented with pride, "people know me almost as generally here as in America."[22]

Watson stayed in Europe until 1784, long enough to witness the early glimmers of revolutionary resistance against the Dutch stadtholder. Watson judged the Dutch Patriots, who pronounced God to be on their side, presumptuous. That claim belonged to the Americans alone, he told Adams, observing: "Seldome, in the history of man, has the interposition of Providence been more distinctly revealed than in the events of our Revolution, when the victory was withheld from the great and powerful, and given to the humble and feeble."[23] Adams, deploring "the uninterrupted Opposition of Family Connections, Court influence, and Aristocratical despotism" that had allied to block Dutch recognition of the Americans, concurred.[24]

Adams invited Watson to his new residence in The Hague. Watson must have wondered about Adams's advice to hold tight to his frugal, practical American values; it required fourteen folio sheets to inventory the gold framed mirrors, damask curtains, furniture, china, silver, and portraits of Adams's elegant residence. Yet even as he indulged in European luxuries, Adams would persist in contrasting the simple American farmers with the effete European aristocrats.

Watson spent his last night in Europe in London with the surgeon William Sharp, brother of the abolitionist Granville Sharp, whom Watson lauded as "a noble enthusiast in the cause of African emancipation and colonization." In Sharp's home, Watson read the published letters of Ignatius Sancho, a leader of the black community in London who had been born aboard a slave ship on the Middle Passage. Watson was "impelled by the interest it excited" in him to seek out Sancho's widow before he sailed. In her small cottage, he met "a family of cultivated Africans, a spectacle I had never witnessed" in America.[25] The London experience, as he described it in his journal, shook his rigid American understanding of race. Sharp entrusted two bundles of books dealing with emancipation to Watson for delivery to George Washington at Mount Vernon in hopes of persuading the American leader to free the slaves. Perhaps Watson read them aboard ship.

Watson returned home, he wrote in his journal, to "contemplate a young empire, blessed with singular advantages, unconnected from its situation with the entangled politicks of Europe, enjoying the freest local governments on earth, and inhabited by a brave and enterprising people scattered over a great continent."[26] He was ready to take advantage of boundless possibilities for getting ahead that he was convinced were to be found only in America; Europe had provided him with the capital to do so.

Watson invested his European wealth in land in the not yet developed regions of northern New York, western Virginia, and Michigan. Based on projects he had observed in his travels, he explored the possibility of connecting the Hudson River with Lake Erie, a proposal deemed so radical that it, along with his calls for free schools and turnpikes, led to his dismissal from the board of directors of the Bank of Albany. These novel ideas, though, struck him as consonant with equality as the Americans had defined it. Equality for Watson meant unbridled economic opportunity. He did not find that in Europe on the brink of revolution. The wide-open opportunity was exceptionally American.

Europeans Witness "The prodigious effects of liberty"

European entrepreneurs shared Watson's eagerness to exploit America's economic opportunities. Was there ever a better moment to expand commerce than with "a new people, a people who enjoy extensive lands nourishing an immense population and laws that are favorable to the rapid growth of that population?" French pamphleteer Jacques-Pierre Brissot and his friend Genevan financier Étienne de Clavière asked.[27] That was the optimistic view advanced by Saint John de Crèvecoeur in his influential journal published as *Letters from an American Farmer*. Crèvecoeur, the son of a French nobleman, had studied in England and served as a lieutenant in the English army defending Canada in 1759, before he married and settled down to farming in New York, cultivating his new identity as James, a simple American farmer, to narrate his journal. Crèvecoeur depicted the Americans as hardworking people who happily spurned the old world's "involuntary idleness, servile dependence, penury, and useless labour" and dedicated themselves instead to "toils of a very different nature, rewarded by ample subsistence" in the wilderness.[28]

Crèvecoeur was no revolutionary. In 1779, as the fighting drew closer to his home in upstate New York, he left his young family and returned to

Europe. Crèvecoeur had sold his American journal to an English publisher for thirty guineas before crossing the channel to France. Although *Letters from an American Farmer* did not elicit much interest in America, it was widely read in Europe, with new editions published in London, Dublin, Belfast, Leipzig, Paris, and Maastricht. Translated into a romantic French prose, Crèvecoeur's manuscript expanded to twice its original length. A countess, Sophie d'Houdetot (the inspiration for Rousseau's *Julie*) introduced him to the American envoy, Benjamin Franklin, who in turn offered Crèvecoeur access to the elite circles of Paris. In 1787, Crèvecoeur, together with Brissot and Clavière, organized the Gallo-American Society "to enlighten Europeans curious about the progress of America."[29]

Brissot, who had always wanted to see America for himself, finally succeeded in 1788 in convincing three European bankers to send him across the Atlantic to explore investment opportunities in the American debt. He disembarked in Boston expecting to meet "a people whom nature, education, and tradition had endowed with that equality of rights which is everywhere else considered a chimerical dream."[30] Letters of introduction from the marquis de Lafayette gave him an easy entrée into the inner circles of American political society. Brissot discussed alfalfa farming with John Adams, books with Benjamin Franklin, and barn designs with George Washington. Only Crèvecoeur was begrudging in his welcome, putting Brissot up for one night and then ushering him to a lodging house around the corner.

Brissot kept a journal during his six-month trip. In the preface, he instructed other aspiring travelers in the practice of journal keeping. "If he wishes nothing to escape him he must get used to noting things rapidly and in such a way as not to miss anything." Travelers should never fall behind in their recording, "for the observations pile up in the mind," but instead must be disciplined about writing every evening. He advised a potential travel writer to climb into garrets, visit stables, and go beyond "the confines of his dignity."[31]

Writing with all the naïveté of a newly arrived traveler, Brissot was easily convinced that without aristocratic titles and "conscious of their liberty," Americans treated each other "as merely brothers and equals." He acknowledged that Europeans habituated to "the depradations of despotism" might struggle "to accustom themselves to the idea of a 'sovereign' people, of a president, or 'elective king,' who shakes hands with a workingman, has no guards at his door, travels about on foot etc."[32] Other European visitors to revolutionary America who extolled the virtues of liberty and equality in the abstract were unwilling to share a bench in an inn with a coachman.

Brissot especially appreciated the openness of unmarried girls in America, whose liberty seemed to him consistent with a virtuous republic. He was amazed to learn that they could ride in a chaise with a young man without fear of seduction. The married women Brissot met in America reminded him of the politically engaged republican women of Geneva. They cared about nothing so much as making their husbands happy and bringing up virtuous children for the new republic, he assumed, and did not indulge in the frequent affairs that characterized the life of French aristocracy. His own wife, Brissot added, was home in Paris reading Rousseau's *Émile*. "Let those who doubt the prodigious effects of liberty on man and on his industry come to America!" Jacques-Pierre Brissot advised readers he hoped would follow him to this new republic. "What miracles they will witness!"[33]

On a tour of the South, though, Brissot came face to face with American institutions that disturbed his idyllic picture. A committed campaigner against the slave trade, he was shocked by the plantations he visited and by his conversations with their masters. He asked his Quaker hosts in Philadelphia, all committed abolitionists, how "men who were taking up arms to defend their own liberty" could "rob other men of this same blessing?"[34] Indolent white plantation owners living off the labor of their slaves were no better than leisured aristocrats in Europe. Although Brissot had intended to hold up America as a land of promise to his European readers, he could not reconcile bondage with revolutionary principles. All he could do was point to the valiant efforts of American abolitionists before the Revolution, including the tailor John Woolman and the multilingual French émigré Anthony Benezet.

Brissot's frustration with American slavery was echoed by European visitors arriving in the new American republic on diplomatic missions from Europe. François Barbé-Marbois, first secretary to the French minister, Anne César de la Luzerne, crossed the Atlantic with John Adams and his son. From their hammocks slung at the back of the *Sensible*, Barbé-Marbois and the twelve-year-old John Quincy witnessed the "keel hauling" of a black slave on a passing corsair. In the journal that he kept, Barbé-Marbois recounted his horror when he realized that the black object he saw falling from the top of the yards into the sea only to be yanked back up into the air and dropped down again was "a miserable negro, entirely naked."[35] A twenty-four-year-old Dutch diplomat, Carel de Vos, on his first trip out of Philadelphia, witnessed a slave auction in Fredericksburg, "an event that was very shocking to us as Europeans and that seemed so contradictory to the principles of American freedom."[36] Black men were rented for ten or eleven pounds per year, he observed, or even traded for tobacco, as if they were beasts. The encounter with slavery jolted de Vos, otherwise a dispassionate observer of architecture, politics, and flora and fauna in the new republic, out of his customary restraint.

Thomas Jefferson's neighbor, the Tuscan merchant Filippo Mazzei, who enthusiastically adopted the American revolutionary cause as his own, confronted the role of slavery in a prosperous agricultural economy as a Virginian farmer. Together with Jefferson, he drew up plans to introduce grapevines and olive, citrus, and mulberry trees to the new world. In his journal, though, Mazzei asked how it was possible "that after the famous revolution succeeded in America, that after the principles were established for new governments that breathed liberty and equality, slavery could still exist in the United States."[37] How could the self-sufficient farmers held up by European philosophers as the ideal citizens of a modern republic limit liberty to white settlers like themselves? Mazzei adapted to Jefferson's Virginia, but not to its treatment of men and women taken from Africa to labor in the New World.

Mazzei's journal, *Historic and Political Research on the United States of America*, was translated into French by one of the staunchest French abolitionists, the marquis de Condorcet, and his wife, Sophie de Grouchy. Mazzei criticized Crèvecoeur's portrayal of American customs as overly idyllic. However, even the optimistic Crèvecoeur's journal had turned dark at the end. Crèvecoeur questioned the humanity of American revolutionaries who could auction Africans like beasts, "the daughter torn from her weeping mother, the children from wretched parents, the wife from loving husband . . . arranged like horses at a fair, they are branded like cattle, and then driven to toil, to starve, and to languish, for a few years, on the different plantations of these citizens."[38] Brissot leaped to Crèvecoeur's defense, despite agreeing with Mazzei that resettlement of blacks in Africa offered the best solution to the deep racial divide in America.

Brissot planned to publish his journal to encourage other entrepreneurial Europeans to follow him to America, but instead got caught up in the French Revolution. He finally published it in 1791 as a lesson to the French on securing their revolutionary liberty and equality and resisting the lure of luxury and privilege. His journal was translated and republished the next year by the American poet and businessman Joel Barlow, who left out everything critical of the United States. It went through five German editions, one Irish, one Dutch, and one Swedish.

Barbé-Marbois, named French consul to America and then tapped as intendant of Saint-Domingue, had to wait for two decades to edit his journal. Exile in French Guiana gave him time to reflect on senators he observed on the Philadelphia waterfront returning from market, fish tucked under their arms. In his journal, like Brissot, he wondered whether Europeans accustomed to "porters, stewards, butlers, and covered carriages with springs" would ever offer "the same resistance to despotism" as Americans.[39] Barbé-Marbois supplemented his original journal entries with information drawn from letters he had written to his wife that she collected for him. It was handed down through generations until it was finally published in an English translation in 1920.

As travelers crossed the Atlantic between the two revolutions, they wondered whether absolute monarchies could navigate their way peacefully toward a republic, or whether that fate was reserved for the New World. Brissot compared the American revolutionaries with French patriots "who extol the Declaration of the Rights of Man while gravely considering the choice of a new cabriolet or a fashionable waistcoat."[40] When the crisis that would topple one of the stablest of the Old World monarchies intensified, he asked whether the French had not become too refined over the centuries for liberty as the Americans had defined their natural rights. Were Europeans perhaps too attached to the luxuries and privileges of the Old Regime to see a revolution through to the end? Could it be that the American people inhabiting their rustic paradise were unique?

Witness to the Fire That Has "consumed all the dusty cobwebs of antiquity": Dumont in Paris, 1789–91

Defying the expectations of almost all of the transatlantic travelers, France roused itself "from its circle of frivolities" to revolt in the spring of 1789. Genevan pastor Étienne Dumont predicted from Paris that liberty and equality, spawned by the Enlightenment and reared in the American "nursery of patriots," would define the new world in France.[41] Dumont had emigrated to Saint Petersburg when the French crushed the Genevan Revolution of 1782. He moved on to Lord Lansdowne's Bowood House in Wiltshire, where he joined a political circle that included the Baron d'Holbach, Mirabeau, Benjamin Franklin, and Joseph Priestly. Word of revolutionary stirrings in Geneva drew Dumont back across the Channel to try to negotiate French support for Genevan reforms.

Dumont decamped at the home of Brissot's friend the Genevan banker Étienne Clavière outside of Paris, collaborating with other Genevan exiles in writing speeches and articles for Mirabeau. Dumont left every few days for Versailles to observe the French Estates General, meeting for the first time in more than a century. "Everything remains to be done and everything is possible," he wrote his friend British lawyer Samuel Romilly, urging him to come to France. "All that was rock solid is now as malleable as wax," he promised.[42] The world was changing, and the new revolutionary wave that would sweep Europe was beginning in Paris.

On his way to join Mirabeau for dinner shortly after his arrival in Paris, the diplomatic Dumont brushed off cautions offered by his hosts about not adhering to French protocol. "A foreigner can form friendships with whom he likes," Dumont explained of his brash conduct.[43] Outsiders, unconstrained by the conventional boundaries of social standing or political allegiance, could meet with everyone. That freedom gave adventurous travelers a unique perspective on the revolutions through which they moved and to which some returned when they went home.

Dumont chronicled "the chaos of confused opinions" that was revolutionary France in the spring of 1789. He reported that the commoners elected as the Third Estate wanted delegates from all three estates to deliberate together in one room, voting individually, rather than adjourning to three separate rooms, with each estate getting one vote.[44] Dumont could not understand why the first two estates, the clergy and the nobility, refused to vote in a common assembly with the commoners. Even from the perspective of a Genevan pastor accustomed to a hierarchical social ordering, this entrenched defense of privilege appeared ridiculous. Why should "a hundred thousand noblemen and eighty thousand priests have the confidence to complain that they would be considered as equal to the other twenty-four million countrymen?" Dumont asked in May 1789.[45] He was frustrated that the privileged orders who made up such a small part of the French population presumed to block reform.

In his journal entry of 18 June 1789, Dumont marveled at the momentous transformation of the French government he had just witnessed. It had happened so suddenly. The Third Estate had arrived in the morning to find the meeting room barred shut. These delegates then proceeded, in Dumont's view, with the impetuosity of the French character, to the tennis court, where they proclaimed themselves the National Assembly two days later. He described the Tennis Court Oath as "nothing less than a declaration of independence," the beginning of the end of the Old Regime. Instead of estates defined by the privileges of birth, the deputies to the National Assembly now referred to classes, "a denomination well calculated to strip those orders of the respect which they derived from their ancient titles," and to set the nobles and clergy "in their proper light as usurpers."[46] Dumont recognized that French deputies to the Third Estate thought of themselves no longer as representatives of orders defined by inheritance but as national citizens with rights. Inspired to hasten a similar dismantling of privilege in Geneva, Dumont set to work to write a new constitution for his native land, which appeared to be launching another revolution of its own.

Dumont regretted that he had spent the fourteenth of July at Versailles and missed the storming of the fortress like Bastille in Paris. He had to rely on others' accounts of the crowds that wrested control of the prison and seized its arms, decapitating the old governor of the prison and mounting his head on a pike. As soon as he could get to Paris, Dumont visited the Faubourg Saint-Antoine, the poor district of the French capital so long in the shadow of the Bastille, and described for his readers firsthand "the whole prison, its dark stair-cases, its mysterious passages, its triple doors plated with iron and fastened by enormous bolts, its cells, which resembled graves."[47] The Genevan émigré rejoiced that the common people of France were claiming their sovereign rights and that their delegates were writing a constitution for the nation.

Identifying as enthusiastically with the French revolutionaries as the French revolutionary Brissot had seven years earlier with the Genevans, Dumont proclaimed: "We may be said in the space of a week to have lived a century." History was moving at such a rapid pace that Dumont struggled to keep up in his journal with the events he witnessed. He apologized for neglecting his journal through much of July 1789: "I have been so much taken up with the astonishing events which have happened here, that I have not had a moment's leisure to write to you."[48] Journal writing required quiet moments for reflection, and these were in short supply in revolutionary Paris in the summer of 1789.

On the night of 4 August 1789, the French National Assembly convened and with little debate voted to abolish all of the feudal privileges that remained from the Old Regime. Rather than voicing his own opinion of the dramatic events about which he was beginning to harbor doubts, in his journal Dumont quoted Mirabeau, who lamented that "it was just like the French. They are a whole month disputing over syllables [in writing the Declaration of the Rights of Man], and then, in one night, they upset the whole of the ancient law and order of the kingdom."[49] Dumont's journal entry for 15 August excused the escalating violence of the French Revolution as the inevitable result of a servile people suddenly freed and declared equal. The French lacked the historical tradition of liberty written into constitutions on which the Genevans, the Dutch, and the Belgians had founded their revolutions. The French themselves admitted that they "had been sunk in slavery for centuries," and so had to turn to philosophical principles instead of experience.[50]

Although he had identified with the promise of the French in the spring of 1789, by August, Dumont had begun to distance himself from the violence of their revolution. Like many of his American friends in Paris, he worried about the democracy fueled by popular revolution. Perhaps the traveling skeptics were right to doubt the aptitude of the French for revolution. The moderation of the constitution writers who had prevailed in previous revolutions was being impetuously trampled underfoot by Parisian crowds.

Disillusioned by the instability of revolutionary France and full of hope for revolutionary Geneva, Dumont left for home in 1790, traveling with Achille du Chastellet, a French aristocrat who had served as an aide de camp in the American Revolution before joining the French army. In January 1789, triggered by a spike in the price of bread, Genevan revolutionaries had torn down the city gates, built barricades, and driven out foreign troops with fire pumps filled with boiling water and soap lye. In a February edict, the Genevans banished all foreign troops from their city and invited the exiles of 1782 to return, though not to take up politics in Geneva again. Dumont celebrated. "Great news! Happy news! Extraordinary news," he wrote in his journal. He lobbied the French, still guarantors of the Genevan constitution, to permit the exiles to return to their offices in Geneva. He hoped after seven years' exile "to finish what the Genevan revolution [of 1782] had only suggested," an enduring revolution for equality and citizenship.[51] The French refused to allow the Genevan revolutionaries to resume their offices.

The problem was not just with the French. Dumont realized as soon as he reached Geneva that his time abroad in Saint Petersburg, London, and Paris discussing the rights of man with Mirabeau, Sieyès, and Romilly had enlarged his "ideas of Liberty" beyond those of the Genevan revolutionaries who had never left their city-state, a common fate of expatriates.[52] He found himself caught between two revolutions: too radical in his republicanism for the Genevans and too moderate in his condemnation of popular democracy for the French. He felt like an outsider to both.

An admirer of the British separation of powers, Dumont traveled back to England from Geneva.[53] Changes should be accomplished through legal means, he was now even more convinced than ever. There, Samuel Romilly pressed him to publish his journal. His personal history of the first year of the French Revolution would serve as a tribute to their mutual friend Mirabeau. Dumont refused. "Of what use are books?" he asked. "Who can write or even think without disgust, when he sees the most enlightened country in Europe returning to a state of barbarism? The howlings of savages are less frightful than the harangues of the representatives of a nation esteemed the gentlest and the most polished of the continent."[54] He was thoroughly disillusioned.

Revolution, so reasonable in America and Geneva, had become too "enthusiastic" in France for Dumont. Even Brissot, who "would have been excellent had he been born in the United States," had been swept away in France "by the enthusiasm of Liberty."[55] There, crowds dictated their unstable democracy. Excessive liberty had degenerated into French license, he observed, and all in the name of his countryman Rousseau. Dumont feared the political leaders of France would never agree to a constitutional consensus, unlike the British in 1688. He added little to his journal on the French Revolution after he returned to Paris on his way to England. "The fire which has been thus kindled," he remarked, had by then "consumed all the dusty cobwebs of antiquity, together with the tarnished liveries of magnificence."[56]

In 1792, Romilly translated Dumont's journal into English. Published as *The Groenvelt Letters*, alleged to be a translation from a German traveler, Henry Frederic Groenvelt, the journal included twelve letters from Dumont and ten from Romilly.[57] Dumont attempted to explain the French violence after the Terror of 1793, while Romilly condemned it. Anonymous publication protected them both from the many British critics of the French Revolution. After Dumont's death, his nephew Jacob-Louis Duval published a more complete edition of Dumont's narrative as the *Recollections of Mirabeau*. Duval claimed in the preface that his uncle's journal was more reliable than "most writings of its kind" because "M. Dumont, a foreigner in France, always refused by a rare feeling of delicacy to take any active part in the events that were taking place before his eyes. He therefore has nothing to conceal."[58] Duval thought that distance lent Dumont's journal more credibility, even if the claim was not exactly true.

Helen Maria Williams in Paris: "Notwithstanding a few shocking instances of public vengeance"

The English poet and novelist Helen Maria Williams picked up the story of the French Revolution where Dumont's journal left off. Williams, however, was less quick to condemn the French than he. Before she left England for France, she sounded the themes of revolutionary universality in her poetry. One of her best known poems, "On the Bill Lately Passed for Regulating the Slave Trade," condemned that commerce, and "An Ode

FIGURE 2.2

Portrait of the English author Helen Maria Williams, by an unknown artist and
published by Dean and Munday. NPG8601, stipple engraving. The journals
Williams published based on her observations provided details of the French
Revolution for the British public. Courtesy of National Portrait Gallery, London

to Peace" celebrated the end of the American Revolution. Her sentimental novel *Julia* invited comparison with Rousseau's *Julie, ou la nouvelle Héloïse*.

Williams arrived in Paris on 13 July 1790, the eve of the first celebration of the Festival of the Federation. She watched the processions of men and women from the provinces assembling on the Champs de Mars, where the hero of the American Revolution, the marquis de Lafayette, now major general of the French Federation, swore the civic oath to the revolution. "How am I to paint the impetuous feelings of that immense, that exulting multitude?" she asked in her journal, intended for publication in England.[59] "It was man reclaiming and establishing the most noble of his rights, and all it required was a simple sentiment of humanity to become in that moment a citizen of the world."[60] John Paul Jones led an American delegation that included Thomas Paine and the poet Joel Barlow. Here, for Williams, was the true manifestation of a cosmopolitan revolution.

Williams followed in Dumont's path, making her own pilgrimage to the Bastille. In her account, she singled out the women in the crowd who, driven by their families' hunger, "far from indulging the fears incident to our feeble sex," had defied "the cannon of the Bastille . . . with a spirit worthy of roman matrons."[61] Williams also reminded her readers of the October 1789 march to Versailles by Parisian women. They had covered the twenty kilometers in the cold rain to demand lower bread prices and an end to the king's veto power. Lafayette followed the women to Versailles with the national guard and persuaded the crowd to spare the royal family. She imagined for her readers the scene of fishwives storming the royal apartments and then triumphantly leading the king, the queen, and the dauphin back to the French capital. She approved. After the historical prologue, Williams turned in her journal to the events of the French Revolution she witnessed herself.

Williams regularly attended the debates of the National Assembly, joining the other women in the galleries. Where Dumont heard chaos and confusion in revolutionary France, Williams saw "the mists of ignorance and error . . . rolling away, and the benign beams of philosophy . . . spreading their lustre over the nations."[62] The ideals of the Enlightenment were being realized in Europe as in America, she rejoiced. In France, at last, "the golden dream of the moralist" had become "historical fact."[63]

It took her longer than most English and American visitors to be disillusioned by the evidence. For a while, Williams reveled in the tumult of French debates driven by philosophical principles, such a contrast to the more restrained English Parliament, which had yet to outlaw the slave trade.

Like Dumont, Williams was especially stirred by Mirabeau, "the professed friend of the African race," when he demanded an end to the slave trade. A convinced abolitionist, Williams pronounced the revolutionary French too enlightened to "persist in thinking what is morally wrong, can be politically right," as the English continued to do.[64] She could not countenance the economic justifications of the slave trade.

Williams returned to England in September 1790 for a brief visit, as the first volume of her letters on the French Revolution was published. She deplored the timidity of the English, who criticized her as they fretted about the violence of the crowds in the streets of Paris. "Alas," she responded to her more cautious readers, "where do the records of history point out a revolution unstained by some actions of barbarity?"[65] Dumont would have answered, in England in 1688.

Most travelers' journals written in the midst of revolutions strove to engage the emotions of their readers, for, as the London salonnière Elizabeth Montagu wrote her sister, "without the accompaniment of Sympathy, a long narrative of frivolous matters is the most tiresome thing in the world."[66] That often meant taking sides in narrating events. Like other members of the large community of American and English expatriates who gathered in Paris in the first years of the French Revolution, Williams felt most at home in Paris with the moderate revolutionaries, the Girondins, who believed in a free market, not the economic leveling advocated by the more radical Jacobins.

Williams discussed politics at the salon of Madame Roland, a prominent Girondin, and entertained a salon of her own on Sundays in her apartment. Traveling revolutionary exiles gathered there to drink tea, including Brissot, Joel and Ruth Barlow from Connecticut, Thomas Paine, the German chronicler Georg Förster, Wolfe Tone from Ireland, and Mary Wollstonecraft, the English feminist. Wollstonecraft, who found Williams's manner somewhat affected ("authorship is a heavy weight for female shoulders"), was nevertheless drawn to Williams "by her simple heart" and her powerful connections.[67] Williams seemed to know everyone in revolutionary politics, including the Jacobin leader Maximilien Robespierre, who stopped by her apartment to share in the political conversation. The adventurous Venezuelan general Francisco Miranda, who would fight for the French revolutionaries before leading campaigns for independence in South America, often visited her, as did the Polish engineer who fought in the American Revolution, Thaddeus Kościuszko. She also attracted John Hurford Stone, a wealthy English coal merchant who managed his manufacturing interests as he promoted abolitionism on both sides of the Channel. They never married, but lived together until his death in 1818.

The expatriates from Britain and America gathered every Sunday and Thursday at White's Hotel in the Passage des Petits Pères. Calling themselves the Society of the Rights of Man, they toasted the victories of the French Revolution with deputies from the National Convention and celebrated French General Dumouriez's victory over the Austrians at Jemappes. They sang "Ça Ira" and the Marseillaise, translated into English by Helen Maria Williams, as well as a parody of "God Save the King" composed by Joel Barlow.

Williams had her critics. Some challenged her amorous liaison with a married man, Stone, others her politics. English novelist Laetitia Matilda Hawkins published a two-volume attack on the widely read *Letters from France*, charging that Williams inflamed "the minds of my countrywomen with notions they had better be without." How, Hawkins wanted to know, could a woman condone the violence of the French Revolution? And why, she asked, would an English author celebrate the demise of hereditary privileges? Hawkins also condemned Williams for her unconditional support of the abolitionists. Above all, she criticized Williams for intruding into politics, properly the domain of the "male genius," which alone could plumb "the depths of science and accumulated wisdom of ages."[68] She insisted that Williams would be more usefully engaged as a wife and mother back in England.

Rather than viewing her politics as unfeminine, the Société des Amis de la Constitution (Society of the friends of the constitution) of Rouen in northern France held Williams up as a model of true domesticity. Earlier, in London, Williams had befriended a young French couple and helped them to marry over the objections of an aristocratic father, an example of revolution in the family. It did not seem to matter to the Rouen revolutionaries that the English author who had publicly come to the aid of the French couple was a single woman living with a married man. They assigned her the role of "Liberty." She would bedeck the altar in Rouen in a dramatic representation of *La famille patriotique* (The patriotic family).

Williams in turn heralded "the considerable role" French women played in their revolution.[69] Rather than be intimidated by Hawkins and the other critics, Williams called on English women to emulate the example of the French and "to intervene in the important questions or interests of human concern."[70] Women had a different role to play than men, Williams explained, because their natures were not the same. In a revolutionary age, she was convinced, the morality of women gave them a particular role to play in politics. "To understand the common good," she argued, "it is not necessary to possess the wisdom of a philosopher, it is enough to have the sensibility of a woman."[71] This sensibility, she believed, distinguished her journal from the stack of eyewitness accounts written by men. She told stories that men overlooked, guaranteeing a substantial audience for her volumes of letters in England.

After a second trip to England, Williams brought her mother and two sisters back with her to Paris, arriving just in time to experience the beginning of the Terror on 10 August 1792. Looking down from their windows on the Rue de Lille, the Williamses saw the Parisians storm the Tuileries. Helen Maria Williams described for her English readers the crowd, after being pushed back several times, mounting a final assault on the royal palace. To escape their vengeance, Louis XVI and his family fled through the passages to the meeting room of the Legislative Assembly. The crowd brazenly pursued the royal family through the royal apartments until the Swiss Guards defending them fired on the insurgents. To end the melee, Louis XVI ordered his guards to put down their arms. He assumed his subjects would then calmly retire. Instead, the crowd massacred the guards, stripping them of their clothing and mutilating their bodies. Crossing the gardens the next day, Williams reported that she inadvertently stumbled over two dead guards, an incident that upset her readers more than it did Williams.

In September 1792, as Prussian troops approached Paris, mobs stormed prisons rumored to house counterrevolutionaries. They tried the prisoners on the spot and killed those they pronounced guilty, mounting their heads on pikes. Williams's good friend Anna Seward, back in England, counseled her, in a letter published in *Gentleman's Magazine*, "to fly that land of carnage." How, she asked, could Williams call "the fire which led the French into chaos the rising sun of Liberty"?[72] Williams dismissed Seward's advice and stayed on, little wavering from the conviction expressed in her first volume of letters in 1790 that "notwithstanding a few shocking instances of public vengeance, the liberty of twenty-four millions of people will have been purchased at a far cheaper rate than could ever have been expected from the former experience of the world."[73] The French had learned from the Americans, who had taken lessons from the seventeenth-century English revolutionaries, and in the end, Williams predicted, they would teach "mankind a lesson, which perhaps the whole human race will be proud to learn."[74]

At the height of the Terror in 1793, though, Williams must have had her doubts as the ruling Jacobins rounded up the Girondins, including many of her closest friends, and charged them as counterrevolutionaries. Also falling under suspicion were the numerous foreigners befriended by the Girondins. Outsiders were not as free, as Dumont had once thought, to flout national customs or bridge political factions. After the night when the Convention called for the arrest of all English expatriates, Williams, her mother, and her sister were relieved to see the dawn in their own apartment. They assumed that as women they had been spared. Later that day, however, they were arrested and escorted by commissioners from the revolutionary committee to the Luxembourg prison. From their cell, they heard that the Girondins were guillotined on 26 October 1793. The Williams sisters and their mother were freed at the end of December. Robespierre ordered all foreigners to leave the capital in April 1794 and, together with Stone, they fled to Switzerland.

After the Jacobin leader Robespierre fell victim to the guillotine, Williams returned to France to publish a third and fourth volume of her letters in 1795 and 1796. She acknowledged, unlike most other American and English visitors, that revolutions cost blood. When other exiles questioned the French Revolution for betraying the promise of the summer of

1789 with a bloodbath, Williams was steadfast in her acceptance of the revolution that swept away the Old Regime of privilege.

In 1795, after six years of upheaval in France, this revolutionary Atlantic world had begun to seem inordinately noisy even to Helen Maria Williams. Remembering her prison cell in Paris, the English writer sighed, "How I envied the peasant in his lonely hut! . . . My disturbed imagination divided the communities of men but into two classes, the oppressor and the oppressed; and peace seemed only to exist with solitude."[75] She had tried to retire to the mountains of Switzerland but discovered there was no escape from politics. There was no way to avoid taking sides in a world divided into two, "the oppressor and the oppressed."

Many of her fellow travelers, including veteran revolutionaries, had been frightened by the violence of the Terror. In comparing revolutions, Brissot observed, "Natives are often too prejudiced in favor of their native land, and foreigners are too prejudiced against them."[76] It was the job of the travel journal writer, he explained, to ask questions abroad to reveal the truth in between. Only the rare travelers who shared in the sociability of revolutionary Paris before the Terror came away convinced cosmopolitans, finding that "truth in between." Williams was one of them.

"Alarmingly republican": Transformed Travelers between Revolutions

The revolutionary French offered shelter, if not security, to revolutionary refugees and aspirants from across the Atlantic world. Thomas Paine carried the American flag in the French Festival on the Champ de Mars in Paris in the summer of 1790, explaining, "A share in two revolutions is living to some purpose."[77] Together with many other foreigners in Paris, Paine claimed a role in what he envisioned as a universal world revolution for liberty. The marquis de Lafayette entrusted Paine with the key to the Bastille. Paine was to convey "this early trophy of the Spoils of Despotism and the first ripe fruits of American principles transplanted into Europe to his great Master and Patron," George Washington.[78]

In the beginning, the French Revolution had appeared to be an extension of the American Revolution onto a continent still infested with monarchs and overrun by aristocrats. Jefferson was one among many Americans who credited the Americans with waking up the French "from the sleep of despotism in which they were sunk."[79] There remained a great deal of work to be done. Paine and Jefferson expected the French to take the lead in that revolution. As late as 1792, a dinner companion commented that "like his friend T. Payne [Jefferson] cannot live but in a revolution, and all events in Europe are only considered by him in the relation they bear to the probability of a revolution to be produced by them."[80]

In the summer of 1789, American and French revolutionaries openly celebrated their shared experiment. Newly arrived in Paris, the American diplomat Gouverneur Morris wrote his friend the comte de Moustier, French minister in New York, that he found "on this Side of the Atlantic a strong resemblance to what I left on the other: a Nation which exists in Hopes, Prospects, and Expectations."[81] The Société de 1789 gathered French moderates, many of them, such as Lafayette, Condorcet, and La Rochefoucauld, closely tied to America, in 1790 to plot universal human progress guided by reason. After the summer of 1791, most visitors from the new United States found fewer reasons to join the new republics in common cause. In June 1791, Thomas Jefferson's aide William Short warned him from Paris that France had become "alarmingly republican."[82] Short was referring not only to the presumed fate of the king after his capture at Varennes on the French border, but to the readiness of crowds to take to the streets of Paris. "Those who court the People have a very capricious Mistress," Morris, newly appointed American minister plenipotentiary for France, wrote Short.[83] It was not just that the French Revolution had taken a radical turn between 1789 and 1792.

With few exceptions, during the French Revolution, American expatriates in Paris frequented the circles of the elite. Morris's French mistress entertained him at the Louvre. A committed republican in America, Morris proved loyal to the royal family in France throughout the Revolution. It was to Morris that Louis XVI entrusted his treasures before the storming of the Tuileries. The American expatriates adapted to their surroundings. They were quite comfortable among the privileges against which Adams had warned Watson and amid which they all lived abroad. America may have been the land of equality, of opportunity, and of the rustic farmer celebrated in French journals, but these travelers feared the common people of France, most often depicted in their journals as unruly and threatening crowds. They noted the differences separating the two continents.

Traveling in the other direction, European travelers who came to America imagining the land of equal opportunity, left disillusioned by the Americans' unwillingness to abolish the institution of slavery.[84] After their visits to the plantations owned by the founding fathers of America, they, too, returned home committed exceptionalists.

The ideas that crossed national borders in pamphlets influenced the course of their neighbors' politics; the revolutionaries who traveled often found that they themselves had been transformed by the experience. That was true of the visitors to America in the decade before the French Revolution, such as Brissot, who noticed coachmen sharing benches with worthier travelers, and of the American expatriates who planted corn in the formal gardens of the Champs Élysées during the opening years of the French Revolution. Watson and Brissot both had ongoing revolutions to which they could return from their travels, the first engaging in commerce, the second in politics. Dumont and Williams did not have that option. Geneva's second revolution of 1789 was as short-lived as the first in 1782, and England seemed inhospitable to revolution in Williams's eyes, if not Dumont's. Writing of revolutionary opportunities yet to be realized, neither of them returned home to resettle comfortably among compatriots. Like the travelers of the next chapter, the experience of revolution set them upon a restless quest for liberty that continued across borders for the rest of their lives.

THREE

The Revolutionary Narratives of Black "citizens of the world"

Travelers fleeing slavery in the newly independent United States in 1782 crossed the Atlantic in search of what they called liberty. Their paths from the American South to Nova Scotia to London and Sierra Leone crossed those of white revolutionaries integrally interested in their plight. Their narratives compiled as they neared the end of their journey revealed the frustrations and disappointments, as well as dreams of the revolutionary era when commerce, religion, and political ideals combined to drive the abolitionists' colonial projects. Settling at last in Sierra Leone, the black travelers' liberty amalgamated different ideals gathered en route through the revolutionary era.

O n his return from Africa, Swedish abolitionist Carl Wadström encountered an astonishing number of intrepid black sailors who, he observed, "expose themselves voluntarily to great dangers, and to many inconveniences of life, only from a hope of obtaining a more extensive Liberty than at present they enjoy."[1] He knew that it was the American Revolution that had set thousands of people of color in motion. He did not realize that they constituted the largest transatlantic migration of the revolutionary era. These travelers fleeing slavery felt less at home in this revolutionary world than the English poets and Genevan pastors who had settled provisionally in Paris.

In search of their own land, transatlantic cosmopolitans "roved" across three continents, in the words of Olaudah Equiano, whose *Interesting Narrative of the Life of Olaudah Equiano, or Gustavus Vassa, the African, Written by Himself* took readers on journeys back and forth across the Atlantic. Freed slaves fearing recapture by the victorious American revolutionaries, they followed the British promise of liberty to Nova Scotia, the West Indies, England, and eventually Sierra Leone. As they journeyed along the margins of revolutions, their vision of "a more extensive Liberty" emerged.

Some of these imperial itinerants kept journals; more composed narratives toward the end of their lives based on their memories of arduous sojourns. The "autobiographical turn" of these black writers almost always originated with the reclaiming of an African identity, some tied to a specific ethnic kinship and others to a mythic African past.[2] That thrust their narratives into the midst of the discussion over the humanity of Africans at a time when European travelers were chronicling the limitations posed by slavery to American liberty and Americans were exploring the explosive possibilities of the new French liberty. Writing as Africans, but also as Christians, these black writers disrupted the preconceived categories held by their white European and American readers.

Narratives written by freed slaves forced their readers on both sides of the Atlantic to confront the experience of human bondage. Their descriptions of the stench of the close quarters on the Middle Passage on slave ships bound for the Americas were even more disturbing to most eighteenth-century readers than the images of carts rolling to the guillotine in Paris painted by American and English visitors to revolutionary France. Equiano recounted in his widely read *Interesting Narrative* stories of masters whose "injustice and insanity would shock the morality and common sense of a Samoyed or a Hottentot," white men who fathered children with their slaves and then worked their own offspring almost to death in the fields, buying and selling them for fifteen pounds.[3] His eloquent narrative undermined readers' fundamental assumptions of the humanity of white Christian men and the barbarity of African slaves.

One of the first white women to record her visit to West Africa, Anna Falconbridge purposefully unsettled the assumptions of the readers of her epistolary journal. Although she complained that the daily writing was "really a fatiguing job, being obliged to sit in bed with a book placed on my knee, which serves for a writing desk," she diligently recorded the incidents of malfeasance, crop failure, and racial disharmony that would call into question the motives of the directors who had sent her husband, a slave ship's surgeon turned abolitionist, to settle a colony of free blacks in Sierra Leone.[4] John Clarkson, a young naval officer and the first governor of Sierra Leone, chronicled his encounters in this new world of free blacks on the African coast that he and the Falconbridges helped to mold.[5] Imperialism and abolition "dove tailed" in this new era of freedom, but the obstacles to an easy fit were many.[6] Falconbridge's narrative was re-printed twice in 1794 and reissued in a new edition in 1802, but Clarkson was afraid of adding fodder to the attacks on the antislavery movement that had aligned itself with imperialism and decided not to publish his account.

By contrast, the two-volume work by his older brother, the renowned abolitionist Thomas Clarkson, *The History of the Rise, Progress, and Accomplishment of the Abolition of the Slave-Trade by the British Parliament,* was widely read at the time and has continued to define our understanding of the antislavery movement in Britain. That was its purpose. Thomas Clarkson attributed the "progress" of abolitionism to Christian altruism, to the convergence of Quaker activists, Evangelicals, and, of course, his own efforts, all informed by a British tradition of liberty.[7] His narrative recorded that history of individual choice and action.

The story of collective action to found a free state on the coast of Africa comes from the narratives, published and unpublished, written by the black loyalists and abolitionists who "roved" over three continents and sailed the seas. The revolutions of the indigenous people of Benna, Moria, and Sumbuya among whom black loyalists settled are rarely mentioned in narratives.[8] All of these life stories, recorded or not, were integrally intertwined with white commerce and political revolutions on the one hand, but on the other, they were mostly invisible to white revolutionaries. Their paths all crossed because their goals interlocked around the tortuous dilemma of slavery. Their narratives carried their readers along on their quest for a liberty whose definition stretched from the American Revolution through the French Revolution to insurrection in Sierra Leone.

"Great liberty from the Lord": Freed Slaves after the American Revolution

In 1789, the first year of the French Revolution, Olaudah Equiano defined himself in print as a free black man. Spending much of his life at sea between continents, "Olaudah Equiano, or Gustavus Vassa, the African," challenged the fixed identities that populated the late-eighteenth-century Atlantic world by claiming multiple ones. "A native of Africa," he wrote, he felt "almost an Englishman."[9] His elegant portrait inside the cover of his autobiography displayed a black man dressed as a European, open book in hand. It was not only his name that slipped from one paragraph to the next in this revolutionary document. Olaudah Equiano or Gustavus Vassa, the African, as he was named by an owner and as he called himself, filled lecture halls night after night to promote his self-published autobiography on tours of Britain. It was reprinted eight times in his lifetime, with translations published in the United Provinces, Russia, and Germany.

In the first paragraph of his chronicle, Equiano reflected, "I believe there are few events in my life which have not happened to many."[10] His was the story of thousands of men, women, and children of color his

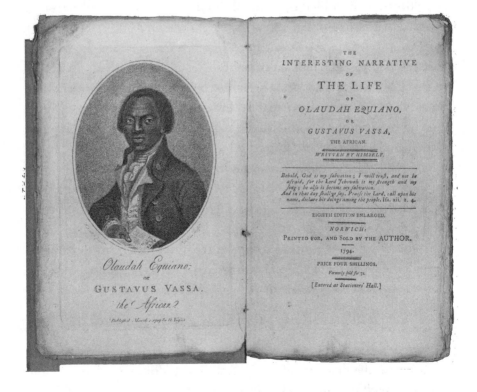

FIGURE 3.1
Frontispiece and title page from *The Interesting Narrative of the Life of Olaudah Equiano*. Readers would have been struck by the elegant portrait of "the African" in European dress. Courtesy of Prints and Photographs Division, Library of Congress

readers had not seen. What made his adventures unique was that he freed himself, and then wrote and published his narrative to document his journey. Equiano wrote out of his conviction that they, as "citizens of the world," had an obligation "to profess universal benevolence. More particularly, "as Christians," freed slaves should "commiserate and assist, to the utmost of our power, all persons in distress, or captivity."[11]

Olaudah Equiano's narrative opened in Africa, in "a country where nature is prodigal of her favours, our wants are few and easily supplied," and where neighbors helped each other to raise houses, expecting "no other recompense than a feast" for their labors.[12] This idyllic African picture turned on its head the prevailing view propagated by sailors and slave traders of a barren continent inhabited by primitive peoples. The Europeans were the ones who introduced barbarism to the prodigious African continent. Equiano recounted that one day, after all the adults had gone off to till the fields, leaving him alone with his sister to mind the house, two men and a woman scaled the walls of their house and seized the two children. Marched for days on end through the forest in a trek toward the sea, Equiano described being sold several times, sometimes serving a new master for only two or three days, before they reached the slave ships anchored on the coast. In a reversal of the commonly told European sailors' stories, Equiano portrayed the slave-trading Europeans, not their African victims, as cannibals and monsters. He defined an African identity that slaves could claim as their own, as he challenged the humanity of the white Christian slavers.

In his *Interesting Narrative*, Equiano recounted in intimate detail his childhood in "Esaka" among the Igbo-speaking people along the Niger River. A recently discovered ship's register and baptismal record, however, listed South Carolina as his birthplace. That led Equiano's biographer Vincent Carretta to speculate that the first chapters of Equiano's journal describing his African origins might be fiction, crafted by a literate black man to convince his white European readers of the evils of the slave trade.[13] The historian James Sweet sees Equiano's shifting African-American-European identity as a record of the fragmented and disjointed lives of men and women of color in the fluid Atlantic world. Douglas Egerton suggests a middle course. "As a boy and man," Egerton writes, Equiano "told so many contradictory stories that even today it remains unclear which were true and which were fictions crafted for self-protection or for propaganda."[14] Compared with a European, "I might say my sufferings were great," Equiano himself acknowledged. "But when I compare my lot with that of most of my countrymen, I regard myself as a *particular favourite of Heaven*, and acknowledge the mercies of Providence in every occurrence of my life."[15] He was not only a freed man, but to add to the ambiguities of his identity, was himself a former overseer of slaves.

Equiano's description of the Middle Passage was one of the earliest firsthand accounts of the slaves' transatlantic passage to be published and read by Europeans. His friend Quobna Ottobah Cugoano, who had been abducted from the Fante village of Agimaque on the African coast while he played with the chief's children, had in 1787 published a blistering attack on the slave trade, *Thoughts and Sentiments on the Evil and Wicked Traffic of the Slavery and Commerce of the Human Species*, but Cugoano avoided the autobiographical detail that seared Equiano's account into his readers' imaginations.[16] Equiano told of being herded on board ship as human cargo by "white men with horrible looks, red faces, and long hair." He feared he had fallen "into a world of bad spirits, and thought that they were going to kill me." When the ship anchored off Bridge Town in Barbados, Equiano reported, white men came on board to assess the African captives who had been divided into parcels. Driven into a large pen on shore as if they were wild beasts, brother was parted from brother, child from parent, husband from wife. "Is it not enough that we are torn from our country and friends to toil for your luxury and lust of gain?" Equiano asked his readers. "Must every tender feeling be likewise sacrificed to your avarice?"[17] Who were these unchristian, inhuman traders in slaves, he asked, challenging his readers' consciences without directly calling for the abolition of slavery.

Transported to Virginia, separated from his countrymen, Equiano was set to work weeding grass and gathering stones on a Virginia plantation, unable to converse with anyone for want of a common language, before being sold to an officer in the British navy who took him to England in 1757. There Equiano was taught to read by two of his master's sisters, who also baptized him. Equiano purchased his freedom in 1766 with the money he had made as a shrewd independent entrepreneur while enslaved. He recalled in his narrative that he, "who had been a slave in the morning, trembling at the will of another, was become my own master and completely free."[18] Manumission returned Equiano to "my original free African state."[19] The Americans had stolen his liberty, turning him into a commodity. He bought back his freedom by working their commercial system. His narrative documented his oppression, but also the resolve and intelligence of the man who had been their slave. It extended liberty from the political term employed by American and European revolutionaries to encompass the freedom to be human.

Equiano's timely narrative troubled the consciences of his British readers just as Parliament opened a new debate on the slave trade. He told the British Parliament that he had written the *Interesting Narrative* "to excite in your August assemblies a sense of compassion for the miseries which the Slave Trade has entailed on my unfortunate countrymen."[20] Ottobah Cugoano's treatise, published two years earlier and translated into French, made the case even more directly against Christians who plied the slave trade in the name of their religion. "The destroyers and enslavers of men can be no Christians," Cugoano explained simply, "for Christianity is the system of benignity and love."[21]

A free man, Equiano settled in London. He had thirty-seven guineas in his pocket. England represented a free state to him. In 1772, Lord Chief Justice Mansfield had sided with an escaped slave, James Somerset, against his master, who had intended to carry him back to the West Indies. Thereafter, slaves who escaped their masters and found refuge in the black community in London were effectively free, even if few found steady employment. The abolitionist Granville Sharp, who had defended Somerset, personally supplied relief as far as his resources would stretch, even though private charity was not nearly sufficient to relieve the plight of the swelling population of free blacks in the British capital.

Equiano intervened himself in 1774 to prevent the transportation from England of a free black sea cook, John Annis, whose master in Saint Kitts reclaimed him. The lawyer whom Equiano hired on Sharp's advice lost the case. The abolitionists could do little more than watch as Annis was dragged back to Saint Kitts, staked to the ground with pins through his ankles and wrists, and flogged. In his narrative, Equiano refused to be discouraged, predicting that the day would come when all the "sable people shall gratefully commemorate the auspicious era of extensive freedom."[22] He did warn of the bloody insurrections that would ensue if full rights were not readily granted the Africans who had been enslaved by Christians throughout the Americas.

It was not long before Equiano set sail again, journeying to Greece, Turkey, Portugal, Naples, Madeira, Barbados, Grenada, Jamaica, Nevis, and the North Pole in search of a passage to India. Throughout the narrative of his travels, he praised "the Lord God on high for all his mercies!"[23] Equiano glimpsed Providence in his narrow escapes from shipwreck and reenslavement. To protect himself from being sold back into slavery, Equiano's friend Cugoano was baptized, taking the name John Steuart. A free man, Cugoano learned to read and to write. He thanked God that through Christianity he had obtained liberty and literacy. Theirs were spiritual as well as physical journeys, recognizable to their readers as stories of struggle and Christian redemption. Equiano concluded that true freedom came to him at last when he "was received into church-fellowship" and "rejoiced in spirit, making melody in my heart to the God of all my mercies."[24] Freedom meant more than being unshackled. It implied salvation in religious terms.

Religious convictions prompted other former slaves to recount the stages of their "pilgrimage" to freedom, away from slavery and also from sin. The conversion stories at the center of the narratives, unpublished as well as published, emphasized the equality of all before God and the possibility of personal salvation. They celebrated individual struggles and divine grace. The religious freedom they portrayed appealed particularly to men and women who had broken the physical chains of slavery but had yet to chart a course for themselves through a revolutionary world.

Boston King was raised on the Waring plantation in South Carolina by parents he characterized in his 1796 journal as God-fearing: his father read Scripture alone in the woods every Sunday afternoon, and his mother ministered to the sick. Put to work in his master's house when he was six years old, at nine he was sent outside to tend cattle, where, contrary to his religious upbringing, he "learnt from my comrades the horrible sin of swearing and cursing." At the age of twelve, he recalled in his narrative, "it pleased God to alarm me by a remarkable dream." King "dreamt that the world was on fire, and that I saw the supreme Judge descend on his great white Throne! I saw millions on millions of souls; some of whom ascended up to heaven; while others were rejected, and fell into the greatest confusion and despair." Chastened, King resolved to serve God and no longer to swear. He wrote down his memories to acknowledge "Almighty God," who "delivered me from the hand of the oppressor, and established my goings."[25]

King won his physical freedom by fleeing the plantation and joining the British in Charleston. "They received me readily, and I began to feel the happiness of liberty, of which I knew nothing before," he wrote, "altho' I was most grieved at first, to be obliged to leave my friends, and remain among strangers."[26] The war for American independence created the conditions for the physical exodus of slaves away from the plantations of American patriots. Lord Dunmore's proclamation promising freedom to rebels' slaves who joined British forces attached liberty to loyalty to the British and their king, not to the cause of the American revolutionaries. The black loyalists who wrested their freedom from the American patriots claimed a liberty rooted in a long British tradition of constitutional liberty.

David George, like Boston King, wrote his story toward the end of his life under the guidance of church leaders in England. He was born into slavery in Essex County, Virginia, in about 1743. The hanging of his brother Dick from a cherry tree, suspended just above the ground, with a pole between his legs, and the whipping almost to death of his mother, the master's cook, led him at nineteen to run away from the plantation. He was quickly captured by Creek Indians and sold to George Galphin, a plantation owner and trader in deerskins. One day in the fields, a black traveler warned the young man given to profanity that if he continued to live "a bad life and had no serious thought about [his] own soul," he would "never see the face of God in glory."[27] Chastened and baptized by a passing preacher, George learned to read from the white children on the plantation. When the American revolutionaries banned whites from preaching to blacks for fear that Christian messages of freedom and equality might incite the slaves to rebel, George organized the first black Baptist church in America. In 1778, as British troops approached Silver Bluff, George's master fled and the black congregation seized the occasion to escape, finding shelter at the British encampment twenty miles upriver. They joined the hundred thousand other slaves who had responded to Lord Dunmore's promise of freedom.

The eventual American victory over the British filled these former slaves not with joy but with "inexpressible anguish and terror," George wrote in his narrative. Rumors flew that as part of the peace settlement they would be handed back by the defeated British troops to "our old masters coming from Virginia, North Carolina, and other parts." George was awakened by nightmares of these American patriots traveling north and "seizing upon their slaves in the streets of New York, or even dragging them out of their beds." Now that he was free, he could not imagine a return to slavery, as King called it, a life "without liberty."[28] In the end, the British ensured that many of the black loyalists were registered in the *Book of Negroes* and allowed to leave the new republic.

More than half of the former slaves who had fought for the British, including George and his family, sailed to Nova Scotia, where the British promised them "freedom and a farm."[29] Land ownership was part of the American understanding of freedom that the former slaves carried with them from the plantations. Independent men owned land. Another three thousand black loyalists boarded ships sailing for Jamaica and Saint Lucia, and two thousand freed slaves ended up in east Florida, which became a Spanish territory after the American Revolution. Most of these Africans were enslaved again when they reached their destination.

The black loyalists who sailed north to Canada settled along the rocky coastline of Nova Scotia. They founded villages in the dense forests, keeping their distance from the land already cleared by white settlers. Although the British government dispensed rations of flour and pork to the newly arrived Canadian settlers, it failed to follow through on the guarantee of one hundred acres for each family. The black loyalists had been promised land allotments equal to "the rest of the Disbanded soldiers," the whites.[30] In that promise, they were disappointed.

That first winter, forced indoors by the continuous blizzards, Boston King recalled, "the work of religion began to revive among us; and many were convinced of the sinfulness of sin, and turned from the error of their ways." King's wife, Violet, "awakened" by the preaching of Moses Wilkinson, the leading Methodist in Birchtown, struggled with the Lord for a year and a half, according to King, until she was freed from her fears and her soul "set at perfect liberty." Unable to find the same freedom, King trekked into the forest, buried three feet deep in snow, with only a blanket and a firebrand. There, he wrote, the devil convinced him that he was "predestined to be damned before the foundation of the world." He returned home and dutifully read Scripture daily at morning and evening prayer meetings until at last, when he least expected it, "the Lord again spoke to my heart, 'Peace be unto thee.' All my doubts and fears vanished away: I saw, by faith, heaven opened to my view, and Christ and his holy angels rejoicing over me."[31] Freed from the doubt that had enslaved his soul, King was still without employment in the midst of a famine so severe that poor people "fell down dead in the streets, thro' hunger." In 1791, he moved his family to Preston and began preaching.

David George, too, "had great liberty from the Lord."[32] He traveled up and down the Nova Scotia coast with his wife and their two children in search of a place to preach. Baptist services, held in kitchens, chapels, or, as in George's case, the woods, were thunderous, emotionally charged affairs, "groanings, screamings, roarings, tremblings & faintings . . . with a falling down & rolling upon the floor, both sexes together."[33] George recalled, "I was so overjoyed with having an opportunity once more of preaching the word of God that after I had given out the hymn, I could not speak for tears." Wherever George went, he wrote in his narrative, his message of freedom and equality attracted large numbers of black worshipers, includ- ing slaves who "were so full of joy that they ran out from waiting at table on their masters, with knives and forks in their hands to meet me at the water side."[34] George established seven "New Light" Baptist churches in outposts throughout Nova Scotia. This was not the Christianity of their former masters, who had preached subordination. Evangelical Christianity promised emancipation for the soul, a hope requisite to life in such harsh conditions.

The black loyalists would continue their quest for a political freedom rooted in land of their own. Their time in Nova Scotia, although marked by disappointment, deepened the black loyalists' attachment to their newly won liberty and to the British king who guaranteed it. They had won their freedom through their loyal service to the British. That British loyalty would be as important to their identity as free people as their ownership of land. Both were their heritage from the American Revolution.

Clarkson and Sharp: "To expose to publick view the cruelties practiced in it"

In May 1787, a small group, among them Granville Sharp, known for his defense of the slave James Somerset's rights before Judge Mansfield, and the well-traveled American abolitionist William Dillwyn, met at the London shop of printer James Philipps to establish the Society Instituted for Effecting the Abolition of the Slave Trade. They believed fervently that limiting importation of slaves to British colonies would lay "the axe at the very root" of the evil institution.[35] Sharp and Dillwyn had met thirty years earlier, when Dillwyn, a Quaker merchant, delivered a letter to Sharp in London from Anthony Benezet, the leading Philadelphia abolitionist.[36] Quaker abolitionists in America had circulated Sharp's letters calling attention to "the present miserable and deplorable slavery of Negroes and Indians, as well as white servants in our colonies."[37] The web of antislavery correspondence stretched across the Atlantic, following the lines laid down by the first Atlantic movement, the slave trade that had bound Africa, Europe, and the Americas since the seventeenth century.

Sharp attested in his memoirs, later edited and published by Prince Hoare, that the abolition of slavery was a moral duty for him.[38] An evangelical Anglican, son of the archdeacon of Northumberland, he shared neither the Enlightenment faith in reason nor the revolutionaries' commitment to the truth as an instrument of conversion. His vision, guided by fear of the coming judgment day, had more in common with that of black loyalists than with that of enlightened philosophers. Thomas Clarkson, son of an Anglican minister and author of a prize-winning Cambridge thesis attacking the slave trade, was convinced of the power of the truth. Believing that "nothing more was necessary than to unfold the true state of the Slave Trade, and to expose to publick view the cruelties practiced in it," Clarkson set out on horseback in the summer of 1787 to gather evidence for a public antislavery campaign.[39] He interviewed captains and inspected slave ships docked in British ports, talking along the way with ships' physicians and former slaves. Late into each night, Clarkson read letters describing the terrible conditions of confinement on the Middle Passage, poured over muster lists, and diagramed the holds of the ships in which slaves had been transported. When he finally did go to bed, he recalled in his influential narrative, "My rest was frequently broken by the visions which floated before me. When I awoke, these renewed themselves to me, and they flitted about with me for the remainder of the day."[40]

In Manchester, Clarkson met Thomas Walker and the radical Deist, lawyer, scientist, and philosopher Thomas Cooper, leaders of the Manchester Society for Constitutional Information, who proposed to petition Parliament against the slave trade. Petitioning had previously been reserved for privileged groups, such as nobles or clergy, with strong claims on government attention, but the Manchester Society planned to collect names of common citizens at mass public meetings. Their drive spread rapidly. By the end of 1788, more than one hundred petitions had been gathered from all over Britain, including slave-trading ports like Bristol. The Manchester petition alone had 10,639 signatures; the petition from York bore 1,800, one quarter of all adult males in that city. The abolitionists' campaign brought workers and artisans into the heart of British politics.

The organizers of the drive refused to allow women to sign their petitions, lest opponents dismiss the cause itself as frivolous. Still, Manchester women lent substantial financial support, their "ladies subscription" contributing almost a quarter of the income of the antislavery society. Too, they summoned men to action that they themselves were forbidden to take, reminding husbands engaged in business "that some attention is due to the Humanity of our Commerce as well as to the Gains of it."[41] Beginning in 1791, women across Britain also boycotted sugar, the largest import from the colonies where slaves labored. Abolitionists assumed that as mothers, women would understand the suffering of the slaves, and as consumers, they would connect that colonial misery to British families' consumption of sugar. Three hundred thousand families of "all ranks" and political persuasions joined the boycott.[42] The arrival in London of black loyalists fleeing American independence brought the problem of the slave trade home to Britain. The London Society elicited and published the testimonies of the first black speakers and writers many Englishmen and women had ever heard or read.[43] Clarkson postulated in his narrative on how quickly "light and information proceed under a free government in a good cause." All it took to begin was one individual who "communicates his sentiments to others. Thus, while alive, he enlightens; when dead, he leaves his works behind him." Accounts such as his would perpetuate the antislavery campaign, "encouraging us in libraries" into the future.[44]

How much more effective were individuals combined in a society. Together, Clarkson noted, the Anti-Slavery Society "had produced a kind of holy flame, or enthusiasm, and this to a degree and to an extent never before witnessed." The society, Clarkson boasted, arrested "the attention of the nation."[45] In 1788, the French journalist Jacques-Pierre Brissot wrote the London Society and asked for permission to join, noting "the intimate relations that link England and France to each other."[46] He promised financial support from Genevan banker Étienne Clavière, but the London abolitionists politely suggested to him that French and Swiss resources would be better spent in France. Rebuffed, Brissot organized the Société des Amis des Noirs, or, as British visitors to Paris called it, the Society of Friends of Negroes.

In February 1788, the philosopher Mirabeau, the journalist A. M. Cérisier, and the marquis de Lafayette joined Brissot at the first meeting of the Société chaired by Clavière. Its annual membership dues of two louis effectively limited the French Société to nobles and wealthy bourgeois, but it did offer honorary memberships to visiting abolitionists. In recognition of "their zeal for everything that concerns humanity, the interest they have demonstrated in abolition, and their influence on the other sex," the Parisian Société admitted women.[47] Their first order of business was to establish correspondence with British abolitionist societies. Brissot read aloud British abolitionists' essays and American Quakers' letters. The French society also reprinted Granville Sharp's *Plan to Abolish the Slave Trade*.[48]

Basing its campaign in the writings of French philosophers, the French Société reminded the National Assembly that the *Declaration of the Rights of Man* had "engraved on an immortal monument that all men are born and remain free and equal in their rights."[49] They had but to "follow nature" and abolish slavery.[50]

So convinced were they of the philosophical inevitability of their cause, the Société did not bother to rally popular support. The Genevan revolutionary exile Étienne Dumont scoffed that in contrast to the London Society, the Parisian Société was "not very respectable for its numbers, its activity, or indeed anything, but the goodness of its intentions, and the virtues of many of its members"; other foreign visitors complained that meetings were tediously formal.[51] Wadström, who kept the Société's minutes while he was in Paris, noted that it was often impossible to assemble enough members for a discussion, and that a number of those who came to the meetings sauntered in over an hour late. The secretary sent out frequent reminders to be punctual. Brissot invited Jefferson to join, but he refused even though his chargé d'affaires, William Short, was active in the Société. Jefferson assured them that no one desired the end of the slave trade and of the institution of slavery more than he did, but that public announcement of his membership in a French society would make him less effective in opposing slavery at home.[52] He hoped French abolitionists would understand his prudence. The leaders of the Société voiced their surprise at the equivocation of the contributor to two declarations of rights.

When the Société did decide to petition the National Assembly, it asked the British, more experienced in outreach, to collect signatures for them. The British refused, but sent Thomas Clarkson to assist. British parliamentarian and abolitionist William Wilberforce hoped that "if an application were made to them judiciously," the French revolutionary leaders might "be induced to take the Slave trade into their consideration, and incorporate it among the abuses to be done away."[53] As soon as Clarkson arrived in Paris, rumors of the presence in the French capital of an English spy intent to "impose equality on the French Nation" led Lafayette to offer Clarkson shelter in a hotel near his own so that he could protect the English abolitionist from the mobs he feared would gather.[54] National suspicions undermined international abolition. Caribbean planters camped out in the French capital lobbied against the Société as a British-inspired conspiracy to ruin the French colonies by cutting off their labor supply.

On 21 August 1789, Clarkson attended his first meeting of the Paris Société, but his expectations that the French, who had abolished feudal privileges on 4 August, would also put an end to the slave trade were quickly dashed. Clarkson was unimpressed by the sparse attendance of members at the Paris Société; even Lafayette claimed he was too busy with the National Assembly in Versailles to attend. Clarkson, though, "found great delicacy as a stranger" and generally kept his own counsel.[55] The politics of the French Revolution seemed to Clarkson to have eclipsed the antislavery movement in Paris. How different from England, where the two movements seemed to evolve together. Not so in Paris.

One evening when Clarkson was dining with Lafayette, or so he recalled in his narrative, they were joined by a delegation from the French colony of Saint-Domingue, six men "of a sallow or swarthy complexion . . . already in the uniform of the Parisian national guard." The deputies led by Vincent Ogé had come to Paris to demand "that the free People of Color be put upon an equality with the whites" and be seated as delegates to the National Assembly.[56] A free man of color, Ogé had been born in the Dondon parish outside of Cap Français, on a coffee plantation owned by his mother, a free woman of color, and his father, a white man. Educated in Bordeaux, he was apprenticed to a goldsmith there before returning to Saint-Domingue. Ogé returned to France in 1788 to fight the construction of a road through his family's plantation and to engage in trade.[57] He was joined in Paris by Julien Raimond, another wealthy free man of color, who had come to France to lobby in 1783. Clarkson thought these delegates of color from Saint-Domingue should be seated in the place of the white delegation.

In the National Assembly, Mirabeau challenged the mandate of the white delegates who claimed to represent the people of Saint-Domingue. Condorcet echoed, asking how a free nation could seat delegates who forcibly kept slaves. Alarmed, colonial planters collected petitions from all of the French ports protesting the claims of the free people of color. The Société in response condemned the colonial planters as aristocratic interlopers "a thousand times more odious than the Nobles."[58] When the Assembly refused to reconsider the exclusion of free men of color, Ogé warned the white revolutionaries, if they would not recognize mulattos as free men, "Our own arms shall make us independent and respectable. If we are forced to desperate means, it will be in vain that thousands are sent across the Atlantic to bring us back to our former state."[59]

Ogé left Paris at the end of 1789, both frustrated by the continuing delays in the National Assembly and inspired by the ideal of the citizen militia whose uniform he had worn so proudly. He tried to charter a ship in Le Havre from a captain who had made it through the British blockades of the American War for Independence, but that fell through. Finally,

Ogé sailed to Saint-Domingue by way of England and America, where he collected funds, arms, and ammunition. Thomas Clarkson received him in London, but with much trepidation, "for the errand of the deputies of colour to France was as odious to the slave-merchants and planters of England, as it was to the white colonists at Paris, and I trembled therefore at the thought of being seen in company with Ogé in London, lest it *should do a serious injury to our cause.*"[60] Clarkson gave him money for his passage to America. Ogé spent two weeks in South Carolina before returning to Saint-Domingue.

Ogé landed near Dondon, where a veteran of the American Revolution, Jean-Baptiste Chavannes, had not only petitioned the Provincial Assembly, protesting the unequal treatment of free colored militia, but had organized an assembly of free colored people. Together, Ogé and Chavannes wrote letters to the governor of Saint-Domingue and the Provincial Assembly demanding that they enfranchise all free citizens "without distinction" of race. Comparing themselves to the French Third Estate, they levied the first explicit attack on the colonial racial order based on the principles of the French Revolution.[61] After soldiers tried to arrest Ogé and Chavannes, three hundred men assembled at Chavannes's house. Their makeshift militia took the town of Grande-Rivière, disarming whites and imprisoning several men overnight in the town jail.

One of the plantation owners captured by the militia threatened the rebels with vengeance from the French army. Ogé allegedly countered that he had just come from France, where he enjoyed "the protection of men in power. Those who dominate the National Assembly are completely devoted to us."[62] What happened next is uncertain. In his own testimony, Ogé referred to only one battle, followed by a long spell of camping out on farms and the flight across the border into Santo Domingo. The narrative that has informed most historians, written by Jean-Philippe Garran-Coulon in 1795, described a two-wave attack on the men of color, the first unsuccessful and the second by a larger force under Colonel Cambefort.[63] Ogé asked the Spanish for asylum, but the Spanish instead turned them over to the French. Ogé and Chavannes were tried, forced to repent their crimes on bended knee, a noose around their necks, tied to a wheel, and broken on a scaffold. Their heads were cut off, mounted on pikes, and displayed on the roads to their homes. Thirty other rebels were sentenced to death two days later. Colonial officials claimed to have found a Wedgwood abolitionist medallion from British abolitionists and an anti-slavery pamphlet from France in Ogé's luggage. They refused to believe that Ogé could have acted on his own.

In France, the Société took up Ogé's cause in the National Assembly, championing him as a defender of the rights of man who resisted oppression in the name of the French Revolution. They recounted his story to make it clear that the villains were the white planters who had perverted the National Assembly's decrees. With rumors circulating in Paris that agents of the Société were trying to rouse revolutionaries throughout the French colonies to follow the American example and that the Société was supplying twelve hundred guns to slaves on Saint-Domingue, soldiers searched the Société's meeting rooms in Paris. They found papers and books, but no weapons.

The defeat of Ogé's rebellion in Saint-Domingue reverberated across the Caribbean. Authorities in Spanish Santo Domingo worried that "innumerable mulattos of the same condition and mode of thinking as Ogé, and perhaps also many discontented whites with depraved ideas," would follow Ogé into the Spanish territory.[64] They summoned troops from Spain and Puerto Rico "to form a Cordon to prevent any communication whatever between the French and Spanish part of the Island."[65] The French were identified as the source of revolutionary contagion that threatened to incite violence throughout the Caribbean.

In the end, though, the French Revolution overran the antislavery movement, at least in the metropole. Jacobins imprisoned or guillotined the leading French abolitionists, including Lafayette, Brissot, and Condorcet, for their political moderation. The Société des Amis des Noirs was silenced, resurrecting itself only in 1796 to stake out an argument in Paris against the slave trade with the backdrop of colonial insurrection.[66]

Sierra Leone: "Civilising Africa"

Abolitionists and imperialists might strike us as strange allies, but at the end of the eighteenth century their beleaguered goals seemed compatible, at least to them. That explains why, in January 1787, two ships left their moorings on the Thames with about 250 poor black passengers on board and sailed for Spitsend near Portsmouth, where they were joined by a third and a naval escort to head for Africa. British antislavery activists saw in this mission a solution to the inconvenience of so many poor blacks lodged in London. If abolitionists believed in colonization, it followed that the resulting expansion of commerce with a free African colony would promote the cause of abolition, or so Equiano, a supporter of the African resettlement scheme, had been convinced. Others believed that the project in Sierra Leone would help to reassert British moral authority in the Atlantic world, an authority undermined by the American Revolution.[67]

Equiano should have been aboard one of the four ships, but they sailed for Sierra Leone without him. Although the company had hired him as commissary, the first black man to serve in an official capacity for the British government, he did not remain in his position for long. He observed the white superintendent pilfering provisions and reported the offense to a naval officer and to his friend Ottobah Cugoano in a public letter published in the *Public Advertiser*. The Navy Board responded to the complaint by relieving Equiano of his position, charging him with inciting discord. Equiano was put ashore. Instead of partnership with the British, Equiano found contemptuous patronizing.[68] His experience sums up the abolitionists' venture into colonization.

The naturalist Henry Smeathman had spearheaded the founding of a colony to absorb the black expatriates sheltering in London, and to promote British commerce. Smeathman, who in his travel journal proposed the fertile land lying in the shadow of verdant mountains of Sierra Leone as a site for colonial development, expected crops would flourish with little attention and a simple hut would protect against the elements. He saw in Sierra Leone a free colony, "a sanctuary for the oppressed people of colour," and predicted that over time the promise of liberty in this African colony would exert an influence "wider than even *American Independence*."[69] From the African shore it would shine as a model of multiracial colonial possibilities, a beacon of Christian liberty.

A skeptical friend sneered in 1783, when Smeathman set off to raise funds for his venture, "Master Termites is gone to Paris to tell Dr. Franklin of his plan for civilising Africa."[70] Benjamin Franklin listened respectfully, but it was Granville Sharp who advanced "much more money than a private

Person in my situation ought to have done," convinced as he was that "the Establishment of a Free Settlement on the Coast of Africa for honorable Trade would be the most effectual means of destroying the Slave Trade."[71] How better to challenge the arguments that slavery was necessary to the economic profitability of a colony than to establish a colony of free blacks engaged in the free trade of sugar and other agricultural products?

How better also to refurbish Britain's image after the American War for Independence? In response to a correspondent who "dislikes the name of *a colony* and wishes rather to promote a *free settlement*," Sharp explained that under "this glorious Patriarchal system of Frankpledge," with its "*Regular Rotation of all the Males* from 16 to 60 with their *own Arms* in their *own Hands . . . Colonies* or even *Kingdoms* and *Monarchies* may be rendered perfectly *free and happy.*"[72] British colonial rule could be compatible with freedom.

Smeathman was not the only traveler who saw beyond the rapacious slave traders infesting the African continent. C. B. Wadström lobbied Swedish King Gustaf III to establish a colony, a New Jerusalem, that would extend full human rights to blacks in Africa. He persuaded the Swedish government to send a team to West Africa to survey the prospects. Thomas Clarkson, who met Wadström and his colleague Andrew Spaarman on their return from Africa, recalled in his journal that the Swedish abolitionists "showed me their journals, which they had regularly kept from day to day" as they traveled through the lands bordering Senegal. "In these I had the pleasure of seeing a number of circumstances minuted down, all relating to the Slave trade, and even drawings on the same object." From the Swedish journals, he "obtained a more accurate and satisfactory knowledge of the manners and customs of the Africans . . . than from all the persons put together whom I had yet seen."[73] The journals chronicled the promise of Africa. Clarkson helped Wadström publish his *Plan for a Free Community upon the Coast of Africa*, with all of the unconscious paternalism common to the antislavery movement. Clarkson agreed with Wadström's declaration that "civilized nations for their own advantage must of necessity act unanimously for the happiness of the barbarous and uncivilized."[74]

The poor blacks in London had not been as easy to convince. Africa for them resonated with the threat of reenslavement. Too many remembered kidnappings. They wanted assurances, official documentation, of protection against slave traders.[75] Black "corporals" finally convinced them that Smeathman's "humane plan" offered them their best option, better than the Bahamas, where they would have been surrounded by slavery, or Nova Scotia, with its harsh climate. Those men, women, and children who did sign on found themselves virtually incarcerated onboard ship through the winter months as the government prepared their provisions.

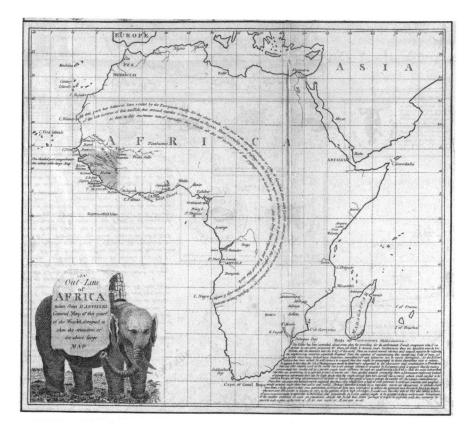

MAP 3.1

Inset from "Nautical Map Intended for the Use of Colonial Undertakings on the W. Coast of Africa . . . more particularly those of Sierra Leona and the Island of Bulama Respectfully Dedicated to the Humane and disinterested Promoters of those & similar Establishments." From Carl Bernhard Wadström, *An Essay on Colonization, particularly applied to the western coast of Africa*. London: Darton and Harvey, 1794. Courtesy of the Houghton Library, Harvard University. Econ 2400.3*

The ships reached the mouth of the Sierra Leone River on 10 May 1787. The settlers negotiated with the local chief of the Temne people, King Tom, for a tract of land along the harbor. The ship-weary settlers disembarked, hacked a passage through the brush, and marched up the hillside to plant a British flag at what was to be known as Granville Town in the "Province of Freedom," the slave-free colony. Following Sharp's scheme, they elected a chief in command to govern a common council made up of household heads. Physical labor was to be shared equally by all of the inhabitants without regard to wealth or race. Arriving too late to build permanent houses before the relentless downpours of the rainy season began, they camped in open tents pitched in the clearing, through which eighteen-foot-long snakes slithered during the day and leopards prowled after nightfall. It was also too late to plant crops, so they were forced to subsist on the meager rations brought from England and what they could barter for from King Tom. By mid-September of the first year, 122 people had perished. Back in London, Granville Sharp despaired at the "melancholy accounts of my poor little ill-thriven swarthy daughter, the unfortunate colony of Sierra Leone."[76] The poor timing of the launch had doused the revolutionary expectation that change would come from this model of prosperous freedom carved by the black settlers themselves from the fertile coast of Africa.

Neighborly relations were almost as troublesome as the weather for the colonists, wedged as they were on the coast between the slave traders who operated from Bance Island and the Temne people inland. Although the philanthropists and colonists referred to the settlement as returning home, their culture differed markedly from those of the indigenous people who lived and traded up and down the coast and inland along the Sierra Leone River. The sources of conflict between the black settlers and the indigenous peoples, including religion, the slave trade, and land ownership, were many. In 1789, the commander of a British naval warship anchored off the Sierra Leone coast tried to mediate "a permanent peace" between the slave traders, the settlers, and the new Temne chief, King Jemmy. Instead, they brought war. Flares from the ship accidentally set an African village aflame. Jemmy's men fired on the naval vessel, sending it back to sea, leaving the settlers to deal with a king intent on revenge. Taking pity on the besieged colony, the slave traders from Bance Island provided the settlers with canoes to travel upriver to Bob's Island as Jemmy razed Granville Town to the ground. In London, the colonial investors blamed the black colonists for the settlement's misfortunes.[77] Their terms of abuse were harsher than those of Sharp's paternalism. The young evangelical banker Henry Thornton replaced Granville Sharp as director of the newly incorporated Sierra Leone Company in 1791. Thornton was firmly convinced that "trade is the great engine by which towns are made to rise up & industry excited in all uncivilized countries."[78] As plans for establishing a commercially viable colony trading in agricultural produce displaced Sharp's dreams of a self-governing "Province of Freedom," the two goals began to appear less compatible. The company chose Alexander Falconbridge, a surgeon and abolitionist, to execute its commercial mission in the colony. Anna Maria Falconbridge, who accompanied her husband to "the wilds of Africa," narrated the journey in an epistolary journal, *Narrative of Two Voyages to the River Sierra Leone.*[79] The youngest of five children whose mother had died when she was little, Anna had hastily married Alexander in 1788, against the wishes of her family and friends. She would come to regret her rash decision. When her husband, a renowned abolitionist, drank to excess, he did not treat her kindly.

As soon as they arrived, Alexander and Anna Falconbridge journeyed upriver to negotiate with the Temne ruler, Naimbana, for the return of the land on which Granville Town had been sited. After seven meetings, including one that so frightened Anna Falconbridge that she swooned in hysterics, Naimbana agreed to allow the English to return to their settlement in exchange for more tobacco, rum, iron bars, and gold-laced hats. Before the rains started, the settlers built huts and planted cassava. Anna Falconbridge complained in her journal about the mosquitoes that swarmed in the settlement and the insects, "rather larger than a locust, covered with a tortoise coloured shell" with "forceps like a lobster," that had stung one of the settlers. She was appreciative, though, that the "tygers and lions" she had heard inhabited the mountains did not venture down to the coastal settlement. "Nature seems to have been astonishingly sportive in taste and prodigality here, both of vegetable and animal productions, for a man cannot stir without admiring the beauties or deformities of her creation," she wrote. She kept three pet monkeys. "Everything I see is entirely new to me. . . . There is such a variety here as to afford a continual zest to the sight."[80] That variety in all that was exotic made for a captivating narrative.

Falconbridge described her solitary evening stroll to an African village where a crowd gathered, staring, she supposed, at her dress. She gaped back at the naked women. Relieved by the approach of a group of women attired in European dress, she soon realized they were concubines, not wives of tribal leaders, further disturbing her preconceptions of colonial paternalism and, in the letters to a fictional friend in Bristol that formed her journal, those of her readers.[81] That was her goal.

With but the addition of a few of her accustomed comforts and some friends from England, Falconbridge wrote after the first few months, she might even consider remaining in Africa. At the approach of the rainy season, however, the Falconbridges returned to Falmouth to procure additional money and supplies from the Sierra Leone Company. In a meeting with Thomas Clarkson, they learned that one thousand blacks had been recruited from Nova Scotia to join the initial black settlers in Sierra Leone. Writing with the advantage of hindsight, Anna Falconbridge dismissed the imperial plan: "It was surely a premature, hair-brained, and ill-digested scheme, to think of sending such a number of people all at once, to a rude, barbarous and unhealthy country, before they were certain of possessing an acre of land."[82] She understood the ambiguities of land ownership and the harshness of the African coastal climate, and was surprised that the company would bring more poor black settlers, this time from Canada. Nova Scotia, after all, had been considered as a destination for the black poor of London who ultimately settled and died in Sierra Leone.

In 1790, the Nova Scotians dispatched a delegate, Thomas Peters, a British veteran of the American Revolution, to plead their unhappy case in London. "Slaves have no more Protection by the Laws of the Colony (as they are at present misunderstood) than the mere Cattle or brute beasts," the black loyalists charged in their petition.[83] Peters told the British government that the blacks in Nova Scotia were so miserable that they would happily settle "wherever the Wisdom of Government may think proper to provide for them as free Subjects of the British Empire."[84] They had subsisted in shelters with makeshift roofs and worked as sharecroppers for white Nova Scotians, all the while deprived of political rights. The secretary of state invited Peters, "the poor Black, to tell his own melancholy Tale," framed in the language of British rights.[85] He was convinced black loyalists would finally find liberty in the Province of Freedom floundering on the west coast of Africa under the direction of the Sierra Leone Company.

With the support of the British government, the Sierra Leone Company promised the black loyalists of Nova Scotia twenty acres for every man, ten for his wife, and five for each child who went to Africa. The government offered to pay the passage of the former slaves on their exodus across the waters to freedom in Africa. John Clarkson, Thomas Clarkson's younger brother, was put in charge of the expedition. He followed Thomas Peters back across the Atlantic to Nova Scotia to recruit the new settlers for Sierra Leone. On leave from the navy, the twenty-eight-year-old Clarkson seemed the ideal man to escort the black loyalists to Sierra Leone from Nova Scotia. Known for his gentle charm and negotiating skills, he was guided by a strong religious faith and a devotion to the abolitionist cause. Thomas Clarkson and William Wilberforce, however, warned John not to discuss abolition while recruiting settlers in Nova Scotia. He was not to call the black loyalists "Blacks or Negroes," but was told to use "Africans as a more respectful way" of speaking of them.[86] That must have surprised the black loyalists.

Clarkson and Peters traveled throughout Nova Scotia and into New Brunswick to promote the exodus to Africa. Boston King, who had just secured a good job as a domestic servant in Preston, agreed to emigrate to preach Christianity. Clarkson then met with David George, now the father of six children, at Merchants' Coffee House in Halifax. George delivered a list of men, women, and children eager to escape the misery of Nova Scotia. After hearing a rousing presentation in Birchtown, another 514 men, women, and children decided to emigrate. Clarkson reported back to the company in October 1791: "I feel myself much interested in the welfare of these oppressed people; indeed I never viewed the business I have undertaken to perform with that degree of awe, that I do at this moment." The former slaves, so often disappointed, had been subject in their journeys to "everything that is base," he wrote.[87] That explained why a staggering number signed on the rosters to leave the Americas behind.

Theirs was more than a simple migration; they traveled as a community.[88] Exceeding the government's most optimistic expectations, more than one thousand black loyalists set sail in January 1792 from Nova Scotia in fifteen ships, including one named the *Ark*, bound for Sierra Leone. Peters made sure that conditions on board were not reminiscent of the transatlantic voyages in the other direction experienced by some of the older Nova Scotians, ordering ventilation holes drilled in the decks and berths added to the ships.

Clarkson commented in his journal that the passengers were mostly "sober, hardworking men, and extremely grateful & rather enthusiasts in religion which I hope to be able to moderate on the voyage, though I commend them for their intentions."[89] With little exposure to the freedom conferred by their evangelical religious faith, Clarkson assumed that a conscientious Anglican clergyman could convert them through prayer in the new African colony. He had come to appreciate the depth of their disappointment with governments in America, but not their religion. He did not really understand, therefore, what they meant by liberty.

Once they dropped anchor, Thomas Peters led the first group of new settlers ashore singing: "The day of jubilee is come; return ye ransomed sinners home." One of the passengers recognized the landing place on the West African coast. The thirty-year-old had been kidnapped as a child and sold to an American slave ship that embarked from the same port fifteen years earlier. He reported that when a party of natives visited the settlement, a woman recognized him as her son, long lost to the slave trade.[90] They had come home to land they could farm and call their own. They would be free at last.

The new settlers from Nova Scotia began to build mud houses with thatched roofs and to organize their own churches. Divided into seven different congregations, each with its own preacher, the Baptists followed David George, while the Methodists were led by Cato Perkins, Moses Wilkinson, and Boston King. Within earshot of the Sierra Leone Company's Anglican minister, David George preached under a canvas tent on the first Sunday in Africa. The spirited religious meetings that often lasted all night and into the early morning annoyed Anna Falconbridge. "I have awoke at every hour of the night" and heard one congregation or another, she complained in her journal.[91] The directors in London, alarmed by the

FIGURE 3.2

A View of Sierra Leone from John Matthews, *Voyage à la Rivière de Sierra-Leone*. Paris: Hautbout l'Aine, 1797. Depiction of the original 1787 "Free Black settlement" of Sierra Leone under the British flag as seen from Saint George's hill looking north to Bullom across the harbor. New York Public Library/Art Resource, NY

exuberance of the Baptist and Methodist congregations in Sierra Leone, dispatched the Reverend Nathaniel Gilbert, the son of a wealthy planter in Antigua, to conduct Anglican services to compete with the black ministers. The directors and the settlers alike little understood the spreading Islamic faith of their neighbors among whom they sought to proselytize.

Many of the settlers from Nova Scotia perished that first year in one of the wettest rainy seasons in West African history. Tornados and lightning threatened the hastily constructed settlement. "Who wonders that Savages adore the Sun," Clarkson despaired in his journal.[92] The fever that killed sixty-seven people en route and confined him to his bed continued to spread through the settlement, infecting eight hundred of the settlers at one point. "It is quite customary of a morning to ask, 'how many died last night?'" Anna Falconbridge explained in her journal.[93] By the end of 1792, only forty white settlers remained alive, giving the settlement the unfortunate name "White Man's Grave."[94] With the rains came swarms of insects, both cockroaches and red ants that ate everything in their path, even chickens and goats.

The Nova Scotians who survived were once again disappointed in their hopes for acquiring the land that was so integral to their definition of freedom. The plots they were allocated by the company were small, one-fifth of the promised size, of poor quality, and not contiguous. Free men in Africa, they had expected to enjoy a new status as peasant proprietors on freehold land, supporting themselves from their own property and selling their excess produce to the Africans. Instead, the company charged them quitrents or annual fees for their land, in essence making them feudal tenants. Without land of their own, they were not truly free.

The settlers had also been promised representation in a government composed of black men, a government in keeping with their self-definition as British subjects. They identified themselves as a self-governing, just community. However, the Sierra Leone Company had dismantled Sharp's system of self-government, destroying with it the promise of racial and economic justice as envisioned by the black loyalists. In its place, the Sierra Leone Company installed eight white directors. "Never were characters worse adapted to manage any purpose of magnitude," Anna Falconbridge commented of the white directors. She did not think them "fit to be guardians and stewards of the immense property required for erecting the fabric of a new colony."[95] John Clarkson, who had won the trust of the blacks in Nova Scotia with his sympathy for their plight, could do nothing to rein in the white directors who drank to excess, stole supplies, claimed the waterfront land for their own houses, and abused the black settlers. The black loyalists had chosen freedom under the empire rather than slavery in a new American republic. They were disappointed to find themselves subject once again to the rule of a white government.

In April 1792, their rations reduced, the settlers deputized Thomas Peters to convey their discontent to Clarkson. The conditions they found in Sierra Leone reminded them of the slavery they had long since escaped in America, Peters observed. Quite simply put, they did not need white rule. On Easter, Peters and Clarkson held a four-hour palaver, or discussion, under a massive silk cottonwood tree. Clarkson had assumed that since he had shared the discomforts of the voyage with the Nova Scotians, the black settlers would accept him as Moses delivering them from bondage. Confronted instead with demands presented by Peterson, Clarkson admitted that he was confused by their "strange notions . . . as to their civil rights."[96] Peters recalled the promises Clarkson had made in Birchtown that they would be "free" in Africa, governed by laws consistent with the British constitution.

The black loyalists saw themselves as founders of a new nation. They were loyalists, but their understanding of liberty in Sierra Leone bore the stamp of the American Revolution. They had incorporated property ownership into their definition of liberty. Property implied independence for them, as it had for Crèvecoeur's farmer in New York.

Surprised by the insubordination of the black loyalists, the company warned the "Nova Scotians" that "on their due obedience to government, under the blessing of Providence, their happiness, their liberty, and perhaps their very lives depend."[97] The black loyalists finally compromised. They accepted freedom as British subjects, on the condition that there was someone "of our Color in it."[98] They declared that they would not be made to pay quitrents, with or without representation. Their revolutionary image of liberty required new laws and a refuge at the end of their long sojourn within the British Empire.

No matter the frustrations that John Clarkson confided to his journal, Thomas, who had not yet read the journal, wrote to congratulate his brother: "The Eyes of England are upon you & this Infant colony. . . . To your lot it falls to be Governor of the Noblest Institution ever set on foot, an institution which embraces no less than an Attempt to civilize and Christianize a great Continent, to bring it out of Darkness & to abolish the Trade in Men."[99] Colonization and civilization could be accomplished together, Thomas Clarkson still believed. And their enterprise would be commercially profitable.

By the fall of 1792, in Freetown, there were twelve streets lined with timber houses raised a foot or two off the ground, and three avenues housing the public buildings, including a school, a church, and a multipurpose gathering place, Harmony Hall. Many of the Freetown householders were women. In fact, women owned three of the six shops and women voted in the elections; other than citizens of New Jersey, they were the only women in the world with that right.[100] Fifteen acres of land had been put into cultivation, twelve with alternate rows of rice and cotton. The settlers had planted a nursery of sugar cane, but insects—ants and "bugabugs"—ate most of the plants.

In December 1792, John Clarkson returned to England to be married. He was sorely missed by the black loyalists, especially because he was replaced by William Dawes, an evangelical and the governor of the penal colony at Botany Bay. Dawes was assisted by the twenty-four-year-old Zachary Macaulay, formerly an overseer of slaves on a Jamaican sugar plantation. Macaulay arrived expecting to temper the "inadequate or enthusiastic notions of Christianity" of the black settlers and thereby to squelch their "false and absurd notions . . . concerning their rights as freemen."[101] His Christianity would teach the "truly unfortunate" settlers to be obedient, he told the directors in a journal that he kept, edited, and posted to London at regular intervals. In this journal, he dwelled on the constant rains and the horrifying variety of insects. Macaulay was even more appalled to find settlers "falling down as if dead" and "bellowing with all their might" as they wrestled with the Devil.[102] Methodists lacked discipline, and "their government is a pure democracy," he complained, boasting of his requirement that all settlers attend Anglican services.[103] These would "do them good."[104] At least on Christmas, the church was quite full. Evidence suggests that the directors were pleased with his reports, especially his detailed discussions of commercial ventures.[105]

Boston King and David George followed Clarkson back to England in 1793 to further their religious education. The Methodists at the Kingswood School near Bristol persuaded King to write down and publish the story of his life.[106] David George met English Baptist preachers and, like King, was encouraged to write his "account" of his journey from American slavery to the wilderness in Nova Scotia to Africa. His narrative of enslavement, escape, and conversion was published in the first volume of *The Baptist Annual Register*. Like the Israelites led by Moses out of Egypt, the black loyalists portrayed their escape not only from slavery, but from a land of bondage, the newly independent American republic. King and George both acknowledged the "goodness of God" that had set them free from "their oppressors."[107] Their narrative written, they sailed back to Africa to confront continuing disagreements over property and quitrents.

Anna Falconbridge had also returned to London in June 1793, traveling with her second husband (her first had died) on a slave ship commanded by her brother. She published her journal, "an uncompromising account" of the failure of the directors of Sierra Leone Company. After

two years in Sierra Leone, she questioned the principles of the abolitionists, including those of her first husband. It seemed to her that these
well-meaning idealists had been merely "sporting with the lives of such
numbers of their fellow creatures."[108] If imperialism and abolition were
not compatible, and she did not think they were, she emerged from her
experience in the free colony of Sierra Leone doubting the latter. Stopping
in Jamaica, she witnessed Thomas Paine and William Wilberforce being
burned in effigy. She lamented her hero Paine's involvement with the
abolitionists. She had concluded that the slave trade would benefit Africa
by spreading Christianity and taming the ambitions of the African chiefs
who subjugated their own people. Equivocating and tired, she was "heartily glad to get rid of this subject, and am surprised how I came to entangle
myself in it."[109] She dismissed the British colonial project in Africa as naïve
and unrealistic.

Anna Falconbridge published her account, daring the directors of the
Sierra Leone Company "to contradict one tittle" of her evidence that vin-
dicated her second husband, if not her first, from charges that held them
responsible for the settlers' unrest and the commercial failure of the colony.[110] Carl Wadström commented that her journal proved "that even the
tender sex, under the influence of conjugal attachment, may be so much
interested in a great undertaking, as to forget the delicacy of their frame,
and to face danger and distress in every terrifying shape."[111] Her narrative
was reprinted twice in 1794, then reissued in a new edition in 1802, and
its success confirmed Thomas Clarkson's adage about popular interest in
the coast of Africa, colonial exploration, and the antislavery movement.

Henry Thornton, the director of the Sierra Leone Company, issued a
175-page report to rebut Falconbridge's journal. It did not prove popular
reading. John Clarkson, whose own Sierra Leone journal, his brother
assured him, would command five hundred pounds from a publisher,
remained silent. Sympathetic to the black settlers who "have been de-
ceived through life and have scarcely ever had a promise made that was
performed," Clarkson worried about setting back the cause of the abolitionists by portraying the settlers' shortcomings.[112] His journal remains in
manuscript form.

For another decade, the black settlers struggled for control over their
colonial government. They now referred to Freetown as "A Town of

Slavery," infuriating the Sierra Leone Company, which held it up as a model of British moral values. Two of the settlers, Cato Perkins and Isaac Anderson, carried a petition to London to deliver to the Court of Directors of the Sierra Leone Company in October 1793, complaining that Dawes treated them "just as bad as if we were all slaves which we cannot bear."[113] When they received no answer to their petition, the settlers followed up, reading aloud passages from Anna Falconbridge's recently published book. "We are sorry to think that we left America to come to be used in that manner," they wrote.[114] In an echo of Equiano's warning, they added that if the directors did not stop abusing them, God would "see the tyranny and oppression" and "attack the Barbarous Task Masters in the Hight of their Pomp and Oppression."[115] News that "liberty had been proclaimed to the French slaves in the West Indies and that America had wholly abandoned the slave trade" arrived in September 1794 aboard a slave brig.[116]

The directors in London replied in their annual report to the charges levied against them that they had sacrificed much to promote the cause of "Christianity and Liberty and Civilization among the Africans." They suggested that the complainants were too suddenly emancipated to realize the limits of "civil rights" or to understand the difference between tyranny and the unavoidable hardships of life.[117] The settlers might have answered that Macaulay and Dawes taught them all they needed to know about taxation without representation and religious interference in Africa.

"Thorough Jacobins" in a "Town of Slavery"

In July 1792, John Clarkson wrote the marquis de Lafayette, pleading with the French not to attack Sierra Leone should war break out between Britain and France. This was no ordinary British colony, he explained; the settlement had been "established on the true principles of Freedom and intended to promote the general Happiness of Mankind."[118] On the coast of Africa, the black settlers had at last found liberty, Clarkson informed the French hero of the American Revolution, adding that if threatened, the residents of Sierra Leone might become revolutionaries themselves. Lafayette, who would probably have shared Clarkson's sympathy for the former slaves, never received Clarkson's letter. He was locked away in an Austrian prison for betraying the French Revolution.

In September 1794, seven French ships disguised as British vessels sailed into Freetown harbor. Governor Macaulay, with just twenty-four guns positioned on rusting parapets to defend the British colony against the hundred French cannon pointed directly at him, hoisted a white table-cloth as a sign of surrender an hour and a half into the bombardment. David George and a crowd of unarmed settlers watched as warehouses, churches, and houses went up in flame. For the next two weeks, French sailors, called "sans-culottes" by Macaulay, plundered the black loyalist settlement, showing no mercy. They looted shops, burned the public library, dismantled the printing press, trampled Bibles, ate and drank their way through provisions, dug up farm allotments, slaughtered hogs, muti-lated dogs and cats, and burned the settlers' crops. They left one child dead, reportedly hacked in half in his mother's arms, two men without legs, and George shirtless. Settlers who could flee found shelter in the Temne villages.[119]

In his journal, Macaulay recalled his personal efforts to convince the French commanders that the black loyalists were "not Englishmen," something he probably believed himself.[120] In their own entreaties to the French, the black loyalists took a different tack and reclaimed their revolu-tionary American identity, "telling them we was Americans from North America." Neither ploy worked. Instead, the encounter with revolutionary France opened new possibilities, both for revolt and for repression, as soon as the ships sailed away. Macaulay, whose own children had escaped only through the kindness of Mary Perth, a black loyalist and shopkeeper, imposed quitrents and a new loyalty oath on the black loyalists and demanded that they share the costs of rebuilding and restoring company property.[121] This resonated among the black loyalists with reminders of decades of injustice in the Americas. A preacher complained in a letter to John Clarkson, "We wance did call it Freetown but since your absence— we have Reason to call it a Town of Slavery."[122] The opportunity for revolt would come soon.

The outspoken French abolitionist Abbé Grégoire apologized for the French attack in an address to the French Academy that eventually found its way to Granville Sharp, carried by "a Swedish gentleman."[123] How was it, he asked, that the French, who had declared the liberty of black slaves in the Caribbean, would destroy a settlement of free blacks established to end the slave trade on the coast of Africa? Sierra Leone shone for Grégoire as a living demonstration that civilization could eradicate slavery by educating and improving the Africans so recently enslaved by the Europeans and Americans.[124] He was disappointed by the action of French revolutionaries.

Rebuilt after the French-set fires, by 1796 the four hundred timber-and-shingle houses of Freetown made it the largest town on the west coast of Africa. Struggles over payment of the quitrent continued, leading the settlers to threaten to ask the Temne for land free of the governance of the Sierra Leone Company. Macaulay complained that the Methodists wanted to throw "off the jurisdiction of the company servants" and name one of their own as "a kind of dictator, who assisted by a council, should rule them after the manner of the Natives around us."[125]

In September 1800, the residents of Freetown took advantage of Macaulay's departure and issued their own code of laws before rising up in armed rebellion. After a decade as British subjects, liberty to them definitely meant the right to rule themselves. They named three justices of the peace, and created a bicameral legislature that recognized the black loyalists and surviving London poor as the proprietors of Sierra Leone.[126] Years earlier, they had reminded Dawes of the fate of the French king, Louis XVI, who had also denied his people the bread and freedom they demanded. Then, that had proved to be an idle threat, especially with British warships to back up the governor just off the coast. Now, to assert their independence once and for all from white rulers, the black loyalists looked inland to Africa and opened talks with King Tom for land. The settlers menaced the whites still in Sierra Leone, threatening to set them afloat upon the ocean in boats without oars or sails. Revolution was imminent here on the periphery of the British empire, with the white company men outnumbered by the rebels who were negotiating for support from Temne and Mori-Kanu warriors.[127]

Just as freedom seemed within reach at last for the black loyalists, five hundred Maroon warriors, free blacks from Jamaica, sailed into the harbor of Freetown aboard a British transport ship under the command, it happened, of Macaulay's brother. The Maroons were in search of land to farm, because they too had failed to thrive among the rocks of the Nova Scotia coast. "A Most unexpected intervention of providence completely changed the face of affairs," Thomas Ludlam, the otherwise not particularly religious new governor, later recalled.[128] Ludlam told the Maroons of the insurrection ashore. Their Maroon commander noted in his journal entry of Wednesday, 1 October, "The evening was spent in a humdrumish way arranging matters for a general attack on the Rioters."[129] It was one of the more ironic twists in the increasingly interconnected and contentious revolutionary world.

The Jamaican barrister Robert Charles Dallas observed with hindsight in 1803, "Had the Maroons been the disciples of revolutionary emissaries, or the abettors of anarchy and equality, they would in all probability have joined the people of their own complexion to extirpate the white tyrant; on the contrary they joined with alacrity in quelling the insurrection."[130] After a stormy night, the Maroons surprised the "Rascals," chasing them into the forest.[131] The Maroons then turned their attention to defeating the native chiefs who had allied with the black loyalists. Their definition of liberty also included property. They, too, had escaped both slavery and the disappointed promises of Nova Scotia, but they also brought military experience from the Caribbean.

The Sierra Leone Company hanged the would-be ruler of an independent Freetown, Isaac Anderson, and banished the leaders of the short-lived Freetown revolution, including George Washington's former slave Harry Washington, from the colony. Sierra Leone was absorbed into the British Empire. The black loyalists' vision of racial and economic justice, their moral sense of liberty, was effectively silenced, to be forgotten as a critical voice in the revolutionary struggles, a movement that drew on cross-cutting revolutionary traditions from three continents.

In London, Lord Wilberforce, known as an outspoken abolitionist and supporter of the colony, responded in horror to news of the insurrection in Sierra Leone. He feared that the black loyalists, transported across the ocean and given land by the British government, had become "as thorough Jacobins as if they had been trained and educated in Paris."[132] These revolutionaries not only abolished slavery but established institutions of self-government and advocated the broad distribution of property in an egalitarian society undivided by race and unified by their deeply felt religious faith. Where could they have imbibed such radical views of their rights, he asked, if not from the French revolutionaries in their famous

Jacobin clubs? After all, was that not how the revolutionary demands of free people of color such as Ogé and the slaves in the Caribbean had been explained? Perhaps, Wilberforce speculated, if British abolitionists had not promised these former slaves the liberty the Americans denied them in the War for Independence, they would not have posed such a threat in this era when the destabilizing example of the French Revolution loomed large. In his mind, the Jacobin threat eclipsed all others.

FOUR

The Press and Clubs: "Politico-mania"

Throughout newly constituted republics on both sides of the ocean, men and women who had never before enjoyed the privilege of considering the affairs of state gathered in public spaces beyond parliaments and state houses to read newspapers and discuss politics. French journalist Camille Desmoulins triumphantly announced to his readers: "the fermentation is universal." The rising volume of revolutionary politics and the ever intensifying news cycle drew readers and listeners to clubs, notably in France, but also in revolutionary Poland, and even England with its pockets of revolutionary agitation. Together, the clubs and newspapers recast the political community between 1789 and 1793.

In the heart of Paris, the artisan Jacques observed hundreds of Jacobins gathering three to four times a week across from his stall in the Rue Saint-Honoré. At the end of December 1790, he decided he had watched long enough. He worked up the courage and followed the other common people of Paris through the doors into one of the many "clubs for the people's use, simply organized and unpretentious." Inside, Jacques found artisans like himself learning to think for themselves. Reading newspapers and listening to speeches, they had emerged from "the shadow of ignorance" cast by the Old Regime, Jacques reported.[1] These were the Jacobins whose specter in Sierra Leone so frightened English Lord Wilberforce.

Jacques the Jacobin did not actually exist. His was a fictional account published in the most widely read of the multitude of new French newspapers, *Les Révolutions de Paris* (Revolutions of Paris) to draw the uninitiated into the realm of politics. If pamphlets opened revolutionary discussions, newspapers amplified the political debate, often escalating the incendiary rhetoric of the clubs. Political news was in such demand that clubs with newspaper subscriptions often regulated the time a reader could monopolize a newspaper before passing it along to waiting readers. Some clubs even chained particularly popular papers to tables and stamped them with special seals so that they could not be removed. Other clubs solved the problem of high demand by reading papers aloud to the assembled multitude. Two centuries after the invention of the printing press, newspapers overtook pamphlets as the mouthpiece of political dissent.

The Genevan philosopher Jean-Jacques Rousseau had observed in 1762 that "the better constituted the state, the more public affairs dominate private ones in the minds of the citizens," because "in a well-run polity, everyone flies to assemblies."[2] A German professor noted the omnipresence of politics: "Everyone is eager for the most recent news of world events, from the Regent, who receives it at first hand from his envoys and messengers, down to the countryman, who hears . . . the newspapers read by his political schoolmates every Sunday in the pub."[3] Clubs, from the Paris Jacobins meeting across the street from Jacques's stall to the London Corresponding Society assembled at Bell Tavern on Fleet Street to the Warsaw Citizens offering Aid gathered in the empty Radziwell Palace, took it as their responsibility to inform or, in their words, to enlighten citizens. They constituted an alternative political sphere.[4]

Before the revolutions, individual wealthy readers typically perused their newspaper alone in the comfort of their home, although some read papers in reading clubs that admitted the elite. European politics had generally been the business of the expensive international gazettes because they were not subject to national censorship. A typical issue of the *Courrier de l'Europe* (Courier of Europe), published in London, featured bylines from Saint Petersburg, Stockholm, Vienna, Madrid, Maastricht, Liège, Brussels, and Paris. Like most eighteenth-century newspapers, it regularly republished translated articles from other journals without attribution.

With the revolutions, circulation exploded. One-third of Londoners read a weekly newspaper at the time of the American Revolution. "These days political newspapers outsell others by a ratio of ten to one," the duc de Choiseul reported from Paris in 1789.[5] John Adams boasted to friends in Congress of his "secret connections" with Dutch journalists who promoted the American cause of liberty to an enlarging reading public throughout Europe. "The Gazettiers in this Country are not mere Printers," Adams told his compatriots, alluding to the old perception of the colonial printer in America as "a mere mechanic in the art of setting and blocking types," without a mind of his own. That image evaporated with the American

Revolution. The Dutch editors, Adams asserted, "are men of Letters and as these Vehicles have a vast Influence in forming the public opinion."[6] Most notably, Antoine Cérisier, the French-born Dutchman, wielded a pen that had "erected a monument to the American cause more glorious and more durable than brass or marble." Cérisier's articles in *Le Politique hollandois* (Dutch politics) "were read like oracles and his sentiments weekly echoed and reechoed in gazettes and pamphlets" from The Hague to Milan, Adams told Congress.[7] Stories of American victories in their War for Independence, recounted in the *Gazette de Leyde* (Leiden gazette), were read by the Polish king's advisers in Warsaw.

From Philadelphia to Warsaw, the press trumpeted news of the humblest hints of insurrection, building to a crescendo with the Jacobin clubs of the French Revolution. The *Gazeta Narodowa I Obea* (National and international gazette), published in Warsaw, also carried all the latest news from revolutionary France, including the regulations adopted by the Parisian Jacobins in February 1790. Accounts of French political debates covered by the *Gazette de Leyde* published in the United Provinces were translated by Thomas Jefferson and reprinted in English in the *Gazette of the United States* of Philadelphia. Stefan Luskina then translated and reprinted them in Polish for the *Gazeta Warszawska* (Warsaw gazette). This overlapping coverage knit the revolutionary world together.

From The Hague, the ever-active Cérisier countered the malicious rumors circulated by the British press that he was a foreign agitator for the American cause. "Someone has said that I was neither a good Englishman, nor a good Frenchman and that I was an even better American than I was a Dutchman," Cérisier informed Adams. "All I know is that I have the principles of liberty too deeply engraved in my heart to ever betray its cause."[8] He had been born not a Frenchman but a "politico-mane."[9] The journalist identified himself simply as a citizen of this revolutionary Atlantic world.

"All the loudest trumpets": The Press and the People of Revolutionary France

The *Révolutions de Paris*, the newspaper that invented Jacques the Jacobin, first appeared on the streets of Paris on 19 July 1789, two months after the Estates General assembled in Versailles. Aspiring journalists had been requesting permission from the French government to publish the proceedings of the Estates General because the set of national gazettes authorized to reprint government decrees, once of little interest but now newsworthy, was severely restricted. International gazettes still imported more news into France than they relayed outward, and elite readers alone could afford these expensive papers.

While Louis XVI's ministers stalled in their discussions of the appropriate role of the press, Jacques-Pierre Brissot, the French lawyer and journalist who had covered revolutions in Geneva and America, deliberately flouted French censorship regulations, publishing and distributing the *Patriote français* (French patriot). Pamphlets had sparked interest in the revolution, he acknowledged, but only the serial publication of "a political journal or gazette" could keep the people in the large French nation informed. According to Brissot, "without the newspapers, the American Revolution, in which France played so glorious a part, would never have been achieved." *Common Sense*, reprinted and disseminated throughout Europe "would have remained . . . unknown and without influence."[10] Other unsanctioned newspapers quickly followed Brissot's into print.

Threatened with arrest for breaching censorship regulations, Brissot promptly ceased publishing, but the philosopher and delegate to the Third Estate the comte de Mirabeau, editor of *États généraux* (Estates general), persevered. "Twenty million voices are crying out for press freedom: Nation and King are unanimous in their wish for help and ideas," he explained. He owed the people an account of the proceedings.[11] A free press was vital to the open discussion that fueled a revolution, he believed. He called on his workshop of Genevan revolutionaries, especially Étienne Dumont, to contribute articles to his new paper. Camille Desmoulins, a poor Parisian lawyer who, from atop a café table had dramatically announced the king's dismissal of the popular financial minister Genevan Jacques Necker, joined the ranks of journalists challenging press restrictions. The French government retaliated by raiding the booksellers and arresting the women peddlers who sold newspapers.

When censorship and suppression failed to check the tide of publication, the French government relented and granted permission to journalists to cover meetings of the Estates General. That opened the floodgates;

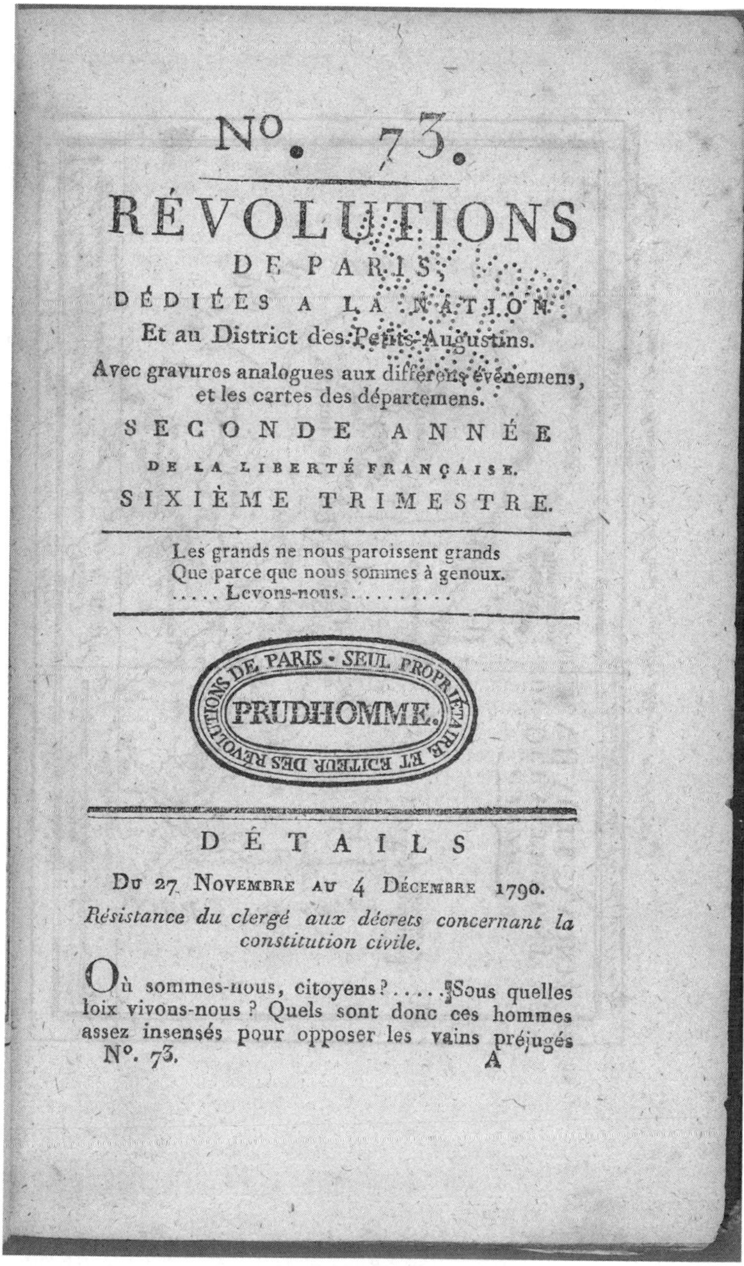

Nᵒ. 73.

RÉVOLUTIONS
DE PARIS,
DÉDIÉES A LA NATION
Et au District des Petits-Augustins.

Avec gravures analogues aux différens événemens,
et les cartes des départemens.

SECONDE ANNÉE
DE LA LIBERTÉ FRANÇAISE.

SIXIÈME TRIMESTRE.

Les grands ne nous paroissent grands
Que parce que nous sommes à genoux.
..... Levons-nous. ....

RÉVOLUTIONS DE PARIS · SEUL PROPRIÉTAIRE
PRUDHOMME.
ET ÉDITEUR DES RÉVOLUTIONS

DÉTAILS
Du 27 Novembre au 4 Décembre 1790.

*Résistance du clergé aux décrets concernant la
constitution civile.*

Où sommes-nous, citoyens? ..... Sous quelles
loix vivons-nous ? Quels sont donc ces hommes
assez insensés pour opposer les vains préjugés
Nᵒ. 73.   A

FIGURE 4.1
Révolutions de Paris. 27 November to 4 December 1790. The story of the artisan
Jacques appears in this issue "dedicated to the nation." With permission of the
New York Public Library

194 new papers appeared in Paris and 90 in the French provinces in the
first year of the French Revolution.[12] The cost of printing one thousand
copies of a popular newspaper was only forty to forty-five livres, the price
of a good meal at a restaurant in the Palais Royal or of a box at the opera.[13]
What was expensive was the paper, so most eighteenth-century editors
sought a format that maximized words and minimized space. With a run
of one thousand copies, editors could expect to break even. In January
1788, only 5 percent of French journals had dealt with political questions,
but by 1789, two-thirds of French journals focused on the debate of the
revolution.[14]

Revolutionary readers in France not only had a choice of newspapers,
they had a choice of political perspective in a world where impartiality was
not necessarily a virtue. One skeptic warned readers, "Those who have
made the revolution also want to retell it; after having tormented and massacred their fellow citizens, they wanted to mislead posterity."[15]
Revolutionary journalists aspired to provide more than "a dry recital of
facts."[16] These were new roles for French journalists who had previously
been content to recount official information without commentary for the
elite. Conservative journalist Antoine Rivarol decried this "liberty of the
press." What could not be said aloud in public "could be conveyed in
print." With their incendiary stories, newspapers, "the artillery of
thought," roused to action people who had never before ventured into
politics.[17] L'ami du Peuple (The friend of the people), edited by Jean-Paul
Marat, targeted "cultivators of the land, the small merchants, the artisans,
the workers, the laborers, and the proletarians," in contrast to the international papers, which were written in a language unknown to tradesmen
and artisans and sold at a price beyond their budgets.[18]

New French newspapers proved more agile than the international
press and better able to capture revolutionary events as they happened.
Their news did not have to travel out of the country to be published and
brought back in again. The Gazette de Leyde countered in vain that as a
foreign press, it "had a little more freedom" to reveal "the truth" than the
French papers, but "the truth" was relative, and speed was essential.

Revolutionary crowds materialized with such seeming spontaneity
that editors of international gazettes initially refused to believe Parisian
reports of the storming of the Bastille. The Gazette de Leyde waited two

weeks for corroboration of rumors that the people of Paris had taken the monument. French journalists, for the most part clustered in Versailles to catch news of the debates of the National Assembly, also missed the Parisian uprising. The popular insurrection in Paris did not go unreported, however. Playwrights and bookbinders joined the fray, eager to report that "the arms used by former monarchs to enslave men under their royal tyranny are now in the hands of wigmakers' apprentices and clerks serving the cause of liberty." The editor of *Révolutions de Paris* was not exaggerating when he confided in his readers, "All of Europe is watching you."[19]

American newspapers published Robespierre's speech in 1789 to the National Assembly on the liberty of the press. Some papers reprinted excerpts, others the whole speech, but all highlighted Robespierre's statement "that the Freedom of the Press will contribute more to the freedom and happiness of the people, than the strength of all your National Militia combined." The French revolutionary leader recognized the liberating power of "the free discussion of every man's sentiments among his fellow subjects," the *Pennsylvania Mercury* reported.[20] American journalists, even those who decried Jacobin politics, concurred, at least in theory, that the business of the press was to inform and, it seemed to follow, to persuade an ever larger public in this revolutionary age.

A journalist, according to Jean-Paul Marat, newly returned from England, had a duty as a sentry to keep watch and "sound the alarm" rousing the popular classes when their representatives in the National Assembly wavered from "good principles."[21] His and other revolutionary papers read almost as serial pamphlets, their publication eagerly anticipated in the provinces as well as in Paris. Jacobin clubs in the French provinces met on days when the mail from Paris was expected, to take advantage of the timely arrival of the press. If floods or storms delayed the post, rumors replaced the news, often full of speculation of counterrevolutionary sabotage.

Many clubs were open around the clock so that members could come by anytime to read newspapers and converse. In 1791, clubs in Rouen, Castres, Strasbourg, and Montpellier each subscribed to more than twenty newspapers, almost all French.[22] Clubs rarely got more expensive international gazettes. Papers on the right, including the *Mercure de France* and the *Gazette de Paris*, did not appear on subscription lists either, the

Jacobins explained, because they spread "the spirit of fanaticism and revolt."[23] Similarly, the Jacobin reading rooms shunned papers on the far left, including Marat's *L'Ami du Peuple*. "It is only from knowing the whole news that truth can be found," Jacobins pronounced, in support of their multitude of newspaper subscriptions, even if they all leaned one particular way.[24]

Clubs and newspapers reinforced each other, acculturating subjects first as revolutionaries and then as citizens. In his paper the *Révolutions de France et du Brabant*, Camille Desmoulins celebrated the propagation of "the great tree planted by the Bretons at the Jacobins," whose branches spread ever outward with clubs meeting throughout France, most linked via circular letters with the "mother club" in Paris.[25] In 1789, the National Assembly explicitly recognized the right of active citizens "to meet peacefully without arms in assemblies to draft addresses and petitions."[26] The Société des Amis de la Constitution (Society of friends of the constitution) originally drew deputies from the National Assembly, "animated by an ardent zeal for the rights of man," to their meetings in the church formerly owned by the Jacobin order. Regulations adopted by the Parisian Société in February 1790 explicitly encouraged participation by "ordinary people." Perhaps inspired by the fictional account of Jacques in the *Révolutions de Paris*, an increasing number of artisans and small shopkeepers joined.

The Jacobins' powerful oratory in this alternative public space eclipsed meetings of the official Legislative Assembly. One of the main attractions at meetings was the reading of excerpts from the press, but lectures were also given on such subjects as "man's nature and his duties to his fellow men."[27] Listeners reported that speeches overflowing with the rhetoric of the Enlightenment moved them to tears and the club to ovations. That earned the Jacobins substantial coverage in the press, disseminating their influence yet more widely and defining them as a monitor on the elected bodies. Politics was not just the government anymore.

Jacobin clubs opened up a public sociability unknown under the Old Regime. In Montpellier, they boasted they "were never divided, their hearts always confiding in each other, they all belonged to one family."[28] Citizens, most of whom had been elected to no formal assembly, gathered to discuss the political future of the world. They replaced the formal

FIGURE 4.2
Jacobin meeting in Paris, January 1792. The crowded assembly hears the
declaration of war. With permission from the Bibliothèque Nationale de France,
Département des Estampes et de la photographie

"vous" with the informal "tu" in meetings. In keeping with this revolutionary sociability, Jacobins visited sick club members with food and
newspapers, and organized celebrations that gathered everyone together.
On Sundays, most clubs opened their doors to the public.

Revolutionary political sociability spread throughout the provinces as
if spontaneously, engaging the French in their revolution. "Organized
around the shared enthusiasm for the public good," the Jacobin societies
encouraged "political discussions that are among the chief delights of a
free people." Around France, "associations of zealous patriots" met three
or four evenings a week in former monasteries, taverns, small theaters, or
offices decorated with the busts of Rousseau, Mirabeau, or Benjamin
Franklin, with speaking platforms poised under copies of the Declaration
of the Rights of Man.[29] French clubs grew from twenty-one to three hundred in 1790, to eleven hundred in 1791, to fifty-five hundred in Year II of
the French Revolution.[30] The network, linked by correspondence, extended to the colonies, with clubs in Pointe-à-Pitre, Sainte-Rose, and Moule in

Guadeloupe, Cayenne in Guiana, and Saint-Louis in Mauritius. "By their very union," the Genevan Étienne Dumont noted, the Jacobins exercised considerable power.[31]

Revolutionary travelers from abroad routinely attended Jacobin club meetings in Paris and throughout the provinces. The Prussian-born Dutch revolutionary refugee Jean Baptiste—better known as Anacharsis Cloots—introduced a motion at the Jacobins in Paris in March 1790, speaking as "Cloots du Val-de-Grace, Baron in Germany, citizen in France."[32] The Jacobins celebrated the success of other revolutions, flying the flags of America and Geneva. Robespierre proclaimed that "different peoples must come to one another's assistance according to their ability, like the citizens of the same State. He who oppresses a single nation declares himself the enemy of all."[33] Their gaze extended beyond France.

The Jacobins had no monopoly over this alternative political sphere. Other clubs, most notably the Cordeliers, coalesced the popular classes unable to pay the membership dues of the Jacobins. At meetings of the Cordeliers, newspapers were read aloud, the enemies of the revolution denounced, and images of a just new world unfettered by economic distinctions pronounced. One English visitor complained about the rowdies in attendance, whose "dress was so filthy and unkempt that one would have taken them for a gathering of beggars."[34] He did not think they belonged in a political discussion. Women as well as wage earners attended the Cercle Social.

In December 1790, Etta Palm d'Aelders from Groningen, in the north of the United Provinces, mounted the speakers' platform at the Palais Royale to address a crowd of four thousand members of the Cercle Social's Conféderation des Amis de la Vérité (Confederation of the friends of truth). It was unprecedented for a woman to speak at all, yet she was asking the French Revolution to defend the rights not only of men but of women as well. "You have restored to man the dignity of his being in recognizing his rights," she began, so why "allow women to groan beneath an arbitrary authority?"[35] D'Aelders, an outsider in Paris, appealed to "all individuals, without differentiation for sex," to recognize "the equality of rights without discrimination of sex."[36] Explaining that French women "burn to show all Europe . . . they are the model of civic virtues," d'Aelders established the first women's club in Paris, the Conféderation des Amies de la Vérité (Confederation of the female friends of truth).[37] The founding members set dues at three livres per month, a sum that effectively excluded women without substantial means.

Even if, as the Girondin Madame Roland remembered, "the Jacobins, like the Assembly, suffered convulsions at the very mention of the word," the king's flight to Varennes in June 1791 energized these more popular clubs and journalists on the left alike to agitate for a "republic."[38] In their campaign to promote American liberty in France, Brissot, Thomas Paine, the Genevan revolutionary Étienne Clavière, and the marquis de Cordorcet and his wife Sophie de Grouchy organized the Société des Républicains (Republican club). Meeting at the home of the American Revolutionary War veteran Achille du Chastellet, they resolved to publish a newspaper, *Le Républicain* (The republican). On 1 July 1791, deputies to the French National Assembly found a declaration signed by du Chastellet affixed to their door. Paine, alleged to be the actual author of the address, informed the French that it was their responsibility as revolutionaries to build a nation where every individual was subject to the same laws and where equality would assure the preservation of liberty. They rejoiced that while the rest of Europe was still bound by aristocratic privilege, at least in Paris, "public opinion is formed in the clubs."[39]

Many of these clubs, including the Cercle Social and the Cordeliers, coalesced under a central coordinating committee in the summer of 1791. They drew up a petition calling for abdication of the king and the declaration of a republic.[40] Thirty thousand citizens arrived en masse at the Champs de Mars on 17 July bearing the signed petitions. The National Guard under Lafayette's command opened fire, killing or wounding sixty petitioners, and the government ordered the arrest of a number of club leaders.

Newspaper editors had "at their command all the loudest trumpets," one of Brissot's enemies complained, noting how easily the rabble was roused.[41] The informal transfer of power from elite institutions to the more popular press and clubs did not go uncontested. In drafting the moderate French Constitution of 1791, Isaac le Chapelier moved that political power be vested in elected bodies and their constituted governments only. Groups of friends could meet, but their debates could not be open to the public. Thereafter, Jacobins could sign their addresses as free citizens, but not as members of an organized group.

Nor was the presence of women on the political stage universally welcomed. When a journalist writing for the *Gazette de la Haye* (The Hague
gazette) died, Etta Palm d'Aelders asked to replace him. The editor refused
on the grounds that "she was only a woman with politics for a hobby."[42]
Women were apparently not included in his ideal of equality. In the new
republic of equal brothers, women were relegated to club galleries to
observe and listen, and not allowed to participate in the debate. Writing
to a friend, d'Aelders protested the French revolutionaries who "desire
the liberation of the slaves in America and uphold the despotism of the
husband."[43]

The Société des Républicaines Révolutionnaires (Society of revolutionary republican women) defended their right to participate in politics,
arguing "that one must recognize one's social duties in order to fulfill one's
domestic duties adequately." They pledged "to instruct themselves, to
learn well the Constitution and laws of the Republic, to attend to public
affairs, [and] to succor suffering humanity."[44] Together with the
Cordeliers, they called on Jacobins to mobilize the sans culottes and arm
them with weapons forged in public workshops.

In September 1793, a detractor denounced the Société des
Républicaines Révolutionnaires, now several hundred strong, to the
Jacobins for inciting disorder among the stalls of the marketplace.
Members had tried to compel market women to wear the revolutionary
cockade. Their leader, Claire Lacombe, "meddles everywhere" the critic
complained, just as Lacombe herself entered the gallery. The president of
the Jacobins pointed to her unwelcome appearance as "proof of the declarations that have just been made against her." He chided other women in
attendance that their true duties were at home. Lacombe was hauled
before the Committee of General Security for questioning.[45]

Tensions escalated. Market women invaded the next meeting of the
Société des Républicains Révolutionnaires shouting "Down with red bon-
nets! Down with Jacobin women! Down with Jacobin women and the
cockades! They are all scoundrels who have brought misfortune upon
France!" The chair "tried in vain to bring people back to their senses using
the arms of reason," but soldiers had to intervene to restore order.[46] The
Jacobins seized the occasion to close the women's clubs as a threat to public order in October 1793. Theirs remained open.

With the decisive victory of the "Mountain" or Jacobins in the National Convention in the summer of 1793, the Jacobin clubs not only came back to life but were officially recognized as an auxiliary arm of the government. This formidable presence when all of Europe was to be "jacobinized" has endured as the image of the Jacobin clubs, overshadowing the more informal institutions that claimed the allegiance of Frenchmen in the first four years of the revolution.

British Sans Culottes: "Manufacturers, Tradesmen and other inhabitants"

Newspaper-reading, pamphlet-writing societies in England predated the French Revolution.[47] What changed under the influence of the French was the involvement of artisans and tradesmen in politics. Their participation in this alternative political sphere alarmed the government as it built up the bulwarks against revolution from across the Channel.

In 1790, a coterie of peers, knights, aldermen, and a few doctors in 1780 organized the London Society for Constitutional Information "to convince men of all ranks, that it is in their interest as well as their duty, to support a free constitution, and to maintain and assert these common rights which are essential to the dignity and to the happiness of human nature."[48] In its first three years, the London Society for Constitutional Information disseminated more than eighty-eight thousand copies of thirty-three pamphlets calling for reform: broader parliamentary representation, fair elections, just taxation, and the abolition of the slave trade.

In December 1791, a quite different set of men in Sheffield, mostly tradesmen, drawing inspiration not only from the Society for Constitutional Information but from the French Jacobins as well, organized a society to answer "the want of knowledge and information in the general class of People."[49] By mid-March 1792, more than two thousand members, divided into sections, were meeting in Sheffield taverns. The Sheffield Constitutional Society published a cheap edition of Thomas Paine's *Rights of Man* to summon still more artisans to the cause of parliamentary reform. Paine offered to donate the profits from the sale to the popular societies.

A Scottish cobbler in Piccadilly, Thomas Hardy, gathered a similar circle of eight London tradesmen at the Bell Tavern on Fleet Street in

March 1792. Hardy recalled later in his memoirs: "They had finished their daily labour, and met there by appointment. After having their bread and cheese and porter for supper, as usual, and their pipes afterwards, with some conversation on the hardness of the times and the dearness of all the necessaries of life, which they, in common with their fellow citizens, felt to their sorrow, the business for which they had met was brought forward—parliamentary reform—an important subject to be deliberated upon and dealt with by such a class of men."[50] Each of the eight members of the London Corresponding Society contributed a penny to the kitty, far less than the dues of the London Constitutional Society. The second meeting drew sixteen members; within a month more than one hundred members had split into divisions, each meeting in a separate London tavern.

The two societies reached out to industrial Britain, encouraging societies in Birmingham, Manchester, Norwich, and Stockport. The political awakening of the "large and respectable manufacturing towns," John Horne Tooke, a London barrister and leader of the London Society for Constitutional Information, explained, would offset "the aristocratic interests of the country" that had long dominated British politics.[51] The London Corresponding Society pointedly identified its struggle with that of black slaves who had been stripped of their rights, appropriating the term "slavery" to describe members' own condition as British laborers. Olaudah Equiano, the leader of London's free black community, revised his widely read narrative in the home of his friends Thomas and Lydia Hardy.[52]

The communication among the rapidly growing membership of the radical societies and their alliance with abolitionists and freed slaves alarmed William Pitt's government. Why, government agents wondered, would the members of the Constitutional Society, propertied and educated at Eton and Oxford, who gathered at Tooke's solicitor's quarters in Chancery Lane for meetings, correspond regularly with tradesmen like Thomas Hardy? More to the point, why would barristers invited to the London Tavern in Bishopsgate Street for "Dinner at Four. Ticket Seven Shillings and Sixpence" defend the right of "the people necessarily separated for the purpose of following their several occupations and attending to their domestic concerns . . . to meet, associate, and communicate together, upon all matters relative to their common good"?[53] Why did the disparate associations consider cooperation not only a right but "a duty they reciprocally owe to each other so to do"?[54] Edmund Burke, author of *Reflections on the Revolution in France*, identified the growing crowds assembled in London taverns as "the mother of the mischief" and a threat to Britain's tradition of peaceful reform.[55]

Thomas Paine toasted the "Revolution of all the world" at the Revolution Society in London, as reported by American journalist Thomas Greenleaf in the *New York Journal*.[56] Peoples were joining together and rising above national prejudices "to assert the unalienable rights of mankind, and thereby to introduce a general reformation in the governments of Europe," speakers at the London assembly proclaimed. Together they would "make the world free and happy."[57]

Even though the London Corresponding Society openly declared "their *abhorrence* of tumult and violence," the government was determined to find a Jacobin conspiracy.[58] Their fears were not completely misplaced. Tooke wanted "to bind all our fellow citizens with us in the strong tyes of mutual interest and general good," building a movement across Europe and America that would join all the people in a vast democracy.[59] An admirer of the tracts of Joel Barlow appealing to a "class of men that cannot write, and in a great measure . . . cannot read," Tooke nominated the American poet for honorary membership in the Society for Constitutional Information.[60] Unanimously welcomed into the Society, Barlow was appointed a steward to plan the April celebration of Thomas Paine in London.[61] Correspondents from the British societies also wrote regularly to their counterparts on the Continent, looking "forward to the day when the two nations, united by Nature, but divided for ages by the intrigues of Courts and the pride of Princes," would "be reunited by the love of peace, and by the reciprocal advantages of a Commerce."[62] Some of these letters were intercepted and ended up in the hands of the government.

A government spy who had been accustomed to follow the "ragamuffins" of the London Corresponding Society was dispatched to monitor the Society for Constitutional Information; he reported his surprise at "the decent and respectable appearance of the persons assembled together."[63] Shadowed by this same spy, Tooke decided to play along and, within hearing of the man, exaggerated the number of Society for Constitutional Information members, spoke of plots for revolution, and boasted of collections of arms and ammunition. When the spy intercepted a letter to Tooke asking, "Is it possible to get ready by Thursday?"—in fact, a dinner invitation—the spy assumed a militia was on the march, and dispatched police. They surprised the impeccably dressed dinner guests at Tooke's Wimbledon estate.[64] This alliance of middle-class reformers with mechanics and artisans new to politics was especially worrisome to the government, given the success of the American War for Independence and the progress of the revolution across the Channel.

In April 1792, James Watt, son of the inventor of the steam engine, and Thomas Cooper, representing the Manchester Constitutional Society, traveled to France to address the Jacobins. As observers of the French Revolution, they witnessed firsthand what "the American Republics have taught us experimentally, that nations may flourish and be happy who have no Bishops, no Nobles, no kings. No reflecting Man," Cooper added, "can look back at the last half Century, or consider the probabilities of the next, without seeing clearly that the Revolution of Europe is at hand." From London, Burke denounced Watt and Cooper for exposing Britain to Jacobinism. Is it a crime to enlighten the people upon the subject of politics? Cooper asked. "Why this dread the People (the Swinish multitude as their friend, Mr. Burke, calls them) should think too much and reason too much on their own rights and their own Interests?"[65] Others derided Watt and Cooper as British Jacobins intent on reducing Britain to "a general confusion and scramble, in which all orders, ranks, and properties are to be confounded."[66] Property aside, that was not far from their goal.

Tensions escalated the next autumn when Joel Barlow and a British lawyer, John Frost, self-identified as "respectable cosmopolitans" representing the London Corresponding Society, addressed the French National Convention. "Frenchmen, you are already free and Britons are preparing to become so," they proclaimed.[67] Carried away by the enthusiasm of the convention, they ventured beyond their prepared text. "Like the faint glimmerings of an aurora borealis, the spark of liberty, [was] nurtured in England during the course of several centuries." In 1776, "a more intense light, similar to that of the true dawn blazed forth from the heart of the American Republic, but at too great a distance to illuminate our hemisphere." The Europeans watched, inspired from afar, but unsure how to apply the new principles in the Old World, Barlow and Frost explained.

"The French Revolution, shining with all the intensity of the sun at its zenith," reintroduced revolution to Europe. "Everywhere, its influence is dispelling the clouds," they concluded before presenting one thousand pairs of shoes to the assembly for French soldiers.[68] French Jacobins wrote back to thank the British, pledging that together they would fight and defeat the "league of tyrants," a coalition that many thought included the British government.[69]

In December 1792, Scottish radicals summoned their English associates to Edinburgh for a "convention," a term purposefully chosen to echo the French. Two hundred sixty delegates from eighty committees represented the British people at this alternative body to the House of Commons. Although the delegates rejected the most incendiary proposals put forward by the United Irish and swore their allegiance to the king, the convention closed with the French oath "to live free or die."[70]

In 1793, the London Corresponding Society and the Society for Constitutional Information together organized a massive petition drive to protest their government's rush to join the Austrians and Prussians in their war against the French. They held out little hope of succeeding, but as Prussian troops approached Paris, they wanted to "assure the French that we entertain the most friendly dispositions . . . towards them."[71] Modeled after the abolitionist petition campaigns, the British societies' drive gathered more signatures from "the Manufacturers, Tradesmen and other Inhabitants" than the number of enfranchised citizens who had voted for the sitting Parliament.[72] Their success in enlarging the political community was obvious. Ten thousand signed the London Corresponding Society petition opposing war with France, eight thousand the antiwar petition in Sheffield, and Edinburgh's petition stretched the length of Parliament itself. The British government monitored the petitioners but ignored the petitions.

The London Corresponding Society also organized a mass meeting to rally support for France in its war against its counterrevolutionary neighbors. Seven hundred ticket holders assembled in the Crown and Anchor Tavern to hear spirited orators denounce the "British gold" that "subsidizes armies of Continental slaves" while "the starving labourer is compelled to sell his life and liberty for bread!"[73] So many people came to a third mass meeting that organizers had to move the crowd out of doors, where bystanders gawked and cried out, "Tom Paine was come to plant the tree of liberty. . . . The French Jacobins were come."[74] (Paine had, in fact, fled to France to avoid arrest.)

In the fall, despite threats of arrest by Scottish authorities, English societies sent delegates "who really wish for a radical Reform in Parliament and the Preservation of the Constitutional Rights" back to Edinburgh to a second British convention.[75] Delegates deliberately echoed the rhetoric of the French Convention. William Pitt's government dispatched the police to disperse the convention and arrest the leaders.

The rhetoric of the London Corresponding Society's final public meeting in the early spring of 1794 at Chalk Farm just north of London eclipsed that of the French Jacobins. John Thelwell, a firebrand who had been addressing gatherings across London, lamented the poverty of British laborers and told them "in plain terms I am a Republican, a down right sans culotte."[76] He spoke of reform, not revolution, but advocated the destruction of the regime of privilege in Britain that allowed the rich to swell their incomes "by monopolising the necessities of life" while laborers paid heavy taxes and languished, untaught, in poverty.[77] Many of the leaders of the London Corresponding Society were not afraid to call themselves Jacobins. The reformer William Fox said he was proud to be associated with the French Jacobins, "if Jacobinism be the progress of human knowledge subverting ancient systems founded on ignorance and superstition."[78] The inflammatory declaration provoked a response.

The government arrested twelve leaders of the British radical societies, including John Horne Tooke, John Thelwell, and Thomas Hardy, and seized their papers. They were accused of organizing a convention "directly tending to the Introduction of that System of Anarchy and Confusion which has fatally prevailed in France."[79] Club members who escaped the first round of arrests fled Britain, some traveling to the Continent, others taking refuge in America. The society leaders were acquitted after long and well-publicized trials, but few British radicals dared to continue their struggle for revolutionary change in Britain. Pointing to the contagion of revolution throughout continental Europe, members of Parliament encouraged the government to prosecute radicals under the terms of the Two Acts, the so-called "Gagging Acts."

The government drove the radical movement in Britain, including the abolitionists, underground, a casualty of the alleged connection to the

French Jacobins. Even though many of these British radicals were actually more outspoken in their populism and abolitionism than the French Jacobins, it was in their alleged association with the French that they were seen as posing the biggest threat to the British government.

The "revolutionary wave" of the Polish Jacobins

The enlightened Polish monarch King Stanislas worried—with good reason, it turned out—that reformers throughout Europe would be tainted by their friendship with the Parisian Jacobins. He had heard that in Italy and Germany foreign radicals said to be "emissaries of the Jacobin Club . . . are distributing profusely thousands of copies of all kinds of pamphlets in French and German best designed to stir up people's minds."[80] This threat of French radical contagion put nervous absolutist governments everywhere on guard, a particular problem for the Polish ruler, lodged as he was between Prussia and Russia. Association with the French revolutionaries could give his powerful neighbors an excuse to invade. A known reformer himself, he was no Jacobin.

The king ruled from Warsaw, the only large city in Poland. His power was limited. Most of the Polish peasants owed their allegiance as serfs to their local lords. These lords, each representing one of the fifty regional assemblies in the national parliament or Diet, could block legislation they opposed. That obviously included reforms eliminating this Liberum Veto. In 1789, after a decade of discussion, 141 Polish towns petitioned the king for the right to representation in the Diet alongside the gentry. Newspapers on both sides of the Atlantic followed "the progress of the Spirit of Liberty in Poland."[81] When debate in the Diet stalled, reformers initiated secret meetings with the king to draft a new constitution outside the parliamentary sessions.

In the spring of 1791, eighty Polish citizens calling themselves the Society of the Friends of the Constitution, after the French Jacobins, assembled at the empty Warsaw's Radziwill Palace to encourage ratification of this new constitution by the Diet.[82] Urged on by an Italian expatriate active in the Society of the Friends, Scipione Piattoli, King Stanislas convened an emergency meeting of the Diet, scheduled for the Easter holiday, when members of the gentry were away at their country estates.

Reformers gathered in Stanislas's chamber at three in the morning. Together they vowed, as had the French National Assembly, not to adjourn until they ratified a new constitution. The club's tactic succeeded. The Diet approved a new constitution.

Stanisław Małachowski, marshal of the Diet, championed the Polish Constitution of 1791 that guaranteed "liberty, security, and all freedoms," rooted as it was in English and American constitutional principles.[83] The Constitution eliminated the Liberum Veto, strengthened the powers of the king, and separated the three branches of government. It did not free the serfs but did recognize the rights of burghers, the urban middle class, and open their path into the gentry. King Stanislas, well "aware of its considerable shortcomings," conceded that the Poles had accomplished what was possible.[84] All the while, he endeavored to assure his neighbors that the Polish revolution was neither democratic nor Jacobin.

Outside observers and the press did not help his cause. The *Gazeta Warszawska* (Warsaw gazette) linked the French and the Poles as two people "sharing a common goal. Both countries want to be free and to know no other laws than those they have given themselves."[85] Jacobin clubs in France that had followed the progress of Polish reform efforts hailed the new constitution that extended liberty to "millions of men in one day."[86] Filippo Mazzei, a Tuscan merchant hired as the Polish king's agent, informed the king from Paris, "Here now there is hardly any talk other than of Poland and her magnanimous, divine Stanislas Augustus."[87] French newspapers heralded the reforms in Poland as the beginnings of revolution in central Europe. The *Moniteur* and *Révolutions de Paris* warned that if other European monarchs did not follow the example of Stanislas, their people might rebel like the French.

Acclaim came from all of the expected quarters, and from others as well. Anacharsis Cloots proclaimed: "The trumpet announcing the resurrection of a great people has sounded to the four corners of the earth, and the cries of joy from a chorus of twenty-five million free men will awaken the peoples long asleep in slavery."[88] Thomas Paine inquired about the possibility of claiming Polish citizenship. His rival, Edmund Burke, who had condemned the French Revolution in his influential *Reflections on the French Revolution*, modestly took credit himself for the Polish constitution. Meanwhile, the American Joel Barlow, who had sent King Stanislas a copy of his recently published *Advice to the Privileged Orders in the Several States of Europe*, praised the new constitution as "if not the best law that you could frame, at least the best that circumstances would admit."[89] The *Pennsylvania Gazette* congratulated the Polish king, whom it recognized as an avid reader of all things American.[90] From London, the *Public Advertiser* warned that "if the new Revolution in Poland is suffered to be permanent, . . . and if the flames should spread, the conflagration, in all human probability, would become general."[91]

The Society of Friends of the Constitution meeting in Warsaw fanned the flames. They pledged to assure the respect due the Constitution in the Diet, the army, the schools, newspapers, and churches. The Society organized public festivals in May 1792 to commemorate the first anniversary of the Constitution before threats from neighboring emperors forced them into secrecy. Just as Stanislas had predicted, the arrival of the French ambassador and his attendance at meetings of the Society of Friends stoked Russian and Prussian fears of a secret revolutionary alliance between the French and the Poles.

Polish newspapers, unlike their French counterparts, devoted the little attention they gave to Polish politics to parliamentary decisions of the Diet, not to the debates of the clubs. There was no exponential growth in the number of newspapers, either, as in Paris. Perhaps the two factors were related. Instead, the *Gazeta Narodowa I Obca* (National and international gazette), published by reformers in the Polish Diet, reprinted documents from the Parisian Jacobins. Their twenty-four-year-old correspondent, Thadée Mostowski, documented "the passage of the people from oppression to liberty" in France.[92] It was said that Ignacy Potocki, the king's cousin and a representative of the Polish reformers, was late to a session of the Diet because he was waiting for the latest news from France.[93]

The visit of a Polish deputy to the French Convention in December 1792, reportedly on mission from Poland to affirm the fraternal brotherhood of the two republics, confirmed Russian suspicions. Russian empress Catherine II assured the Prussians that she would put an end to "this pernicious epidemic."[94] That was just what Stanislas had feared all along. In May 1792, Russian troops invaded Poland and called for the dissolution of the Diet. They justified their intervention with the Act of Targowica, an aristocratic denunciation of the Polish Constitution of 1791.

King Stanislas capitulated as Austria, Prussia, and Russia occupied and partitioned the country. Newspapers around Europe got this news from the *Gazeta Warszawska*. British editors applauded the courage of the Polish people and their king. "The Revolutions of Poland differed essentially from the Revolution in France," the *Public Advertiser* clarified for its readers to elicit their sympathy. "The change in Poland was not from a state of slavery to that of licentious liberty [as in France]. No! It was the united struggle of a brave, of a free people to rescue themselves from the insulting overbearance of a despotic neighbor."[95] Although many Polish revolutionaries fled to Dresden, Leipzig, and Paris, a Polish resistance movement mobilized within Poland. They told the French foreign minister that they intended to drive out Russia and Prussia and to restore an independent government guaranteeing the freedom of the common people of Poland. Their first revolution had demonstrated to them "how unsatisfactory moderately employed means are when enemies of humanity impose ever-present barriers against their freedom."[96] They chose Thaddeus Kościuszko, the Polish hero of the American Revolution, as their leader.

Kościuszko, now an honorary French citizen, visited Paris in January 1794. He left the French capital with vague assurances of French support for a second Polish revolution. French foreign minister Pierre Lebrun envisioned "squadrons of battleships on the Baltic Sea" as Sweden and Turkey joined France in liberating Poland.[97] Kościuszko traveled to Italy to divert attention from plans afoot in Poland. In Italy, Kościuszko encountered the seemingly ever-present Mazzei, who offered to arrange his transport to America. Kościuszko feigned interest, another ploy to confuse his enemies, but returned secretly to Poland. There he pledged, "in the face of heaven and before all the human race, and especially before all the nations that know how to value liberty above all the blessings of the universe . . . to deliver the land of our fathers from a ferocious oppression, and from the galling yoke of the ignominious bondage."[98] He began to prepare a coordinated assault against the Russians.

Forced by events to attack before they were ready, Kościuszko's troops defeated the Russians at the village of Racławice after an uprising at Cracow. That signaled the beginning of the insurrection that spread throughout the country in April 1794. It was not clear whether the Poles were fighting only to secure independence from the Russians or had launched a second revolution. Kościuszko realized that a revolution that pushed beyond the reforms of 1791 would alienate moderate reformers, whose support he would need to govern. However, to mobilize the Polish peasants on whom he relied in battle, their scythes converted to pikes, Kościuszko had to promise equality. The Polaniec Proclamation of May 1794 was a compromise document. It proclaimed the peasants free, but required them to report their movements to public authorities. Even if Kościuszko sympathized with the Jacobins instead of the moderates, circumstances in Poland forced him to bend toward the middle class to counter the power of the gentry.

After the 1794 uprising in Warsaw, a new club explicitly following the model of the French Jacobins, Citizens Offering Aid and Service to the National Magistrates for the Welfare of the Country, pledged to democratize this second Polish revolution. Meeting in the former Jesuit colleges and in the cloisters of the Capuchins, the club drew its members predominantly from the intelligentsia of Warsaw. Shopkeepers and tradesmen gathered in clubs of their own in popular cafés on Mostowa Street in Warsaw, on Szewska and Florianska streets in Cracow, and in Vilno. The British ambassador in Warsaw anxiously reported seeing club members emerge from their gatherings fully attired in Jacobin clothing and insignia, inspiring massive crowds in demonstrations staged before the palace to demand equality. King Stanislas asked Kościuszko to disband the incendiary clubs, but the Polish revolutionary leader refused. Revolutionary clubs were needed, he asserted, wherever "the people were not respected by the government or when the excessive moderation of the government towards evil doers and the slowness of justice chilled them."[99] In defiance of the king, Polish Jacobins continued to build altars to the fatherland, to wear Phyrgian caps, and to sing civic hymns from the French Revolution. Catherine vigorously denounced "the wanton Warsaw horde established by French tyrants."[100]

The Poles fought the Russians and the Prussians through the summer, casting themselves as heirs to earlier revolutions. No foreign aid materialized, not from the French or anyone else. That left the Poles, closely watched by Americans and Europeans, on their own. Even though clearly overpowered, the optimistic Polish Jacobins still aspired to launch "a revolutionary wave that would flood all the countries from the Don to the Oder rivers."[101] The Polish army dispatched "several hundred apostles of liberty" into Russia to foment revolution.[102] In October 1794, the Poles lost the battle of Maciejowice, and that sealed their fate. Kościuszko was captured by the Russians, who marched on, massacring between ten thousand and fifteen thousand citizens in the suburb of Praga alone before the Poles capitulated for a second time. The Russians, the Austrians, and the Prussians once again partitioned Poland, dismantling the embryonic reforms instituted by the revolutionaries and their king.

Revolutionaries throughout the Atlantic world once again heralded the martyrs to the cause of liberty. A Dutch poet dubbed Kościuszko the Polish George Washington, "the son of freedom," for freeing the serfs.[103] The Jacobins in Paris announced that Kościuszko's time in Paris and his visit to the National Convention in particular had inspired in the Polish patriot "this sacred fire of liberty, this hatred of tyranny and this love of the people, without which an insurrectionary chief is nothing but a tyrant."[104] Few of them doubted that revolution would return to central Europe, led, they expected, by a new hero inspired by their revolution.

"The party from which the mischief is expected to arise"

French journalists had cause to describe Paris as the fount of liberty after 1789. Their revolution not only outlasted all the others, except the American, but inspired imitations. The idiosyncratic editor of the *Annales politiques, civiles, et littéraires* (Political, civil, and literary annals), Simon-Nicolas Linguet, who had spent time in Poland, Britain, the United Provinces, and the Austrian Netherlands, foresaw the imminent defeat of "tyranny, this monster, who under so many different names crushed enslaved Europe" and celebrated the liberation of the people who would govern themselves "without Pope, without Kings & without Queens."[105] Camille Desmoulins dedicated his Parisian newspaper to the "fraternity that must unite all free peoples."[106] He linked the preeminent French Revolution to the Portuguese who were awakening from their slumber, to revolutionary movements stirring in Spain, and to the "Philosophy and the spirit of liberty scaling the Alps."[107] The *Courrier de l'Europe* reported in 1791 that "the yet undefined watchword *liberty* has electrified everyone."[108] That was before the second defeat of the Polish revolutionaries and the suppression of the British radicals. Even those setbacks, though, would do little to dull their optimism.

The press and the clubs together transformed politics in the revolutionary age. Citizenship required a free press and voluntary associations. They invited the people, not just deputies elected by a limited franchise or officials appointed by a monarch, into politics. These new citizens did not just vote; they expected to be integrally involved in the governing of their society. This was the public sphere more broadly defined by clubs, based in the popular sovereignty of an expanded citizenry that read or listened, and joined in a revolution. The political community had ceased to be the privileged domain of "some," of the elites.

André Chénier, editor of the *Journal de Paris* (Journal of Paris), charged that the French Jacobins, with "more zeal than enlightenment," had forgotten "that in a well-administered state all of the citizens do not control public affairs." Vesting their trust in "the sovereignty of the people," the Jacobins in their clubs and newspapers incited mobs, "brazenly called the people," to claim a role in running the state.[109]

"Experience shows us that the people are not the terrible monster that the supporters of despotism portray," the editor of a Dutch newspaper countered.[110] Joel Barlow more maliciously suggested in his *Advice to the Privileged Orders* that it was pointless for "some" to worry about the dissemination of revolutionary news to "the party from which the mischief is expected to arise," because that party had "knowledge of them already."[111]

The experience of French revolutionaries had solidified the conviction that there was only one truth. Writers on the left especially, but also the right, shared an optimistic faith with the leaders of the clubs that if the truth was published, it would convince. "If only the liberty of thinking and writing was given to everyone, errors would collapse of their own weight, and the truth and the general interest alone would float on the ocean of public thought," the editor of *La Cocarde nationale* (The national cockade) suggested.[112]

The revolution transformed the press. It was not just the staggering increase in the volume of newsprint. Before 1789, journalists covered political events in sparse prose, often from a safe distance. The French

Revolution enlisted journalists as political participants; they in turn demanded engagement from their readers. Partisan newspapers read by like-minded people hardened political divisions not only in a revolution with a guillotine, but in ones surrounded by imperial armies.

This political opening attracted admiration and imitation among France's neighbors, from London to Krakow. The London Corresponding Society foresaw an alliance "not of crowns, but of the people of America, France, and Britain."[113] Jean-Paul Marat, happy to imagine himself "the father of the clubs," envisioned these popular clubs as an educational forum for "men well versed in politics who are vigilant day and night watching over their interests and defending their rights."[114] Their revolution would become more contagious as the public sphere opened. Politics would travel across national borders through the press, linking one popular association to another.

The threat of conflagration in the volatile age of upheaval meant that connections with the French Jacobins, whether real or imagined, was sufficient to alarm the powers interested in preserving the established order. Burke dedicated himself to keeping "the French infection from this country; their principles from our minds and their daggers from our hearts." He warned his "countrymen to beware of these execrable philosophers, whose only object is to destroy every thing that is good here, and to establish immorality and murder by precept and example."[115] In Poland, as in England, suspicion of alliances triggered by revolutionary club members' travel to Paris roused the forces of order to quell the revolutionary tide. The French Revolution that inspired neighboring revolutions also caused their demise.

With the Prussians and the Russians on the move in central Europe, the Republican Society of South Carolina worried that "the European potentates" threatened "nothing less than American vassalage, in some form or other."[116] United by their common interests, American clubs up and down the Atlantic Coast called on revolutionary people everywhere to fight against "Aristocracy and Despotism" and for "the lasting improvement and happiness of the human race as they are founded in the equal rights of man."[117] When the French consul gave the society in South Carolina a stone from the Bastille, members promised to engrave on it the infamous French cap of liberty.

They did not anticipate that citizenship, redefined by revolutions on both sides of the Atlantic, would be more dramatically expanded by the revolution in the Caribbean. That wave of revolutions shaking the institution of slavery and disrupting the slave trade would challenge many of the very revolutionaries who had redefined the public sphere in America and Europe.

FIVE

Rumors of Freedom in the Caribbean: "We know not where it will end"

Mobility incited rebellion in the ever-changing and volatile Caribbean. Outnumbered, the whites who controlled the plantations and colonial administrators who profited from slave labor in Jamaica, Saint-Domingue, and Guadeloupe felt surrounded and constantly under siege. News arrived with an irregular rhythm dictated not by politics or newspaper coverage but by unpredictable travel. Rumors and the fear they stoked, though, flowed as freely as people through the islands.

Events in the metropole have excited significant fermentation in the Windward Islands," a French agent in Saint Lucia warned the minister of the marine in October 1789.[1] Principally in the French colonies of Guadeloupe, Martinique, and Saint-Domingue, but also on the Caribbean islands colonized by British, Spanish, and Dutch planters, momentous discussions of liberty circulated with the ocean currents. Slaves worked to death on colonial plantations kept alive traditions of insurrection, some based on memories of African unrest, others indigenous to the colonies. Among the islands of the Caribbean, where 80 percent of the population was enslaved, liberty and citizenship took on new meaning. That did little to allay the suspicions rampant among white officials and planters that a vast network of clubs and their printed propaganda were the agents carrying the revolutionary contagion to the colonies from the metropole.

Vessels carried newspapers and correspondence into the Caribbean harbors, where black and white sailors transmitted tales aloud to a population denied literacy. A British traveler visiting Barbados reported the throngs of men and women meeting a packet ship arriving from England: "Each wishing to be first, and all eager to learn the reports, the vessel was beset on every quarter before she could come to anchor, and the whole bay became an animated scene of crowded ships and moving boats."[2] The harbors launched waves of rumor and intrigue that traveled inland. The informal markets that flourished on the docks brought sailors into regular contact with slaves working locally. Rumors of liberty granted abroad coursed through markets, dances, and horseraces. In Sunday gatherings on plantations, slaves heard tales of colonial masters' denial of that freedom and of brazen escapes from plantations. White masters and their overseers testified to the transmittal of rumors based on news from Europe. They knew less about the heritage of freedom and rebellion carried from Africa or engendered by conditions on their own plantations.

In 1788, more than five hundred ships manned by nine thousand seamen carried goods and people in and out of Jamaica, while more than seven hundred ships with almost twenty thousand sailors traded in Saint-Domingue. The French minister of the marine, César Henri de la Luzerne, complained that the colony teemed with troublesome outsiders, "Majorcans, Minorcans, Italians, Maltese and other seafarers."[3] Sailors preparing for return voyages across the Atlantic or recovering from illness contracted at sea typically outnumbered rooted residents in port cities, their disorderly behavior the subject of frequent complaint.

The relaxation of commercial restrictions and opening of colonial ports in the late eighteenth century encouraged not only trade in goods but also the dissemination of information among the colonies. Illegal trade flourished, eluding all attempts at control. So did stowaways, often finding a freedom at sea denied them on land. Language differences that limited intercourse between Europeans posed less of a barrier to the men and women transported from Africa and accustomed to communicating across linguistic divides.

Slaves vastly outnumbered the white planters and colonial officials on every island in the Caribbean. The slave population of Saint-Domingue, for example, had almost doubled between 1770 and 1790, increasing from 379,000 to 650,000.[4] That raised not only the profits of colonial plantations and France's economic dependence on them but also the threat of insurrection. "Thousands of slaves" imported into the "disorder" of a decade of revolution portended trouble.[5] Male slaves and sailors accused of disorderly conduct were routinely rounded up in coastal cities.

MAP 5.1

Map of "the West Indies exhibiting the English, French, Spanish, Dutch &
Danish settlements. Collected from the best authorities by Thomas Jefferys,
geographer to His Royal Highness the Prince of Wales," London, 1760. Courtesy of the Library of Congress, Geography and Map Division

Free men and women of color on whom the plantations depended
were even more worrisome than the slaves. The free population of color
had grown significantly: in the poorest of the French colonies,
Guadeloupe, increasing from 10 to 18 percent of the free population between 1687 and 1789; in wealthy Martinique from 7 to 33 percent; and in
the more heavily populated Saint-Domingue, from 6 to 40 percent.[6]

Traders and peddlers, they supplied plantations with market goods. They carried produce harvested by the slaves back to the markets, as well as news of insurrections. Often raised by at least one white parent, these free men and women of color moved more easily among the white population than their unequal legal status would suggest. To white planters, they always seemed on the edge of rebellion. In addition, almost every free man between the ages of sixteen and sixty was armed, which gave the authorities reason to worry.

Slaves in port cities slipped into the ranks of free blacks and mulattoes employed as artisans in the harbors. Inland, individual slaves freed themselves by fleeing plantations. They established their own communities in rugged mountainous regions throughout the Caribbean, often trading arms and provisions with slaves on plantations. Lines demarcating race and freedom were always slipping in this fluid region.

"We love the Revolution," a veteran of the War for American Independence from Martinique wrote, "but we must tell you frankly that the colonies will be lost, . . . if you do not maintain the line of demarcation that separates the recently emancipated from the free man and the slave from the emancipated."[7] He feared the promise of liberty would echo too loudly in the colonies. A white deputy from Saint-Domingue sitting in the National Assembly in France went farther, arguing that the "absolute difference between the society of France and the colonies" meant the rights of man should be suspended in the colonies.[8] Georges Danton therefore urged the French National Assembly "not to exceed the boundaries of wisdom" and to filter the news headed to the colonies. The Committee of Public Safety and Committee of the Colonies would be advised to limit the transmission of information across the Atlantic to those revolutionary principles "useful for humanity without endangering it."[9] That proved impossible.

Word of the meeting of the Estates General in Versailles in May 1789 did not arrive in Saint-Domingue until the autumn of 1789. The slaves and free people of color heard what they expected to hear, that the king of France had abolished slavery. For decades, slaves in Saint-Domingue had looked to the king for protection. Based on the provisions of the century-old Code Noir, he could restrain renegade masters.[10] Masters and colonial authorities tried in vain to set the story of the revolution right. That rumor would not be silenced. And anticipation of revolutionary rights could be quelled no more than could patterns of trust. The promise of liberty flowed in with the tide; threats of insurrection flowed out just as regularly.

Ships carried news of revolts in the Caribbean back to North America and Europe. Unlike their American and European contemporaries, few of these Caribbean revolutionaries left behind written records. Talk may have flowed easily in the colonies, but it was rarely recorded, and when it was, the person was usually in authority. In Saint-Domingue, only a few dozen slaves could read and write; in Guyana only one slave in 1794 was literate. None of them had the luxury of time to compose their memoirs or to write letters, especially the literate slave in Guyana; he was executed in 1796.[11] That most of the slaves in Saint-Domingue spoke Creole, not a written language before the mid-twentieth century, meant that only a few proclamations and even fewer letters were written in the language of the majority of the population. British, Spanish, and French colonial officials sent "distressing accounts" of "the disorders," often in an attempt to counter "the false rumors" that had arrived with other travelers ahead of them.[12] Read between the lines, the rumors relayed by white officials and plantation managers testify to their own fears, and to the revolutionary aspirations of the vast populations of enslaved and freed men and women of color of the Caribbean.

Rumors on Jamaica: "The Disaffected amongst us"

In July 1776, just days after the American Congress endorsed the Declaration of Independence, white masters in the British colony of Jamaica uncovered plans for an insurrection on their plantations. Their trusted drivers, craftsmen, and domestic servants, in league with their field slaves, were allegedly plotting to claim their own freedom. British troops had abandoned the garrison to quell rebellion in the North American colonies at the same time that the commercial fleet sailed to England with the annual harvest. Before the rebels could load their guns and set fires on the hilltops to signal the launching of the insurrection, an attentive overseer, suspicious of a slave fingering his master's guns, forced a confession that led to the plot's unraveling. Fear escalated as news of the foiled insurrection spread amid the vastly outnumbered population of white masters and colonial officials.

The whites did not hesitate. The colonial government identified forty-eight slaves as miscreants and rounded them up. The Jamaican government tried the ringleaders, including the notorious three-fingered Jack, and executed them two days later. Within the week, another twenty to thirty conspirators, slaves and free men of color, were seized, along with a large quantity of guns and ammunition. In trials that stretched into September 1776, 135 slaves from forty-three plantations, including some of the most trusted domestic workers, were accused of plotting to slaughter their overseers and to set fire to their plantations. It appeared to the whites in power that the rebels were alarmingly well organized.

Rumors of a plot to poison the water supply at Montego Bay coursed through the colony before the end of the summer. Investigations implicating 8,618 slaves reached all the way inland to the isolated Maroon settlement at Trelawny Town.[13] A British officer told the governor that he had heard from a free man of color that the Maroons, the escaped slaves who had carved out their own communities in the mountainous interior of the island, "had invited the Coromantee Negroes in the Neighbourhood to join them" in rebellion. The governor called up the colonial militia to march with British troops. Although it turned out to be "all a Made up Story, not containing a Syllable of Truth," the governor cautioned, "there is now an apparent Spirit of insolence among the Slaves, over the whole Island, and in several Parishes."[14] He called a war council, declared martial law over the whole island, and summoned British war ships to show force along the coast, confirming the worst fears of the plantation overseers scattered around the colony. "Our apprehensions are great," because "we know not where it will end," General John Grizel of the Hanover militia reported to England.[15] It took little to set off fresh rounds of rumors that further escalated fears.

While the North American colonies chafed under British rule, the Caribbean colonies requested additional British troops to be stationed among them. The West Indies remained loyal to the British, on whom they depended for protection. With more than 200,000 slaves and free people of color on the island and only 12,737 white residents, maintaining order was a constant struggle.[16] To minimize the threat of insurrection, the Jamaican Assembly called for closer white oversight over all the plantations, inspection of fortifications, and a strengthening of the colonial militia. Maroons found guilty of encouraging slaves to escape from their plantations were to be deported.[17] The Assembly forbade slaves from keeping horses, hoping to limit the spread of conspiracies beyond the distance that could easily be walked.

Jamaica housed half of all the inhabitants of the British West Indies, and its ports controlled half of the trade. Planters there had cleared and cultivated vast plots of land by importing shiploads of slaves from Africa. Ninety-four percent of its population came from Africa. In 1739, colonial officials had signed a treaty allowing Maroon communities in the interior mountains to govern themselves in return for their assistance in rounding up runaway slaves who headed in their direction in search of freedom. Plantation owners, few of whom considered the islands their true home, assumed that they could trust these independent blacks, who enjoyed some rights and shared in the relative prosperity of the bountiful sugar trade. That uneasy trust evaporated in 1776.

That the slaves and free people of color would have imbibed the spirit of revolution rampant in the Americas seemed obvious in retrospect to whites in the British colony. They feared that Jamaican merchants' petitions in support of their trading partners, the American revolutionaries, had encouraged slaves to revolt against their petitioning masters. "Dear Liberty has rang in the heart of every House-bred Slave, in one form or other for these Ten years past," a Jamaican doctor wrote a friend in Edinburgh. The moment the masters joined the revolution, they found their slaves "fast at our heels. Such has been the seeds sown in the minds of our Domestics by our Wise-Acre Patriots."[18] He blamed the slave insurrections of 1776 on white Jamaicans who had "been too careless of Expressions, especially when the topic of American rebellion" was raised by "the Disaffected amongst us," often in earshot of the domestic workers and slaves serving dinner.[19] He did not see the conditions on Jamaican plantations that had given rise to slave revolts since 1673, including Tacky's Rebellion in 1760, when slaves wrested control of a number of plantations before they were subdued several months later.

Contributing to the Jamaican unrest in the 1770s, but also largely unacknowledged by contemporaries, was a shortage of food, a result of drought and the American war. In the second half of 1776, the price of essential food rose dramatically in the British West Indies.[20] Starvation stalked the islands. American privateers who disrupted Atlantic shipping added to the economic distress of the trade-dependent Caribbean colony. The combination of island populations deprived of basic necessities by a war-torn Atlantic, but regularly nourished by word of insurrections for freedom around the Atlantic, proved potent.

The newly arrived governor, Lord Effingham, cautioned whites about "what the gossiping of Idle Folks may produce."[21] Overheard table conversation was the alleged cause of the Jamaican uprising in 1776. Other British officials worried that literate domestic slaves had intercepted and opened letters. It was especially alarming that their slaves seemed to hear the news before their masters. The owner of a remote plantation realized that his slaves knew of an uprising in Montego Bay, some thirty miles away, even before the rider on horseback arrived to relay information to him. Somehow his slaves had learned every detail of the insurrection. How was this intelligence possible? His plantation lay off of the public roads and he kept his own slaves under close supervision within the bounds of his plantation. What, he wondered, was this "unknown mode of conveying intelligence amongst Negroes?"[22]

He might have learned from observing Mingo, a fisherman and driver sentenced to life in prison for instigating rebellion in the 1780s. Mingo escaped in 1791 and hosted a dance to confirm the rumors of his free state. Mingo not only was at liberty but had established a community "with about eighteen other Negroes men slaves and three women of different Countries and owners," a slave boasted. "All the Negroes know of this Town," he reported, alluding to the multitude of surreptitious gatherings unseen and undetected by whites.[23] Their network flourished in ways that whites could not even imagine.

An upholsterer in Montego Bay, Robert Parker, reported that he awakened one night, looked out his bedroom window, and was alarmed to see "four Negroes . . . very earnest in discourse." He overheard them talking in hushed voices with "two more Negroes that were on the other side of the Bridge," speculating on the number of guns and soldiers the white planters could mobilize against them.[24] The slaves, it seemed, had a formidable chain of oral communication, even if it had produced little actual unrest.

After the defeat of the British in America, thousands of white loyalists and their slaves flooded into the nervous peace of Jamaica. They were followed by the less welcome ships carrying at least a thousand black loyalists from Savannah. Landing in Jamaica, free blacks such as George Liele, a Baptist minister, made clear that they had no intention of challenging the British Empire. Even though he professed his loyalty to the king, Liele was regularly harassed, forbidden to preach, and imprisoned on charges of sedition.[25]

No significant insurrections troubled the calm of Jamaica over the next decade, but white planters were nevertheless convinced that the slaves were plotting, stirred by discussions of the slave trade in Parliament in London. The British abolitionists had published their parliamentary testimony in booklets said to be carried by ship to the Caribbean, obvious fodder for the revolutionaries of color in Jamaica. After the debates over abolition of 1788 in London, the governor of Jamaica paid "particular attention to prevent any disturbance in Consequence of the rumours which must necessarily be spread among the Negroes."[26] An aborted uprising in April 1788 confirmed the planters' fears of a universal conspiracy to free the slaves. After 1789, French ships allegedly brought revolutionary printed materials that were supposed to be distributed hand to hand through the island.

Rumors fanning Caribbean revolutions did not proceed along a direct path. Otherwise, Jamaica, with its busy ports, would have been more vulnerable to the spread of slave revolts. Since Jamaican planters focused their fears not on insurrections bred by the harsh regime of plantation slavery but on "the contagion of revolutionary principles," they could not relax if there was revolution anywhere in the Atlantic.[27] By word of mouth, slaves, "immediately informed of every kind of news that arrives," knew all about the August 1791 uprising in Saint-Domingue, the military commander in Jamaica reported.[28] It took less than two weeks for that news to arrive. Planters reported overheard talk among their slaves affirming that "Negroes in the French country were men" with rights just like the whites.[29] Although white correspondents consciously limited explicit references to riots or emancipation decrees in their letters, slaves were heard adding verses to folk songs to celebrate the uprising of the "Negroes in the French Country."

Instead of igniting a slave revolt, however, the French Revolution had the opposite effect in Jamaica. It actually bolstered the institution of slavery in the British colonies. The curtailing of French trade in the Caribbean allowed the British West Indies to recover from the damages imposed by the American Revolutionary War. As the Jamaican economy prospered, it soaked up thousands of new slaves; twenty-five thousand unwilling laborers sailed into Kingston in 1793. English-language newspapers, including the *Savanna la-Mar Gazette* and *St. George's Chronicle and New Grenada Gazette*, featured the French Revolution with large headlines, but other than the revolt of the Trelawny Maroons in 1795–96, the British colony remained quiet in the years after the French Revolution, in marked contrast to its French neighbors of Saint-Domingue, Martinique, and Guadeloupe.[30]

The "cauldron of insurrection": Saint-Domingue

In the winter of 1788–89, Louis XVI ordered that every press in Saint-Domingue be dismantled "in order to keep the flame of liberty from spreading to the Colonies" from revolutionary France.[31] Newspapers had sprung up to cover not only the National Assembly in Versailles but the two colonial assemblies in Saint-Domingue, and the king's ministers worried that the ever-smoldering discontent among slaves needed little encouragement to ignite. Throughout the French Caribbean, the French revolutionary decrees of liberty accorded well with the emancipation struggles indigenous to the plantation colonies dependent on slave labor.[32]

Unfortunately for the king's ministers, news traveled on and off the island without newspapers and pamphlets. Seamen, "well fed on the incendiary slogans of the clubs" in France, transmitted tales in harbor taverns and on docks, where they labored alongside slaves and free men and women of color in this simmering "cauldron of insurrection."[33] Stories spread quickly inland in Saint-Domingue, as in Jamaica.

Alexandre Stanislas Wimpffen, a French aristocrat who had fought under the comte de Rochambeau, commander of French forces in America, traveled to the Caribbean on the eve of the French Revolution. He complained upon landing in Saint-Domingue of the heat: "The smallest effort here is exhausting, the least exertion is real work."[34] Strategically located at the entrance to the Gulf of Mexico, the mountainous island supported 120 sugar plantations in 1710.[35] The conversion of the economy to sugar plantations depended on slaves, whose population rose from just over three thousand in 1690 to half a million in 1789. Wimpffen acknowledged that although he "shared the sentiments of writers who denounced the loathsome traffic conducted on the coast of Africa," after a month in Saint-Domingue, it was clear to him that the colonies "could not exist without slaves."[36]

Slave uprisings had traditionally been a problem in the colony, but there was relatively little violence in the 1770s and 1780s. On the eve of the French Revolution, however, Saint-Domingue was anything but a unified society. Lines of allegiance were not necessarily defined by wealth or race. The island's free people of color on Saint-Domingue, many of them slave owners, numbered almost thirty thousand in 1789, roughly equal to the number of whites. While they owned one-third of the plantations and controlled substantial wealth, they did not enjoy equality with the island's whites. European-educated Julien Raimond had represented their commercial interests in Paris since 1783. The son and grandson of indigo planters, he owned hundreds of slaves and an impressive plantation house but was considered a man of color because one of his four grandparents was an African.[37] Excluded from white society, the free people of color did not necessarily empathize with the plight of the slaves, either. Raimond identified himself as a Frenchman.

Word that the Estates General had been called to Versailles transmitted excitement to the French colonies. Propertied free persons of color petitioned to claim their rights, too. Only after the Third Estate named itself the National Assembly in June 1789 did the free people of color hear that their petitions for representation had been denied. By then, six white delegates had made their way to Versailles intent on securing colonial independence from France. They would follow the example of American independence from the European metropole. The philosopher Mirabeau challenged their legitimacy, reminding the National Assembly that slaves and free people of color had been denied the right to participate in elections. The white delegates were more concerned by the rumors, printed in the *Journal de Paris*, that the king had contested the validity of their credentials.[38]

Word of the 14 July storming of the Bastille did not reach Saint-Domingue until the fall of 1789. When it did, crowds swarmed onto the streets of Le Cap. The national guard, composed of Patriot planters, arrested François Barbé-Marbois, the French agent appointed by the king before the revolution. Previously stationed in Philadelphia, Barbé-Marbois was known to whites in the Caribbean for his alleged leniency toward people of color. In 1788 he had called a slave owner to account for the torching of two of his slaves, appealing to "considerations of humanity."[39] The planters dispatched him on a boat for France. The revolutionary whites in Saint-Domingue also made sure that they alone wore revolutionary cockades.

Fear of a slave insurrection gripped the colony. In response to reports that four French abolitionists had landed in Saint-Domingue and assembled three thousand slaves above Le Cap, French troops were sent to disperse the gathering. They found empty fields. White planters called for the lynching of a judge of mixed race, and several whites were imprisoned for harboring abolitionist sentiments. "Never has a more general fermentation reigned in the spirits here; it is to be feared that it will be communicated to our most distant possessions, especially in this colony under my command," a colonial agent warned in his letter to Paris.[40]

Abolitionists and their opponents, slaves and their masters, all anxiously awaited news of the contentious debates over slavery in the National Assembly in the autumn of 1789. Initially deferred to a committee, the first decree touching on rights for persons of color was passed by the Assembly on 8 March 1790 and granted significant autonomy from French authority to the colonial assemblies, institutions elected by whites intent on maintaining the status quo. In its instructions, the Assembly gave the right to vote and hold office to all property-owning "persons" at least twenty-five years of age who met tax and property requirements. The Assembly left the definition of "person" to the colonial assemblies, an obvious opening for trouble in Saint-Domingue.

While rumors seemed to fly, substantiated news and official proclamations lumbered slowly over more restricted routes. The delay in relaying decrees to the colonies and reports back to France presented few problems in normal times. During a revolution, much could change in the months it took agents and news to travel across the Atlantic. In the summer of

1789, while Parisians stormed the Bastille and inaugurated the National Assembly, oblivious French colonial agents carried on trade as before, under the terms of the Old Regime.[41] News going to Paris from Saint-Domingue arrived just as sporadically, with opposing officials often sending conflicting accounts. French agents in Port au Prince consequently advised the minister in Paris not to act precipitously based on partial information spread by travelers but rather to wait for the rumors to dissipate.[42] That would have required more patience than was to be found in revolutionary Paris.

When the March decrees granting some colonial autonomy finally arrived in Saint-Domingue in the spring of 1790, the colonial assembly meeting of the Western Province that had already drawn up its own set of decrees called a whites-only election. Free people of color audacious enough to demand inclusion were arrested. The assembly of the Northern Province sent its militia to disperse the rogue assembly. Their meeting surrounded, in August 1790, eighty-five delegates from the assembly seized a ship, the *Léopard*, anchored in the Port au Prince harbor, and sailed to France with their archives, some printers, and the national guard, to plead their case for complete colonial autonomy. They renamed their rogue vessel *The Savior of the French*. When they arrived after weeks at sea, the National Assembly refused them a hearing, but their presence in France called attention to the disorder in France's richest colony.[43]

Louis Elie Moreau de Saint-Méry, a prominent Parisian lawyer representing Martinique as a deputy to the Assembly, urgently proposed that no further legislation be considered by the French unless the colonial assemblies themselves formally requested it, leaving the colonies to deal with their slaves and free people of color as they saw fit. Robespierre responded indignantly. "Perish the colonies if they are to be maintained at the cost of your freedom and glory." He asked "the Assembly to declare that the free men of color shall enjoy all the rights of active citizens."[44] Camille Desmoulins put it more succinctly: "Perish the colonies before the principle."[45] A decree granting citizenship to some free persons of color passed in May 1791. Only free persons of color who had been born to two free parents were granted their rights. The compromise angered Robespierre and the Abbé Gregoire because it was so restrictive. The planters who gathered at the Massiac Club in Paris were not happy, either. They feared that any change threatened slavery on which the colonies' economy was based. The decree was never officially sent to the colonies.

Slaves living on the two hundred sugar plantations in the Southern Province of Saint-Domingue, near the port city of les Cayes, got word of this much debated French decree. What they heard was not that rights had been granted only to free persons of color born to free parents but that the king had granted all slaves their freedom for three days a week. This persistent rumor assumed mythic proportions in the Caribbean, where slaves for decades had looked to royal authority as the only possible restraint on overreaching masters.[46] When they did not get the three days allegedly promised in the king's emancipation decree, the slaves blamed their masters. This was not the first time the slaves had heard of royal benevolence blocked by intransigent planters. In the summer of 1791, plantation managers wrote the Club Massiac from Saint-Domingue that even the sight of the revolutionary cockade set off slave rebellions.[47] Two hundred slaves had reportedly taken up arms and threatened to kill their masters who denied them their three days of liberty.

The liberty espoused by the French further fueled the yearning of the slaves for freedom. Slaves had traditionally congregated Sunday nights on plantations, some with permission from their managers, others with forged passes. In the summer of 1791, a white planter overheard the assembled slaves discussing the premise of Louis XVI's proclamation that freed them from labor. Unable to believe that slaves could organize an insurrection on their own, he suspected that abolitionist pamphlets and engravings from France had been smuggled from the ports, infecting slaves on his and surrounding plantations. Other planters claimed that they had actually discovered texts in the hands of their slaves. Even if few slaves were literate, all it took was one person to read aloud to spread the idea that European revolutionaries had acted to alleviate the plight of slaves in the Caribbean.

"Listen to the voice of liberty which speaks in the hearts of all of us," Boukman Dutty, a coachman, is said to have proclaimed in August 1791 at Bois-Caïmen, halfway between Gallifet and Le Cap, to two hundred delegates, two from each of the plantations in the central region of the Northern Province.[48] In a raging storm, a tall black woman wielding a long knife danced and sang an African chant repeated by the assembled masses. She stabbed a pig and passed around its blood in a wooden bowl. A document, allegedly signed by the king, that granted slaves freedom three days a week and banned the use of whips was read aloud. White masters and colonial authorities were said to have refused to comply with the royal decree, but it was rumored that royalist troops were on their way from France to the island to enforce it. The only account of this gathering was written by Antoine Delmas, a surgeon on the Gallifet plantation who emigrated to the United States. He claimed to have seen the slaves slaughter a pig, drink its blood, and swear to secrecy. Before they dispersed, Boukman gave the signal for slaves throughout the region to rise up and set their plantations on fire, according to Delmas.[49]

In the middle of the night on 21 August, a group of slaves woke the manager of the La Gossette plantation, whispering that they had come to talk with him. As he rose from his bed, they assaulted him. Wounded in the arm, the manager escaped and got word to the larger Gallifet plantation. The next morning, a band of whites, backed up by a judge from Le Cap, interrogated the slaves. Under pressure, the slaves divulged plans for a rebellion against whites suspected of denying them the promised freedom.

Knowledge of the plot was of little help in preventing an insurrection.[50] The next day, slaves deserted their plantations in Acul. A band of slaves led by Boukman attacked an apprentice guarding a refinery, shot the overseer, and then massacred the refiner in his bed. Slaves from the neighboring Flaville-Turpin estate set the Clément plantation on fire, sparing only the doctor and his wife. Armed with torches, guns, and sabers, the rebellious slaves moved on to surrounding plantations. The next night, the revolt spread westward to the Limbé parish. The insurgents, reported to be two thousand strong, roamed from one plantation to the next, burning buildings, killing whites, and setting the cane fields aflame. They established military camps on each plantation they overran.

News of the revolt traveled rapidly, just ahead of the insurgents. A white merchant compared the fear that gripped whites on the surrounding plantations to "the effect of epidemical disease."[51] No precaution would assure immunity. The violence that the Abbé Raynal had predicted for the Americas if they did not abolish slavery had come to pass. Just as Raynal had foreseen, the black masses were wreaking vengeance on

FIGURE 5.1
"Révolte des Négres à St. Domingue." Engraving of the August 1791 slave revolt
by G. Jacowick, depicting the ferocity of the slaves setting fire to the plantations
of Saint-Domingue. Published by J. Chateigner between 1796 and 1798 in
Brussels at the time of a widespread revolt by Belgian peasants. With permission
from the Bibliothèque Nationale de France

the whites who had kidnapped them from their homes in Africa and
enslaved them. The overwhelming majority of slaves had arrived in
Saint-Domingue less than ten years before the insurrection, and many
had fought in African armies. They had been captured by British and
French slavers from the Angola coast and Lower Guinea, both regions
at war. Their military prowess stunned whites guarding plantations in
their path.[52]

Clutching a sword, a lone sentry rode bareback into Le Cap to spread
the alarm. "To arms, citizens, our brothers are being slaughtered and our

properties are being burned," he alerted anyone on the streets. "All the slaves of the plain are advancing with fire and iron in hand!"[53] Few of the residents of the capital believed the messenger at first, having heard false cries before. Soon enough, the stream of refugees from burning plantations corroborated his story. Terror escalated with each new rumor of plots to burn the capital itself to the ground. As the insurgents drew closer, residents could smell the fires. Smoke stoked the rumors.

To keep sailors in the capital for defense against the insurgents, municipal officials banned ships from leaving port. They stationed cannons around the perimeter of the city, but these proved ineffective against the insurgents, estimated to be ten thousand strong.[54] By nightfall, the streets of the capital were deserted, but the dread penetrated the homes of terrified whites. "One feared being slaughtered by one's servants," a resident of Le Cap testified.[55] All suspects of color were summarily executed, whether they were captured insurgents or domestic slaves overheard predicting "that soon the blacks would put the whites in their place."[56] By September, all of the plantations within fifty miles of Le Cap had been reduced to ashes, but the capital was spared. Sugar production ceased.

White planters dispatched desperate pleas to Jamaica, Cuba, Santo Domingo, and the United States for military aid.[57] A member of the colonial assembly even wrote William Pitt, inviting the British to invade and secure the property rights of white plantation owners. The besieged plantation dwellers subsequently welcomed a British warship into the harbor at Le Cap. The slave revolts obviously worried French colonial officials, but it was the link with the separatism encouraged by the British that bore ominous, if ironic, echoes of the Americans' appeal to the French against their British enemies. They hoped the British would help to preserve the institution of slavery on which their plantation economy was founded. In the end, little foreign aid arrived in Saint-Domingue, other than from a few American ships anchored in the harbor.

The effect of the August 1791 insurrection in the Caribbean, especially the French colonies, but throughout the Spanish and English islands and into Latin America as well, was incendiary.[58] What might otherwise have passed in the Spanish colonies as local uprisings that could easily be put down by masters reinforced by troops were exaggerated by officials alleging connections with the French Revolution.[59]

In the region, instead of dampening the sugar trade, the insurrection had just the opposite effect. The burning of sugar cane on Saint-Domingue, the island with a virtual monopoly on sugar production, opened up trade of the commodity. The slave trade expanded dramatically throughout the Spanish Caribbean even as violence threatened to spread from Saint-Domingue. In 1794, the discovery of four passportless French sailors in the port of Rio de Janeiro caused the viceroy Conde de Rezende to order deportations and searches to squelch "the pernicious consequences of the present revolution."[60] He informed Lisbon that his agents had found a cache of French revolutionary pamphlets and anonymous correspondence warning of slave insurrection. Spanish translations of the Declaration of the Rights of Man were burned in public, as were pamphlets proclaiming "Viva la Libertad."

Stories of the revolt traveled to France along the slow route of official reports, but were also relayed in private correspondence. Jacques-Pierre Brissot questioned the veracity of the "disastrous news." Despite rumors of revolt, "the implausibility of the details, the immense discrepancy in the number of revolting blacks, the silence of the French agents, the refutations given by people who have received subsequent letters all cause us to dismiss the exaggerated scenes that terror has spread," he testified.[61] Who could imagine in a colony divided into plantations that fifty thousand slaves could coalesce? Was it not suspicious, he suggested, that the news came from an English ship at the moment when Frenchmen were preparing to emigrate to the colony? Like the whites who spread and believed rumors in the colonies, Brissot was skeptical that the slaves could act for themselves. He counseled prudence and trusted that the free men of color would maintain the peace.

Planters' representatives in Paris loudly demanded that French troops be sent to quell the slave revolt that they blamed squarely on revolutionary abolitionists in France, refusing to believe that the initiative for the revolts came from the slaves themselves. Abolitionists not only had goaded the slaves to rebel with their arguments against slavery, the planters charged, but had actually led the insurgents into battle. The violence and terror seemed to escalate with every retelling. A description of the rebels' attack on the Gallifet plantation presented to the National Assembly in France in November 1791 and translated into English in a pamphlet in 1792 pictured an impaled white child carried aloft on a stake by the insurgents. The child symbolized the destruction of the insurrection, even though neither of the two eyewitness accounts of the attacks contained such an image. This same report described other horrors—a carpenter tied between two boards and sawed in half, a woman raped on the body of her dead husband, and a policeman nailed to the gate of his plantation, his limbs chopped off one by one with an axe. Another letter from Saint-Domingue described a rebel captured by soldiers with French pamphlets in his pocket alongside tinder, phosphate, and lime. He wore a sack of hair, herbs, and bits of bone from a voodoo ceremony around his chest. What better proof could there be that the incendiary slogans of the French Revolution had ignited the insurrection in Saint-Domingue, the correspondent asked. What better proof that insurgent slaves were heathens and barbarians?

Interrogated about their motivation for revolting, captured slaves declared that like the revolutionaries in France, "they wanted to enjoy the liberty they are entitled to by the Rights of Man."[62] They had heard of the storming of the Bastille and of decrees granting all men their rights. Some insurgents claimed the king of France as their revolutionary ally. Others spoke of royal promises to free the slaves, whether they harkened back to the images of glorious African kings or had heard rumors of the French king's support of a reform of the labor conditions on the Caribbean plantations. The few leaders of the revolt who left written accounts referred to reforms in the implementation of slavery on the plantations. That the insurgents killed masters and burned their plantations suggests that the majority of the insurgents, who left no records, expected to free themselves.[63]

Moreau de Saint Méry was shocked that the slaves had the audacity to insinuate that the liberty and equality proclaimed in France applied to them. It was all part of a "so-called plan of true happiness that would end up setting the whole world ablaze." The free men of color, including Vincent Ogé and Julien Raymond, had all been indoctrinated by Jacques-Pierre Brissot and the Society of the Friends of Blacks in collusion with the English abolitionist Thomas Clarkson, Moreau charged. Their incendiary speeches to the National Assembly, reprinted as pamphlets and carried aboard ships to Saint-Domingue, Martinique, and Guadeloupe, threatened "the public fortune, the tranquility, and the grandeur of France,"

Moreau complained.[64] The ominous "concordance" in the actions of the English and French abolitionists, he prophesied, would destabilize the once flourishing French colonies, all to England's economic gain.

Thomas Clarkson defended the Society from the charge of rabble rousing, laying the blame for the 1791 uprising in Saint-Domingue on the slave trade itself. The French Jacobin Jean-Paul Marat tried to help by championing the slaves' right "to overthrow the cruel and shameful yoke under which they suffer," even if that meant "massacring their oppressors to the last."[65] While Clarkson's intervention stoked fears of international conspiracy, Marat's words corroborated planters' claims that the radical French revolutionaries were fomenting a slave insurrection. Even the playwright Olympe de Gouges, who had celebrated slave resistance in her play *Zamore et Mirza ou l'heureuse naufrage* (Zamore and Mirza, or the fortunate shipwreck), was alarmed. "Men were not born in irons and now you prove them necessary," she wrote upon hearing of the violence that wracked Saint-Domingue.[66]

Through it all, the colonial administration continued to function. Civil commissioners had sailed from France before news of the August insurrection reached Paris. They carried a decree passed by the French Assembly on 24 September 1791 giving local assemblies control over internal colonial questions, including the rights of slaves and free men of color. In November 1791, they arrived to a maelstrom in Saint-Domingue. They were shocked by the killing and recriminations that confronted them. The commissioners set about interviewing slaves and masters and collecting evidence to take back to France. They made speeches, too, though the colony in upheaval proved an awkward stage for announcing the establishment of a constitutional monarchy in France and the granting of a general amnesty to all the French revolutionaries. Leaders of the slave insurrection wanted to know whether the amnesty applied to the colonies. The commissioners did not have the luxury of sending the question to France and awaiting a response. After the colonial assembly asserted preemptively that amnesty was intended only for true revolutionaries—meaning whites, not people of color—the commissioners tried, without success, to negotiate a compromise between the insurrectionaries and the colonial assembly.

Events were happening so quickly, the governor of Saint-Domingue acknowledged, that he would need daily ships sailing for France to keep the minister apprised. Most of the news, he apologized, was alarming.

Two hundred white soldiers had been killed, "assailed from all sides by blacks they could not see," leaving the insurgents as "the absolute masters of the plateau."[67] Governor Blanchelande blamed the climate for fueling the "effervescence" of the "rebels" who continued to destroy the "tranquility" of the once prosperous colony.[68]

In March 1792, planters in the Southern Province fled their homes as their plantations fell to armed bands of slaves. Ten thousand to fifteen thousand slaves had reportedly joined the insurrection in the Cul de Sac plain, inspired by the August 1791 uprising. Most frightening to the masters was the alliance of slaves and free men of color. Together they posed an unimaginable threat to the outnumbered whites on the plantations and in the towns. "For too long France has endured innumerable troubles that have devastated the most flourishing and the richest colony in the universe," a group of French merchants cried out from the Caribbean. "Saint-Domingue has become a vast furnace for burning fortunes."[69] The commissioners who returned to France transmitted eyewitness accounts of the revolts and chaos that had engulfed the whole colony and threatened to spread throughout the Caribbean.

"What will stop the revolt of the slaves in Saint-Domingue?" a deputy asked the National Assembly.[70] Brissot and his allies in the colonial ministry gave an answer their questioners did not like. The colony would be saved only by giving free people of color their rights. On 4 April 1792, the National Assembly decreed that "men of color and free blacks must enjoy, with white colonists, equality of political rights."[71] The debates over slavery would take another two years; events in the colonies would finally force the hand of the French revolutionaries.

Guadeloupe: "Noises of seditious proposals"

The fear of "explosions" had preoccupied colonial authorities in Guadeloupe after the population of slaves more than doubled between 1750 and the 1770s. By 1790, out of a total population of 107,226 residents, 90,130 were slaves.[72] Anxiety increased again when unrest in Saint-Domingue redirected the French slave trade from the prosperous island to its more economically marginal neighbor, further exacerbating white fears.

In the autumn of 1789, the first French ship to arrive in Pointe à Pitre at the end of the stormy season at sea brought news of the transformation of the Estates General into a National Assembly from Versailles. So many French colonial officials were stationed in Guadeloupe that official information was more quickly imported and exported onto the island than on the larger Saint-Domingue. Here too, rumors traveled faster. Youths took to the streets and men donned the revolutionary cockades carried by ship from France. They foisted the revolutionary symbol on all local officials. The governor gave free people of color permission to wear cockades, but slaves wearing revolutionary insignia were to be whipped.

News of the French Revolution spread from the harbor inland to the sugar-producing regions in North Grande-Terre and sparked insurrections in the capital of Guadeloupe, Basse-Terre. Whites led these first demonstrations. The emancipatory language of the French Revolution resonated among the poorer whites, predominantly clerks from the colonial administration and soldiers, but also young white overseers from the surrounding plantations, dockers, and seamen, who had been denied representation in the colonial assembly of Guadeloupe. Their grievances were heard by a colonial government that counted on them to help maintain order, and they were included in an enlarged white constituency in December 1789. The first act of their assembly was writing a new constitution, completed in August 1790. It protected the rights of plantation owners. Free men of color had also petitioned parish assemblies in Guadeloupe for the right to vote. In 1791, in another concession prompted by fear of slave revolts, the colonial assembly accepted their offer to help white property owners maintain order in exchange for the right to vote.

Anxious informants warned the governor, Charles François de Clugny, in April 1790, that slaves in Trois Rivières had been overheard saying that since the French had dethroned their king, they too should overthrow their masters. White masters in Guadeloupe complained, as they had in Jamaica, that domestic slaves heard the word "liberty" idly exchanged between careless white patriots. As in Saint-Domingue, the governor blamed the unrest on "the philanthropists," abolitionists who "beguile slaves with the false idea of liberty." To halt "the plot," the governor sent troops to Trois Rivières to round up the alleged insurgents. Hundreds of slaves were condemned to hard labor; six free men of color were singled out as organizers and executed. The governor assured the minister in France that he had no doubt that rigorous interrogation would "yield further details."[73]

On the island of Marie Galante, a dependency of Guadeloupe to the southeast of Basse-Terre and Grande-Terre, Bonhomme, a free man of color, warned an Englishman that blacks would "take power and replace the whites."[74] Bonhomme, a native of Saint-Domingue who had been educated in France, cited the Abbé Raynal's legendary prediction that if the French did not abolish slavery, a black Spartacus would seize power in the Caribbean. Based on the Englishman's report, Bonhomme's house was searched, charts detailing the number of slaves and free people of color on each of the Caribbean islands were seized, and Bonhomme was tried and executed.

In March 1791, Governor Clugny received news of an uprising of "negroes" in Sainte-Anne. Blaming this plot, too, on loose talk by whites, he decided it would be wise not to disseminate any French decrees that could be overheard or misconstrued by people of color.[75] The news blackout seemed to work. In June, he reported to France: "Calm is restored again."[76] The relative tranquility allowed the French commissioners stationed in Guadeloupe to reflect on the unrest in long reports sent to Paris. From the moment they arrived, the commissioners had heard from the governor of plots fomenting within the military and "noises of seditious proposals" on the plantations and in the cities.[77] The problem appeared to be Governor Clugny's runaway imagination. Given his close relations with white planters, he repeatedly jumped to the conclusion that the slaves were on the verge of revolting. Any time persons of color spoke, the commissioners reported, the governor expected plantations to be burned and their masters murdered in their sleep. In fact, trouble arrived from a different direction.

In the summer of 1792, encouraged by rumors of the victory of the counterrevolutionaries and the king in Paris, royalists in Guadeloupe armed free people of color and slaves in the colony. Slaves had often looked to the king as an ally, so it seemed natural that they would support the royalists. Naval officers loyal to the king allied with colonial separatists sitting in the assemblies of Guadeloupe and Martinique took over both colonies. In August 1792, they replaced the revolutionary tricolor with the white flag of royalty. From France, an expedition of two thousand troops sailed on 10 August 1792 to extinguish the royalists' rebellion in Guadeloupe. They embarked just hours before crowds dethroned the king in Paris, so would not learn that France was a republic until long after they landed in Guadeloupe.

Word of the September decrees abolishing the monarchy and establishing the new French republic did not reach Guadeloupe until December 1792. The news arrived aboard ships bearing additional troops under the command of Jean-Baptiste Lacrosse, who launched his assault on Guadeloupe with pamphlets. Revolutionary decrees proclaiming "The name of citizens unites us all" were posted for all to see. Free men of color responded by joining the militias and voting in the elections of 1793 for a new colonial assembly. Local officials replaced the white flag of royalty with the tricolor and reported the victory to the National Convention. Lacrosse added, without modesty, "I dared to do everything and I succeeded."[78]

Lacrosse planted trees of liberty, and the citizens of Guadeloupe swore an oath of loyalty to the French republic. He also reestablished the Jacobin societies disbanded by the royalists, adding men of color who promised to keep a vigilant eye on the colony. In March 1793, "the new citizens of Guadeloupe" praised Lacrosse, named provisional governor of Guadeloupe. "An odious faction, enemy of the French Revolution, misled us about the extent of our rights. You have raised your voice, you have shown us in full light the favor that our mother country has bestowed on us; you have made us conscious of our rights."[79] Lacrosse was convinced that the era of rumors was over, at least in Guadeloupe. Addressing himself to "Citizens of all colors," he vowed to print and circulate all the news that he could verify to be read by every revolutionary and to discredit the counterrevolutionaries.[80] Decrees dispelled rumors.

The widely disseminated words of the philosophes meant something quite different in Guadeloupe than in France, the procureur to the Conseil Souverain of Guadeloupe responded in alarm. He complained of the French revolutionaries who "talk of freeing the slaves and have applied the ideas of Montesquieu, the Abbé Raynal and others, but who did not understand the inherent danger lurking in discussions of rights and freedom on islands inhabited predominantly by slaves.[81] Plantation owners lived in fear, convinced that armed slaves would butcher all the whites on the island, as it was rumored they were doing throughout the Caribbean.

In April 1793, two hundred fifty slaves from Trois Rivières, allegedly armed by their masters to march against the republicans in Basse-Terre, instead turned against their masters. Word of the planned insurrection traveled through Basse-Terre, readily traversing the property lines drawn by whites that separated one plantation from the next.[82] A contingent of "assassins," still covered in blood and fully armed, approached the new governor, Victor Collot, a veteran of the American Revolution. The governor threatened to arrest the insurgents, but the Assembly of Guadeloupe refused, grateful for the protection of the slaves against royalist plots. Sailors arriving in Baltimore in May 1793 reported that "the Negroes had killed a number of whites of that island a few days before the brig [left] that place."[83] It was rumored that in a rural section of the parish, slaves led by "an unknown individual who was seen walking around saying that since a liberty tree had been planted, there should be no more slaves" had indiscriminately massacred all the whites.[84] In fact, the slaves had attacked only the known royalists, bypassing the plantations of revolutionary patriots. They trusted white patriots and free men of color, even if they were skeptical about the frequently repeated, yet unfulfilled, promises of freedom.

White republicans on Guadeloupe were not as ready to trust their slaves, especially with insurrection brewing in Saint-Domingue and with England at war against France. Few whites in the Caribbean were as convinced as their compatriots in France that armed service to the nation "would awaken honor in the souls of these new men, and would prepare them by degrees to be admitted into the class of free men."[85] In July and August 1793, municipalities in the sugar-producing area around Sainte-Anne and Point à Pitre reported another wave of rumors alleging that French decrees were being withheld from the slaves by their masters. "Walk with us; blacks are free," free men of color had been overheard whispering to slaves.[86] It seemed to whites only a matter of time before slaves in Guadeloupe rose up as they had done in Saint-Domingue. After receiving word of "an insurrection of blacks in the heights surrounding Sainte-Anne, who are heading downtown," the mayor sounded the alarm.[87] White planters fled their plantations for the safety of the reinforced forts, where they told tales of rebels who stopped them en route and demanded their guns. Commissioners reported that alarms spread easily, preying upon the fears of "weak" whites and "ignorant" blacks.[88]

News traveled too slowly across the Atlantic for revolutionary times, the new French administrator, Victor Hugues, complained when he arrived in Guadeloupe from France. "None of the laws emanating from the National Convention are known here, other than the abolition of slavery."[89] The English filled the vacuum, "corrupting the public spirit by spreading distrust and fanning the winds of false news to alarm the feeble, timid citizen and the peaceful farmer."[90] Hugues, who had sailed in the Americas, worked as a merchant in Port au Prince, and served as a judge of the French revolutionary tribunal in Rochefort, dispatched three commissioners to Paris to retrieve a printed set of laws from France. But white émigrés got to Paris first and relayed stories of Hugues's reign of terror. Hugues countered with his own reports to convey his "exact and sincere description of events."[91] The conflicting accounts collided in Paris.

Hugues had arrived in Guadeloupe with French republican troops and called on citizens of all colors to enlist in his army. After the British surrendered, Hugues promised to pay slaves salaries if they would return to their plantations, where they were to sing the Marseillaise and shout "Long live the Republic." In response to the widely circulated rumors about days free from work offered by royal decree, Hugues granted the ninth day of the revolutionary French week to slaves to attend to their own private affairs and the tenth day as a day of rest.

A gradual abolitionist, Hugues tried to strike a compromise between reinstating slavery and declaring freedom. He ended up alienating both plantation owners and French abolitionists, each suspecting him of siding with their opponents. Hugues did not believe that the Directory's constitution of 1795 could be applied to the colonies; social equality there would lead to laziness and violence. "Who will be able to contain 90,000 strong and robust individuals, embittered by long suffering, terrible tortures, and horrible punishments?" he asked, refusing to give the right to vote to freed slaves as in Saint-Domingue. "Who will be able to contain the natural ferocity of the Africans when it is compounded with their desire for vengeance?"[92] He also promised white émigrés who had fled to the United States that he would respect their property rights if they returned.

Revolutionary Reform: "The lost sentinels of the Republic"

In the summer of 1792, Governor Blanchelande urged the newly appointed French commissioners sailing to Saint-Domingue to suspend the publication of all newspapers in the colony.[93] Political gazettes such as *L'Ami de la Liberté: Ennemi de Licence* (The friend of liberty: Enemy of license) were corrupting public opinion and leading the people daily to new excesses. *L'Ami de la Liberté* "was not only read with avidity by free people of colour," according to the editor of a competing paper, "but Negro Slaves were Subscribers to it, and it is well known that Negroes on a Sunday have frequently clubbed together a quarter dollar to purchase it, in order to have it read to them."[94] That could only lead to more trouble. After a year of insurrection, the king lamented that Saint-Domingue, "once the object of envy among all the nations of Europe . . . now offers the eye only a vast field of disorders, of pillage, fire, carnage, crime, and revolutions."[95]

The new French commissioners, Léger Félicité Sonthonax and Étienne Polverel, ignored the governor's warnings. Outspoken abolitionists as well as experienced journalists, they arrived in Saint-Domingue with their own printing press and the April decree guaranteeing full rights to free men of color. The reputations of the new commissioners preceded them to the French colony.[96] Sonthonax had supported seating the deputation of the men of color in the place of planters in the National Assembly, and Polverel had proclaimed that nature had made all men equal. As Sonthonax and Polverel understood their mission, they had been charged by the assembly with restoring political tranquility and enforcing existing laws so that political equality would reign in "this unfortunate colony."[97]

The commissioners' problems began with their landing in the colony. Colonial officials, who would have been happy had their ship gone missing at sea, neglected to tell them which ports were in revolt and which well disposed to receive them.[98] Accompanied by a convoy of six thousand soldiers, the commissioners tried in vain to reassure the whites that they intended only to grant rights to the free people of color, not to destroy slavery. The violence of 1792 had linked these two revolutionary outcomes in the minds of whites as well as persons of color.

Planters not only feared talk that flowed so freely but were concerned about "that guilty silence" that might shroud new slave plots.[99] They worried about rumors and the lack of rumors, too. Silence could signal tranquility, but it could also mean that slaves had effectively muffled their plots. The whites were on edge, threatened by their own slaves and by the free people of color who might align with them. "The most ghastly plot" often lurked, yet unknown, in the shadows.[100]

From their vantage point on the ground in Saint-Domingue, the commissioners cautioned the French National Convention that something needed to be done for the slaves or the French would lose Saint-Domingue. Either their pleas for further reform sank somewhere in the mid-Atlantic or the Convention simply ignored them, preoccupied by more pressing questions in the metropole. Feeling completely cut off from France, Sonthonax cast the French agents in the colonies in 1793 as "the lost sentinels of the Republic."[101] On their own authority, Sonthonax and Polverel issued a proclamation in May protecting slaves from Sunday work, a lingering demand, and inviting them to submit complaints about harsh treatment at the hands of their masters to local officials. To ensure that it would be observed throughout the French colony, the proclamation was translated into Creole, read to the slaves, and posted in a central spot on each plantation.

The governor who replaced Blanchelande, François Thomas Galbaud du Fort, had no sooner landed in May than he was besieged by planters complaining of the emancipators, Sonthonax and Polverel. Their stories confirmed the preconceptions of the absentee landowner, who was no friend of the abolitionists. The governor called the commissioners to meet him in Le Cap. That encounter spawned radically divergent accounts that echoed through the colony and eventually made their way to France. In one frequently recounted story of the meeting, Galbaud reprimanded the commissioners for their leniency, telling them their souls were as black as the slaves they intended to free. It was not only what happened in the closed meeting between the governor and the commissioners that was in dispute, but whether they actually met at all. In a very different version, the commissioners refused to come to Le Cap. Galbaud's wife allegedly advised the governor to return to Paris to unmask the commissioners before the National Convention and raise troops to avenge the insults suffered by the whites at the hands of men of color and their insolent commissioners.

Whatever happened, the commissioners imprisoned the governor, who was to be deported to France on a ship anchored in the harbor. Tensions simmered between the white sailors on the hundred ships anchored in the harbor and the free people of color in town. The crews complained of armed attacks on shore by men of color whose "words smell of revolt."[102] Galbaud did not wait for word from Paris. Backed by prisoners and sailors, he attacked Le Cap on 20 June. They rowed from ship to ship in the harbor, rallying support. Shops in town closed, their owners having heard "that the sailors were going to land, and that it was going to be quite a show, that they wanted to kill all the mulattoes, and send the commissioners to the National Convention."[103] The white sailors' attack on Government House was unsuccessful. They were beaten off by forces led by Jean-Baptiste Belley, a free black officer. In their attempt to invade the upper town, they were ambushed at every building, "every window a hostile gunport," one white volunteer reported.[104] Galbaud's forces did capture the arsenal. The outcome of the battle was uncertain at the end of the first day.

Rumors of emancipation ran rampant in the chaos. On 21 June 1793, Polverel and Sonthonax, backed by black troops, proclaimed the French republican commitment to shattering "all chains."[105] In a carefully worded proclamation, the commissioners offered freedom and citizenship to all "black warriors" who would "fight for the Republic" against its enemies. One of Galbaud's supporters cited the proclamation as "the decisive blow" that turned the battle. For the first time, European officials offered freedom to all male insurgents willing to join them.[106]

On the morning of 21 June, prisoners and sailors, thousands strong, attacked the city again. Galbaud's forces had sounded the general alarm, but only fifty whites showed up to join them. In the chaos, prisons were flung open and emancipated insurgents from 1791 took up arms on the side of the commissioners. The commissioners escaped from the besieged Government House to Haut du Cap. Even though that left the city open to victory for Galbaud, rumors that "thousands of blacks were coming from Haut-du-Cap and that they were going to exterminate all of us" swept through Galbaud's forces who ran for the ships.[107] Galbaud reportedly had been seen jumping into the harbor shouting frantically for assistance.

Whether set by sailors or slaves, fires, fueled by the sugar and coffee stored in the harbor, consumed Le Cap, the richest city in the colony. Against orders from Sonthonax and Polverel, but claiming that they were cut off from French authority, ships made ready to sail, carrying off the frightened whites. The streets of Le Cap, barely "recognizable between the ruins that were still smoldering, were filled with bodies of all colors," a white resident still in the city reported.[108] To restore order, Sonthonax and Polverel promised to liberate the families of soldiers in July. Rumors of general emancipation circulated widely.

On 24 August 1793, fifteen thousand people assembled at an open-air meeting in Le Cap and voted to emancipate slaves in the Northern Province of Saint-Domingue. A witness reported that the assembly presented its proclamation to Sonthonax, who received it "as the expression of justice and humanity."[109] On 29 August, echoing the popular vote, Sonthonax proclaimed: "Men are born and live free and equal in rights." In the words of a new citizen, "General Liberty has just been proclaimed in the island." Together all races on Saint-Domingue would "live free or die."[110] Polverel, stationed in the Western Province, had also freed soldiers. He was surprised to receive unofficial word of the general emancipation by Sonthonax in the North. Petitions demanding freedom, spurred by news of emancipation in the North, spread through the West and the South and ignited new slave insurrections, leaving Polverel with little choice. He followed Sonthonax and freed slaves in the regions under his control. Both of the commissioners cautioned freed slaves, however, that they would have to prove themselves worthy of their freedom and citizenship by laboring for a share of the produce on their plantations.

Shortly thereafter, Sonthonax organized the election of a tricolor delegation including three white deputies, three deputies of mixed European and African descent, and three deputies born in Africa and raised in slavery. The delegation set off for Paris with the news of the slaves' emancipation. They sailed by way of Philadelphia, a city full of former governor Galbaud's supporters, who swarmed the docks when they landed. The crowd threatened Louis Dufay, a white delegate, who was spirited to safety through side streets by a woman sympathetic to their cause. Before the former slave Jean-Baptiste Belley could disembark, members of the crowd boarded the ship and wrested his sword, watch, papers, and money from him. They tore the cockade from his hat, protesting that revolutionary insignia were to be worn only by whites. The rest of the delegation made it to New York, where they boarded two separate ships bound for France, hoping that at least one would make it to Paris with the news of the emancipation of slaves in Saint-Domingue. Three deputies did. While anchored in Bordeaux, they were imprisoned briefly, but they finally reached Paris in February 1794. News took time to travel its often circuitous route, depending on travelers who could be held up.

At the Convention, a deputy proclaimed to loud applause: "Equality is consecrated: a black, a yellow [mulatto], and a white have taken their seat among us, in the name of the free citizens of Saint-Domingue."[111] The next day, in a speech to the Convention, Louis Dufay told the story of the battle of Saint-Domingue. That news was a long time in coming. On 4 February 1794, the Convention declared "slavery is abolished throughout the territory of the Republic; in consequence, all men, without distinction of color, will enjoy the rights of French citizens."[112] One of the most outspoken of the abolitionists, the Abbé Grégoire, recalled the "sudden emancipation pronounced by the decree of 16 pluviôse An II" as "the political equivalent of a volcano."[113] After years of discussion of gradual emancipation and its deleterious economic consequences, it had taken revolutions in the Caribbean to abolish slavery. Decreed by the French Convention, for the first time on either side of the Atlantic, citizenship knew no color line.

"The cruel period of waiting and anxiety"

The day that the printed version of the National Convention's abolition decree finally arrived in Saint-Domingue, Toussaint Louverture, a free man of color who commanded four thousand troops, abandoned the Spanish to fight for the French. Louverture had issued his own proclamation of liberty and equality on the same day that Sonthonax abolished slavery in the Northern Province of Saint-Domingue, both in advance of the French Convention. "We are Republicans and therefore free by natural laws," Louverture assured skeptical soldiers who had heard rumors that white commanders would force them back into slavery at the end of the fighting.[114] It was said, and often repeated, that Louverture had read the passage written by the philosopher Denis Diderot in the Abbé Raynal's *History of Two Worlds* that predicted a black Spartacus would rise up to avenge the enslavement of Africans in the Caribbean. Observers claimed they had seen black sailors carrying the works of Raynal, presumably bought from abolitionists sailing ships from Bordeaux.[115]

The ship that transported the first copy of the French emancipation decree to Saint-Domingue also conveyed an order recalling the commissioners Sonthonax and Polverel to France to face charges levied by white planters. Such were the entangled politics of the colonies and the metropole, each reacting to the other with a time delay. While the commissioners had been working in Saint-Domingue to establish order by imposing the policies decided in Paris, the white Colonial Assembly had sent its own deputation to Paris to argue that the colony would not thrive without the institution of slavery. Each set of commissioners almost succeeded in its cause, and both were arrested by the Committee of Public Safety.

Rumors were fed by what a French commissioner in Guadeloupe identified as "the cruel period of waiting and anxiety" that separated events from correspondents eager for news in this unstable revolutionary world.[116] Necessarily, it was itinerants, not always the most trusted and reliable of agents, who passed along the fragments of information. In the summer of 1793, for example, the colonial assembly in Saint Lucia waited with "unperturbable tranquility" for the arrival of enemies they heard from sailors were gathering in Martinique to lay siege to their island.[117] They waited for nearly a year. Throughout the Caribbean, threats of invasion from without and insurrection from within were exacerbated by the lack of reliable news and cross-cutting allegiances of empire, race, and class.

Rumors worked both ways. They justified the often-exaggerated precautions taken by whites in the government and on the plantations to protect the colonial order. Read against the grain, white accounts also suggest that rumors kept alive the promise of revolution for slaves throughout the Caribbean.[118] The rumors, which replaced reliable information, contributed to the revolutionary transformation of the Caribbean on currents that flowed in and out along the channels between the islands, but also back and forth between the metropolitan governments in Europe and their slave-dependent plantations in the New World.

To colonial officials and planters, anything out of the ordinary appeared an ominous signal of insurrection. Revolutionary city councilors in Havana interpreted the shortage of pigs as a sign that Cuban slaves had heard of the insurrection in Saint-Domingue and stopped work. The Cuban authorities assumed that a lively communications network linked the slaves.[119] The cause of the pork shortage was much more mundane, but everyday events assumed legendary proportions in a time of heightened anxieties. For example, a Capuchin friar named Jean Baptiste, "the curé des nègres," was said to have prophesied the coming of the king of Angola at the head of an African army ready to free the slaves of Martinique and take them home to Africa. Throughout the revolutionary period, his preaching was blamed for violence, whether a convenient scapegoat for anxious whites or the source of an oral lore that spread and incited slave insurrection.[120]

War further intensified the tensions and amplified the rumors. The guillotining of Louis XVI and consequent European war severed the already unreliable official communications networks linking the colonies to the metropole. The imperial wars of the 1790s continually reshuffled Caribbean identity. Territories were handed from one power to another. The English occupied Tobago; they captured Martinique in March 1794, Saint Lucia in April, and Guadeloupe in June, before news of the French abolition of slavery reached the Caribbean. The next year, French troops regained control of Guadeloupe and Saint Lucia with the aid of free colored and slave support. Thereafter, little news made it across the Atlantic, a vast battlefield in the war between France and its neighbors Britain and Spain. In June 1795, Spain signed the Treaty of Basel, ceding Spanish Santo Domingo to the French. News of the transfer did not reach the colonies until the end of the year, and Louverture did not occupy the territory until 1800. Although the Spanish agreed to disband their black fighting forces, the "valiant warriors" decided on their own to sail in four ships for Havanna. Cuba, not anxious to have former slaves tainted by French ideals of liberty and equality at large, sent them on to the Isle of Pines off shore to be "civilized."[121]

Warships and privateers, especially the French corsairs, subsequently almost completely disrupted the commercial trade that carried news with it. The tensions were many and cross-cutting: royalists vs. republicans, whites vs. people of color, masters vs. slaves, and colonies vs. the metropole. In the minds of revolutionaries in power, counterrevolutionaries infested the Caribbean. Royalists from Guadeloupe and Martinique were said to have signed an agreement promising to turn the two colonies over to the British if the Bourbons could be restored to the French throne. From Guadeloupe, the commissioners lamented, "Government doesn't even exist here and the Military interferes in everything."[122] Beset, these colonial correspondents attacked their enemies as the most "perverse leaders" who spread "disastrous anarchy."[123]

Sonthonax and Louverture competed to represent themselves as the force responsible for abolishing slavery, each claiming to have been "the first to dare proclaim the Rights of Man in the new world."[124] The tales they told collided with stories disseminated by other itinerants, the white planters who had taken refuge in Kingston, Philadelphia, and Paris. Governor Collot, who was deported from Guadeloupe to Philadelphia by the British in 1794, had no sooner arrived in America than he delivered a report indicting his successor, Commissioner Hugues. He accused Hugues of spilling the blood Collot had spared as a governor. Collot boasted that he alone had maintained order in the Caribbean "without money, troops, a navy, laws, a guide in the midst of hatred and passions at an immense distance from the foyer of the enlightenment, in a country without any public spirit other than that of interests, and where there were as many different opinions as nuances of skin color."[125] Injustice had many voices, he declared to the Americans, but the truth just one.

Leonora Sansay, the wife of a Saint-Domingue planter who also sought refuge in the United States, chose a different vehicle for conveying this truth, the "desolation" and "distress of the unfortunate people" inflicted on whites in the Caribbean. In her semiautobiographical epistolary novel *The Secret History; or, The Horrors of St. Domingo*, she described events that she knew "would fill with horror the stoutest heart, and make the most obdurate melt with pity."[126] Lending credence to the stories recounted by other white refugees from Saint-Domingue, she stoked her readers' imaginations with accounts of sexual intrigue and racial violence. "Unfortunate were those who witnessed the horrible catastrophe which accompanied the first wild transports of freedom!" she concluded.[127]

SIX

The Revolutionary Household in Fiction: "To govern a family with judgment"

In the midst of a revolutionary world that redefined and redistributed rights, female novelists recast families. In the United Provinces of the Netherlands and Britain, both urban and merchant-centered, Mary Wollstonecraft, Mary Hays, Betje Wolff, Aagje Deken, and Isabelle de Charrière found French inspiration for new domestic arrangements freely contracted by individuals. Conscious of the social possibilities promised by political revolution, these Dutch and English novelists probed the sensibilities of young women, as they created new families in a turbulent world.

The domestic order described in Betje Wolff and Aagje Deken's novel *Sara Burgerhart* drew readers to the authors' tidy thatched cottage north of Amsterdam seeking counseling for their troubled households caught up in the swirl of revolutionary upheaval. So many young women made the pilgrimage to the small village of Beverijk that friends referred to it as the "Nun's cloister at Lommerlust." There, Wolff passed summer mornings in the garden before she retreated to her book-lined hermitage to write, a round wooden chair set before a writing desk and double doors open to the roses, jasmine, and chickens. Few of the visitors noticed that Wolff's companion was not a prosperous merchant like Hendrik Edeling, the ideal husband portrayed in the novel, but Deken, the daughter of a cattle farmer. Although the fictional Sara Burgerhart found her calling in raising her five children, no young voices were to be heard in the authors' refuge at Lommerlust.

Rousseau's portrait hung over Wolff's desk in Beverijk. For Dutch as well as British writers, the Genevan philosopher's widely read and often-discussed book *Julie, ou la nouvelle Héloïse* and *Émile* defined the context for their explorations of the possibilities opened for women by revolution. According to Rousseau, women had emerged from the state of nature as sensitive, passive, irrational, and nurturing beings, the complement to independent, rational men. "A perfect man and a perfect woman ought not to resemble each other in mind any more than in looks," the philosopher explained.[1] Destined by their nature to bear children, in civilized society Rousseau's women loved finery, were alluring to their husbands, had wit but lacked genius.

The characters of Julie in the novel that took her name and Sophie in Rousseau's educational treatise *Émile* both meet tragic ends, unable to master the natural sensibility of their tender hearts or to fit within their families. The young Julie is sensitive and in love with her tutor, but her father intends her to marry his aristocratic friend. She pledges to obey her father and husband, assuring them both a happy family. The character of Sophie was explicitly created by Rousseau to marry the independent and reasonable hero of *Émile* and bear his children. "Thus the whole education of women ought to relate to men," Rousseau advised his contemporaries. "To please men, to be useful to them, to make herself loved and honored by them, to raise them when young, to care for them when grown, to counsel them, to console them, to make their lives agreeable and sweet—these are the duties of women at all times and they ought to be taught from childhood."[2] Sophie's upbringing guides her to be modest and reserved, and to cherish her reputation for virtue. As the plot of *Émile* inexorably unwinds, Émile and Sophie marry and are happy until their first child, a daughter, dies. To distract Sophie, Émile takes her to Paris. Marital infidelity—first his, then hers—follows their visit to the vice-ridden city. Dying is the only way out for Sophie, as it was for Julie, who drowns saving her child.

Wolff, Wollstonecraft, Hays, and de Charrière's female protagonists all struggled as mightily, as did Rousseau's sentimental heroines, to secure their place in an era of individual freedom and male self-determination. Educated by experience, the characters pondered and negotiated their own fates. Not all of them expired, and when they did die, unlike Sophie and Julie, it was not for transgressing a social code. Instead, as the women writers adapted Rousseau's plots to their ends, their female protagonists left the world as victims of legal or psychological oppression, exemplifying for Wollstonecraft the particular burdens women bore as a result of social and legal inequity.[3]

In the preface to her first novel, Wollstonecraft confessed, "I could have made the incidents more dramatic, would I have sacrificed my main object, the desire of exhibiting the misery and oppression, peculiar to women, that arise out of the partial laws and customs of society."[4] Little high drama—no pirates, kidnapping, wars, or even revolutions—enlivened the novels of Hays, de Charrière, or Wolff and Deken. The Countess Flahaut, a French author and the mistress of both the American ambassador in Paris, Gouverneur Morris, and the French diplomat Charles Talleyrand, explained in the preface to her novel, *Adéle de Senange*, published in London in 1794: "The point of this work is not to paint characters who leave the common path; . . . I want instead to show what is not seen of life, & to describe the ordinary movements of the heart that make up the story of each day."[5] Revolutionary drama resided in the details of everyday life. Questioning the constraints on a wife's relation with her husband was part of the project of challenging the Old Regime. Hays, Wolff, Deken, and de Charrière, like Wollstonecraft, saw writing novels about women and their families as a revolutionary act in itself, rendering the domestic political.

Literary critics and historians who have connected the fictional sensibility of novels to what historian Lynn Hunt labeled the "family romance" of eighteenth-century revolutions have focused on the American and French revolutions.[6] Historian Sarah Knott depicts revolutionary Americans, preoccupied "with selves and social relations," and their intimate novels that revealed the sentiments of love and friendship, of passion and virtue.[7] "French revolutionaries attempted to use the state to remake society," Hunt explains, and in doing so ripped "the veil of deference off society."[8] In contrast, Knott continues, "American revolutionaries sought, with greater suspicion of the state, to use society to remake itself."[9] The morality that infused Dutch and English accounts of daily domestic life on the margins of revolution, as with the French writers studied by Carla Hesse, created the "new terms of existence" for women to reside in Hunt's republic of brothers.[10]

The legislation of the French revolutionaries that attempted to remake the family commanded the attention of the novelists. Wollstonecraft, the most politically outspoken, wrote for them all when she described the French Revolution as "the most extraordinary event that has ever been recorded."[11] She crossed the Channel from her home in England in December 1792 to witness the transformation for herself. The Dutch-born Isabelle de Charrière visited Paris on the eve of the French Revolution, and Wolff and Deken sought exile in provincial France after the Prussians crushed the Dutch Patriot Revolution in 1787, not returning to their home until the French had supported a second successful Dutch revolution in 1795. Only Hays remained in England, a sometime-recluse. Even though she saw revolutions as "ruinous and dreadful to those actually engaged in them," she ventured that "posterity will, I have no doubt, reap the benefit of the present struggles in France."[12]

France offered a new vista of social transformation. Well-read novelists from the two prosperous, commercial societies of England and the United Provinces imagined companionate marriages based on sentimental unions. One of the many visitors drawn to Wolff and Deken's cottage at Lommerlust, the Dutch playwright Lieve van Ollefen, asked rhetorically in verse:

> Who has ever seen such a selection of books
> On a rural cottage wall? Who would
> think to seek so many wise men
> in a woman's hermitage?

To his response, "No one but a Dutchman," van Ollefen could have added the equally urbanized English.[13]

Betje Wolff published 5,094 pages on her own, contributing another 4,758 with Aagje Deken.[14] She read more, including the novels of Samuel Richardson and Rousseau. Commercial printers, recently deregulated in some countries and flourishing almost everywhere at the end of the eighteenth century, encouraged novelists, increasingly including women, to write, and the ever more literate public to read. The number of European women writing novels doubled every decade from 1750 to 1800, despite the exclusion of women from institutions of higher education everywhere.[15]

In novels—perhaps more than in pamphlets, journals, narratives, newspapers, or rumors—geographic place, language, and national manners mattered. Characters inhabited specific places governed by particular customs. And yet the discourse of fiction in a revolutionary era transcended

FIGURE 6.1
Betje Wolff's garden and library at Lommerlust in Beverwijk, where she wrote
Sara Burgerhart. Lieve van Ollefen noted the shelves filled with books on the
walls. Courtesy of the Rijksmuseum, Amsterdam

national boundaries. In novels, sometimes translated and more often reviewed and discussed, locally grounded images of reworked families traveled more widely than did some of their authors, striking home throughout
the Atlantic world. Reflections of revolutionary aspirations, they were
agents of change. That transformation in the family pivoted around wom-
en, first addressed in treatises on homely virtues.

Betje Wolff and Aagje Deken's Motherless Mothers with "Duties to satisfy"

"To be useful is our genius," Betje Wolff counseled the readers of
her advice manual, *Proeve over de Opvoeding* (Examples of upbringing)
published in 1779.[16] Her guidance for young mothers among the prosperous Dutch merchant class was practical, her tone cheerful. She addressed

them informally "as we would converse among friends in a room surrounded by our children at play." She promised neither to echo the male
philosophers nor to bore her busy readers with tedious abstract treatises.
These mothers had too many young children underfoot to spend time
deciphering John Locke's "costly book," *Some Thoughts Concerning
Education*. Instead, although she admired the seventeenth-century English
philosopher's views, Wolff wrote down-to-earth cautionary tales, advising
Dutch mothers when to chastise, how to praise, and what to read aloud
to their families. In keeping with Locke's environmentalism, she counseled the Dutch mothers to model good behavior for their children, allowing the young to learn directly through experience. Her widely read
advice manual assumed intimate and loving families. Was "anything else
necessary to make a Woman happy?" she asked rhetorically.[17]

Economische Liedjes (Economic songs), published by Wolff in 1781,
provided more exemplary scenes of a family life Wolff herself would never
know. Betje Wolff had been married, but her own household offered no
model to be followed. Born in the Dutch port of Vlissingen in 1738, she
was the youngest of six children of a wealthy spice merchant; her mother
died when she was little. In poor health herself, Wolff took up writing to
pass time. She almost foreclosed her own marriage prospects as a teenager
by running away with a soldier, who abandoned her to pursue a military
career in the East Indies. Her family and friends took her back, but with
shaking fingers and bowed heads. In 1757, she struck up a correspondence
with Adrianus Wolff, a Dutch Reformed preacher and widower who
shared her philosophical interests. The night in 1759 when they finally
met in person, they decided to marry. She was twenty-one, he fifty-two.
Their relations were "not familiar," she wrote; the husband and wife lived
together as "good friends."[18] This was no ideal companionate marriage.

She had never imagined she would end up in a village of twenty-eight
hundred people tucked away on an isolated polder, five hours from
Amsterdam at the best of times, and unreachable when it rained. "My
life has ended up to be very austere, as you would say, stuck with an old
peasant pastor!"[19] Wolff yearned to travel, but her husband was older and
rooted to his pastoral duties, so she filled her attic with books and her
mind with stories. She read Rousseau's *Julie, ou la nouvelle Héloïse* (*Julie, or
The new Heloise*), *Émile, ou de l'éducation* (Emile, or Education), and the

Profession de foi du vicaire savoyard (Profession of faith of a Savoyard vicar), as well as the epistolary novels of the English writer Samuel Richardson. She had less use for the rationalism of the French philosopher Voltaire. Wolff complained of "the deep loneliness that is my lot."[20] The year after Wolff published a parody of the Dutch Reformed Church in which her husband preached, the couple went their separate ways. Adrianus Wolff died in 1777 and Betje Wolff invited an aspiring poet, Aagje Deken, to come live with her, banishing the loneliness that had afflicted her throughout her childhood and married life.

Together they wrote the epistolary novel *Sara Burgerhart*. It was an instant success in the United Provinces in 1782, reprinted eleven days after its first publication; a 1787 French translation marked the only publication outside of the Netherlands. Wolff and Deken offered Sara to their Dutch readers as a model to be emulated of a marriage of friends. In their preface, they cautioned against translation, thinking the novel would not travel well.[21]

The story of an orphan who survived youthful indiscretions to marry an upstanding merchant, the protagonist, Sara learns from her experiences. Left after her parents' death to the care of her mother's pious and shrewish sister, twelve-year-old Sara reminisces about the "golden days" of her youth, when she had played in the garden while her father, a tea merchant, smoked his pipe and her mother read, all deeply in love with one another.[22] She finally escapes her aunt's control and takes up residence with a widow Spilgoed, who acts as a surrogate mother.[23] The words "worthy," "respectable," and "duty" reverberate not only through the widow's lessons, but through all of the letters addressed to Sara by the sensible burghers of her very practical Dutch world.

Throughout much of the novel, without the guidance of a mother, Sara fends off the young men who swarm around her "like mosquitoes to the light." She knows nothing of love, she confesses, but has no desire to learn, either. "I am completely happy as I am," Sara says as she brushes off one of the suitors.[24] Independent, Sara is content in the society of her female friends who read in one another's company, converse, take long walks, and correspond in a world separate from men. A prosperous young merchant, Hendrik Edeling, informs the widow of his love for Sara but is given little reason for hope. The widow informs this eligible suitor that

Sara thinks of men and marriage less than if she lived in a convent. Undeterred, the earnest Edeling asks directly in a letter addressed to Sara whether he "dare to hope for the favor of one who is dearer to me than my own life." In response, she will only call him her friend, confiding in her best friend, Anna, "Freedom is happiness." A friend of her father's counsels Sara that it is time to look for a man who is honest and respectable, sensible, able, and good-natured to be her husband. "Understand, my child, that from your choice, your happiness in life depends."[25] Adult women are dependent on men.

Sara's story is told solely through correspondence, without the intervention of a narrator. Both authors had written so many letters during their isolated lives that they easily adapted the epistolary style of Richardson and Rousseau for their own. Letters allowed them to reveal the personal development of the young women who were their characters. As cool and reasoned as are Sara's responses to the men seeking her hand, her letters to her female friends, Anna Willis and Aletta Brunecr, brim with impatient passion. Female friendship binds them in a way that love letters with men can only attempt to imitate.

Over time, heeding the counsel of her father's friend, Sara comes to appreciate Hendrik Edeling. Before she can avow her love, however, she is abducted by a rich rake with whom she foolishly walked unaccompanied. The predatory aristocrat would have raped her but for the timely intervention of his gardener's daughter. In a feverish state of semiconsciousness following her misadventure, she whispers to the hovering Hendrik that she is no longer worthy of marriage. She blames herself for being so careless and for assuming that men—especially, it seems, dashing aristocrats—could be friends. Hendrik assures her that she can rely on his "strength that he will use only to protect her from the dangers of the world."[26] He will be no tyrant, but a companion. Over time, they grow to love each other in the image of her parents, smoking a pipe and reading in the garden. "I have chosen my best friend to be my husband," Sara confides in the widow.[27]

Wolff and Deken were not looking to revolution to change women's lives. For the time being, at least, they found the conditions for individual fulfillment within Rousseau's family as they reinterpreted and reshaped it. Even if Rousseau defined the subordination of women to be "natural" in the family, Wolff and Deken were convinced that he had opened new possibilities for the wives of merchants, and new happiness for mothers. In marked contrast to Rousseau's works, though, Sara's good sense triumphs over the obstacles thrown up by society. By the end of the novel, Sara has learned "what it is to be a mother." At home with her five children, the young Dutch wife of a prosperous merchant no longer has time to walk out with friends, all of whom are also married with children, because she has "duties to satisfy that earnest reflection tells me are true." Sara muses as she remembers her life's experiences: "And how natural it is that a woman finds her diversions in her household and that she values her husband's company above all others."[28] Sara has learned, as Mary Wollstonecraft would counsel, "to govern a family with judgement."[29]

Two English Heroines, Mary and Emma, Adrift In "a thorny and a pathless wilderness"

Mary Wollstonecraft published *Thoughts on the Education of Daughters* in England in 1787, the year of the Dutch Patriot Revolution. She earned ten pounds and ten shillings for the small book addressed to English parents. Practical, like Wolff's treatise on child rearing published a decade earlier, Wollstonecraft's manual also followed John Locke, advising parents to model behavior for their children to emulate.[30] Like Wolff, Wollstonecraft did not write from her own family experience.

Mary Wollstonecraft was born in 1759 in Spitalfields in East London, the second of seven children. Her father, an alcoholic, abused her mother and squandered the family's savings to establish himself as a gentleman farmer. Before she was old enough physically to leave home, Wollstonecraft confided to her journal: "I commune with my own spirit—and am detached from the world."[31] Self-educated, Wollstonecraft learned by experience. She made her own way in a world that spurned independent women, as it would the heroines of her novels.

"Mary, the heroine" of her first novel, entitled simply *Mary*, was raised by a caring mother to be compassionate and to think for herself. Over her mother's deathbed, her insensitive father gives Mary in marriage to the boorish son of a friend. "It was the will of Providence that Mary should experience almost every species of sorrow," the narrator informs the reader.[32]

Immediately after the wedding, her husband leaves to tour the Continent, so Mary sets off on her own for Portugal to care for an ill friend. There she meets Henry, and it is clear that although her husband has freedom to roam the world as an individual, Mary does not.

In the preface to her novel, Wollstonecraft condemned other authors whose little-thinking characters contentedly inhabited "an insipid paradise," instead of striking out to create their own worlds. Samuel Richardson's popular heroine Clarissa and Rousseau's beloved Julie considered the opinions of others, usually fathers or husbands, before coming to any decision. In contrast, Wollstonecraft's metaphysical heroine Mary examines ideas for herself on their own merit. Her "tumultuous passions" battle with "cold reason" as Mary is torn between her increasing friendship with Henry and her loveless marriage. Mary almost chooses Henry, clearly forgetting, as the narrator reminds the reader, "that happiness was not to be found on earth," at least not for women. If she "built a terrestrial paradise," it certainly would "be destroyed by the first serious thought."[33] Mary can envision the ideal family, but realizes it is not possible in this life.

Mary ultimately decides to return from Portugal to England and to dedicate herself to alleviating the misery of the poor. That worthy plan collapses when Henry, in declining health, follows her, seeking her care. "Wherefore am I made thus?" Mary despairs. "Vain are my efforts—I cannot live without loving—and love leads to madness." Her husband's precipitous return leaves her wishing "involuntarily, that the earth would open and swallow her." In the end, the narrator reports, "her delicate state of health did not promise long life." Mary "was hastening to that world *where there is neither marrying* nor giving in marriage," her escape from a claustrophobic society with no place for her.[34] Neither the heroine nor the narrator could imagine liberty for reasoning women who could still be forced against their will into marriage. And such a marriage foreclosed all other options for friendship with men.

Wollstonecraft's own fortunes improved with the publication of this first novel. She wrote her sister that the publisher of her novel, Joseph Johnson, had offered her regular wages as a staff writer as well as lodging. He "assures me that if I exert my talents in writing, I may support myself in a comfortable way. I am then going to be the first of a new genus—I tremble at the attempt."[35] A multitude of other women wrote romances, poems, conduct manuals, and literary criticism, but they only scraped by with their piecework. She fit readily into the circle of radicals who gathered around Johnson, including the future leader of the Society for Constitutional Information John Horne Tooke, the philosopher William Godwin, Thomas Paine, the American poet Joel Barlow, and the chemist Joseph Priestly. On the editorial staff of the *Analytical Review*, in a series of bold yet anonymously published articles, Wollstonecraft sympathized with the black loyalists' economic plight in London, followed the Temne prince Naimbanna's voyage from Sierra Leone to England, and heralded slave rebellions in Saint-Domingue. Her message was clear: what slaves could do, so should white women. Nevertheless, in her writing she disguised her gender; women did not typically comment on politics.

At Johnson's London bookshop in Paternoster Row, Wollstonecraft met an admirer and aspiring author, Mary Hays, who asked Wollstonecraft to read the manuscript of her *Letters and Essays, Moral and Miscellaneous*. Wollstonecraft responded critically, especially irritated by the "vain humility" of Hays's preface. Hays had not only apologized for her own intellectual inadequacy as a woman but had thanked all of the men who had contributed to her success. Wollstonecraft advised Hays to write clearly and courageously and to eschew expressions that would mark her as a female writer. Despite Wollstonecraft's initial scolding, their friendship flourished.

Hays was one year younger than Wollstonecraft, born in 1760 to a family of Dissenters in a London suburb. At seventeen, she had fallen in love with a fellow Dissenter, John Eccles, who became her mentor and teacher. Families and friends on both sides disapproved of the relationship, so they corresponded in secret until Eccles's premature death. In mourning, Hays withdrew from society to read philosophy, history, theology, and selected novels, including Rousseau's *Julie, ou la nouvelle Héloïse*.

In 1788, she ended her self-imposed "widowhood" to publish her first monograph, *Cursory Remarks*, under the pseudonym Eusebia. Hays's defense of public worship beyond the established church won the attention of Dissenters and radicals, in particular, the philosopher William Godwin, who offered to serve as a mentor. Hays sent him her manuscripts in twenty-page packets that they met regularly to discuss. "How often have you poured the light of reason upon my benighted spirit!" Hays wrote, thanking Godwin for his critique.[36] However, no sooner had Hays asked

FIGURE 6.2

Portrait of Mary Wollstonecraft reading, an unusual pose for a woman's portrait.
Illustration from *Century Magazine* based on the oil painting by John Opie,
1790–91. With permission of the Art Archive at Art Resource, NY

Godwin whether it was possible in their society for a woman to live independently, to be happy without the love of a man, than she fell in love with Cambridge mathematician and Dissenter William Freund. He apparently harbored no amorous feelings for her, leaving her heartbroken. Godwin encouraged Hays to write a novel to work through her unrequited love.

Emma, the love-sick protagonist of *Memoirs of Emma Courtney*, asks, "Should I desist from my present pursuit, after all it has cost me, for what can I change it?" With no parents to guide her, Emma was raised by an indulgent aunt and uncle. She grew up with the company of ten to fourteen novels a week, leaving her "as a human being, loving virtue, while enslaved by passion, liable to the mistakes and weakness of our fragile nature."[37] When she falls desperately in love with Augustus Harley, she casts herself as Rousseau's Julie of *La nouvelle Héloïse*. She sends Harley increasingly desperate and cloying letters, only to learn that he is already secretly married. On the rebound, Emma accepts the proposal of Mr. Montague, whom she holds high in "rational esteem," if not love. She resolves to assist him in his medical practice and she has his baby. But friendship proves an inadequate bond for a family, as in Rousseau's *Julie, ou la nouvelle Héloïse*. Mr. Montague discovers the depth of Emma's past passion for Hartley, a glaring contrast with the reasonable friendship she has offered him as her husband, and dies. "I have no home," Emma tellingly sobs at the end of the novel, "I am an alien in the world—and alone in the universe."[38] She has no family.

Alone, Emma is miserable. She ventures forth "with caution . . . and dread" into a world that appears to her as "a thorny and a pathless wilderness." Unlike Wollstonecraft's Mary, who resolves to forge a life of good works independent of her husband or her friend, Emma openly acknowledges her need for a husband to guide her. "That I require protection and assistance, is, I confess, a proof of weakness, but it is nevertheless true," she laments.[39] Hays intended her novel to be read by young women as a "warning, rather than as an example." In the end, Emma blames society for her predicament. "I feel, that I am neither a philosopher, nor a heroine—but a *woman, to whom education has given a sexual character*. It is true, I have risen superior to the generality of my *oppressed sex*; yet I have neither the talents for a legislator, nor a reformer of the world."[40]

Comparing herself to Rousseau's Julie, who drowns after the appearance of her former lover, Emma recognizes her inability as a woman to control her heart.

A Cosmopolitan Voice: Isabelle de Charrière

The novels of Isabelle de Charrière, although influenced by her reading of her compatriots' novel *Sara Burgerhart*, held out even less hope for women in families than did Wollstonecraft's or Hays's tragedies. De Charrière grounded her novels in a world that would have been recognizable to her Dutch, French, Swiss, and English readers, but unlike the other novelists, her characters reflected the cosmopolitan culture of the nobility of the Old Regime.[41] De Charrière informed her intimate correspondent James Boswell that the ideas for her novels came from "every country," not just her native Holland.[42] As a young girl, she dreamed of claiming "the whole world as my nationality."[43] Her characters, however, never escaped the trap set within their own minds.

Born in 1740 in the heart of the United Provinces, Isabella van Tuyll van Serooskerken, daughter of the president of the provincial Dutch nobility, was raised in the castle van Zuylen. Belle rejected each of the steady stream of suitors seeking her hand, until at thirty she announced her decision to marry her brother's mathematics tutor, Charles Emmanuel de Charrière, a phlegmatic Swiss gentleman of intelligence and somewhat limited means. He was as surprised as everyone else by her choice. "She has too much spirit for me," he confided to a friend. "She is of too high a birth and she has too much money."[44] They moved to the principality of Neuchâtel to live in the family manor with his father and two unmarried sisters. She hoped for children, but had none, so she too passed her time writing letters, meeting friends, and reading.

In 1784, Isabelle de Charrière published *Lettres de Mistriss Henley Publiées par son Amie* (Letters of Mistress Henley published by her friend), a novel set in the England of Wollstonecraft and Hays. An orphan, Mistress Henry has been raised by an aunt in thoughtless luxury and is expected to marry a nephew who would inherit the family estate. This seemingly well-orchestrated future crashes down around her when the nephew dies suddenly. "I lost everything that a woman could lose," she despairs.[45] Suitors pursue her, but she turns them all down before finally choosing to marry a twenty-five–year-old widower with a five-year-old daughter. It seems a sensible decision to the reader. Describing him as the model husband and the wedding as the perfect ceremony, Mistress Henley yearns to be the ideal wife. As with Wollstonecraft's and Hays's heroines, Mistress Henley finds herself bereft of sensible guidance, fancifully envisioning herself either as "the most respectable of Roman matrons" or as one of "the wives of our barons from the feudal past." Alternatively, she imagines herself ensconced in a romantic cottage high in the mountains, attired as one of the "shepherdesses living simply, sweet as their lambs and gay as the singing birds."[46] Her life turns out to be a disappointment.

Mistress Henley arrives at her husband's country house after their wedding with delicately ornamented clothes and fragile accessories for her husband's daughter. He abruptly questions her gifts, saying that the fancy clothes would restrict a young girl in the countryside from running and playing. He is right; she admits her error. Disappointed and determined to do better, Mistress Henley engages the eager child, teaching her to recite fables. Her father would rather she master history. In a letter to a friend, Mistress Henley acknowledges that she alone is to blame for her unhappiness. She can do nothing right, no matter how hard she tries. Visitors admire Mr. Henley as the most reasonable husband and congratulate his wife on her good fortune in marriage. She admits to her husband that any reasonable woman in her situation would be content, but she fears that she possesses none of the qualities to make them happy together.[47] She aspires not to the dependence depicted by Rousseau but to autonomy, to the friendship of an equal marriage. Her husband accepts the world as it is; she yearns for something beyond her reach.

The small domestic matters that unite Rousseau's heroine Julie to her husband Wolmar are a source of torment for Mistress Henley. She despairs at her pregnancy, obsessed by her fear that nursing the yet-unborn child will compromise her own delicate health. When her husband responds with concern for the fetus but none for her, Mistress Henley realizes that she is condemned to spend the rest of her life with a man who will never understand her. He turns down a seat in Parliament and a title, declaring his preference for the simple life of the countryside, and she is so overcome with disappointment that she faints, collapsing to the floor.

In contrast to Wollstonecraft's *Mary*, no tyrannical father has forced Mistress Henley to marry. Hers has been a sensible choice, not unlike Emma's decision to marry Montagu. But Mistress Henley's psychological struggle is more desperate than the social constraints encountered by Hays's Emma. Mistress Henley knows she cannot fit into her husband's rational, ordered, but alien rural paradise, the aptly named Hollow Park. There is no room for her as an autonomous individual in his perfect family. Her personal liberty is incompatible with even the reasonable and virtuous husband she had chosen. All is not well in her sensible world without revolution.

A mother and her daughter are similarly wracked by internal conflict in de Charrière's novel *Lettres écrites de Lausanne* (Letters written in Lausanne). Domestic happiness looms just out of their reach. The thoughtful mother explicitly counsels her daughter not to trust philosophers whose words "can be strung together one after the other to invent characters, laws, educations, and impossible domestic happiness." Philosophers, in short, "torment women, mothers, and girls. Only imbeciles listen to their moral lessons."[48] Rousseau's nuclear family may have offered an asylum to men in revolutionary times; in the end, it traps women in claustrophobic private dependence.

A "natural result of our revolution": Old Families, New Women

Wollstonecraft's *Maria, or The Wrongs of Woman*, literally has no ending. William Godwin published the unfinished manuscript after Wollstonecraft died in childbirth. The reader is introduced to Maria being "buried alive" in a "mansion of despair" by her husband, who is plotting to seize control of a legacy left to their newborn child. Maria's darkness is broken only by reading Rousseau's *Julie, ou la nouvelle Héloïse*. The target of criticism in Wollstonecraft's *Vindication of the Rights of Woman*, here the novel opens a new world for Maria. "How I panted for liberty," Maria exclaims after she finishes Rousseau's novel.[49]

Maria seeks redress in the courts, but her pleas for the freedom to return home and raise her young daughter are rejected by a judge who sneers: "We did not want French principles in public or private life." Why, he asks, could she not simply "love and obey the man chosen by her parents and relations?" The narrator answers the judge directly that only "moralists" would "insist that women ought to, and can love their husbands because it is a duty," leaving the reader with little doubt that tyranny is entrenched within the family. At the end of Wollstonecraft's novel without a conclusion, a domestic revolution seems to be the only alternative open to women. But that was apparently outside the realm of novels.[50]

Wollstonecraft, like Hays and de Charrière, depicted women ensnared in families that little resembled an enlightened paradise of reason, but they also created heroines to challenge tyrannical fathers, to repel insistent suitors, and to govern themselves without absent husbands.[51] Other than Sara, they all succumb in the end, an unhappy fate that probably did not surprise readers, even in a revolutionary era that proclaimed liberty to be individual happiness.

In the novels, marriage causes suffering for women. A wedding was not the resolution of a life without a mother's guidance for any of the female characters in *Maria*; each tells a story more miserable than the last. None of the "deserted females, placed within the sweep of a whirlwind," has known a true home. "Was not the world a vast prison, and women born slaves?" the narrator asks the reader rhetorically.[52] Only Sara in Wolff and Deken's 1782 novel can reason her way out of her plight to find happiness within a family.

The novelists' own lives confirmed the cautionary tales of their novels. Other than Betje Wolff, who vowed not to marry again after her husband died and who told friends, "Never again think of Betje Wolff without thinking of Aagje Deken," all of the novelists' attempts to secure the companionship sought by their heroines were thwarted.[53] Mary Hays's dissenting suitor died, and her second love, William Freund, took no notice of her. Wollstonecraft pursued two loves, Henry Fuseli and Gilbert Imlay, without success. Her friend and husband in the last year of her life, William Godwin, acknowledged her comfortless solitude.[54] More than one of the novelists might have fit Godwin's characterization of Wollstonecraft: "Her ardent imagination was continually conjuring up pictures of the happiness she should have found, if fortune had favoured their more intimate union. She felt herself formed for domestic affection, and all those tender charities, which men of sensibility have constantly treated as the dearest band of human society," but instead, she "felt herself alone, as it were, in the great mass of her species."[55] Although none of these authors experienced the roles of wife and mother idealized by Rousseau and expected by the middle class in England and the United Provinces, it was their unorthodox positions that gave them the time to write about heroines and their families and allowed them to see from the perspective of outsiders.

More dramatically than their fictional characters, the novelists' own lives, all negotiated through the course of at least one revolution, challenged conventions. At the same time, they confirmed the cautionary tales of their novels. Their futile searches for liberty within families, like those of their characters, demonstrated Mary Wollstonecraft's motivation in calling for a "REVOLUTION in female manners" in her *Vindication of the Rights of Woman*.[56] Wollstonecraft addressed the *Vindication* to the French, the revolutionaries she believed would transform society. "Public spirit must be nurtured by private virtue," Wollstonecraft asserted, echoing Rousseau's *La nouvelle Héloïse*.[57] She condemned Rousseau for making his character Sophie dependent, flighty, and oversensitive. To be virtuous, in private, as in public, women had to be taught to reason. "This was Rousseau's opinion respecting men. I extend it to women," Wollstonecraft explained.[58]

Wollstonecraft lamented that a married woman's "sphere of action is not large, and if she is not taught to look into her own heart, how trivial are her occupations and pursuits."[59] Wollstonecraft's critique of Rousseau's limited expectations for women educated only for marriage summed up the plight not only of Rousseau's characters but of Hays's, de Charrière's, and even Wollstonecraft's own. Rather than rejecting domesticity, Wollstonecraft strengthened women's role at the center of the family by demanding that women, like men, be taught to reason. She took Rousseau's argument for political independence and applied it to the family, where women resided. The divine right of husbands made no more sense in an enlightened age than the divine right of kings, she reasoned, counseling friendship as the revolutionary antidote to tyrannical dependence. This reasoning friendship was Wolff and Deken's ideal in *Sara Burgerhart*. It did not work for Emma, wracked as Hays's character was by remembered passions.

The heroine of de Charrière's novel *Trois Femmes* (Three women), suggestively named Émilie, after Rousseau's hero, is cast out of her family and ventures alone into a postrevolutionary world. She resembles Voltaire's Candide leaving the castle in Westphalia to travel the world, except that she has no guide, not even a misguided one like Pangloss. There is little optimism here. How, de Charrière asked, will women create lives if the restrictive laws of the Old Regime that rendered women dependent on propertied men are struck down in revolution? What resources had the French Revolution deployed to enable women to be independent? That was a question none of the other authors ventured to answer or even to ask.

Hays's protagonist Emma observes with bitterness: "Those who deviate from the beaten track must expect to be entangled in the thicket, and wounded by many a thorn."[60] That was the lot of these female novelists and of most of their characters in revolutionary times. Hays wrote nine books after *The Memoirs of Emma Courtney*. Her last novel, *The Victim of Prejudice*, was the most deeply pessimistic. "Mine has been a singular and romantic life, its incidents arising out of a singular and romantic mind," Hays reflected. "I am not suited to the times and the persons among which I have fallen, and I will say—that I have deserved a better fate."[61] In contrast to the pamphleteers and journalists of other chapters, mostly men brimming with confidence who boldly narrated their adventures and disseminated rumors, these novelists were stalked by self-doubt.

Wollstonecraft, who left a politically hostile England for France in 1792, telling her friends that she would be gone about six weeks, rejoiced in the revolutionary asylum she had chosen: "A new spirit has gone forth, to organise the body politic."[62] She renewed her acquaintance with Thomas Paine and the Americans Ruth and Joel Barlow, and befriended Helen Maria Williams. "We indulged little in common chitchat," Williams observed. "The women seemed to forget the concern to please, and the men thought less about admiring them."[63] It must have appeared to Wollstonecraft a living example of her domestic revolution.

Isabelle de Charrière challenged Wollstonecraft, wondering whether women educated to be independent individuals would be content to be legally subordinated in the family. Many of Rousseau's disciples—and there were many, female and male—shared de Charrière's doubts about the harmony of two similar, equally powerful individuals in one family. Women who would be men's wives should not also be revolutionaries themselves, Wollstonecraft's critics cautioned.

Isabelle de Charrière was also more ambivalent about the revolutionary politics of France than was Wollstonecraft. Although de Charrière applauded the Declaration of the Rights of Man, which leveled privilege, the characters in her novels were disappointed by human nature when poor revolutionaries pillaged bakeries in search of bread. "I cannot resolve to be very democratic, even in the bosom of a tyrannical monarchy," de Charrière confessed to a friend, "nor to be very aristocratic within even the most chaotic of republics."[64] De Charrière agreed to write a pamphlet in 1793 about the Swiss revolution. The government official who commissioned the pamphlet suggested that she take on the guise of an outsider. That pose came naturally to de Charrière, an aristocratic Dutch woman living in revolutionary Neuchâtel. With some insight, de Charrière's longtime correspondent, James Boswell, observed that she preferred fiction to facts, the life of the mind to the external world.[65]

In June 1793, frightened by the violence of the Terror and pregnant with her daughter Fanny, Wollstonecraft moved out of Paris to the village of Neuilly. "Let them stare," she said of women shocked by her pregnancy.[66] But it was difficult. She admitted to her friend, the American Ruth Barlow, that while she still held the revolutionary French nation in high esteem, she was tired of being surrounded day and night by self-righteous revolutionaries. At the height of the Terror, Wollstonecraft wrote a history of the French Revolution, seemingly to convince herself that the French Revolution was worth the turmoil it had engendered. Wollstonecraft, though, admitted that she was "grieved—sorely grieved" by the "blood that has stained the cause of freedom at Paris." Still, she held out hope. "Out of the chaos of vices and follies, prejudices and virtues, rudely jumbled together, I saw the fair form of Liberty slowly rising, and Virtue expanding her wings to shelter all her children!"[67]

Wolff and Deken, who had actively engaged in political commentary in the United Provinces before the Patriot Revolution was crushed, fled to Trevoux in provincial France. They thought they had buried themselves "so deep in France, in such a little city, that we did not fear violence."[68]

Wolff grew fat, Deken thin, they reported, even though "all of Europe is in revolt and France is abundantly partaking of it."[69] In their third novel, they alluded to the French Revolution in only one footnote and made it clear in letters home that they had no use for the bloodshed, a position that got them into trouble, charged with hoarding sugar and called before a revolutionary committee.

In 1795, French troops marched into The Hague and proclaimed a new Dutch republic, giving the novelists another revolution. Liberty trees sprouted all over the country, and with support from the French, the Batavian Republic was declared. Wolff and Deken returned in August 1797 to reclaim Wolff's widow's pension. Betje Wolff's longtime admirer who had visited her at Lommerlust, the playwright Lieve van Ollefen, prophesied the emancipation of the revolutionary Dutch, families and all. In his play *Het revolutionaire Huishouden* (The revolutionary household) the father of six skilled and sensible daughters teaches them the male occupations of cobbler, tailor, and painter. He boasts that his daughters will be good and useful friends to their husbands, not the "trifling fashion dolls" treasured by the French aristocracy of the Old Regime. Women's new roles, he proclaims, will be "the natural result of our revolution."[70]

Wolff lent her support to this revolutionary transformation of the family in a final fictional autobiography, *Geschrift eener bejaarde Vrouw* (Writings of an elderly woman). Women were born to take care of the house and to be responsible for the upbringing of children, she explained, echoing Wollstonecraft, whose *Vindication of the Rights of Woman* had been translated into Dutch in 1796 by a theologian. According to the laws of nature, Wolff elaborated, a girl learned arithmetic by counting the window panes in her house and the fingers on her own hand. The study of history guided children to ask why all power should be vested in the hands of the aristocratic few. Little girls in the United Provinces looked out at the wider world and wondered how revolutionary Americans could treat slaves as animals rather than as men. In Wolff's postrevolutionary world, they were convinced that the freedom derived from nature was the right of all.

In this last work, Wolff defined a middle course for individual women after the revolution, neither confined to narrowly defined household tasks nor dismissed as useless learned ladies. That was the way of nature; women had an equal right to follow their genius, cobbling, tailoring, and painting alongside their male companions. Like men, women could govern themselves and contribute to a community. As in the novel *Sara Burgerhart*, Wolff's hopeful voice in *Geschrift eener bejaarde Vrouw* had few echoes, even among the other novelists caught up in the orbit of the French Revolution.

SEVEN

Correspondence between a
"Virtuous spouse, Charming friend!"

Correspondence gave husbands, wives, lovers, and friends a toehold in this mobile society when revolution disrupted traditional social bonds. Men and women alike, in revolutionary France as in newly independent America, relied on letters for the companionship of spouses called to serve in distant lands they imagined only through letters. The letters of French diplomat Louis Otto courting the young Philadelphian Nancy Shippen; of Ruth Barlow from Connecticut and her husband Joel Barlow posted in France and Algiers; of Thomas Short, Jefferson's secretary in Paris, and the duchesse de la Rochefoucauld; and of the quintessential transatlantic couple, América Francès de Crèvecoeur and Louis Otto, to the contrary reveal the commonalities as letters shrank the distances separating lovers and spouses.

R evolutionary virtue was in the air and gender a favorite topic of revolutionary travelers writing letters home. Diplomatic postings and commercial ventures required long absences generating voluminous correspondence, often across the Atlantic. Husbands, wives, and lovers professed their devotion and friendship to those left behind in the sentimental terms of novels as they decried the distance that their letters were meant to bridge. In correspondence intertwining private sentiments and public affairs, itinerant spouses and lovers described revolutionary leaders they met in salons and heard speak in parliaments, speculated on business opportunities, and documented the trials of daily lives and intimate relationships, sometimes strained and other times emboldened by revolution.

Letters exchanged across the Atlantic reminded recipients of Wollstonecraft's counsel in the *Vindication of the Rights of Woman* that husbands and wives share responsibilities at home and beyond. Family correspondence not only described the challenges of everyday life apart during the revolutions, it guided futures to be lived together. Like the novelists, these husbands, wives, and lovers envisioned a domesticity not confined to the home that was often quite different from the lives they had left behind before the revolutions. Most thought that future was within their reach.

Correspondence was limited for the most part in the late eighteenth century not only to the literate but to the elite with the time to sit at a writing table with a quill pen and ink set, and with the funds to post or to receive letters.[1] Regular letter writing allowed physically separated family members to exert control over their family networks and commercial infrastructure.[2] In their letters, correspondents worked out their politics in private. Generally just the well placed saved their letters for posterity. Others of lesser means sent letters occasionally, but few have survived.

Letters were typically written on folded sheets of paper. Postage was charged to the recipient by the page, so to spare expense, correspondents usually wrote addresses on the outside sheet rather than on separate envelopes. The pages were sealed with hot wax to lessen the chance, especially in wartime, that they would be opened en route by probing authorities. So unreliable was the post that correspondents often numbered their letters to alert their recipients if one went missing. Even when correspondence arrived safely, letter writers despaired at the time it took their news to wend its way to the intended recipient, especially across the Atlantic. "Is it possible, Sir, that my letter of the 27th June did not reach your hands before December! I cannot tell what became of it all that time & where are now four or five others I wrote since?" the comtesse de Damas complained from northern France to her friend St. John de Crèvecoeur in New York.[3]

In a revolutionary world without an international postal system, letters were frequently entrusted to travelers known to be heading in the general direction of the recipient. Some were carried as merchandise on cargo ships across the Atlantic, lodged amid the textiles, wood, and coffee. When letters reached port, the sender had to organize connections on land. A monthly "packet" boat service devoted specifically to the transport of mail cut the transit time between New York and England from eight to four weeks in the middle of the eighteenth century. The newly appointed American chargé d'affaires in Paris, William Short, insisted that members of the American legation use the nascent national postal service rather than relying on acquaintances who might lose letters or forget to deliver them. Correspondence from America to France was to be sent in care of the French consul at New York who would put it aboard the monthly French packet ship. Letters sent from Virginia took roughly two months to reach him in Paris by that route.

If a letter arrived at its destination, it was often read aloud to assembled family members and friends. Letters were not necessarily private affairs in the eighteenth century.[4] American poet, businessman, and diplomat Joel Barlow purposefully left his diplomatic letters open so that his wife Ruth could read them herself before she delivered them to their designated recipient. Some writers explicitly asked recipients to share their letters, adding asides intended for various acquaintances. Others urged discretion. The duchesse de la Rochefoucauld asked her lover, William Short, not to write to her too often while she was in Paris; she received her letters there in the salon surrounded by curious company, sometimes including her husband. The German-born French diplomat Louis Otto similarly advised the young Nancy Shippen, whom he was courting, about the "indelicacy" of displaying romantic correspondence to her family that he intended for her alone.[5]

Despite the expense and time required for correspondence to travel, husbands and wives who were separated frequently complained of neglect at the hands of their absent spouses. From Paris, the recently arrived Joel Barlow despaired that he had not yet heard from his wife, Ruth, back in Connecticut. After a six-month silence, he moaned: "I really thought you dead and wished myself so."[6] Their letters document the expectations of intimate friendship.

Correspondents, especially wives, had manuals to guide them in the art of letter writing at the end of the eighteenth century. They were instructed: "Write freely, but not hastily; let your Words drop from your Pen, as they would from your Tongue when speaking deliberately on a Subject of which you are Master, and to a Person with whom you are intimate."[7] These manuals modeled this language of the heart. Conventions guided the flow of feelings, often expressed as physical sensations. The studied eloquence expressed in phrases of sensibility was reminiscent of the epistolary novels letter writers were reading.[8] Reflecting on their own social relationships, the correspondents echoed philosophers such as John Locke, Jean-Jacques Rousseau, and Francis Hutcheson in their depictions of affectionate companionate marriages.[9]

Living among families constituted differently from the customs the correspondents had always assumed only magnified the separation. The travel that disrupted these letter-writing families caused diplomats, merchants, and philosophers to see their own relationships anew. It transformed families traveling between America and France, even if writers rarely discussed "politics" in their letters subject to inspection by others. Their letters worked out politics, within the family and beyond it, over the decades of revolution.[10]

Nancy Shippen: "Doom'd to be the wife of a tyrant"

Two newly arrived French diplomats riding through Connecticut in the autumn of 1779 chanced upon a pair of young women weaving willow baskets alone in a shaded glen. "On their heads were straw hats decorated with wild flowers and ribbons, bouquets of cornflowers were on their bosoms. . . . Our imaginations were transported into the vales of Arcady," the French emissary François, marquis de Barbé-Marbois, wrote home, enraptured.[11] Young American women rode unescorted, and, he soon discovered, innocently "bundled" in bed with young men, even French travelers.[12]

Barbé-Marbois and Louis Guillaume Otto had accompanied Anne César de la Luzerne on a diplomatic mission to America. Barbé-Marbois, who would go on to serve as the ill-fated intendant of revolutionary Saint-Domingue, was thirty-four years old. Otto, born in 1754 into a distinguished German Protestant diplomatic family, had just finished legal studies at Strasbourg. Sailing with the French diplomats to America in 1779 aboard the *Sensible* were John Adams and his son John Quincy. The senior diplomats Luzerne and Adams enjoyed the comfort of two cabins on board, while Barbé-Marbois, Otto, and the younger Adams slung their hammocks in quarters at the back of the ship.

After a voyage discussing religion and American women, reportedly the favorite topics of John Adams, the French diplomats were received in Boston harbor with a thirteen-gun salute. The French Alliance of 1778 had given Americans reason to welcome the French. Congress discussed at length the proper etiquette for receiving them in Philadelphia, debating even the number of horses to pull the carriage.

Otto and Barbé-Marbois explored the East Coast before settling into diplomatic life. Regions that just one hundred years earlier were "savage and almost deserted," Barbé-Marbois wrote, "today are peopled, fertile, and covered with orchards."[13] Impressed by the diligence of hardworking Americans, Otto and Barbé-Marbois were surprised to see senators returning from the market, fish and vegetables tucked under their arm. Reflecting on the connection of virtue and revolutionary politics, Barbé-Marbois wondered in a letter to a friend whether their French acquaintances, "people who have porters, stewards, butlers, and covered carriages with springs, would have offered the same resistance to despotism" as the revolutionary Americans.[14] In contrast, these independent farmers and landowners were poised to be virtuous citizens, or so the French travelers assumed. Barbé-Marbois and Otto's enthusiasm for American egalitarianism waned somewhat when they found themselves sitting next to their coach driver on the rough-hewn benches of a village inn. They missed the social distinctions of Old Regime Europe that consigned common laborers to separate tables.

Settled in Philadelphia, de la Luzerne, assisted by Otto and Barbé-Marbois, lived up to the French reputation for gracious diplomacy. The men attentively paid court to the daughters of important Philadelphia families, from whom they claimed to learn a great deal about politics in the new republic. "You could not make an afternoon's visit to a *whig* or *tory* family in the city, without being sure to meet with this political 'General' or one of his 'Aides de Camp,'" the marquis de Chastellux, a French general, remarked of the diplomatic trio in his memoirs.[15] An American visitor to Philadelphia wrote her sister-in-law that although the French minister was a domestic man himself, he "sacrifices his time to the policy of the French Court," hosting "a Ball or a Concert every week and his house full to dinner every day."[16] The first summer, in addition to entertaining smaller soirees for the Philadelphia elite, the French delegation opened the gates of the Chestnut Street mansion to Philadelphians of all ranks for a festival to celebrate the birth of the French dauphin in Versailles. The next morning, Barbé-Marbois was horrified to discover that a goat, a sheep, and several cows wandered in and "took possession" of the garden, eating the leaves off his fruit trees and magnolias and uprooting the creeping vines and saplings he had planted along the winding paths.[17]

Fifteen-year-old Nancy Shippen, daughter of Dr. William Shippen, chief physician of the flying camp of the Continental Army, caught the twenty-four-year-old Otto's eye at one of the French diplomats' earliest functions.[18] She had just graduated from Mistress Rogers's School for Young Ladies in Trenton, New Jersey, where she practiced her needlework, making a pair of cuffs for George Washington. Nancy returned home an accomplished harpsichord player, in addition to having perfected her marking stitches, her tambour work, her letter writing, her penmanship, and her French. Such an education, American republicans were convinced, would make "our women virtuous and respectable; our men brave and honest, and honourable—and the American people in general an EXAMPLE OF HONOUR AND VIRTUE to the rest of the *World*."[19] Nancy had learned "to be industrious," which her mother explained, "makes so great a part of a female," and had improved "in humility, patience & love." When her mother reminded Nancy that "much depends on you being improved," she had marriage in mind, although probably not to a Frenchman.[20] Her cousin Peggy had just married Benedict Arnold and come into possession of one of the grandest houses in Philadelphia.

In 1781, four regiments of Rochambeau's army, hair done in queues and grenadier hats topped by plumes, marched into Philadelphia, en route from Newport, Rhode Island, to Yorktown, Virginia. Their route took them through swamps, into skirmishes with British Loyalists, and across rivers without bridges. They rested for two days in Philadelphia, their visit arranged by the French legation of Barbé-Marbois and Otto. The marquis de Lafayette noted that much of his time in Philadelphia was taken up by teas, walks, dinner parties, and balls with dances named "the success of the campaign," "the defeat of Burgoyne," and "Clinton's retreat." The French officers spent their last afternoon at the Shippen house, where they were pleasantly surprised that unmarried women danced with the officers while their mothers nonchalantly chatted in the next room. Nancy Shippen sang and played harpsichord, accompanied by Louis Otto on the harp and Lafayette's brother-in-law the vicomte de Noailles on violin.

Otto took to walking past the Shippens' elegant three-story red brick Georgian house on Fourth Street every day. Nancy suggested a rendezvous with him at the corner of her garden, but guided by his French manners and concerned for her reputation, he rejected "your contrivance of the corner." He could not countenance this American freedom and reported her forwardness to her mother. He proposed "a more proper time to make confidences" in the company of her parents.[21] He began visiting regularly on Tuesdays and Saturdays, when the couple played harpsichord together.

In between visits, Otto sent her poems; she replied with verses of her own. Part in fun, but also in the interest of discretion, because, as another of Shippen's suitors reminded her, even in America, "illiberal custom prevents a correspondence between the sexes," Otto signed his flirtatious letters "John-Wait-Too-Long," "Lewis Scriblerius," and "Mr Reciprocity," and dated them from "Patience island in Elysium" and "In the Other World."[22] Although the French diplomat complained of struggling to write in English, "a language that is not my own," he seemed to have no difficulty expressing his sentiments.[23] He asked Shippen to read his true feelings "in my Eyes, in my whole conduct—or if it is possible—read them in your heart."[24] After he left her house, he rhapsodized in fluent English, "Your image is entirely present to me, all my thoughts are so entirely directed towards you that I see or feel nothing in the world but you."[25] In this language of sentiment, as practiced on both sides of the Atlantic, he was fluent.

Otto soon encountered a rival, Lieutenant-Colonel Henry Beekman Livingston, a distinguished veteran of the Continental Army and an heir of the wealthy Livingston family of New York. At first, Livingston visited only on Mondays, but soon he was coming every afternoon. Sometimes, Livingston and Otto appeared at Shippen's door at the same time. Livingston sent Shippen letters, but they lacked the grace of the sensitive French diplomat. The wealthy New Yorker tried to speak the language of the heart, but it did not come naturally. At 3:30 one morning, for example, he "scrawled a few lines," noting, "the writing, which at Best [is] Bad, is now worse, from the Dimness of a Lonesome Taper, emblematical of your Lovers Situation with this Difference that it Burns at one End, I all over."[26] The awkwardness of his phrasing must have struck Shippen's ears as labored.

Whether or not Shippen had encouraged Livingston, one of the most eligible and experienced bachelors in the colonies, she confided her concern about his increasingly relentless attention in a letter to Otto. The French diplomat replied in the persona of "Milady Old-fashion," an apt characterization of his view of their cultural differences, and chided Nancy Shippen for her part in encouraging her other suitor. He accused her of leading Livingston on "only in order to gratify your vanity" without considering "the consequence of your Behavior." He reminded her that even in America "a young lady who is first introduced in the world ought to act with greatest precaution." Milady Old-fashion acknowledged that Nancy found herself now "in a great perplexity how to disintegrate yourself" from the relationship with Livingston. Rather than openly scorn the unwanted suitor, Milady advised Nancy Shippen to be disagreeable and contradictory. Surely in America, as in France, that strategy would cause Livingston to lose interest and move along.[27]

Dr. Shippen, Nancy's father, observed in a letter to Tommy, her younger brother away at school, that "Nancy is much puzzled between Otto & Livingston. She loves the first and only esteems the last." Dr. Shippen, however, had come to favor Livingston over Otto as the surer financial prospect. Livingston would not have to wait to make his way in the world before marrying, as would Otto. "A Bird in the hand is worth 2 in a bush," Dr. Shippen reasoned, and besides, he concluded, "they are both sensible."[28] Her father consequently limited Otto's visits to the house to twice weekly. At the same time, Mrs. Shippen, leaning the other way, wrote directly to Otto to encourage his courtship.

Otto openly avowed his sentiments in his next letter, hoping to oust his rival. "I shall tell you so often how much I love you that you will be forced to answer: and *I too, I love you, my dear Friend!* No harmony in the world could equal these words flowing from your Lipps.' "[29] When Nancy Shippen did not reply to his letter, he left Philadelphia, expecting that his absence would force her to declare her affection. His ploy succeeded, and in March 1781, Nancy apparently agreed to marry him.

Dr. Shippen responded to the news by banning Louis Otto from the Shippen house for four days. Otto tolerated the enforced separation at first. "I made today a very pleasant discovery in our parlour," he wrote. "I can see two of your windows and one chimney. . . . I assure you never was a chimney so interesting for me."[30] He dropped off his recently composed "Strasbourg Menuet" on her doorstep with a note signed "Mr. Runaway." The subsequent days passed more slowly. "Was it a dream, my dear Nancy? Or did I really hear you pronounce that heavenly yes?" he pressed.[31] He was "so unhappy" he moaned, beseeching her to "forgive me, dear friend, I was never less master of my feelings." After she accused him of misinterpreting their relationship, he asked how he could possibly "misunderstand you? I should as well misunderstand my own feelings. I have studied your conduct since I have the pleasure of knowing you, nothing escaped my watchful eye. Lovers are quick sighted."[32] He was sure that she favored him and convinced that in America, lovers, not their parents, made the decision to marry. It was, in fact, more complicated than that, and not as different from France as he assumed.

Passing by the Shippen house the next evening, through their parlor window Otto saw Henry Livingston holding Nancy Shippen's hands. Horrified, he wrote, "You seem'd to be very happy yourself and this unhappy Discoverie mad[e] me for one moment, the most miserable creature in the world."[33] Shippen confirmed Otto's fears: Livingston had proposed to her and she had accepted. Otto was stunned. Why, he wondered, "in this free Country, a Lady of Sixteen years who is handsome enough to find as many admirers, and who had all the advantages of a good education must be married in a hurry and given up to a man whom she dislikes?" Had he, the perceptive French diplomat, misunderstood the unspoken rules of American courtship? "By the polite attention of your parents, your candour, your pleasing behaviour and your complaisance in listening to my broken language," he had thought she favored him. After all, he had been allowed to spend "allmost every Evening alone in your Company," a sure signal of Nancy Shippen's affection and her parents' intentions. He would not have expected her "to refuse an advantageous Establishment for my sake," but he reminded her that "being myself of a Family worthy to be Connected with any one in the Continent and in such circumstances as to be entitled in a few years to an honorable appointment," he too would be an eligible partner in marriage. He blamed the influence of wealth. "Your P . . . knows that my Fortune cannot be compared with that of [Livingston] and . . . therefore he prefers him."[34] That was the stark American reality: money. Otto was not alone in noting its power in the New World.

FIGURE 7.1
Nancy Shippen Livingston from a miniature attributed to Benjamin Trott.
Smithsonian American Art Museum, Gift of Natalie Brooks Sears Shippen and
William Brush Shippen

"I am yours forever, though perhaps you will never be mine," Otto added on the last tear-stained page of his letter.[35] Rather than acting as "common souls" who "know only the transition from love to indifference," he asked her to "be my friend as you was before and let me believe that I occupy always a part of your heart as much as religion and decency will allow you." For his part, he promised her "a thousand times that I will adore you for ever and that shall be my only comfort in a life that will grow painful by the remembrance of my disappointment."[36] Dr. Shippen prevented them from meeting on the eve of the wedding, fearing the power of Otto's words. They continued to correspond.

On the occasion of her marriage, Dr. Shippen reminded his daughter of her new obligations as a wife, adding that her family's happiness depended on her. His advice echoed that of the father in *The History of Emily Montague*, an epistolary novel written in 1769 by the Canadian author Frances Brooke. The fictitious father cites Madame de Maintenon, the devout companion of Louis XIV, who told her daughter how to preserve affection within a marriage, acknowledging that "the caprice, the inconstancy, the injustice of men, makes the task of women in marriage infinitely difficult."[37] That advice would prove prophetic for Nancy Shippen Livingston.

As Henry Livingston's wife, Nancy moved to the two hundred–acre Livingston Manor, which extended fifteen miles along the North River in New York. There she was expected to adapt to the routines of her new husband and his family. Nancy's brother Tom, surprised to receive no letter from the newlyweds, wrote her, painting for "myself the most pleasing scenes. I shall with pleasure view my dear sister at one time walking or fishing with her dear husband on the banks of the Hudson, at another conversing with him about domestic or foreign affairs, playing with him at Draughts or Chess."[38] Nancy Shippen Livingston was soon pregnant, but her husband refused to allow her to visit her parents. She begged them, in increasingly desperate letters, to come help her in New York. She finally got her way, and the baby, named after Livingston's mother, was born in Philadelphia.

Nancy Shippen Livingston's life bore little resemblance to the images of postrevolutionary or republican American marriage of a husband and wife united in friendship as depicted by European diplomats or imagined by her brother. Instead, her letters home would have provided source material for a novel by Mary Wollstonecraft or Isabelle de Charrière. After two years of disguised references and whispers, Nancy Shippen Livingston learned from her mother-in-law of Livingston's plans to install his illegitimate children, of whom there were apparently several, in their household to be raised alongside their daughter.

At the same time, still jealous of Otto, Henry Livingston accused his wife of infidelity. Nancy Shippen, an avid reader of novels, cast her husband as the rake in her letters to her family. In her journal, she gave family members fictional names, as if they were all characters in the novel that was her life. Imagining the trials of her own married life in the sentimental terms of novels such as Goethe's *Sorrows of Young Werther*, Nancy Shippen Livingston attempted to negotiate a way to survive in her husband's world on the banks of the North River, far from her own friends and family. Finally, in 1783, she returned to her parents.

Until the day Henry Livingston's threats of legal action forced her to send the baby to the Livingston estate to be raised by his mother, Nancy Shippen Livingston's life back in Philadelphia centered on "sweet Peggy," her infant daughter.[39] Thereafter, she languished as a married woman without a husband, a child, or a household. She had nothing to do, no role to play, she confided to her new friend, Eliza Livingston, a distant relation of her husband. If her husband, a known rake, fit the bill as the "Estated ruffian" of a Henry Fielding novel, then it followed in her mind that she was the virtuous female in distress, the wronged wife.[40] Although she ached after her daughter, Nancy Shippen Livingston was so convinced that her husband would make her miserable at home in New York with his taunts of infidelity that she chose to endure solitude in Philadelphia.

Mrs. Livingston assured her daughter-in-law that she would not release her granddaughter from her care to live with Henry Livingston, no matter how fervent his assurances of good behavior. She could never "permit a child of one of the first families in the United States to be in a family without a white woman in it," the older woman wrote.[41] Some of the illegitimate children who drove Nancy Shippen Livingston from New York seem to have been the offspring of her husband's relations with the domestic help on the Livingston estate. Deprived of her daughter, Nancy Shippen Livingston lamented in letter after letter: "My distress is greater than I can express. . . . I feel that she is close twisted with the fibres of my heart."[42] During the rare intervals that Peggy was entrusted to her own mother's care, Nancy Shippen Livingston was forced to spirit her daughter from one safe house to another to evade her husband.[43] Peggy could not be sent to school out of fear of abduction, so Mrs. Livingston, "determined to spare no cost to make her an accomplished woman," hired tutors for her in French and music, and guided her correspondence.[44] Nancy Shippen Livingston taught her daughter practical housekeeping skills when they were together. Apart, she instructed Peggy "to make a daily exercise of writing to me; it will improve you & make me as happy as I can be without you."[45] She closely monitored her daughter's penmanship, spelling, and epistolary style, all deemed critical components of a young woman's education.

Otto returned to Philadelphia from France in August 1785, now the French chargé d'affaires. "Now must I be wretched in the reflection of what I have lost. O! Had I waited till the obstacles were remov'd that stood in my Father's way, then had I been compleatly happy," Nancy Shippen Livingston confided in her journal. Instead, she was "a wretched slave—doom'd to be the wife of a tyrant I hate but from whom, thank God, I am separate."[46] Nancy Shippen Livingston countered the reality of her disastrous marriage with visions of Louis Otto, whom she imagined as her friend in an affectionate marriage. She blamed her father for arranging the marriage to Livingston, the wealthier suitor, but it appears from her correspondence that she had freely acquiesced in what was presented to her as a choice.

Nancy Shippen Livingston did follow her father's advice about propriety and the behavior of married women and stayed away from the French legation on Carpenter Street.[47] In their clandestine correspondence, however, Nancy Shippen Livingston and Louis Otto avowed their friendship for each other. "I am constantly checked by the apprehension of saying too much or too little—too much for you to read, too little for my feelings," he wrote her in the style of his earliest letters.[48] She refrained from inviting Otto in for tea when he passed by her parlor window, noting that "prudence forbids it" and "it wou'd displease my husband."[49] The farther her husband strayed from accepted standards of behavior, the more Nancy Shippen Livingston was intent to prove her virtue. At times, she chafed against her father's strictures, asking her journal, "When will the time come, that I can be free and uncontroul'd?"[50]

In her journal, Nancy Shippen Livingston quoted the passages her father had copied from Frances Brooke's novel for her wedding. She echoed Brooke's comment that Madame de Maintenon "must be allowed to have known the heart of man—tho' I cannot agree with her that women were only born to suffer & obey."[51] Abigail Adams drew on the same passage in her letter to her husband, John, "to remember the ladies" when the Continental Congress drew up their "new Code of Laws." Neither of them accepted that women were born just to obey their husbands. "That we are generally tyrannical, I am obliged to own," Brooke's male protagonist acknowledges, but he adds, "such of us as know how to be happy, willingly give up the harsh title of master, for the more tender and endearing one of friend." That was the problem. Legally, husbands had power over their wives, who were obligated to submit. And yet, Brooke explained, and Nancy Shippen Livingston copied in her journal, "Equality is the soul of friendship: marriage, to give delight must join *two minds*, not devote a slave to the will of an imperious lord."[52] Equality and submission proved difficult to reconcile. Her marriage was so far from her sense of this ideal of equal friendship that she endured separation from her daughter and society rather than live with her tyrannical, adulterous husband. A wife in the new republic, she yearned for an ideal she could not attain.

Nancy Shippen Livingston "was very much affected" by a story she heard "of a young lady who was sacrificed to the avarice & ambition of her parents to a man she hated & her death was the natural consequence of her misery." She read into the anecdote parallels to her own life. It did not matter that she named her parents Lord and Lady Worthy in her journal, nor that she had encouraged Livingston's courtship. In her journal, she reflected on the tale of the sacrifice, composing a self-portrait. "She had a soul form'd for friendship—she found it not at home, her elegance of mind prevented her seeking it abroad." In the end, as Nancy Shippen Livingston worried would be her own fate, "she died a melancholy victim to the Tyranny of her friends & the tenderness of her heart."[53]

In 1789, Nancy Shippen Livingston wrote her uncle inquiring about the possibility of divorce. Despite the intervention of well-placed relatives, a private bill in the New York legislature, and her mother-in-law's advice that she petition as a "femme sole" from Philadelphia, she could not overcome the obstacles erected by one of the wealthiest men in New York. Her husband cited Otto's earlier courtship as evidence of her infidelity. The revolution that established a people's right to separate from tyrants was of little help to Nancy Shippen Livingston in her marriage. Denied recourse through the legal system, the wronged wife depended on friends to console her in her struggles. Two years later, her husband sued her for divorce on the grounds of desertion. He won his case. In postrevolutionary America, republicanism presumed harmony, but not gender equality.

While Nancy Shippen Livingston fought Henry Livingston in the courts, her closest friend, Eliza Livingston, confided in a letter to her that she had taken up correspondence with Louis Otto. Their marriage in 1787 gave Otto entrée into the homes of the leading public figures in New York. Ever aware of the American social hierarchy based on wealth, the French diplomat related that the views of his new social circle "carry much weight in public deliberations."[54] An American visitor to the home of the newlyweds reported that they lived "in the style of a nobleman. His servants and attendants were numerous."[55]

Within the year, Eliza Livingston Otto died in childbirth.[56] St. John de Crèvecoeur was a pallbearer at her funeral, alongside diplomats from the United Provinces, Spain, and Britain. "Every former prospect of happiness being at once vanished, I am wandering thro this world," Otto wrote Nancy Shippen Livingston. Like her, he lamented, "I was born for the peaceable enjoyment of domestic Life."[57] Both of them imagined the different course their lives might have taken had she not submitted, as she explained it, to her father's wishes. Would that Nancy Shippen and Louis Otto had contracted the marriage of friends so idealized in revolutionary America. Instead, Nancy Shippen Livingston ended up estranged from her parents, whom she increasingly held responsible for her ill-fated marriage. Her daughter chose to join her when she turned sixteen and could legally leave her grandmother's house, but by then Nancy Shippen Livingston was completely overcome with melancholy. Both turned to religion, and mother and daughter malingered together, estranged from society.[58]

"More philosophy than you can imagine": Ruth and Joel Barlow

"Virtuous wife, Charming friend!" Joel Barlow wrote his wife, Ruth, "Since your tenderness convinced you to give in to my desire that you join me in Europe and share my misfortunes, you have deserved my homage, my recognition, and my eternal love." The Connecticut poet and veteran of the American War for Independence–turned–European businessman and French revolutionary, Joel Barlow assured his wife, friend, and confidante, who trailed behind on his diplomatic and commercial adventures, "You are in truth, a world for me, the goodness who is my fortune, the comfort for all my unhappiness that gives sweetness to my life."[59] By return mail Ruth sent him political advice and discussed the practical details of daily life in his absence. Calling him the "most estimable of friends & most beloved of husbands," she countered the argument that marriages "loose the ardour of love & that we grow old and indifferent that love is lost in friendship."[60] She avowed, "My love & tenderness for you is even greater than on our marriage day."[61] Each protested formulaically in letters that "words are not sufficient to express my feelings," but their correspondence overflowed with sentiment.[62] Here perhaps was the ideal of friendship in marriage for which Nancy Shippen Livingston yearned. Love for them was friendship, at least when they were apart.

At the beginning of their relationship, during their courtship, Joel was the more prolific letter writer. A schoolteacher in New Haven, a career considered appropriate for a Yale graduate without family connections, he soon quit and signed on as chaplain to the third Massachusetts Brigade, a position that left more time for reading, writing, and pursuing young women. One of them was the daughter of his landlord, the blacksmith Michael Baldwin. Baldwin promptly sent Ruth away to discourage the attentions of the young man without secure economic prospects. American fathers might not be tyrants, but few had relinquished control over their daughters' marriage prospects. Economic prospects loomed large in their calculations.

Joel pleaded with Ruth to "come home," but also corresponded with Elizabeth Whitman, a poet residing in Hartford. While Ruth ignored Joel's entreaties, Elizabeth sent back long, soulful letters, asking: "What shall I say to all the tender things it [your last letter] contains but that my heart beats in delightful unison to every tender sentiment?"[63] She proposed a correspondence "in which all disguises are thrown off."[64] Joel seems to have lost interest in "Betsy" as he pursued the more elusive Ruth. "I read your letters and contemplate your perfections till I have grown sick of myself and despair of any merit myself unless it can be perceived from my connection with you," he wrote Ruth, admitting, as her father suspected, "I have done nothing worth mentioning since you left me. I have wrote letters and read letters and I have read yours a dozen times. I live with your Brother and do nothing."[65] Occasionally, she responded.

In 1781, Joel and Ruth were secretly engaged. Neither consulted family. Joel left New Haven to spend the winter with the army "at a frozen distance from the dearest object under heaven," and advised her to "be resigned" to the separation.[66] He announced their marriage to Ruth's father a year later. Countering her father's potential objections to the fait accompli, he reasoned in language befitting the new republic: "To take a daughter from any family upon the principle of mutual affection is a right always given by the God of nature wherever he has given that affection." Besides, he assured Mr. Baldwin, "My affairs are now in a good situation."[67] Mr. Baldwin would have preferred a husband with more stable financial prospects for his daughter, but Ruth and Joel had decided that in America, young women could freely choose their own companions, and young men did not require inheritances to earn their way.

The couple settled in Hartford, and Joel started writing poetry. All was well, it seems, until he traveled to Philadelphia and Ruth failed to write him during his three-week absence. In retaliation, Joel wrote her facetiously of a Quaker girl with black eyes and ten thousand pounds who was tempting him "to cancel all former obligations."[68] Ruth did not write him when she traveled either, and he threatened to go find another wife so "you need not be at the trouble of ever returning."[69] At the end of another chiding letter to his absent wife he mentioned that he had moved house while she was away. Their letters as husband and wife had not changed significantly from the pursuit of a partner in courtship. With humor, each tried to guide the other toward a future life together that they imagined, but struggled in this era of dislocation to realize.

In May 1788, Joel Barlow, enticed by the prospects of a career in European business, agreed to represent the Scioto Associates' Ohio land scheme in Paris.[70] On his first transatlantic voyage, he complained in his long letters to Ruth of the bad food, omnipresent fleas, and the seasickness he suffered in the wretched, dark cabin on the filthy packet ship. From Paris, he wrote of celebrating the fourth of July with Thomas Jefferson, composing brochures to encourage French emigration to Ohio, studying French, attending the opera, and discussing revolutionary politics.

As documented by his and others' correspondence, American diplomats and businessmen moved easily in aristocratic circles in Paris, often centering around Jefferson's house. Barlow was careful to assure his wife that although friends "conceive me to be rioting in the luxuries of Europe, I should be infinitely more happy to be locked in a prison in America, where I might hear the cheering voice of my Ruthy thro the grate."[71] His letters to his wife continued to echo the prose of courtship, but the backdrop was now the French, not the American, Revolution. He would be no less involved in the second than in the first.

Barlow sent a packet of letters to his wife with the first group of Scioto settlers, who sailed to America in January 1789. He was full of enthusiasm for the settlement, unlike Louis Otto, who, upon hearing rumors about the emigration of twelve thousand Frenchmen and women to the swampy lowlands at the mouth of the Great Kanawha River, chided his countrymen for abandoning their revolutionary homeland.[72] Otto need not have worried about the exodus. The first Scioto settlers were so disheartened by the threats of starvation in the Ohio wilderness and scalping at the hands of the Indians that their letters to France discouraged further emigration, and the Scioto scheme crumbled.[73] Rather than elaborate on the failure of the scheme, Barlow simply informed his wife: "The sudden and glorious revolution has prevented my completing the business." His interests had clearly turned to politics in France. He promised to recount in letters all that had "passed under my eye" so that she could share the triumphs of this second revolution.[74]

Once it was clear to Joel that he would stay, he entreated Ruth to join him in Europe. "There is no more difficulty in it than in going from Hartford to New Haven," he assured her, adding, "the difficulties have been principally in imagination." To calm her fears, perhaps inspired by his own accounts of the ocean voyage, he reasoned, "Many wives have done the same thing."[75] He urged Ruth to get advice from Abigail Adams on what to bring and suggested that she hire a good maid. Ruth finally sailed to London, where she was greeted not by her husband as planned, but by yet another letter, this time informing her that he had been detained in Paris for at least a week. She waited a month.

By the time Joel finally made his way to London, Ruth was out of sorts, tired of being "pent up in a narrow dirty street surrounded with high houses." She was especially annoyed at having to appear at all hours in public, always well dressed and with no time to call her own. "No person can have an idea of extravagance & luxury, folly, wickedness & wretchedness without coming to Europe," she complained in letters to her "dear friends" at home in Greenfield, "that dear delightful village" she had left behind.[76] Her husband might be happy conversing with aristocrats and attending political assemblies, but she missed her life in Connecticut.

The publication of two works, his poem "The Conspiracy of Kings" and his essay "Advice to the privileged Orders," and his translation of Brissot's *New Travels in America* in March 1792 won Joel Barlow a following in London radical circles. Rather than stay in London, Joel soon abandoned Ruth again to travel on diplomatic business, this time on behalf of the French. He sent her details of treaty negotiations and passed along advice, instructing her to avoid card games—especially debilitating for sedentary women—and to take daily exercise, "running or jumping in the garden." He explained, "It's your friend who advises it, your husband who commands it."[77]

In November 1792, Joel Barlow, who had entrusted his proposals for a new French constitution to Thomas Paine to deliver to the French National Convention, decided to go to Paris himself to extend fraternal greetings to the revolutionary citizens of France. Acknowledging the "intense light" that "blazed forth from the heart of the American Republic," Barlow looked to "the French Revolution, shining with all the intensity of the sun at its zenith," to reveal "the practical results of that philosophy whose principles had been sown in the dark."[78] His address received a standing ovation. He wrote his wife, "It is really no small gratification to me to have seen two complete revolutions in favor of liberty."[79] Thomas Jefferson congratulated Joel Barlow on his "endeavors

to bring the transatlantic world into the world of reason," but Ruth
Barlow, stuck in London, took a different tack. She warned her husband,
"You did wrong in going to Paris."[80] Their British friends now shunned
her as the wife of a radical. She warned him to reply through a
Mr. Leavenworth, as all mail between them would now be opened by
British authorities. She was also tired of the separation, and added for
good measure that her health had suffered because of his rash political
adventures in France. She pointed to the tears that stained the page,
but concluded with the formulaic "I would always wish you to act from
your judgment & feelings without paying the least regard to mine."[81]
Clearly that was not the case.

In March 1793, Joel Barlow sent his wife a passport so that she could
join him in France. He addressed his letter to "Mrs. Brownlow" and sent it
through a chain of emissaries, including John Paul Jones's sister. Ruth
Barlow was apprehensive. Joel Barlow had witnessed the execution of his
ally Brissot and been called to testify before the Revolutionary Tribunal
about his friendship with the Venezuelan general Francisco Miranda.
Besides, his business dealings had all failed. The Barlows lived frugally
at the Palais Royal Hotel, up four flights of stairs that wound through a
casino. Late one night in December 1793, Thomas Paine appeared at their
door with police agents. Paine was under arrest and designated Barlow
to accompany the agents back to search Paine's house. There, Barlow convinced them that the papers strewn around were of no consequence. In
fact, they were the first half of Paine's just completed *Age of Reason*; Barlow
published the important work for Paine.

In the spring of 1794, in need of funds, the Barlows moved to Altona,
a city administered by the Danish monarchy, to engage in shipping and to
escape the French Terror. A trading center on the Elbe near Hamburg,
Altona had long been home to refugees, but never so many as during the
French Revolution, when four thousand foreigners took up residence in
the prosperous Danish port. The Barlows refused to socialize with the aristocratic French émigrés who had fled revolutionary France, but found a
whole community of revolutionary sympathizers with whom to dine and
converse. St. John de Crèvecoeur was there with his son Ally, as was Mary
Wollstonecraft. Looking back, Barlow reminisced that he had been truly
happy those two years with his "beloved at my side, she who had always

refreshed and soothed me."[82] They re-created their American household in relative calm in the midst of revolutionary Europe.

In January 1796, Joel Barlow left his wife behind again, this time on diplomatic mission to Algiers to negotiate a peace treaty with the three Barbary states and to obtain the release of Americans captured by the Barbary pirates.[83] From a Spanish inn en route he wrote his wife, "The pigs disputed my right to come inside, knowing that I was to sleep with them." Eventually, "they let me climb to a little open room where I could enjoy their odor mixed with that of the kitchen and the stable."[84] From Alicante, he sailed for Algiers, which he reported "is doubtless, in all respects, the most detestable place one can imagine." Narrow alleyways passed for streets, houses were poorly built, and the people were hostile.[85] Although the dey threatened to throw the American delegation out of Algiers and to declare war on the United States, Joel Barlow was more worried by the lack of correspondence from his wife. Finally, twenty-nine letters arrived, bundled together in a packet. He was temporarily relieved.

Then came the plague. Expecting to succumb, Joel Barlow sent what he thought would be his last letter to his wife. He wrote to inform her she had lost "a life which I know you value more than you do your own. I say I know this, because I have long been taught, from our perfect sympathy of affection, to judge your heart by mine." Throughout their marriage, as often apart as together, he had relied on "the energy of your virtues, which gave me consolation and even happiness." He reflected on "our various struggles and disappointments while trying to obtain a moderate competency for the quiet enjoyment of which we used to call the remainder of our lives."[86] Barlow recovered and promised his shaken wife in Paris, "This absence has contributed to my reformation. I will return to you a new man." He vowed not to leave her again. "My first and constant care will be to make my wife perfectly happy."[87] She assumed that meant returning at last to Connecticut.

In their letters at least, theirs was a marriage of friends. Both spouses complained of neglect in sentimental terms, but at the same time each carried on individually, as Ruth Barlow affirmed, "with perhaps more philosophy than you can imagine."[88] Apart, like other traveling American merchants, poets, and diplomats, the Barlows kept before them a model of their lives together. A 1789 issue of the *Massachusetts Magazine* described the ideal citizen of the republic as a good husband who treated "his wife with delicacy as a woman, with tenderness as a friend."[89] Virtuous, wise, patient, and capable husbands and wives in the new republic expected to live in "heaven on earth," their house a "paradise."[90] From the Barlows' letters, it seems that American families offered rooted republican couples a haven in revolutionary times, or that was, at least, what mobile revolutionaries, whose letters often went missing in the erratic post, imagined and hoped to re-create when they returned.

Joel and Ruth Barlow each complained that he or she wrote more letters than the other returned. A typical letter from Ruth opened: "Cher Amie, I wrote you a long letter this week, yet I am scribbling again. This is my eighth letter. I have had but five from you."[91] Joel answered: "If someone asked me what I do in Marseille, I will say, I write letters to my wife, that's all I'm doing."[92] He claimed that correspondence was his solace in his life away from her. In language reminiscent of the most sentimental of novels, he cajoled his wife, whom he blamed for the lapse in correspondence: "Once you start writing, I can't believe that you won't write all the time. It is such a pleasure. It is the time when I pour my soul onto the paper for you to swallow, that your image is before me, opening my letter. I can hear you reading it. I can see the glimmers of pleasure in your face, the tears of joy even, and sometimes the gay smiles excited by the words that have no value other than that they come from the hand of your friend."[93] Nineteen days later, when he still had received no letters, he was to the end of his patience. "If only I knew you were happy, I would be tranquil. But how could I know that when you don't tell me."[94] The silence between letters seemed "eternal."[95] Even if reason told him that she was probably healthy and happy, he complained, as did other corresponding spouses: "Love did not reason, tenderness always wanted to worry about the fate of its object."[96] To get back at her, he threatened to conceal the details of his life from her, as she did from him. By 1796, they were writing each other in French, "a gentler language" than "that barbarous language," English.[97] All the while, in both languages, they negotiated the relations of power in their marriage.

"Eight of your charming letters" arrived in Algiers, Joel Barlow, ever the exacting recipient, noted, but "there is no 45 nor 39." He suspected, "you lovely creature, you never wrote them. You misnumber very often. I know by the dates."[98] She complained in turn that her weak eyes made it difficult to write and sometimes friends stayed so late that she was too exhausted to sit at her writing desk before bed; besides, she explained, "I write you so often that I have to keep repeating the same sentiments and anecdotes."[99] She recited for her husband her daily schedule, rising in the morning at nine, eating breakfast and reading newspapers until eleven or twelve, riding or walking until two, taking a French lesson and studying until four, then spending half an hour dressing for dinner and having company in or going out to seek company after dinner. That had become her routine, on her own away from home, an American wife in revolutionary Europe. Joel and Ruth were still negotiating in 1800.

Ruth Barlow showed her husband's letters, full of terms of sentimental endearment, to her friend in Paris, Mary Wollstonecraft. In a letter to her sister, Wollstonecraft complained, "I was almost disgusted with the tender passages which afforded her so much satisfaction, because they were turned so prettily that they looked more like the cold ingenuity of the head than the warm overflowings of the heart." As much as she liked Ruth Barlow, Wollstonecraft objected to her sentimentality. The American wife was "a little warped by romance," it seemed to Wollstonecraft.[100] Still, Wollstonecraft contentedly imagined the Barlows enjoying "the peaceable shades of America" after all the "alarms" of life apart in Europe.[101]

"Required by the institutions in the midst of which we live": William Short and the Duchesse de la Rochefoucauld

In the interval between the American and French revolutions, another American diplomat, the Virginian William Short, followed his "adoptive father" Thomas Jefferson across the Atlantic to Paris to serve as his secretary. Young and single, Short lodged with a family in Saint Germain to improve his French and, Jefferson suspected, to pursue the daughter of the house. Only after Jefferson was appointed to succeed Benjamin Franklin as minister to France was Short awarded an official diplomatic position. Then he moved with the rest of the American legation to the Hôtel de Langeac, an elegant three-story building surrounded by vast formal gardens on the corner of the Champs Élysées and the rue de Berri.

The center of American social life in Paris, the residence afforded Jefferson space to grow corn from Cherokee country. Frequent French visitors included neighbors: the duc de la Rochefoucauld, a fervent supporter of the American Revolution, and the marquis de Condorcet, a philosopher and secretary of the French Academy of Sciences. Although stimulated by the intellectual life of the French capital, in his letters to friends at home Jefferson expressed his distaste for the aristocratic society of Parisian salons. "Intrigues of love occupy the younger, and those of ambition, the elder part of the great," he complained to Anne Bingham of Philadelphia. "Conjugal love having no existence among them, domestic happiness, of which that is the basis, is utterly unknown."[102] In his correspondence, Jefferson perpetuated the stereotypical contrast of the bored, aristocratic French mistresses indulging in political intrigue with hard-working American housewives who "fill every moment with a healthy and useful activity."[103] Bingham rose to the defense of French women, who, "you must confess . . . are more accomplished and understand the intercourse of society better than any other country."[104] To Jefferson's mind, that public voice was not advantageous to women or society. Be wary of the "the voluptuary dress and habits of the European women," Jefferson advised young Americans in Europe, warning them to eschew romantic attachments abroad and return home to "the chaste affections and simplicity of American girls" to marry.[105]

Soon fluent in French and known for his "happy and ever-obliging" nature, Short was invited to these fashionable Paris salons that Jefferson disdained. In the summer of 1785, the duchesse de la Rochefoucauld d'Enville and her son, Louis Alexandre, called "the pearl of all dukes" by Crèvecoeur and a friend of Benjamin Franklin and Lafayette, invited the surviving Enlightenment philosophers and French veterans of the American War of Independence to their thousand-acre estate, la Roche Guyon.[106] Thomas Jefferson, his former Virginia neighbor and Tuscan native Filippo Mazzei, and William Short traveled the forty miles from Paris together. Once there, Short ignored the other guests, including the marquis de Condorcet, the chemist Antoine Laurent Lavoisier, and the marquis de Lafayette, passing the afternoon instead in the company of the duc de la Rochefoucauld's wife. Twenty years her husband's junior, Alexandrine Charlotte Sophie de Rohan-Chabot, known as Rosalie, shared a philosophical interest in reform with her husband and her mother-in-law, who also happened to be her grandmother. She seems to have had more in common with Short.

Back in Paris, where the Liancourt and Rochefoucauld families owned adjoining houses on the Left Bank of the Seine, Short took to dining alone with the younger duchesse de la Rochefoucauld after the theater and accompanying her to the salons of Paris. Rumors of Short's new romantic interest reached friends in America, but they assumed that he was courting Jefferson's daughter Martha. None suspected he was seeing a married duchess. Jefferson, who knew better, encouraged Short to travel abroad with two friends, one of them Nancy Shippen's younger brother, Thomas, presumably to forget an affair that Jefferson found inappropriate. Short left, but he soon returned to Rosalie.

In the summer of 1789, Short and the other Americans in Paris circulated freely among the French revolutionaries. Lafayette brought friends to Jefferson's table to discuss the transmittal of revolution across the Atlantic and the writing of a French declaration of rights. Even the king's own cousin founded the Boston Club to debate the ideals of the philosophes. Jefferson traveled daily to Versailles to monitor meetings of the Estates General. He appreciated the courage of the commoners in demanding an equal voice with the privileged orders in June 1789.[107]

In September 1789, Jefferson returned to America with his daughters, leaving Short as the chargé d'affaires. Always homesick for America while in Paris, Jefferson brought back to Virginia his French steward, macaroni, figs, vinegar, a harpsichord, cases of wine, carriages, anchovies, and a waffle iron. He counseled Short, who seemed to be enjoying life in Paris with the duchess, that "a young man indeed may do without marriage in a great city" for some time, but it would not endure. Only marriage to an American would produce "durable happiness."[108] Short assured friends that he would come home to Virginia to earn his fortune and find a suitable wife once Jefferson returned to Paris.[109] Jefferson never came back to France, so Short stayed in Paris. He grew increasingly disenchanted with the endless debates and disorganization of the French revolutionaries, especially the Jacobins, as his ties to the duchess deepened.

The duchess remembered the summer of 1791, with frequent visits from Short to her estate, as an American idyll. The two lovers spent afternoons picnicking in a meadow or strolling together across the hillsides. They gardened and raked hay in the July sun on her estate. They canoed on a millpond on the Seine and passed long evenings together, "when our hearts swelled with the tender outpourings that are the charm of love."[110] She must have known, though, that theirs could not be understood as a typical courtship in the new American republic. She was already married and an aristocrat.

Friends of the duchess among the French revolutionaries looked to the civil institution of marriage to transform their society. Affectionate bonds between a husband and wife freely chosen would form the foundation of their unified republic, too.[111] The duchesse de la Rochefoucauld probably harbored few illusions about fulfilling her duties as a wife on either side of the Atlantic. As would become clear to Short, her aristocratic code of conduct differed as dramatically from the domestic expectations of the Americans he would have overheard gossiping about her in Short's Parisian circle as they did from French revolutionaries advocating divorce.

Short found himself in a no-man's-land between the American code as articulated by Jefferson, his adopted father, and the duchess, his lover. Short refused to abide by the unspoken French expectation of discretion and visited the duchess at La Roche even when her husband was home. In vain, she entreated her American lover to "put yourself in my place." He enjoyed greater liberty as a man and as an American in France. "With no family nor entourage in this country, you do not understand what one owes to duty here," she chided him.[112] She regretted deeply the need for subterfuge and secrecy "required by the institutions in the midst of which we live," but she expected that as an accomplished diplomat, he would realize the importance of adhering to the traditional morality of the French aristocracy, rather than acting the brash American.[113]

The question of discretion was made moot when Short's diplomatic posting in Paris came to an abrupt end. He had hoped to succeed Jefferson as American minister in Paris. That appointment went to the aristocratic Gouverneur Morris. Short was named minister resident at The Hague in 1792 and sent from there on mission to Madrid. Distance increased the necessity for correspondence between Short and the duchess, especially as negotiations in Madrid dragged on for three years. The duchess informed Short that her grandmother and other relatives were impressed by his thoughtful letters and sent "a thousand compliments."[114] She did warn Short to address his letters clearly to "madame" so the postman did not accidentally hand them to her husband. That had happened once, and she was relieved that it was one of his less passionate letters.

The duchess reported to Short on the meetings of the National Assembly she attended. By 1791, she had begun to question whether the philosophes who assumed men were basically good were not mistaken in their assessment of human nature, or at least of the French. She was not the first to have doubts about the French as revolutionaries. Still, the duke and duchess de la Rochefoucauld assumed they would be safe from the revolution forty miles outside of Paris at La Roche. As liberal nobles who had openly supported the revolution, they expected their aristocratic lives to continue unaffected. In letters to Short she described her daily routine: she rose at nine, read Short's letters and the newspapers, and got out of bed at ten. Dressing and breakfast took another two hours. She walked in the gardens, lunched at three, and retired to her "island" to read and write letters in privacy. Dinner was served at ten. The next day, the routine began again, starting with the mail.

The violence of August 1792 drove the duchess, her husband, and her grandmother into hiding for a month in an old Norman spa in Forges. Returning in September to La Roche, they were recognized by a passing army officer, who decided to transport the duke back to Paris to be charged with treason. A crowd gathered. They pelted the aristocrat with rocks before soldiers armed with sabers hacked him to death. His grief-stricken wife and mother returned to the chateau to news that the duchess's brother, one of the king's guards, had been killed in the September Massacre in Paris. After reading his lover's letters, Short railed in his correspondence with America against "the despotism of the multitude."[115] Jefferson urged Short to moderate his criticism of the Jacobins, reminding him from America: "The Liberty of the whole earth was depending on the issue of the contest!"[116] Personal circumstances had convinced Short otherwise. He was less concerned about "the Liberty of the whole earth" than with the safety of the duchess.

Short did not wait long after de la Rochefoucauld's death to ask the duchess, now a widow, to marry him. She refused, citing the need to care for her grandmother. As perplexed by the cultural differences as Otto had been at Nancy Shippen's choice of Livingston, Short returned to his post in Madrid. Long intervals separated their letters, but rather than blaming each other's negligence, as the Barlows did, Short and the duchess assumed the letters had been delayed or gone missing en route. They sent several copies of each letter by different routes in the hope that one might make it to its destination. Gouverneur Morris, at home himself in the society of French women, let them stash their love letters in the American diplomatic pouch, but his successor, James Monroe, refused.[117] "What a cruel situation we suffer when the greatest happiness we can hope for is the hope that we will receive at uncertain intervals a few words cautiously written and regularly scrutinized by the officers of the postal service of the different countries through which our letters pass," the duchess wrote Short.[118] How tragic it was, she lamented, that her greatest happiness during the whole day was to "pick up the sheet of paper, and to cover it with black scribbles! And at the same time, how extraordinary that it is possible to find such a strong attraction in such an otherwise insipid occupation, that it is enough of a diversion to soothe the pain inseparable from the parting of two people who are so dear to each other."[119] Tied to him now only by correspondence, the duchess who had refused the offer of marriage did not "know whether to rejoice or feel afflicted that I have come to know you."[120] Both had learned the language of sentimental correspondence.

Short dreamed of "finishing our days" in America but wrote Jefferson that he feared "the future partner of my life" would not be "happy and contented . . . in your neighborhood."[121] Released at last from his diplomatic post in Madrid, a persistent Short traveled to La Roche to propose again to the duchess. She again refused. After her grandmother died, Short asked the duchess one last time to marry him, but she still declined. She seemed to know she could not be happy as an American wife. Short finally traveled back to America alone. Without any political connections other than Jefferson, who told him that he had been too long away to represent American interests abroad, Short had no diplomatic future in Europe. An aristocrat, the duchesse was not willing to settle into the domestic contentment of an American wife as it had been so often described to the French. Unable to reconcile their two cultures, the aristocratic French of the Old Regime and the diplomatic American of the new republic, Short and the duchess went separate ways.

"Thoroughly trained in all household arts": América Francès de Crèvecoeur, an American in Revolutionary Europe

Born to a family with powerful connections on both sides of the Atlantic, América Francès de Crèvecoeur, St. John de Crèvecoeur's eighteen-year-old daughter, attended a ball given in New York for President Washington by the French minister, the comte de Moustier. Louis Otto, Nancy Shippen Livingston's former suitor and a recent widower, met her there. The couple was married in 1790 at Saint Peter's Church in New York. Thomas Jefferson served as principal witness. A diplomat in attendance pictured them as the model transatlantic revolutionary couple, one French, the other American, together embodying the contentment of a marriage of friends settled into domestic calm in the midst of revolution. They may have seen themselves that way, too.

América Francès, known as Fanny, was the oldest child of Michel Jean de Crèvecoeur, the French aristocrat who had transformed himself into J. Hector St. John, a humble American farmer. In 1780, Crèvecoeur had left his daughter behind on their farm in upstate New York with her mother and younger brother while he returned to Europe with his oldest son, allegedly to secure their inheritance. Although no letters from his family arrived for him in France, he dispatched letters by every possible conveyance to New York, or so he claimed. He even entrusted letters in 1781 to five young Americans to carry back across the Atlantic. The sailors had recently been released from prison in Britain, and he had rescued them on the French coast. He addressed his letters to his family via the governor, the sheriff, and Gustave Fellowes, the father of one of the young American sailors.

Crèvecoeur still had received no news when he returned to America as French consul in November 1783. On landing in New York, he finally heard that Indians had raided his family's farm and killed his wife. He did not know the fate of his children. Only later did he learn that, spurred by Crèvecoeur's desperate letters carried by his sons, Gustave Fellowes had tracked down América Francès and her younger brother. Finding them huddled together in the snowdrifts of upstate New York, Fellowes took them by sleigh to his home to Boston. Fellowes had sent a letter in December 1781 to Crèvecoeur in France, informing him of the rescue of his children, but it never found him and was returned to New York in 1784. One of Crèvecoeur's friends happened to find Fellowes's letter among the papers at the post office left behind by the British. That led Crèvecoeur to Fellowes and his children.

As narrated by Crèvecoeur, it was a story worthy of a sentimental novel.[122] "Cruel death had taken their mother;—the misfortunes of war had driven their father to Europe;—the flames of Savages had reduced their paternal house to cinders;—the subsistence that he had left them was destroyed;—and then [Fellowes] came to their aid,—he took them under his roof, & placed them among his own . . . all because five Americans had escaped their imprisonment in England."[123] Four feet of snow prevented Crèvecoeur's immediate departure for Boston. The evening that Crèvecoeur finally arrived at the Fellowes home, neighbors gathered to dance in celebration to the accompaniment of violins. "To this image of domestic happiness, must be joined those of order, of economy, of cleanliness and of industry," Crèvecoeur wrote of the Fellowes household, adding for the benefit of European readers, "this happiness was to be found in almost every American house."[124] What a contrast to the salon-centered lives of the French aristocracy, such as the comtesse de Houdetot, Rousseau's muse, whose company he had recently enjoyed.

A nineteen-page poem, "The Sassafras and the Vine," preserved in a packet of Crèvecoeur's family papers, celebrated, in the most sentimental terms, the father's "sweet love . . . thou blooming source of ev'ry heartfelt joy" for his daughter. The stable paternal tree supported the vine faithfully through its tender years.

> Look here my child—he with complacence said,
> See how this tree the feeble vine doth aid
> So have I cherish'd, so supported thee
> And thus dependent was thy life on me.[125]

The daughter clung to the love of the father long after he had died. This poetic image, attributed by archivists to América Francès, so different from the reality of her own youth, fit Crèvecoeur's view of his unfaltering love for his children in the American wilderness. One of Crèvecoeur's most faithful correspondents, Marie Louise Aglaé Andrault de Langeron, the comtesse de Damas, responded from France: "I am not sure if I need to rein my imagination to fit the bounds of truth, but it shows to me your American families as little Paradises where no ambition, jealousy, anger, nor any rash passion was allowed to enter. These American families are inhabited by all that is kind & pure in human souls, enlivened by education & good breeding. How far from it are our own polite countries."[126] She subscribed to her correspondent's idyllic representation of family life in the New World, a family life she aspired to emulate as an aristocrat in revolutionary France.[127]

Crèvecoeur sent his sons to Paris to be educated, but Fanny stayed behind with the Fellowes family in Boston, where she was "thoroughly trained in all household arts and brought to an understanding of every culinary possibility."[128] Together with Abigail Fellowes, she practiced harp and spinet daily, and assisted the kitchen staff in making bread, dressing chickens, and cooking omelettes. She learned to sew, knit, and mend clothes. Hers was an education in keeping with the image held by the comtesse de Damas of American home-centered, domestic self-sufficiency.

In a "Melancolik letter dated July 11th," Crèvecoeur disturbed the idyllic imagination of the comtesse de Damas with a "dreadful account of miss fanny's illness & dangerous situation." The countess, visiting the comtesse de Houdetot when the letter arrived, replied that she lacked the "words to express the painful sensations I felt on reading it." Fortunately, her hostess had received a second letter in the same bundle with news "of your dear child's recovery."[129] Fanny had gone to stay with a family in Connecticut. A mutual friend noted that as she recovered in Connecticut, outings on horseback "could not help but have a good effect on her temperament and character," although he worried that Fanny still experienced the world as if it were just "a magic lantern" passing before her eyes."[130] It is not clear from friends' letters whether her detachment from the world around her was the result of an illness or of an accident. Health was such a preoccupation of correspondence focused so intently on individual experience that it is difficult to distinguish the debilitating from the passing.

In the same letter, the countess congratulated Crèvecoeur on "the event you seem to foresee." She hoped it would afford Fanny "all the joys that attend virtuous unions." In marriage, she envisioned Fanny as "a mother of children as dutiful, prudent, and industrious as herself. O happy, thrice happy your country where people are to chuse for themselves, to consult their hearts & call of their affections, & in the most solemn act of their life, can hope for the greatest & purest felicity."[131] Crèvecoeur's letters describing his family and his journal would have done much to create that impression of blissful courtships and unions of individuals freely chosen. It accorded well with the European view of a simple rustic life.

After their marriage, Louis and Fanny Otto traveled to France, arriving in 1792, just in time to learn that the French government had recalled its diplomats. Otto managed to secure a new position as chief of the first division at the Office of Foreign Affairs under François Deforgues, who was arrested in April 1794. Otto, taken into custody in July, was freed three weeks later, only to be arrested a second time and taken to Luxembourg prison. Freed a second time, he returned to the small Paris apartment he shared with Fanny, their one-year-old daughter, Sophie, his father-in-law, and a boarder. Crèvecoeur led a retired life for fear of arrest, but he did visit his imprisoned friend Thomas Paine. Joining their circle was Joel Barlow, whose Scioto scheme Crèvecoeur had supported. Barlow served as their postal link, forwarding Crèvecoeur's letters from Paris to one of his sons, then in America. Crèvecoeur also served as a conduit for the active Franco-American exchange, supplying books to Benjamin Franklin and translating French documents for George Washington. The world of American expatriates in Paris was tightly knit.

In 1796, to escape the threat of ever-changing politics and menacing crowds in Paris, Louis Otto and his father-in-law bought a small estate at Lesches, near Meaux, north of Paris. There, together with one of Fanny's brothers, they devoted themselves to cultivating the land. Fanny took charge of the poultry yard, while Otto's mother tended the orchard. With no agricultural experience, Otto looked to Crèvecoeur for advice on the rotation of crops, lumbering, and growing vegetables.[132] Louis and Fanny Otto edited a translation of Crèvecoeur's *Travels in Pennsylvania* in 1800. It was as if they were living out Voltaire's aphorism from *Candide* to "cultivate your garden." Or, rather, they had translated an American life onto the edges of the French Revolution.

In 1798, the Abbé Sieyès, newly appointed as ambassador to Berlin, disrupted their rural idyll, inviting Louis Otto to serve as his first secretary. Fanny Otto was devastated by her husband's absence. Now she was the wife awaiting letters "with great impatience," eager for "news of all that is dear to me." How strange it was that one sheet of paper could make her so happy, she confided in a letter addressed to her husband, echoing the Barlows, Short, and the duchess. When her husband's first letter, eleven days en route from Berlin, finally arrived, she claimed to have read it eight times through, kissed it a thousand times; she promised to be more patient, to endure his absence as would a true heroine.[133] She asked her husband to calculate the intervals carefully between his letters, so that she would not watch for them in vain. After Louis Otto protested in his next letter that he had been days without a letter from her, she asked indignantly how her husband could imagine her capable of not writing, knowing how important their correspondence was to both of them.[134] The problem was obviously the post.

Fanny Otto pleaded with her husband to write to her more often than she wrote him, rather than just responding to her letters. "You write so well!" she cajoled. "You paint with so much energy and truth the sentiments of your heart, that mine takes from them new forces to support the pains attached to my situation."[135] Otto had extensive experience. He responded by sending her two letters in one week, and she rejoiced: "Do I need to tell you how happy that made me, how gay? . . . All is laughter, all smiles at me. I find pleasure everywhere."[136]

Fanny complained in her increasingly desperate letters that she could not be happy without her husband at home. "My reason is too weak to quell these painful sentiments that agitate me without ceasing and that my heart pleases itself to nourish."[137] She protested her husband's injunction that she refrain from writing when she was unhappy. "How can I do that" with you away, she asked. "I would then not write you at all, because I am always sad waiting for your news. . . . My heart is anxious."[138] As their year apart passed, she seemed to grow more "tranquil." She promised her husband to "be more reasonable in the future."[139] She hoped "to be worthy of you in conducting myself as a reasonable being" and blushed, "thinking of my past weakness."[140] She asked him to share her feelings, but not to blame her for her sensibility.

Louis Otto served his wife as a model of reason, but also of sentiment. She thought they commingled in the ideal man, as in the ideal woman. In this, she echoed French revolutionary orators such as Jacques-Pierre

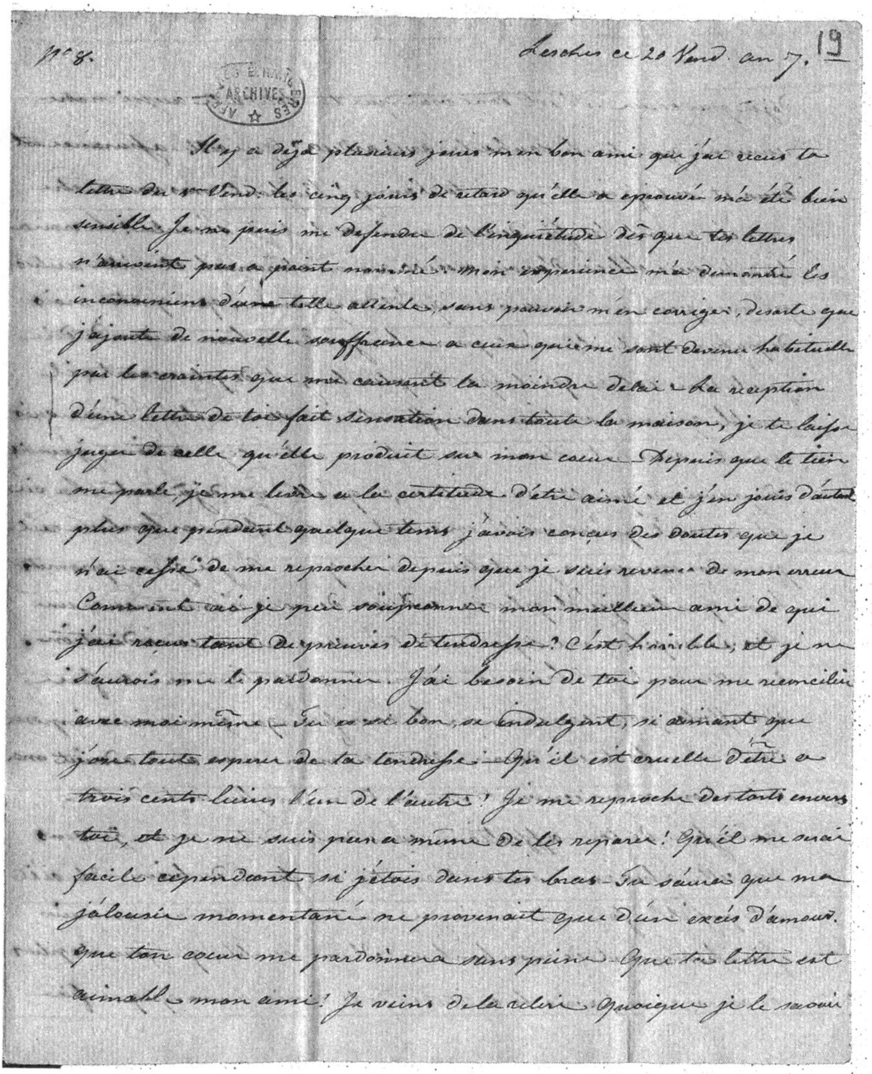

N° 8. Lesches ce 20 Vend. an 7. 19

Il y a déjà plusieurs jours mon bon ami que j'ai reçu ta lettre du 10 Vend. les cinq jours de retard qu'elle a éprouvé m'a été bien sensible. Je ne puis me défendre de l'inquiétude dès que tes lettres n'arrivent pas au point nommé. Mon expérience m'a démontré les inconvénients d'une telle attente, sans pouvoir m'en corriger, de sorte que j'ajoute de nouvelles souffrances à celles qui me sont devenues habituelles par les craintes que me causent le moindre délai. La réception d'une lettre de toi fait sensation dans toute la maison, je te laisse juger de celle qu'elle produit sur mon cœur. Depuis que le tien me parle, je me livre à la certitude d'être aimé et j'en jouis d'autant plus que pendant quelque tems j'avois conçus des doutes que je n'ai cessé de me reprocher depuis que je suis revenue de mon erreur. Comment ai-je pu soupçonner mon meilleur ami de qui j'ai reçu tant de preuves de tendresse? C'est horrible, et je n'aurois pu le pardonner. J'ai besoin de toi pour me reconcilier avec moi même. Tu es si bon, si indulgent, si aimant que j'ose tout espérer de ta tendresse. Qu'il est cruelle d'être à trois cents lieues l'un de l'autre! Je me reproche des torts envers toi, et je ne suis pas à même de les réparer! Qu'il me serait facile cependant si j'étois dans tes bras. Tu sauras que ma jalousie momentanée ne provenait que d'un excès d'amour. Que ton cœur me pardonnera sans peine. Que ta lettre est aimable mon ami! Je viens de la relire. Quoique je le savois

FIGURE 7.2

Letter from América Francès Saint John de Crèvecoeur Otto to her husband Louis Otto, Lesches, 20 Vendemaire, An 7 (11 October 1798). She complains that it has been five days since she has heard from "her good friend," and she is worried. She reflects on her happiness on receiving a letter and knowing that she is loved. Acquisitions Extraordinaires 135, Archives des Affaires Étrangères, Corneuve. With permission from the Ministere des Affaires Étrangères

Brissot and Charles-François Oudet, who believed that affectionate marriage nourished virtue and kindness.[141] Louis Otto responded to one particularly emotional letter from his wife that if only they had loved each
other less, "she would be more reasonable, and he less tormented."[142] Still,
his situation was so different from hers, she argued, because he could lose
himself in his diplomatic obligations. Her daily preoccupations on the
farm were limited to hiring a chambermaid, looking for her parents' wedding certificate, and coping with the harvests. Her life centered on her
husband and he was away, reachable only through correspondence. Her
brother Ally, who worried about her, wrote Otto: "Your poor vine needs
her sassafras nearby to breathe—she vegetates far from him. We give her
our ceaseless attention and caresses to sustain her, but cannot replace the
soul of her life."[143] He reported that Fanny was often feverish with worry.
She relied on the sociability of her marriage even more because he was
away, while business and politics filled his daily life abroad. Like Nancy
Shippen, she could not contemplate a life without the daily presence of
a husband.

Why would he make his wife "miserable when both could be happy,"
one of Fanny's friends asked Louis Otto? The solution seemed so obvious
to Fanny's friend. They should live together in their home, rather than relying on letters in this revolutionary era when the post often went missing.
She apologized for being so bold, "but that is how we women reason," she
explained, blaming men's "reason" for the isolation that made her
American friend so miserable. Instead of asking Fanny to join him in
Berlin, "you think of this, you think of that, you reflect, you compare, you
believe one thing is good and another would be better," and are incapable
of acting.[144] The friend, meanwhile, advised Fanny to trust her own reason
and not defer to her husband. Finally, Fanny Otto did move to Berlin, at
the invitation of her husband.

In 1800, the Ottos were dispatched to London and then to Munich,
where Louis again played a role in treaty negotiations. Otto wrote his
mother from Munich that their home was tastefully furnished and that
Fanny "devotes herself tirelessly to the care of the household."[145] The couple enjoyed walks in the countryside, especially through the English gardens on the edge of the city, and every two days attended the theater,
where they had a loge. Fanny had a horse. Their daughter Sophie learned

German readily, Fanny Otto wrote her mother-in-law. Sophie could already speak French, English, and Italian, knew Latin, Greek, and Hebrew, and read Shakespeare and Schiller. She loved dance and horseback riding. A visiting diplomat noted that the way to get into good graces of Otto was to compliment his wife, "of whom he is strongly enamored," and to admire the talents of his daughter in music and public speaking.[146] The Otto household in Munich seemed to friends to be a model of what cultured Europeans believed to be American domesticity.

In a letter to Fanny, Louis Otto acknowledged that his reason united with his sentiments to persuade him to renounce "the ambition to plunge back into the whirlwind of political affairs in France."[147] He carried on, discussing the new cook and what varieties of wheat to sow. An Austrian visitor commented that Louis Otto, a diplomat of the Old Regime, had taken on the habits "of a man who has spent lots of time in America and in England and savors his domestic life with its comfortable and simple manner, its republican principles, and the calm of reasoning."[148] Although they were not often apart in their later years, when they were, Louis Otto addressed his letters full of politics to his wife, "Ma bonne amie" or "Ma bonne Fanny." He called her "the best of wives and the most loved."[149]

In 1812, Sophie married one of Louis Philippe's ministers, Pelet de la Lozère, whom she met at a diplomatic reception in Paris, and they settled in France. Her nineteenth-century biographer cited her "refined distinction" as evidence of the diplomatic circles in which she had been raised. At home in elite society, she was known for the noble simplicity of her household. She combined, it seems, "the imagination, initiative, and will" of her mother and the diplomatic skills and conscience of her father, leading her to a life of religious devotion.[150] Hers, unlike Peggy Livingston's, would be lived within a family.

At home, together again, without the need for correspondence, the private lives of her parents disappeared from the historical record.[151] With her husband at her side, Fanny's letters were addressed to friends and family, some in France and more in America. They described the couple's walks in the country and their patronage of the opera. At long last, after the revolutions, they had created a transatlantic family that Short and the duchess could not even imagine.

Revolutionary "Companions"

Louis Otto complained in 1785 of the naïveté of the revolutionary Americans who believed fervently "that they can make the entire universe enjoy what they call the rights of humanity."[152] Away from Europe, in their primeval forests on their own side of the Atlantic, Americans seemed to be convinced that they could create a republic to accord with man's true nature. That included reshaping the family. Correspondence between husbands and wives, lovers and friends, not only recorded that transformation but contributed to it. Where better to effect reform that would change the world than within the family?

In the decade between the American and French revolutions, European travelers filled correspondence to friends in Europe with stories of the companionship of husbands and wives observed in the brick houses of the new American republic. The progress of the French Revolution did little to undermine the stereotypical contrast between rustic Americans and aristocratic French frequenters of salons. American diplomats and merchants who chose aristocrats, not artisans, as their friends in Paris persistently sent home letters expressing their indignation at the affairs of the French, whose marriages so little resembled their own. Americans in Paris like the Barlows saw the relationship of William Short and the duchesse de la Rochefoucauld as typical of the corrupt French ways that they imagined had been little disturbed by the Revolution. Jefferson obviously did, too. He was happy when Short returned to America without the duchess, even if he never married.

Rosalie's cousin, the duc de la Rochefoucauld Liancourt, a delegate to the Estates General in 1789, toured North America from 1795 to 1799. Like Barbé-Marbois and Otto before him, the duke remarked upon the freedom of unmarried American women who left their homes without an escort, which "to French manners would appear disorderly." These "natural" and independent young Americans, he observed, "enjoy the same degree of liberty which married women do in France, and which married women here do not take." American women loved their husbands, he scoffed, simply "because they have not considered that they can do otherwise."[153] The duc did not notice disappointed wives such as Nancy Shippen Livingston, who regretted their free but poorly considered decisions.

These travelers also did not notice revolutionary changes in French families. French revolutionaries assigned republican marriage the task of transforming French citizens. The marriage of América Francès de Crèvecoeur to Louis Otto was typical on both sides of the revolutionary Atlantic, where public virtue nurtured by private relationships was seen to be the antidote to the aristocratic cabals of the Old Regime. Although the travel journals had highlighted differences separating the rustic domesticity of the Americans and the court-centered etiquette of the French, correspondence between husbands and wives suggests more similarity than contrast in the revolutionary changes.

The language of sensibility, whether expressed in English or in French, reflected transitional, not transformed, societies. Individuals were negotiating their places not only within their families but in the revolutionary community in formation for more than a decade. Their correspondence suggests that little was set or certain in their lives. Neither of the revolutions, not the French or the American, had remade the family. Instead, letters exchanged between revolutionary partners reveal the contested possibilities of that transformation in progress. In the midst of the chaos of a decade of war, the correspondents all staked a claim on peace and the tranquility of a home.

EIGHT

Decrees "in the Name of the French Republic": Armed Cosmopolitans

The ever-changing French revolutionary governments dispatched a steady stream of ambassadors, commissioners, residents, and representatives to serve as the "eyes and arms" of Paris. Always on the move, shuffled, rearranged, and recalled, this array of civil and military agents transmitted the French Revolution to the Swiss, the Genevans, the Belgians, the Italians, the Dutch, and the Irish from 1793 until the end of the eighteenth century. Cannons and bayonets had become the order of the day, a dramatic departure from the idealistic, peace-promoting universalism of the revolution's earliest days.

The first deputies elected to the new French National Assembly announced to widespread applause that in this revolutionary era all men would live as brothers. Schooled in the cosmopolitanism of enlightened philosophers, revolutionaries on both sides of the Atlantic in the 1770s and 1780s proclaimed their intentions abroad to be peaceful. Old Regime despots backed by their legions of mercenaries had waged wars of imperial conquest. Republicans would instead dispatch diplomats such as Benjamin Franklin and Louis Otto in the service of liberty. They saw the dawning of an era of "universal peace."[1]

Shunning the diplomatic institutions of the Old Regime, the French in 1789, like the Americans in 1786, rejected war as hostile to their revolutionary aims. "Each nation has the right to decide its own laws," the marquis de Condorcet proclaimed, warning potential aggressors that to resort to force was "to make yourself the enemy of the human race."[2] Jacobin Maximilien Robespierre stated what by then seemed obvious, that no government should "assume that by invading a foreign people they could be convinced to adopt your laws and constitution." In an often-quoted addendum, he explained, "No one likes armed missionaries."[3] The new nation expected its neighbors to respect its sovereignty. France, however,

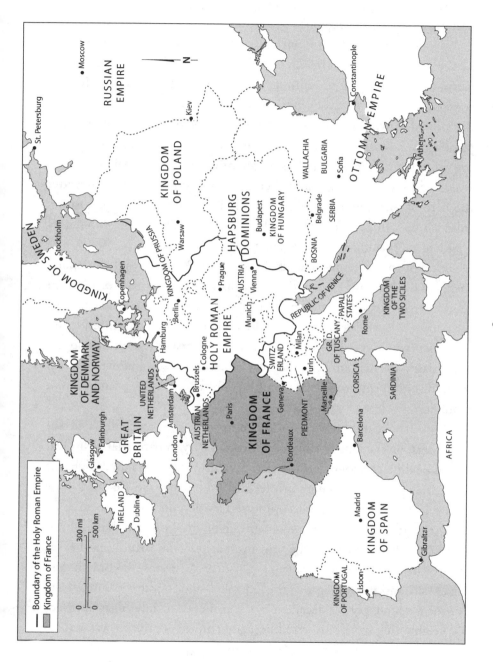

MAP 8.1

Europe, 1789. Map by Bill Nelson

did not have, as the Americans did, an ocean to shield it from either its friends or its enemies. By its continued existence, then, the revolutionary nation threatened its neighbors.

In celebration of its first anniversary, French revolutionaries gathered in the pouring rain on the Champ de Mars and declared the French Revolution a universal revolution. The French National Assembly welcomed processions of revolutionary refugees from Geneva, Italy, Poland, the United Provinces, Ireland, England, and Prussia. At the center of the parade grounds, on the Altar of the Federation, stood a woman symbolizing the constitution and warriors representing the patrie, their arms outstretched to receive the assembled celebrants of universal law. Lafayette, the hero of the hour, approached the altar on a white charger. Visitors from across Europe agreed that at that moment, "all national differences vanished, all prejudices disappeared."[4]

One of the foreigners chosen in 1792 to represent French departments in the National Convention, Anacharsis Cloots, loudly proclaimed the Universal Republic of Humankind. According to the Prussian-born Dutchmen, henceforth there would be no national boundaries; no foreigners would inhabit his new world. With greater reserve but no less enthusiasm, the marquis de Condorcet called on the revolutionary French to grant citizenship to all who took up residence in the cosmopolitan republic.

Propelled by this buoyant optimism in 1792, the French declared war on tyrants, on the king of Bohemia and Hungary in particular.[5] This war would be different, they clarified. The revolutionaries would not fight for territorial gain, as the king's armies did under the Old Regime. They would bring liberty to peoples oppressed by despots and aristocrats. By August 1792, French soldiers were fighting on five fronts: in the southeast against the Piedmontese, in the southwest against the Spanish, in the east against the Prussians, in the north against the Austrians, the British, and the Dutch, and at home against the federalists and counterrevolutionaries. For the remainder of the decade, French armies were fully engaged invading neighboring kingdoms, republics, and empires, venturing as far afield as Egypt and the Caribbean.

French revolutionaries elaborated this armed mission in revolutionary decrees. Printed in Paris, the decrees were dispatched to the Genevans, the

Belgians, the Germans, the Italians, and the Irish—to anyone whose territory lay within the ever-expanding range of their armies levied en masse. The promise of French military aid was as audacious as the universal revolution was bold. The decree of 19 November 1792 extended fraternity to all peoples who desired their freedom. Decrees issued on 15 and 17 December went farther, compelling rather than inviting peoples liberated by revolutionary armies to be free like the French. Armies and their agents plastered decrees on doorways and proclaimed them in town squares.

Diplomatic correspondence, including policy-changing decrees, did not flow any more smoothly over land than it had across the sea to the colonies in the Caribbean. Politics, more often than storms, disrupted the spread of decrees over the mountains and plains of Europe. French foreign agents sent to Italy, Germany, Ireland, and Switzerland frequently introduced their reports to Paris with what became almost a stock phrase: "For several months we have received no letters."[6] An executive commissioner to the army complained: "Nothing is more disagreeable for the principal agent of the government to receive not a single dispatch, not a single response, and to learn government measures only through intermediaries or subordinates."[7] By the time diplomatic communiqués arrived in Cologne or Milan, orders dispatched with urgency from Paris were often irrelevant.

So much changed so precipitously, in committees in Paris and abroad, that French diplomats, many of them holdovers from the monarchy, struggled to implement revolutionary foreign policy on the ground.[8] Foreign minister Charles-François Dumouriez instructed foreign powers to dispense with the formality of the Old World and to address Louis XVI simply as "His Majesty, The King of the French."[9] A few months later, with their king out of the way, French officials asked foreign governments to strike all honorary titles from their correspondence.

On assignment as minister plenipotentiary in Switzerland, a seasoned diplomat, François Barthélemy, informed Paris that he had been barred by the Swiss from entering his official residence in Soleure. He received an official response from Paris in March 1792 informing him that the foreign minister to whom he had addressed his correspondence had been denounced in the National Assembly and arrested. The new minister of foreign affairs wrote two weeks later describing the "revolution" in the ministry in Paris. He assured Barthélemy, then wandering homeless through the Swiss cantons, that he would read Barthélemy's letters with the same interest as his ill-fated predecessor and share them with the king. A few months later, when Parisians stormed the Tuileries, massacring the king's Swiss guards, Barthélemy's Swiss informers urged him to hole up out of sight. The third foreign minister to whom he reported was unconcerned and unsympathetic. Pierre Lebrun simply ordered Barthélemy to stand his ground, reminding him that he was stationed in the Swiss cantons to carry out French revolutionary policy and to disseminate its decrees.[10] Theirs was a bellicose universalism anchored in patriotic nationalism.

Contradictions proliferated, catching French diplomats and Belgians, Genevans, Italians, Germans, and the Swiss and Irish unprepared. The clash in revolutionary assumptions is evident in correspondence linking Paris with its agents. The lines dividing friends from allies, like every other dichotomy in this turbulent era, were ever shifting, further confused, not clarified, by war.

Ending "the reign of error" in the Belgian Provinces and Geneva

In August 1792, within months of the French declaration of war, Prussian forces, flanked by Austrian contingents, invaded France. They captured the French fortress at Longwy in four days. Only Verdun stood between the duke of Brunswick's armies and Paris. It seemed that the French Revolution would perish, as had all of the other European revolutions, crushed by neighboring empires.

One month later, revolutionary France was on the offensive, spurred by the patriotism of the Brissotins in the Legislative Assembly. Singing "Ça Ira" and "La Marseillaise," and proclaiming "Vive la Nation," the Army of the North, under the command of General Charles Dumouriez, and the Army of the Center, under General François-Christophe Kellermann, stopped the Prussians in the deep mud and icy rain at Valmy. "From this place and this time forth, a new era in world history opens," Johann Wolfgang von Goethe wrote.[11] The German writer expected imperial mercenaries across Europe to fall to the French revolutionary volunteers inspired by liberty.

French armies under Dumouriez's command invaded the Austrian-ruled Belgian provinces in November 1792. Their goal was not only to remove the Austrians but also to release an oppressed people from the grip of the nobles and the church. French soldiers posted decrees and handed out proclamations inviting the Belgians to join them in planting trees of liberty. "As long as you establish the sovereignty of the people and renounce the rule of all despots, we will be your brothers, your friends, your supporters," the French general promised his neighbors.[12]

Peasants and artisans alike helped the French chase Austrian carriages fleeing through the countryside and back toward Vienna. Enthusiastically welcomed by former Brabant revolutionaries as liberators in village after village, Dumouriez and his armies saw themselves as true Belgian heroes. In that spirit, Dumouriez refused to accept the keys to the city of Brussels, advising citizens not to "allow any foreigner to dominate you. You were made to be independent."[13] He did not ask himself what would happen if the liberated peoples chose to go their own way, following a path that diverged from that of the French Revolution. Such hostility to the revolution seemed inconceivable, at least initially.

It was the exuberance, not the reluctance, of the Belgian welcome that worried Dumouriez. Belgian crowds burned the Austrian coat of arms and invited the French general to the first meeting of the Société des amis de liberté et d'égalité (Society of the friends of liberty and equality) popularly known as Jacobins, at the Church of the Jesuits. Thousands of Bruxellois gathered to toast the end of "the reign of error" and to proclaim the dawn of a new era illuminated by the light of liberty.[14] Seasoned by his experience as foreign minister, Dumouriez counseled moderation and called for the election of a Belgian provisional government.

Within days, all that changed. Former Brabant revolutionaries from 1789 accused the French revolutionaries in 1792 of imposing their democracy on the Belgians. The worried general informed the minister of war in Paris that victory celebrations might have been premature. "The cabal of priests and the old Estates still rule three-quarters of the country," he despaired.[15] Delegates from the newly elected provisional government in Brussels traveled to Paris to remind the French "that before the 16th Century, in Europe it was only the Belgians and the Swiss who knew true liberty."[16] The Belgians had no need for French tutors or a military occupation. The French Convention thought otherwise.

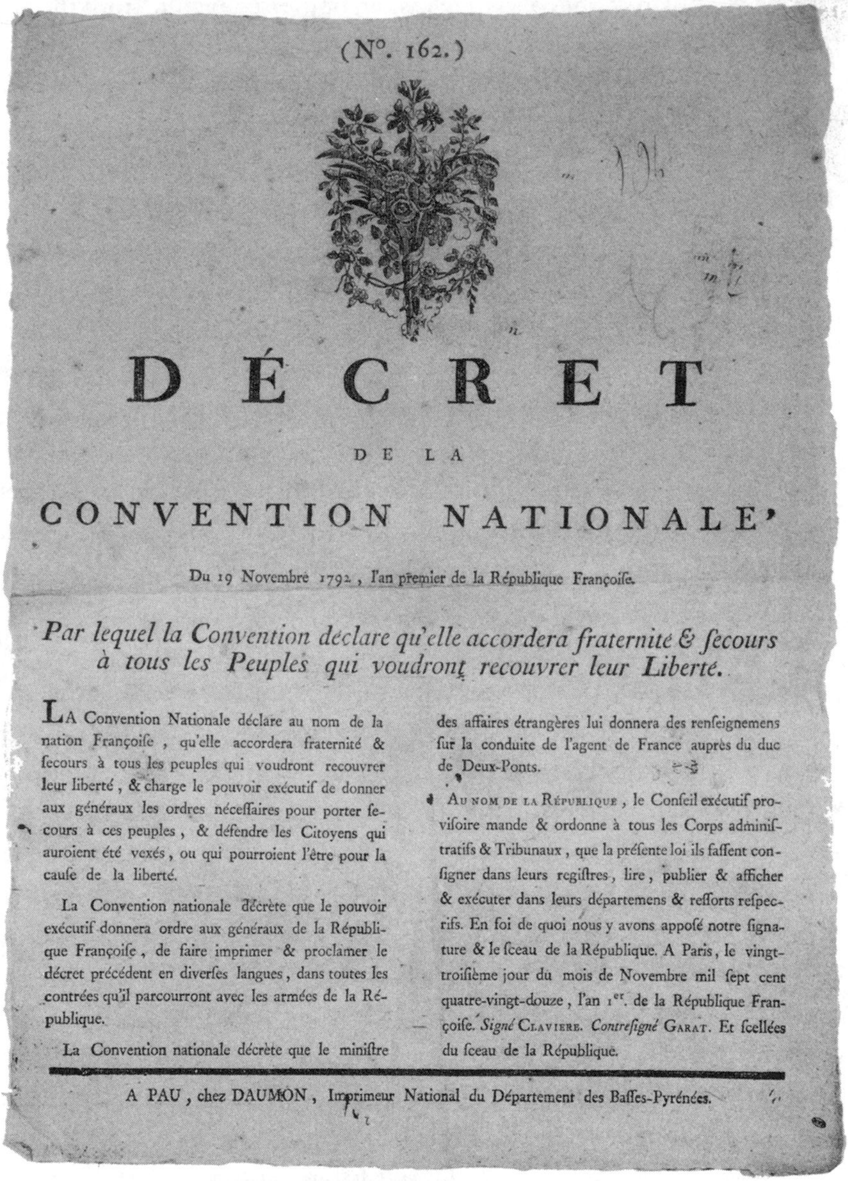

DÉCRET

DE LA

CONVENTION NATIONALE,

Du 19 Novembre 1792, l'an premier de la République Françoise.

Par lequel la Convention déclare qu'elle accordera fraternité & secours à tous les Peuples qui voudront recouvrer leur Liberté.

LA Convention Nationale déclare au nom de la nation Françoise, qu'elle accordera fraternité & secours à tous les peuples qui voudront recouvrer leur liberté, & charge le pouvoir exécutif de donner aux généraux les ordres néceffaires pour porter fe-cours à ces peuples, & défendre les Citoyens qui auroient été vexés, ou qui pourroient l'être pour la caufe de la liberté.

La Convention nationale décrète que le pouvoir exécutif donnera ordre aux généraux de la Républi-que Françoise, de faire imprimer & proclamer le décret précédent en diverfes langues, dans toutes les contrées qu'il parcourront avec les armées de la Ré-publique.

La Convention nationale décrète que le miniftre des affaires étrangères lui donnera des renfeignemens fur la conduite de l'agent de France auprès du duc de Deux-Ponts.

AU NOM DE LA RÉPUBLIQUE, le Confeil exécutif pro-vifoire mande & ordonne à tous les Corps adminif-tratifs & Tribunaux, que la préfente loi ils faffent con-figner dans leurs regiftres, lire, publier & afficher & exécuter dans leurs départemens & refforts refpec-tifs. En foi de quoi nous y avons appofé notre figna-ture & le fceau de la République. A Paris, le vingt-troifième jour du mois de Novembre mil fept cent quatre-vingt-douze, l'an 1er. de la République Fran-çoife. Signé CLAVIERE. Contrefigné GARAT. Et fcellées du fceau de la République.

A PAU, chez DAUMON, Imprimeur National du Département des Baffes-Pyrénées.

FIGURE 8.1

Decree from the French National Convention, 19 November 1792, extending
fraternity to all peoples who desire to be free

The National Convention issued a decree on 19 November 1792 in direct response to resistance encountered by the French army and its agents in the Belgian provinces. Foreign minister Pierre Lebrun dispatched three diplomats to the Belgian provinces to monitor the enforcement of the decrees, and the Convention sent four of its own agents to assure the provisioning of the occupying army. Dismayed, Dumouriez appealed to the Convention, recalling the cosmopolitan proclamations of 1789 and 1790. Now the French were forcing the Belgians into Jacobin clubs and pillaging property, he complained, "leaving their new brothers without physical or moral liberty."[17]

In December 1792, from his post on the French finance committee, Pierre-Joseph Cambon called for a declaration of war not only against despots but against anyone defending the Old Regime. Neighboring peoples who harbored priests and nobles were to be treated as enemies of France. Cambon criticized Dumouriez, in particular, "for announcing grand philosophical principles" but not enforcing the decrees. Cambon's plan to "declare revolutionary power in any country that we enter" prevailed over Dumouriez's objections.[18] It took several weeks for December decrees that threatened French intervention to reach the Belgian provinces. The National Convention had delayed the printing of the threatening decrees because of significant opposition in Paris. Influential deputies, including Jacques-Pierre Brissot, argued that the Belgians themselves should ratify the decrees. Belgian mail carriers refused to deliver post from France.

"When you entered the Low Countries to pull us out of slavery, we all followed you, but you have reversed our rights, laws, Religion, Estates, courts & privileges," a Belgian anonymously chastised the French occupying forces. "You have revolted an entire Nation by your despicable sacrilege."[19] The Provisional Representatives sent another delegation to Paris, this time to condemn the December 15 decree as destructive of Belgian sovereignty. As a free and sovereign people, they expected to choose their own path, elect their own representatives, and act according to their general will, without French interference. However, there is no evidence that the three men arrived in Paris to deliver their message. They seem to have decided their mission was futile and disappeared into villages en route.

While Dumouriez was fighting in the Low Countries, another wave of French troops marched south toward Savoy. Their route took them through the Swiss cantons, a strategically important gateway to southern Europe. The French monarchy had a history of meddling in the affairs of its mountainous neighbors, Geneva in particular. With French soldiers camped just outside their gates, Genevans appealed to the cantons of Bern and Zurich to lend military protection "against this unjust aggression."[20] The Genevan General Council posted placards on walls throughout the city calling residents to arms. As a last resort, the Council empowered an emissary, François Ivernois, to meet French general Anne-Pierre Montesquiou, stationed outside the city. Ivernois did not hesitate. He accosted General Montesquiou as he arrived back in camp at four in the morning. The exhausted general was more diplomatic than Ivernois had any right to expect, sending a courier to Paris to request written confirmation of French intentions to march around, not through, Geneva.

Troops from Bern and Zurich arrived in Geneva before the written assurances came from Paris. That worried the French representative in Geneva, who hastily withdrew to the safety of the French encampment. The Genevan council assured General Montesquiou of its peaceful intentions. He forwarded the Genevan assurances to the minister of foreign affairs in Paris, but cautioned the Genevans not to expect too much of his diplomatic intervention. He was, after all, "as a citizen of a free country, no more than an intermediary." The general warned, prophetically, that in the end Geneva would be no "freer or happier than France wanted it to be."[21] It turned out that he was Geneva's strongest advocate. Worse would follow.

In November 1792, Montesquiou received orders from Paris to invade Geneva with his army of four thousand men. Montesquiou refused, protesting that he would not "act like Louis XIV."[22] Diplomacy should have changed with the revolution, he argued. No more willing to accept direction from Paris than Dumouriez, in accord with his own ideas of the foreign policy befitting a revolutionary republic, Montesquiou personally negotiated a treaty with the Genevans. Stunned, the National Convention in Paris denounced the independent general's "shameful transaction." They sent General François Kellermann, himself accused of cowardice for not attacking the German city of Trier, to replace the insolent general.[23]

Exiles from the Genevan revolutions of 1782 and 1789 joined the fray as the Brabant revolutionaries had in the Belgian provinces. Some urged the French to invade and free their compatriots from aristocratic rule, while others protested against violations of Genevan sovereignty. Étienne Dumont, the Genevan revolutionary who had worked with Mirabeau, wrote from London to remind Kellermann of the long Genevan tradition of independence and republican governance. Brissot, who had witnessed the defeat of the first Genevan revolution, joined those exiles clamoring for French intervention. The Genevan Council also sent delegates to Paris, not trusting the power of a written memorandum. Was national sovereignty not a French revolutionary principle, they asked. Relying on Montesquiou and Ivernois as diplomatic conduits, the delegates relayed increasingly desperate news from their meetings with French deputies and ministers back to Geneva. Pro-French Genevan exiles had promised the French access to the sizable Genevan treasury as a reward for intervention. Lebrun, who had repeatedly denounced "the miserable politics" of the equivocating, aristocratic Genevans as a threat to "French liberty," was tempted.[24]

As a last resort, to preempt French intervention, the Genevan Council staged its own revolution in December 1792. After granting citizenship to 5,423 people, a decades-old demand, and declaring all residents of Geneva equal, the sitting council turned over power to provisional revolutionary committees. Placards posted in the streets proclaimed a pointed variation on the French "Liberty, Equality, Fraternity," reading "Liberty, Equality, and Independence." The Genevans left the French little reason to invade the revolutionary republic as they celebrated their third revolution in a decade. This time, in a marked departure from Old World diplomacy, the French congratulated them on the "happy changes."[25] A Genevan National Assembly of 120 members elected by universal male suffrage took their seats in an amphitheater with raised banks of seating constructed to resemble the Paris Convention. A bust of Jean-Jacques Rousseau sat on the president's table, and trees of liberty were planted around the city.

In 1793, the newly named Genevan ambassador to France assured his fellow citizens that their independence had never been more secure than in the hands of the French revolutionaries. The adjutant general of the French army of the Alps also conveyed a decree from the French resident, expressing his affection for the small republic. Over lunch in Geneva, General Kellermann told the newly elected Genevan assembly that the

French harbored no feelings other than those of friendship and fraternity toward the Genevans who had proved themselves worthy revolutionary allies. They need not be alarmed by perfunctory French troop movements in the vicinity. He did not inform them that he had written the French Convention, requesting permission to invade the city-state.

At stake in Paris was more than the defense of revolutionary France. The French were committed to coming to the aid of all peoples who "wished to recover their liberty." Against the backdrop of the Terror in France, boldly independent generals defined the revolutionary mission of the French abroad. By the end of 1793, the French were fighting not only the Austrians and the Prussians but Britain, Spain, and the Netherlands. The Committee of Public Safety in Paris proceeded to direct the wars by decrees, dispatching its representatives on mission south to Italy and east to Germany.

The Rhineland and the Italian Peninsula: "A true milk cow" and "the most fertile plains"

The French armies that invaded Germany in 1792 had been forced to retreat in 1793. Assessing blame, Merlin de Thionville, the new French commissioner serving with the Armies of the Rhine, scoffed that in 1792, generals had been seduced by "the promises of cosmopolitan universalism" and had naïvely assumed Germans would welcome them as liberators. Merlin took pride as a French revolutionary in being "a free republican, always free." He added in a significant proviso, "before extending liberty to others, I want to derive the benefits of the French constitution myself."[26] The next time, the French would use Prussian tactics against the Germans, seizing everything in the path of the armies and living off conquered territory. That strategy would not be limited to German territories.

Merlin was not alone in dividing his world into the revolutionary French and the "others." This assessment was a long way from the idealistic vision of a universal republic voiced in the National Assembly in 1789 or celebrated at the Festival of the Federation in 1790. German and then Italian resistance to the armed extension of the French Revolution over the next five years would widen that gap. Foreign intransigence would also bring other foreign agents around to Merlin's view of the French revolutionary mission. A determined Committee of Public Safety took over the direction of foreign policy in general and the wars in particular in the spring of 1793. It had been decided. Dissension did not work in wartime.

French armies invaded Germany again in August 1794, advancing through Trier and routing all of "the émigrés, monks, priests, nuns and all the other eminences" in their path. The French were welcomed, at least initially. In Koblenz, municipal authorities, bedecked "in full regalia" and led by the mayor, handed the French the keys to the city. The French accepted them. From the heights above the Moselle and Rhine rivers, the revolutionary army surveyed "the rich and abundant country." Below them the generals beheld "a true milk cow for the French Republic."[27] The mission to liberate the Germans would more than pay for itself. French soldiers inventoried goods left behind by aristocrats while their officers announced "the dawning of the beautiful day for which mankind has longed." They invited the Germans "to become our brothers and free men!"[28]

French armies advanced north along the Rhine to Cologne, where the city council met them. The council offered lodging and rations to the troops, asking the French in turn to respect their republican constitution, religion, and property. In a series of formal letters sent to Paris, they reminded their guests that the city of Cologne, free before the French arrived, expected to remain free after the French left. The French representative promised in his reply to respect Cologne's traditions and laws, but he also asked for an inventory of all public revenues and assets. He assured the city fathers, "Our most fervent wish is always to spare the people the calamities of war that tyrants inflict."[29]

The goodwill did not last the week. French soldiers plundered the rich collections of the municipal library of Cologne, and the council protested in outrage that the books and engravings belonged to the people of Cologne. The French representative reassured them that they had simply relocated their treasures to Paris, where revolutionary allies could enjoy them. Indirect diplomatic channels to Paris produced no response, so municipal officials from Cologne wrote the National Convention directly. "Who should a free man address," they asked "if not the representatives of the people who established the foundation of the reign of liberty?"[30] As a last resort, Cologne sent a deputation to present its protests in person to the Provisional Government established by the French military in Bonn, a government Cologne had not previously deigned to recognize. The French would not hear their protests.

French diplomats and generals alike professed surprise that the liberated German people had not risen up to join them in overthrowing "the monarchical oppressors and tyrants of the universe."[31] Instead, agents reported, Rhinelanders, like Belgians, had obstinately clung to their old ways. They even refused to accept their responsibility for feeding the French army, forcing the French to extract requisitions. Germans who could not appreciate liberty would be treated as a conquered enemy.

In December 1794, ignoring pessimistic reports from military and political agents, the French Committee of Public Safety opened treaty negotiations with Prussian King Frederick William II. In the Treaty of Basel, Prussia ceded the left bank of the Rhine to France, giving the republic, in the words of the Abbé Sieyès, "a virtually insurmountable barrier" to the east.[32] At last, observers predicted, revolutionary France, its boundaries set, would be able to rest. The secretary of the Prussian Royal Academy, André Riem, called on German princes to surrender to the inevitability of French rule. That was supposed to bring peace.[33]

After the fall of Jacobins Robespierre and Saint-Just, between July 1794 and October 1795, forty-eight members of the Convention rotated through the Committee of Public Safety. Representatives to the Army of the Pyrenees lobbied "to secure the limits of the Republic with our military triumphs" by taking possession of new territories "in the name of the people."[34] Pragmatic expansionists prevailed in the Committee, setting additional French armies in motion. A rebalanced Europe would be stable and peaceful, they promised, looking to the future to justify their strategy in the present.

The Directory, established in the fall of 1795 by moderate revolutionaries, inherited the war aims of the Thermidorian Committee of Public Safety. The directors pledged again to secure France's "natural frontiers." The Directory, though, had to contend just with the British at sea and the Austrians and Sardinians on land. The other enemies of the revolution had all been defeated. In the spring of 1796, the Directory sent another young general, Napoléon Bonaparte, into the field, this time to northern Italy. As before, the directors expected his army to live off aristocratic riches, church treasures, and the agricultural bounty of the land as it advanced down the Italian peninsula. "Yours will be an admirable operation from a financial point of view that in the end will upset just a few monks," the Directory promised.[35] Bonaparte needed few words of encouragement. He predicted the Italian campaign not only would pay for itself but would be the decisive battleground of the French Revolution.

After hard-won victories in the Piedmont in April 1796, Bonaparte led his forces onto the plains of Lombardy, forcing the Austrians to retreat before them. In his famous address to the "naked and starving" Army of Italy, he directed his army's attention "to the most fertile plains in the world. Rich provinces, the spectacular cities, all will be in your power. There you will find honor, glory, and riches."[36] Positioning two cannon at the bridge at Lodi, Bonaparte cut off the enemy, allowing French troops led by General Masséna to march into Milan in May. "Today, I see myself for the first time, not as a simple general, but as a man called to influence the fate of the people," Bonaparte declared.[37] Henceforth, he vowed, he would set his own course. When the Directory ordered him to share command with General Kellermann, Bonaparte adamantly refused. He sent wagonloads of loot from his Italian campaign to placate and silence the directors in Paris. Kellermann bowed before Bonaparte's bravado and lent him ten thousand soldiers to reinforce his army.

Bonaparte's rapid march through the Piedmont and Lombardy more than paid for itself. Bonaparte's soldiers collected Petrarch's manuscripts and paintings by Leonardo, Correggio, and Michelangelo to ship back to Paris. French civilian authorities in Italy complained to Bonaparte that sacking municipal treasures and imposing levies on the bourgeoisie would alienate their only supporters and drive rural landowners into the counter-revolution. Bonaparte ignored their concerns. When a small coterie of French soldiers who had remained behind to maintain order were found murdered and hanged from the newly planted trees of liberty, Bonaparte marched back and burned the closest village.

French troops marched out of Milan without the traditional army convoys of provisions. As long as the army kept moving, it could live off the land. Along their route, soldiers pillaged farms for sustenance, and military agents confiscated goods. Two deputies from the Piedmont traveled to Paris to appeal for leniency, but the Directory was too busy celebrating Bonaparte's victories to receive them. "It is not up to you to open a discussion of peace terms," Charles Delacroix, minister of foreign affairs, sneered.[38] The French would dictate terms to the Italians, including provisioning the invading French army. As the Directory speculated about the treasures that could be removed from churches and the contributions that could be exacted, it instructed Bonaparte to confiscate English ships in the port of Livorno and to make Parma pay for its resistance. In Rome the pope was instructed to pray for the success and prosperity of the French Republic.

French civilian agents who arrived in the newly conquered territories in the wake of Bonaparte's military campaign received little specific guidance from Paris on handling disgruntled residents, and what they received was too late to be relevant. The Directory acknowledged that it had "not yet arrived at any plan for regulating certain questions."[39] General Christophe Salicetti, a Corsican Jacobin, installed himself and his wife at the luxurious Palace Greppi in Milan. He proceeded to secure loans, print proclamations, and disseminate decrees to "revolutionize Italy." Many of the Italian revolutionaries who supported Salicetti, however, were unrepentant Jacobins, a political position decidedly out of favor with the French directors, who distrusted foreign revolutionaries and their allies.

The rhetoric of 1789 that had peaceful peoples coexisting in a revolutionary world must have seemed far away to Italians, especially those who counted themselves supporters of the revolution. Seven years into the revolution, they would have wondered what had happened to the principles of liberty and sovereignty. Had the war to extend the French Revolution by defeating despots and displacing aristocrats and clerics so depleted the resources of the republic that national survival of the republic competed as a revolutionary objective with liberation of oppressed peoples beyond French borders? Could these goals be reconciled? These were the questions yet to be answered in the increasingly problematic politics of Italy.

Victories on the battlefields of Italy allowed the Directory to declare an end to papal rule over Bologna and to establish the Cispadane Republic One and Indivisible. A constitution for the republic, ratified by a popular vote in April 1797, vested sovereignty in "the citizens as a whole" and guaranteed property rights. The republic lasted only three months before

Bonaparte incorporated its territories into his Cisalpine Republic, merging six Italian regions. Bonaparte himself appointed a directory for the new republic. Legislators who refused to ratify his constitution were replaced. Revolutionaries from clubs in Milan and refugees from Venice and Sardinia abolished the nobility and guilds, confiscated lands from the church, published a constitution, and organized an army.

Foreign minister Delacroix cautioned the Directory that republics established by revolutionaries and supported by an invading army would command little serious support in Italy. As he balanced the conflicting objectives of winning Italians over to the revolutionary cause and exploiting the wealth of Italy, Delacroix bluntly asserted, as Merlin had before him: "The interests of the [French] should be the deciding factor."[40] Under such conditions, the Directory's agents who had written off "the mass of the people" as "totally deprived of enlightenment and energy" wondered whether "it was possible or even advantageous for the French republic to republicanize Italy as the generals were trying to do."[41]

The French elections in March 1797 produced a moderate-royalist majority advocating negotiations with the two remaining adversaries, Austria and Britain, but Bonaparte was not ready to make peace. What was needed, he decided, was a coup. With the assistance of his emissary, three directors ousted their peace-seeking opponents from the Directory and the legislative chambers, leaving in place a government favorable to republican expansion. Bonaparte understood that it was the state of war that allowed the Directory to survive. Peace was not possible in that political context.

A series of coups followed in the Cisalpine Republic. When General Louis-Alexandre Berthier, a veteran of Rochambeau's army in America and Bonaparte's chief of staff, challenged the French Directory's strategy, he was replaced by General Guillaume Brune, a veteran of Dumouriez's army and a proponent of revolutionary imperialism. Brune refused to cooperate with the Directory's diplomats and openly allied with Italian Jacobins. The Directory responded by replacing the French commissioner to Italy, then recalled his replacement, and finally ordered Brune back to Paris.

In the Rhineland, General Lazare Hoche, another young upstart like Brune, pursued his own independent, but very different, policy. He refused to allow French agents, few of whom spoke German or understood local traditions, to impose a regime on the Germans who had proven themselves ill-fitted for a republic. On his own initiative, General Hoche slowed down the revolutionary march of the French, reinstating the old municipal governments throughout the Rhineland in March 1797. He won the support of the recalcitrant Germans by reducing their tax burdens and restoring property to the clergy. In September 1797, the Directory ordered Hoche to change course and ally not with German moderates but with the more radical revolutionaries in Rheinbach, Koblenz, Cologne, and Bonn to establish the Cisrhenian Republic.

"The intention of the French is clearly to turn all Europe into republics," Axel von Fersen, the Swedish noble who had fought with Rochambeau in America but betrayed Dumouriez's plans for Belgium to the Austrians, predicted.[42] The Cisrhenian Republic lasted less than a month and died in a flurry of decrees. The Directory recalled General Hoche. Before leaving, Hoche called the attention of his successor, General Augereau, to what he saw as the ultimate revolutionary goal: "founding a republic on the left bank of the Rhine to be a friend and ally of France."[43] That was, however, no longer the Directory's intention. Republics had proved to be poor military provisioners.

By 1797, The French army had exhausted the resources and political patience of the Rhineland. The left bank of the Rhine had been occupied and marched over for so long that it yielded little, despite continued pressure from agents dispatched to provision the army. These agents complained that they could not overcome the superstitions and prejudices of the German people mired in their "Gothic routines."[44] Annexation was the only option left to wring more resources out of the Germans.

Renouncing any expectation of self-government, François Rudler, an Alsatian sent by the Directory to the Rhineland, simply eliminated the Old Regime by administrative fiat. He issued 625 decrees in one day. In November 1797, to prepare Germany for annexation to France, he abolished the nobility, guaranteed freedom of religion, reorganized the schools, and proclaimed equality as the foundation of a new system of justice. Rudler ordered the French commissioners stationed in Aachen, Coblenz, Trier, and Mainz to produce German petitions in support of annexation. Although they gathered the requisite signatures, all of the "spontaneous" petitions bore the same phrases: gratitude for the abolition of feudalism and celebration of the French flag that flew from the towers of the former German empire. The commissioners hoped that Rudler would not notice that only fifteen percent of the eligible males had signed. He did. In his report to Minister of Justice Lambrechts in Paris, Rudler protested the recalcitrance of Prussian regions where Hoche had allowed old ways to persist.

German revolutionaries who dreamed of a Cisrhenian republic told a different story. "The ambition of a conquering Republic knows no limits," the German journalist A. G. F. Rebmann complained.[45] He had supported the first French military incursions into Germany, but he did not understand the French claim to natural borders. The Germans, more moral and philosophical than the French, needed to be allowed to make revolution on their own terms, these Cisrhenian revolutionaries argued. Why not "follow the lofty example" of the Cisalpine republic, municipal officials in Bonn asked.[46] What had happened, they asked, to the French revolutionary ideal of a Europe of sister republics? Had the universal republic been completely eclipsed as a goal? The answer ultimately was yes, but France would try one last time to win over its neighbors.

Ireland: "A capital opportunity"?

In October 1797, Bonaparte signed the Treaty of Campo Formio. The treaty did more than secure the natural border of the Rhine to protect the French Republic and procure the Rhineland to feed its armies; it altered the relationship of French civil and military authorities in the field. The Directory gave more authority to the military and took tighter control of its political agents abroad.

Britain loomed large across the Channel, with England as the yet unchallenged enemy and Ireland the unfulfilled republican hope. The French had been betting on an Irish revolution since 1791. That year, against great odds, under the leadership of thirty-year-old Theobald Wolfe Tone, Catholics and Protestants had come together as United Irishmen to fight at the very least against unfair taxation and the concentration of power in the hands of an elite, or even for Irish independence from England. Revolutionary pamphlets flooded Ireland over the next few years, some indigenous, others borrowed. It seemed to one Irish barrister that Thomas Paine's *Rights of Man* was "in every one's hands and in every one's mouth."[47] Calls to imitate the French were everywhere. The French watched as revolutionary momentum ebbed and flowed.

In 1794, the French Marine Ministry sent Anglican clergyman William Jackson as its agent to explore the revolutionary potential of Ireland. John Hurford Stone, English businessman, French revolutionary, and partner of Helen Maria Williams, introduced Jackson to radicals throughout England, including John Horne Tooke of the Society for Constitutional Information. On his own, Jackson befriended John Cockagne, a spy who had infiltrated the porous British radical network. Cockagne kept William Pitt informed of all of Jackson's activities. Among the Irish rebels, only the widely traveled Archibald Hamilton Rowan, a founding member of the Dublin Society of United Irishmen, took Jackson's proposals seriously. Rowan, however, was locked away in prison. But he was not out of contact with the revolution, it turned out. Rowan took full advantage of the generous terms of aristocratic imprisonment that provided for food to be sent from his home and for visitors and pamphlets from the United Irishmen to be received in his cell. It was there that Jackson and Cockagne met with Tone to discuss the overthrow of English rule in Ireland.

Tone reluctantly agreed to draft their declaration, a denunciation of the English and plea for Irish independence. Rowan took Tone's carefully phrased entreaty and embellished it with incendiary calls to arms, all under Tone's signature. Without Tone's knowledge or permission, Rowan passed Jackson a copy to send to an agent in Hamburg, who forwarded it to the French minister in the United Provinces, who in turn dispatched it to France. The packet was intercepted, as Tone could have predicted it would be, and Jackson was arrested and convicted. Jackson committed suicide in prison. Implicated in the treasonous scheme, Rowan convinced his jailor to allow him to visit his wife one last time before his probable hanging. She had prepared an escape. From their house, he slid down knotted bed sheets to the back garden, mounted a horse that was saddled and waiting, and rode to the Channel. There he found a boat and sailed to France. Intercepted by the French and imprisoned as a British spy, Rowan was freed by Robespierre.

The calamitous misadventures scared Tone but did little to set back French planning for an Irish revolution. Rowan, soon a regular at White's Hotel and a close friend of Mary Wollstonecraft, joined the chorus of exiles lobbying the Committee of Public Safety to attack Britain. Robespierre's death at the guillotine convinced Rowan to seek safety in a more tranquil republic. He arrived in Philadelphia on 4 July 1795; he survived the rough crossing, but his bear, raccoon, and opossum did not.[48] Tone was already there. The two Irish radicals kept their distance from American politics, which struck them as, if less bloody, at least as fractious as the French. American politics seemed excessively subject to the unsavory influence of money.

In 1796, Tone returned to Europe to join the committee of Irish expatriates in Paris, his voyage financed in part by James Monroe, the American minister in Paris. By December, decked out in a splendid French adjutant general's uniform, Tone sailed with fifteen thousand French troops aboard the eighty-gun flagship *Indomitable*. It was one of the largest naval expeditions of the French revolutionary wars. Had it not been for the weather, it might have succeeded. The French ships slipped past the British fleet into Bantry Bay on the southwest coast of Ireland, but there, in becalmed seas, the flagship was separated from the rest of the fleet. Once the winds finally picked up, they swirled to hurricane strength, chasing the French ships, commanded by indecisive and inexperienced naval officers, back to France. Eleven vessels and five thousand men had been lost without ever engaging the British, sinking any immediate hopes for a second invasion. The Directory might send some arms across the Channel, but it looked to the Irish themselves to beat back the English and "to proclaim the Independence of their island."[49]

Tone sat for two months on board the Dutch flagship *Vryheid* (Freedom), waiting for the wind to change and launch a Dutch invasion. Finally, Bonaparte himself summoned Tone to discuss invasion plans. "Our Government must destroy the English monarchy, or expect itself to be destroyed by those intriguing and enterprising islanders," Bonaparte wrote the French foreign minister in October 1797. "The present moment offers a capital opportunity," he added.[50] Bonaparte put General Kilmaine, an Irishman who had come to Paris as a student and then fought in the American Revolution, in charge of preparations. Irish émigrés in Paris relayed the excitement rocking Parisian theaters and cafés to the United Irish at home. Thomas Paine contributed funds and drew up plans for an amphibious assault by small gunboats. The United Irishmen waited intently for news of the embarkation. It never came. Before the invasion was launched, the Directory turned its attention to Egypt. The directors had decided that Bonaparte would confront the English in the Middle East, not Britain.

In May 1798, news reached Paris that the Irish revolution had begun on its own. Tone hurried to Paris from Le Havre. Lady Pamela Fitzgerald, a French exile married to the leader of the United Irishmen, sent reports through her sister about the best places for debarkation along the Irish coast. The United Irishmen boasted that half a million people had sworn an oath of allegiance to the revolutionary cause, most having taken up arms. The Earl Camden, Lord Lieutenant of Ireland, warned London that "even a small body of French will set the country ablaze."[51] The French, though, had neither the ships nor sailors ready to launch another cross-Channel invasion in response to the insurrection breaking out in Wexford. They had to resort to cutting down trees lining the avenues to the port to build the flat-bottom boats required to supplement the two vessels lent by the Dutch. Most disastrous of all, General Jean-Joseph Humbert impatiently sailed ahead of the other ships. His still unpaid, inexperienced sailors commanded few supplies. Humbert's soldiers did have pamphlets in hand as they marched ashore. "The moment of breaking your chains is arrived. Our triumphant troops are now flying to the extremities of the earth, to tear up the roots of the wealth and tyranny of our enemies," they announced to their fellow "citizens of the world."[52] Townspeople who saw French frigates sail into the harbor assumed they were British until they saw the blue and green uniforms. The Directory had ordered the ragged band to wait for the second fleet to arrive before engaging the English. Humbert, like so many other French generals before him, ignored his orders. Humbert's Army of Ireland met the English at Castlebar. The eight hundred French soldiers, supported by about six hundred Irish recruits, were vastly outnumbered. Defeat seemed certain until one wing of the English army inexplicably broke ranks and fled. Other English divisions followed, surprising Humbert with victory. The French established the Provisional Government of Connaught. At a victory ball, according to now well-established French custom, the general assessed the local citizens two thousand guineas to support his war. Ignoring the chorus of Irish complaints, Humbert marched on to the next battle. At Ballinamuck, Humbert confronted twenty thousand English troops commanded by General Cornwallis. Luck was not on their side this time. In the rout, the English captured and executed the Irish leaders.

Encouraged by the news of Humbert's first battle, French reinforcements, three thousand strong, once again with Tone in tow, sailed in September 1798 for Ireland. The British anticipated their arrival. Beset by a severe storm as they approached Ireland, few of the French ships made it past the British blockade and into the harbor. The French ships that broke through met news of Humbert's defeat at Ballinamuck conveyed by the local postmaster. Their pamphlets proclaimed in less exuberant tones: "Let not your friends be butchered unassisted; if they are doomed to fall in this glorious struggle, let their deaths be useful to your cause, and their bodies serve as footsteps to the temple of Irish Liberty."[53] The French sailed home, defeated for a third time. Revolutionary wars, it seemed, could not be won by decrees and proclamations alone.

Each side blamed the other. The Irish were disappointed that the French, who had long promised them aid, were unable to deliver it. The French military complained that they had been misled by the Irish exiles in Paris to expect revolutionary support from Protestants and Catholics alike. That had not materialized, either. After the failure of the third Irish invasion, French generals concluded that the Irish were not only oppressed by the English but engaged in their own civil war, Protestants vs. Catholics. The dispirited leaders of the United Irishmen countered that the French knew only how to subjugate revolutionaries, not to liberate them. French generals had proven that throughout Europe, they charged.

The evolving contradictions had consequences. The Irish were not the only revolutionary neighbors to ask whether the cosmopolitan French Revolution of 1789, embraced and energized by revolutionaries from every corner of the Atlantic for a decade, had finally been overwhelmed by calculations of French national interest. Others also wondered what had happened to the Enlightenment conviction that reason transcended national borders. Did the Irish experience prove that revolutionary France was just one more pragmatic European power calculating territorial gain?[54]

"Switzerland is fulli revolutionated" "in the Name of the French Republic"

The answer to the Irish question was not clear-cut. French revolution-ary strategy guided a foreign policy in transition under duress. Increasingly, decrees and dispatches were posted by French diplomats abroad critical of generals who disagreed with agents on the ground who disregarded committees and directors based in Paris. For the last five years of the eighteenth century, ever-changing revolutionary politics dictated the course of the war, while the levée en masse redirected the revolution in Paris. The military campaigns built one on another, pulling not only France but most of Europe into an unending war that ricocheted from one front to another, seemingly out of control.

Under the Directory, the French revolutionary armies had over-reached themselves, marching beyond the territory the French could rea-sonably govern. Historian Albert Sorel bluntly summed up the Directory's problematic strategy for revolutionary war: "Incapable of understanding the sentiments of a people who were not French, or a party that was not their own, a liberty they did not arbitrate, a justice they did not distribute, an independence that was not that of their own government, the Directory treated the emancipated republics as a conquered land."[55] That set off a downward spiral. The French commissioners in Italy, Germany, the Low Countries, and the Swiss cantons engendered distrust of their fundamental revolutionary principles as they established republics and then annexed territory to the French republic.

In January 1799, General Jean Championnet, still a confirmed Jacobin, took Naples. Overstepping the Directory's orders and defying its civil commissioner, he created the Parthenopean Republic. The Directory recalled Championnet to Paris, where they arrested him. The Parthenopean Republic survived longer than its creator, until June 1799.

New European republics bore little resemblance to the vision of earli-er revolutionaries. To propagate liberty, the French revolutionary armies lived off the land; the exploitation of scarce resources mobilized wide-spread resistance against France. The expense of provisioning the army alienated residents, even the most ardent revolutionaries. Escalating resis-tance to French rule in turn created an ever more pressing need for the

French army to maintain order, and that led to more substantial requisitions. The directors changed governments, constitutions, generals, and agents abroad, but did not find a way out of this spiraling escalation of the revolutionary war. Nowhere was that more obvious than in the Swiss cantons.

In 1793, François Barthélemy had worried about the fate of the Swiss cantons. He reminded French foreign minister François Deforgues, who had replaced Lebrun (arrested and accused of treason by the Jacobins), of the agreements negotiated by "your predecessor."[56] He also warned the diplomatic newcomer of the consequences of an independent diplomacy waged by overzealous and powerful French generals. French diplomats had credited Barthélemy's "attention and his conciliatory spirit" with keeping the peace in the independent-minded republic.[57] He had weathered the shifts in French foreign policy by interpreting orders from Paris loosely in the light of his experience and his own relations with the Swiss. He had also encouraged the Swiss to "speak honestly and tell me everything in their hearts," noting: "I responded with the same abandon."[58] That seemed to work as long as there was minimal interference from the military and few decrees or agents wended their way across the mountains from Paris.

Deforgues promised Barthélemy that France would respect the neutrality of Switzerland just as it did that of the United States. That guarantee held for almost five years, a relatively long time amid the chaos of the militarized revolutionary foreign policy. During that same period, the Belgian provinces would be taken back by Austria, reconquered and occupied by France, and finally annexed to the French Republic.

In 1797, revolutionaries in Basel renounced their traditional oath of loyalty to Bern, established a national assembly, proclaimed their independence, and planted a tree of liberty. Revolutionary crowds set fire to chateaux in the surrounding countryside, inspiring popular uprisings in the Valais, Fribourg, Solothurn, Schaffhouse, Zurich, Toggenbourg, Thurgovie, Gossau, Lucerne, Basel, Rheinthal, Sargans, Gaster, and Uznach. The sound of gunfire drew French troops commanded by General Ménard into the village of Thierrens in the Vaud. "You know that Switzerland is fulli revolutionated (new things, new terms)," Brillat Savarin, the French writer just returned to Europe in 1797 from three years in America, informed a friend in his less than perfect English.[59] The Directory recalled General Ménard, sending General Brune to the Vaud with instructions to rely on decrees rather than arms. No sooner had Brune issued his first proclamations and opened negotiations with Bern than he received orders from Paris to attack the city in retaliation for the incident at Thierrens. The confused general wrote Paris requesting more precise instructions. The Directory replied in March, sharply cautioning Brune against negotiations with oligarchs and ordering him to march on Bern without delay, to occupy the city, unseat the government, and raid its treasury. Brune, on his own initiative, assured the Swiss that they were all republican brothers. Frédéric-César de La Harpe, a Lausanne lawyer who had taken up residence in Paris, advised the French directors to be more explicit in their directions to the confused diplomats in the Swiss cantons.[60]

The Directory united the cantons on 22 March 1798, proclaiming the Helvetic Republic, One and Indivisible. Peter Ochs, the mayor of Basel and a leader of the "French party," drafted a unitary Swiss constitution that decreed the equality of all the residents of the republic and abolished the remaining legal distinctions between citizens. Directors in Paris revised Ochs's constitution and offered it to the newest republic. La Harpe, echoing earlier cautions from Germany and Italy, warned the French foreign minister, Charles Talleyrand, of the unrest brewing in the new Swiss republic. He blamed the generals and their soldiers who were not only taxing the Swiss to provision the Army of the Rhine "in the Name of the French Republic" but raping women and defiling the countryside.[61] Named the new Swiss president by the French, Ochs counseled his countryman against open defiance. A few weeks later, Ochs complained to La Harpe that despite his attempts to find common ground between the French and the Swiss, the cantons were rife with distrust and he felt personally threatened. The Directory, unsympathetic to his plight, forced Ochs to step down, replacing him with Philippe Secrétan, the onetime Brabant revolutionary who had returned to the Vaud.

The civil commissioner to the French army, Director Reubell's brother-in-law Rapinat, waded into the disorderly republic, declaring null and void any Swiss decrees that contradicted French orders. He closed Swiss clubs, imprisoned journalists, and replaced reluctant officials with men known to be French allies. Before long, the Directory recalled

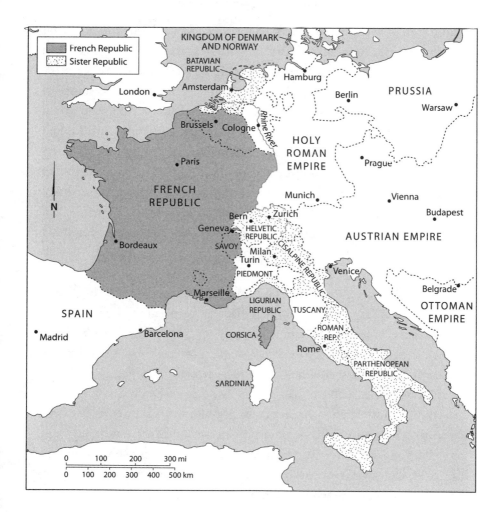

MAP 8.2
Europe, 1799. Map by Bill Nelson

Rapinat and overruled his draconian decrees. To the French request that La Harpe preside over his country, he warned them privately, "it is not in my character to be the creature of any foreign government."[62] At the same time, he cautioned Swiss revolutionaries that "without the assistance of the Grand Nation, the rights of the people and the name Helvetic would be obliterated."[63] After consultations in Paris, the Directory sent Rapinat back to Switzerland more determined than ever to establish his authority over the Swiss. More troubling to the Swiss than the implications of Rapinat's return was the French expectation that the Swiss field an army. Swiss delegations traveled to Paris reminding the French that Switzerland had been neutral for centuries. Talleyrand did not listen, ordering more than twenty thousand Swiss troops into battle against the Austrians in Italy.

In Geneva, the independent republic did not last, either. In January 1798, to put an end to the continual disputes between the French agents and the government of the city-state, the Directory pulled the offending French deputation out of the city, but also closed off routes to foreign trade. French soldiers remained behind to patrol the streets.

One morning, the troops awoke to find that the French flag flying above the empty French resident's house had been stained black. The Genevan city council immediately promised to hoist a new flag and offered a reward for the apprehension of the perpetrator. Five thousand contrite Genevan citizens processed to the French residence to apologize, hoping to stave off French retaliation. It came anyway. Two months later, on behalf of the Directory, the French resident presented the Genevan council with a Treaty to Reunite the Republic of Geneva to the French Republic. The Genevan council appointed an extraordinary commission of 130 members to respond to the French treaty, and the stalling began. The commission read the decree aloud at its first meeting. Discussion spilled over to a second and third meeting before the exasperated French resident ordered them to meet with him. With a stern face and "an extreme coldness," he informed the Genevans that "it was time to finish this affair."[64] They were to have their response to the French treaty to him by noon. Such an important decision could not be rushed, they replied, listing all the Genevan committees and councils that still had to be consulted. The French resident angrily and unilaterally announced the unification of

Geneva to France. He called the councilors into his office to reflect on their options, under the surveillance of French troops. Four meetings later, the Geneva commission complained in a letter to Paris that the resident had acted without appropriate powers. The resident replied that his instructions from Paris were in the mail. At a tenth meeting, he ordered them to address him directly and to stop sending complaints to Paris. As the Genevan council met to consider whether to extend the term of the extraordinary commission, sixteen hundred French troops entered the city by three different gates and occupied the city hall atop the hill. While soldiers milled outside the door, the commission declared the end of Genevan independence. Geneva would be a French department, the Léman. No one was happy.

Swiss deputations wrote the French Directory of the suffering of the common people in their cantons as the French continued to wage war, but the Directory was in no position to lend material or moral assistance to anyone. Local officials complained of "the numerous troops of unclothed and starving people who line the roads of Switzerland. . . . Whole families are emigrating, but where to go? Misery reigns everywhere. Like a contagious illness, the troubles grow every day."[65] Who would have thought a decade earlier, in 1789, when the Genevans and the French each revolted and threw off the tyrants of the Old Regime, or even a few years later in 1793, when Robespierre paid homage to the Americans and the Swiss as the two freest republics, that it would have come to this, revolution at the point of a bayonet. Chosen to represent Basel to the French Consulat, the author of the constitution of the ill-fated Helvetic Republic listened as Bonaparte announced in Paris, "Mr. Ochs, the Revolution is done."[66]

"Two thousand leaders that must be removed": The Caribbean Epilogue to an Armed Revolution

But it was not done. In 1798, the Directory sent General Gabriel-Marie-Théodore-Joseph Hédouville to promulgate French legislation across the Atlantic in the colony of Saint-Domingue. Vested with civilian authority, Hédouville arrived to find a Caribbean ravaged by war. The British, who had deplored the French strategy of freeing the enslaved as "unprecedented . . . unjustifiable and barbarous," ultimately followed the

French practice of recruiting slaves to reinforce their dwindling forces in the Caribbean.[67] Death from disease, especially yellow fever, had taken three out of every five British soldiers. Six thousand black soldiers who had been promised their freedom joined the British.

Hédouville's mission went terribly wrong. To pacify the colony in anticipation of the arrival of fresh French troops, he tried to neutralize two military leaders—Toussaint Louverture, commander of the freed slaves, and André Rigaud, at the head of legions of free people of color—by setting them against each other. That strategy failed. While Hédouville won over Rigaud, Louverture, on his own, negotiated the terms of a British surrender and retreat from Saint-Domingue. Like the British, Louverture knew the limits of the power of Paris in the Caribbean in 1798.

Hédouville was no more successful in reestablishing order on the plantations of Saint-Domingue. His orders to the former slaves to sign three- to five-year contracts with their masters reverberated with echoes of slavery. Black soldiers returning from years of military service, some as officers with experience commanding their former masters, resisted the return to plantation labor. Hédouville tried to make an example of a high-ranking black officer. The officer, Moïse, called on Louverture for assistance. Together, Moïse and Louverture's troops surrounded Le Cap, driving the agent of the French Directory and his accomplices onto ships to sail back to France. Julien Raimond, the one remaining commissioner from the time of Sonthonax and a longtime proponent of rights for free people of color, and Jean-Baptiste Belley, a member of the tricolor delegation that had secured emancipation in 1794, left for France with Hédouville.

The civil war between Louverture and Rigaud that Hédouville hoped to instigate broke out after he left. The unrest in the French colony suited France's enemies, who exploited it to gain trading rights. Louverture, afraid that the return of French forces to support Rigaud would doom emancipation for the slaves, initiated negotiations with the British and the Americans to normalize their formerly clandestine commercial trade. The British and the Americans also agreed secretly to aid Louverture's military efforts. An independent Saint-Domingue, they assumed, would weaken France by cutting it off from the profits of its colonial plantations, and would reduce the possibility of the rumored French attack on Jamaica.

Louverture wrote to the Directory to secure official support of his command, sending his letter with a white officer, Colonel Vincent. Before Vincent arrived in Paris, Bonaparte had felled the Directory. He had no intention of responding directly to the black leader. Instead, Bonaparte sent a commission of three, including Vincent and Julien Raimond, carrying proclamations that exempted the colony from French legislation and that established a new set of "special laws." They arrived in May 1800 bearing assurances from Bonaparte that he would not violate their freedom, and army flags on which had been sewn an acknowledgment that liberty came from France.

Louverture had not waited for approval from Paris to solidify his authority over the island. He ordered Moïse into battle against the Spanish to enforce the terms of the Treaty of Basel and called for electoral assemblies to form a new assembly to write a constitution for the island. In their minds, "the Revolution had violently reversed all that constituted the old administration of the island of Saint-Domingue."[68] Vincent returned to France again, this time with the new constitution confirming the abolition of slavery and naming Louverture governor for life.[69]

Bonaparte responded with military force. He negotiated for British and American support to reimpose slavery in the colony and to restore the slave trade. They obliged, thus freeing the French to turn their military might on the colony. Bonaparte mobilized twenty thousand troops under his brother-in-law, General Victor-Emmanuel Leclerc, a veteran of battles on the Rhine, in Italy, and in Ireland, to take possession of the ports, fight against the black generals, and disarm the black population of the once prosperous colony. The naval fleet carried the largest army yet to cross the Atlantic. Peace in Europe, Bonaparte informed Louverture, had allowed him to direct his full attention to Saint-Domingue.[70]

Leclerc arrived in Le Cap in February 1802. Refused permission to land, he seized it "with indignation," only to discover that the port had been evacuated and burned to the ground.[71] His proclamation to the residents of Saint-Domingue, printed in two columns, one French, one Creole, promised that the French would guarantee liberty for the blacks. Bonaparte urged the citizens of Saint-Domingue to join their "friends and their brothers in Europe," all of whom had "embraced the French and promised them peace and friendship."[72]

Louverture tried to warn military leaders in the west and the south that the French had come to reimpose slavery, but all of his dispatches were intercepted by forces in league with the French. The defection of key black leaders finally forced Louverture to negotiate. When he arrived to discuss terms with the French, they arrested him. Even without Louverture, word of the French decree reinstituting slavery in Guadeloupe rallied resistance in Saint-Domingue. One of Louverture's allies who had defected to the French told a general that the insurrections were spreading like fire throughout the colony. They were not, as the French wanted to believe, just the work of brigands; instead, he warned, "the danger is in the general opinion of the blacks" aroused by the decrees.[73] General Donatien-Marie-Joseph Rochambeau, experienced in American combat as an aide to his father, complained to Paris that despite executing all blacks he suspected of organizing the insurrections, he could not quell the incessant talk of killing whites and burning their cities. Leclerc realized that even though they had deported Louverture, the French still confronted "two thousand leaders that must be removed."[74] Leclerc appealed to Bonaparte not to do anything that even hinted of the reintroduction of the slave trade in Saint-Domingue, because "under those conditions, Citoyen Consul, the moral force that I have established here will be destroyed, and I will be able to do nothing by persuasion, and I do not have sufficient force at my command."[75] Leclerc sent an officer back to Paris to describe in person the appalling conditions in the colony.

French officers in the Caribbean continued to report back to Paris, as they had from Koblenz and Milan, in letters bemoaning the difficulty of their mission. The resistance in Saint-Domingue was unlike anything the French generals had met before. Even as French soldiers proclaimed to the blacks that they were all friends and brothers, the blacks kept firing at them. In Europe or America, their enemies were the troops raised by the British, Austrians, and Prussians. But for the black soldiers, defeat of the revolution in Saint-Domingue meant slavery or death. Bonaparte's expeditionary force was overwhelmed by the combined forces of the mulattoes and blacks united under Jean Jacques Dessalines. Rochambeau capitulated in November 1803. Dessalines promulgated a Declaration of Independence of Haiti from France on 1 January 1804.

At the end of a chapter that began with the revolutionary French Republic declaring war on emperors, Haitian revolutionaries secured their independence by defeating the armies of the soon to be crowned emperor of the French. Led by Jefferson, the Americans established a total quarantine of Haiti.[76] They were intent on limiting the revolution that threatened to return to their shores. The American leaders, like the French, were ready to declare an end to the revolutionary era.

NINE

Revolutionaries between Nations: "Abroad in the world"

Revolutionaries on both sides of the Atlantic heard the "universal cry of liberty" as governments changed all around them. By the end of the eighteenth century, the tumultuous course of the French Revolution and the events leading to the establishment of an independent Haiti governed by men of color had convinced many Americans of the uniqueness of their own political moderation. Revolutionary regimes solidified and returning revolutionaries found themselves homeless, adrift between the new nations.

Benjamin Franklin returned to America from France in 1785. Even the British ships docked at the wharfs of Philadelphia saluted the homeward-bound American diplomat. Philadelphians conveyed Franklin to the three-and-a-half-story brick house on Market Street that he had built twenty years earlier but rarely occupied. Much had changed in the city and its people while he was abroad in Paris, but he would have recognized the landmark taverns and statehouse. Settled back into his library surrounded by his books and scientific inventions, Franklin looked forward, with an optimism characteristic not just of him but of his era, to the day when "not only the love of liberty, but a thorough knowledge of the rights of man, may pervade all Nations of the Earth." A traveling philosopher would then be able to "set his Foot anywhere on its Surface, and say, 'This is my Country.' "[1] A decade lived in Europe between revolutions had buoyed Franklin's enlightened faith that the days of universal citizenship were not far off. How wrong he was.

But in 1789, the year of the Brabant and French revolutions, and a year before his death, Franklin expounded on his expectation that the liberty and rights of man launched in America would continue their journey around the Atlantic world. He was not alone in celebrating the diffusion of revolution across the Atlantic. From Virginia, Thomas Jefferson wrote

Thomas Paine in Paris in praise of the courage of the bold French revolutionaries, who had demonstrated a "coolness, wisdom, and resolution to set fire to the four corners of the kingdom and to perish with it themselves, rather than to relinquish an iota from their plan of a total change of government."[2] Even the Federalist-leaning *Gazette of the United States* proclaimed in capital letters: "THE ERA OF FREEDOM—OF UNIVERSAL LIBERTY! She first broke her chains in the Western world, and having fixed her temple in our favored country, she is spreading her salutary reign throughout the world. Europe bows to her sway."[3]

Stories from revolutionary France actually garnered more inches in American newspapers than domestic politics. The *Pennsylvania Mercury*, for example, reprinted Robespierre's 1789 address to the National Assembly on liberty of the press, telling their readers that the French revolutionary leader believed freedom of the press to be more useful to a republic than a militia.[4] Americans avidly followed the course of the French Revolution, initially at least, because the French seemed to be echoing the Americans. That exaltation did not last.

On one side of the Atlantic, violence spilled onto the streets of Paris, on the other, founding fathers framed a constitution in Philadelphia, or so it seemed to Americans in the last decade of the eighteenth century. Alexander Hamilton feared that the example of France might unhinge "the orderly principles of the People of this country" and take America, too, to "the threshold of disorganization and anarchy."[5] Rancorous debates in the halls of Philadelphia that might otherwise have struck Americans as unnecessarily acrimonious appeared civil when compared in the press to massacres on the Champs de Mars. Distinctions drawn on national lines played to the public imagination, increasing the separation already defined by an ocean. "In America no barbarities were perpetrated—no men's heads were struck upon poles—no ladies bodies mangled," the once sympathetic *Gazette of the United States* commented in January 1793, adding for good measure: "The Americans did not, at discretion, harass, murder, or plunder the clergy—nor roast their generals unjustly alive."[6] All the Americans did, it seemed, was argue, and that made them exemplary.

If Parisian Jacobins sent their political enemies to the guillotine, in their colonies, violence had escaped all bounds, with slaves disgorging their masters. And that threat was closer to home. Tales recounted by "the unfortunate colonists from Saint Domingue," as L. E. Moreau de Saint Méry called them, stoked the already active rumor mills in the United States. The deputy from Martinique to the French National Assembly had himself escaped the guillotine before emigrating to Philadelphia. Arriving on the shores of the United States, "the land of liberty," in waves in 1793, 1798, and 1804, revolutionary exiles from the Caribbean evoked all the danger of revolution run radical.[7] These distinctions stoked an American nationalism rooted in the founding myths of the primeval American wilderness far removed from the corruption of the luxuriant old world.

The fragment of the Bastille displayed in the window of Moreau de Saint Méry's Philadelphia bookstore attracted crowds. They came to gawk, not to applaud. Benjamin Franklin's grandson Benjamin Franklin Bache, who operated a bookstore in the same Philadelphia neighborhood, knew that all too well. With the printing equipment he had inherited from his grandfather, Bache edited the *Aurora and General Advertiser*. No longer an admirer of all things revolutionary, the *Gazette of the United States* attacked Bache for his pro-French journalism as "the most infamous of the Jacobins . . . Printer to the French Director, Distributor General of the principles of Insurrection, Anarchy and Confusion, the greatest of fools, and the most stubborn sans-culotte in the United States."[8] A little more than a decade after Benjamin Franklin had returned from France so full of optimism, his grandson was arrested, charged with libel for his criticism of President Adams, and accused of exciting sedition against the United States.

"He that is not for us is against us": Revolutionary Justice

In *Common Sense*, the pamphlet that helped ignite revolution in 1776, Thomas Paine, looking forward, had envisioned an America that would "receive the fugitive, and prepare in time an asylum for mankind."[9] Quite the opposite happened. In the 1790s, the British editor of the Philadelphia-published *Porcupine's Gazette*, William Cobbett, spurred a campaign against Paine and his fellow "mongrel cosmopolites."[10] Revolutionary itinerants, especially those who had supported the French, were easily cast as radical foreigners. Traveling abroad aroused suspicion.

Returning to America in 1802, Paine was not heartily welcomed as Franklin had been a decade earlier. In a public letter addressed to the

American people, Paine wrote that he was happy at last to be returning "to the country in whose dangers I bore my share, and to whose greatness I contributed my part." He had expected to come back sooner, he explained, but could not leave France in the midst of its revolution, whose principles "were copied from America." What he wrote next, though, sealed his fate in America. "While I beheld with pleasure the dawn of liberty rising in Europe," he added, "I saw, with regret, the lustre of it fading in America."[11] He understood the gap separating the two revolutions differently than did Hamilton. He called American liberty into question.

That Thomas Paine had been named a French citizen in 1792 and elected to the National Convention just confirmed Cobbett's allegation of dangerous cosmopolitanism. Coupled with political moderation, cosmopolitanism had already gotten Paine into trouble in France. Threatened with the guillotine, from his prison cell, Paine appealed to George Washington for help. The American president refused to interfere in French politics to save the British exile. Ultimately released by the French, Paine very publicly held Washington responsible for his brush with death. In response to Paine's charges, a number of American newspapers called on their readers to choose between Washington and "that degenerate moral and political monster, Tom Paine." The editor of the *Virginia Gazette* pictured Paine in revolutionary Paris, allegedly "displayed during his state of intoxication in a cage along with a Bear and a Monkey."[12]

Ignoring the scandalous press, Thomas Jefferson invited his old friend to return home to America. French diplomat Louis Otto reported that despite the invitation, Paine had to wait for eight months in port before he could find an American captain willing to transport him across the Atlantic.[13] As described by a witness to Paine's arrival in Baltimore in 1802, the American revolutionary credited with launching the War for Independence was denied admittance to one inn after another. "In this dilemma Tom was kept wandering thro the town for some time."[14] Equally devastating, Paine, who had vested his hopes in the democratic franchise, was denied the right to vote in New York in 1806. Turned away from the polling station, he was admonished by the clerk, "You are not an American."[15] Although he settled on a farm in New York, Paine did not feel at home in a more religious and censoring America but rather felt himself cast "once more abroad in the world."[16]

Thomas Paine was not alone. Many revolutionary heroes seeking asylum were also rebuffed and cast adrift at the end of the last decade of the eighteenth century. Thaddeus Kościuszko, the acclaimed Polish soldier who had engineered some of America's most significant victories in the Revolutionary War before leading two revolutions for Polish independence, had turned down an invitation to join a Polish Legion fighting in Italy upon his release from a Russian jail in 1796. Suffering from wounds that had festered in prison, Kościuszko hoped instead to retire from politics in America. As he set sail from Bristol, a military band serenaded his ship with a medley of "martial airs from every land where the soldier's banner had waved."[17] The band played for some time.

Crowds in Philadelphia welcomed the "illustrious defender of the Rights of Man, the unfortunate General Kosciuszko," unhitching the horses from his carriage that was then "drawn by citizens" themselves through the streets of Philadelphia, according to Benjamin Franklin Bache's *Aurora General Advertiser*.[18] "Here was the hero on whom "the eye of despotism cast its malignant glances," other papers reported.[19] "I look upon America as my second country," Kościuszko responded to the Philadelphians' tribute.[20]

A few weeks after Kościuszko's arrival, the *Gazette of the United States* warned its readers that the Polish general was in league with the French. The Federalist paper cited as evidence a roster of visitors to his rented rooms in a small boarding house on Third Street in Philadelphia. In the *Porcupine's Gazette*, William Cobbett portrayed Kościuszko as a mercenary who had returned to the United States solely to claim recompense for his wartime services to the country. Was not liberty truly its own reward, Cobbett asked.[21] Kościsuzko was so demoralized by the partisan attacks that he left America under cover of darkness to return to Europe.

Even as the *Gazette of the United States* reminded Americans in their postrevolutionary republic that "he that is not for us is against us," they prided themselves on their civility.[22] Cobbett, the English reformer turned counterrevolutionary, drew a contrast between their free press and court-driven justice and the mob violence that riddled the waning years of the French Revolution. In America, itinerant cosmopolitans who dared to disparage national leaders might be sent packing, but in

France they frequently found themselves carted away by tumbrel to the guillotine.

That was the fate of some other traveling revolutionaries. When he lived in England in the decade between the American and the French revolutions, Jacques-Pierre Brissot had dreamed of assembling the Confédération universelle des amis de la liberté et de la verité (Universal confederation of the friends of liberty and the truth). In November 1792, he was denounced in France by two journalists with whom he disagreed, the Jacobin Louise de Kéralio and her husband and fellow journalist François Robert. Placed under house arrest, Brissot escaped but was recognized in the provinces. He was guillotined as a counterrevolutionary on 31 October 1793. The marquis de Condorcet, accused as a traitor to France and driven into hiding for half a year, was also arrested as he fled Paris; he died in prison in 1794.

In 1795, two years after Anacharsis Cloots had foreseen the future of "the Republic one and universal," where "factions would be crushed by the weight of universal reason," he, too, was charged with treason by French Jacobins.[23] Unlike Thomas Paine, his cellmate in the Luxembourg Prison, Cloots died at the guillotine. Until the end, Cloots held to his belief in the universalism of revolutionary nationalism. As he mounted the scaffold, Cloots cried out, "Hurrah for the fraternity of nations! Long live the Republic of the world!"[24] The decree of revolutionary year II had purged foreigners, including Cloots and Paine, from the National Convention. The revolutionary French defined citizenship by political beliefs, not birthplace. Cloots and Paine did not hold the requisite beliefs and were cast out as foreigners.[25]

The reach of French exclusionary justice extended across the Atlantic to the colonies in the Caribbean. The revolutionary leader Toussaint Louverture, arrested by General Leclerc in 1801, was forced to board a ship ironically named Le Héros bound for France. The hero of Saint-Domingue was imprisoned by Bonaparte in the Jura Mountains. He died there in 1803, a year before Haiti won its independence.

Few of the pamphleteers, journal writers, editors, or even diplomats who strayed from their homelands ever fit comfortably back into the politics they had left behind. Itinerants in a revolutionary age, they had ventured abroad, as did Elkanah Watson, "biting my lips with astonishment, exclaiming in silence . . . what a contrast in customs & manners among

Nations."[26] Contemplating comparisons, a few returned counterrevolutionaries, but more came home more committed revolutionaries than before, unable to settle down at home or abroad. Franklin was unusual in his ability to engineer elegant compromises in the Constitutional Convention soon after his return to Philadelphia. He would be remembered as a founding father. Most of the other revolutionary travelers found themselves out of step with national politics. Everything had changed so dramatically at the end of the eighteenth century.

The Irish revolutionary Wolfe Tone, after sailing with French troops, did return home. He died in Provost's Prison in Dublin in 1798. Louis Otto, the French diplomat who had married América Francès de Crèvecoeur, also returned home. He was arrested twice by the French when he arrived in Paris. When time restored his diplomatic reputation, he served out the revolution abroad in Europe. Offered a post in America, Otto claimed that his wife's health prevented their transatlantic crossing. They did not return to France, either.

Thomas Jefferson's secretary, William Short, left Paris in the last years of the French Revolution to return home to Virginia. He assured Jefferson that he had given up all hope of ever settling in a home together with his French lover, the duchesse de la Rochefoucauld. She had survived the revolution in France and joined her estates to those of a French marquis in a second marriage of convenience. Short visited her en route to Russia, but returned to America alone and politically adrift.

The Barlows, who stayed in Paris longer than most other expatriates, finally sailed home together to America, as Ruth had always wanted, but only for a brief respite. In 1811, Joel Barlow accepted an appointment as minister to France to negotiate a treaty with Bonaparte. Ruth accompanied Joel to Paris, where she once again waited as he traveled alone to central Europe. He died in Poland of consumption; it took two weeks for the news to reach Ruth in Paris and another three months for word to get back to America. She returned home, this time alone, to a country that seemed to resemble more her husband's pessimistic portrait of a chaotic democracy where "ye live united, or divided die" than the universal republicanism Joel Barlow had idealized when they lived in France.[27]

The transformation of the revolutionary decades that displaced so many travelers was illustrated by Washington Irving's "Rip Van Winkle," the well-known American story of a "simple, good-natured fellow" of Dutch descent who falls asleep in the Catskill Mountains of New York in the 1770s. Rip travels through time, not space. When he awakens twenty years later, everything has changed. Described from Irving's postrevolutionary perspective, Rip van Winkle's world has changed as drastically as the societies visited by other revolutionary time travelers, such as those sent by Louis Sebastien Mercier and Betje Wolff into the year 2440. Rip van Winkle awakens after the revolution to discover that even the sign above the inn "was singularly metamorphosed. The red coat was changed for one of blue and buff, a sword was stuck in the hand instead of a scepter, the head was decorated with a cocked hat, and underneath was painted in large characters, GENERAL WASHINGTON."[28]

Two centuries later, in 1968, Martin Luther King, in his last Sunday sermon, delivered in the National Cathedral in Washington, D.C., reminded his listeners of Rip van Winkle standing under this transformed sign. In this new society, Rip "was completely lost. He knew not who he was," King preached, in slow sonorous tones. Such was the power of a revolution. The whole world had changed while Rip van Winkle slept. As King spun out the allegory for his time, "All too many people find themselves living amid a great period of social change, and yet they fail to develop the new attitudes, the new mental responses that the situation demands." The great civil rights leader called on his people, all of his people, to remain awake, not to "sleep through a revolution."[29]

The eighteenth-century revolutionaries who traveled across mountains, oceans, and national borders were wide awake. It was the others, their neighbors, who slept, at home. Transformed by the revolutions they witnessed and joined, itinerants who tried to return home did not find the familiar landmarks as Rip did. Their neighbors, some of whom slept—as, King reminded us, people do during a revolution—failed to recognize the travelers or to countenance their beliefs.

This revolutionary dislocation at the end of the eighteenth century was perhaps most dramatically symbolized by John Frederick, son of Naimbanna, the Temne king. Influenced by the black loyalists settling along his west African coast, Naimbanna sent his three sons away to be educated, one to France, one to England, and the other to Turkey to study with Muslim clerics. The twenty-three-year-old John

Frederick traveled to England on the *Lapwing* with Anna Falconbridge in September 1791.

Onboard ship, Falconbridge taught the prince to read; in England, he was tutored by teachers chosen by John Thornton of the Sierra Leone Company and the abolitionist Granville Sharp. They guided him in journal writing so he could record his travels, both physical and moral, as he converted to Christianity and monogamy.[30] John Frederick recorded his visit to hear debate in the House of Commons on the slave trade. He told of his self-imposed restraint when confronted by a slave trader. Although he had learned the principles of Christian forgiveness, he could not "forgive the man who takes away the character of the people of my country," he noted in his journal.[31] Escorted a few weeks later by his guides to the top of Saint Paul's Cathedral, so close to the wrathful English God, he wrote, he was scared, but he hid his fear from his English companions. He was careful not to appear too much in awe of English institutions and practices. He did not want to reinforce popular English contempt for Africa and its customs. As for many of the other journal writers in this revolutionary era, his path abroad was a solitary one. John Frederick struggled to hold onto his African heritage while adopting European ways.

On news of his father's death in 1793, John Frederick, now a devout Protestant, boarded a ship intent on bringing his newfound Christianity back to Africa, fulfilling the hopes of his English sponsors. En route from Europe to Africa, confined by storms to a cabin washed over by waves, the prince came down with a fever. As he lay delirious in his waterlogged cabin, his English shipmates concluded that John Frederick had fallen ill because he had been away too long from the African climate. His body had lost its ability to tolerate the tropical heat. John Frederick, the son of a Temne chief, had adapted to Europe too completely to return to Africa. Ever a foreigner in England, he had been rendered by travel an outsider in Sierra Leone, too. The man who was to be the next king of the Temne people expired the day after his return to Sierra Leone from England. The colony's Anglican minister performed the funeral services, but John Frederick was buried according "to the manner of the country."[32]

Only the rare itinerants could shift identities seamlessly as they moved from place to place. The articulate former slave Equiano was among the most agile, identifying himself in his narrative as both an African and an

Englishman. Another writer of memoirs, Dutch Patriot Gerrit Paape, returned home in the company of the French after a decade abroad and secured appointment as a civil servant in the Dutch ministry of education. His use of satire against all manner of enemies and allies abroad had redounded to his favor. It could just as easily have gone the other way. When shifting politics finally stabilized, itinerants were among those least able to conform.

Cosmopolitanism on the Atlantic, "the world's highway"

Nationalism marginalized many of these itinerants who had incorporated ideas and ideals from various nations and cultures. Even those revolutionary travelers who sought to "find a peaceful retirement [in America] from the tempest which agitates Europe," Noah Webster charged, could not secure a place in a nation that was convinced that it "alone seems to be reserved by Heaven as the sequestered region.[33] Still fewer travelers lasted out the decade in Paris. In France, revolutionary fraternity implied submission to the "grande nation."[34]

Richard Price, the articulate British supporter of the American and Dutch Patriot revolutions, saw nationalism as a stage to be transcended. While acknowledging "the love of our country" as "certainly a noble passion," he hoped that it would "give way to a more extensive interest," promoting "universal benevolence." In his future world, "every man would consider every other man as his brother, and all the animosity that now takes place among contending nations would be abolished."[35]

Similarly, in September 1791, a month after the slave revolt in Saint-Domingue, a white abolitionist, Jacques-Pierre Brissot's friend Claude Miliscent had compared exclusive nationalism with his own cosmopolitan ideal. In the newspaper that he edited in Saint-Domingue, *Le Creuset*, Miliscent complained that it was unnatural to "prefer one people over another." For him, "The true philosopher was a cosmopolitan, the friend of all men from whatever country." In the century of the Enlightenment, it should have been clear to his readers that "nationalism leads to egoism and to slavery."[36] Cosmopolitanism, in contrast, favored the universal liberty that crossed not only national borders but also racial divides. It embraced others.

This cosmopolitanism was very much a part of the worldview of many revolutionary itinerants at the end of the eighteenth century. Paine, campaigning for international recognition of the freedom of the seas in his 1792 pamphlet *Letter to the Abbé Raynal*, depicted the Atlantic as "the world's highway."[37] Eight years later, from Paris, undeterred by all that had conspired to drown out his internationalism, Paine persisted in drawing up plans for an "unarmed Association of Nations" that would boycott the economies of aggressor nations.[38] Other resilient cosmopolitans, too, many of them homeless between nations, continued through the more contentious 1790s to be inspired by their visions of a universal citizenship undivided by hostile nation-states.[39] At the same time that Webster defined American exceptionalism, the *Independent Gazetteer* encouraged citizens of new republics to shed "partial prejudices respecting nations, names, and colors" and to "advance the increasing welfare of the human species of every class without exception, in all quarters of the globe."[40]

In 1795, the philosopher Immanuel Kant from Konigsberg defined a federation of free, republican nations in his *Project for a Perpetual Peace*.[41] Based on the right of hospitality, individuals as world citizens would nowhere be foreigners. As his inspiration, Kant cites the satirical inscription on a Dutch innkeeper's sign, upon which a burial ground was painted. Besieged by the wars of revolutionaries on a mission, many of Kant's contemporaries envisioned an era of peace based on universal right that transcended borders.

Throughout the cascading Atlantic revolution, cosmopolitanism coexisted, however uneasily, with emerging national citizenship in the pamphlets, papers, clubs, correspondence, and treatises with legs.[42] In common with Peter Ochs from Basel, who had observed the Festival of the Federation with his sister in Strasbourg, these revolutionary travelers were convinced that "the revolutions of America, France, and Poland obviously belong in a chain of events that will regenerate the world."[43] This regeneration was noted by the writers of travel journals and memoirs and echoed in rumors. Its effects were read in novels. Correspondence documented the transformation.

Itinerancy encouraged eighteenth-century cosmopolitanism. It depended on translation and transplantation, on travel among national cultures rather than dwelling within a single one.[44] Cosmopolitanism, like the itinerancy that nourished it, belonged not so much to the largest republics that endured into the nineteenth century as to the peoples of smaller states who knew changing governmental regimes. Theirs were ever-changing and unstable lives; in that upheaval lay the openness of itinerancy.

Writer Mary Wollstonecraft, traveling to Sweden to escape the violence of the French Terror directed at foreigners in 1794, condemned the settled ways of some of her English compatriots. "Travellers who require that every nation should resemble their native country, had better stay at home," she suggested. The few travelers in French coaches, who instead could be merrily sustained by "a cold roast capon, 2 bottles claret, a little salt and a loaf of excellent bread," were the only ones open to "inquiry and discussion." Wollstonecraft cited that open flexibility as the most admirable "characteristic of the present century."[45] Thus nourished, she expected the cosmopolitan understanding of these travelers might someday "in a great measure destroy the factitious national characters which have been supposed permanent, though only rendered so by the permanency of ignorance."[46]

Wollstonecraft's words from the end of the revolutionary eighteenth century continue to reverberate. In this global era, they remind us that the roots of internationalism are as old as the nation-states. Struggles for human rights have connected the Atlantic world for more than two hundred years. Like the pamphlets, journals, memoirs, newspapers, clubs, rumors, novels, correspondence, and diplomatic proclamations that chronicle them, the struggles remind us of the impermanence of the borders that obstruct the travel of restless itinerants and their ideals.

Chronology

1778 David George escapes slavery

1779 St. John de Crèvecoeur leaves New York for France

1779 Elkanah Watson of Connecticut arrives in France

1779 John Paul Jones drops anchor in Texel in the United Provinces

1779 Six hundred free men of color arrive from Saint-Domingue to fight for the Americans under French Admiral d'Estaing

1780 London Society for Constitutional Information organized

1780 Nancy Shippen marries Henry Livingston

1780 Fourth Anglo-Dutch War

1781 Joan Derk van der Capellen publishes *To the People of the Netherlands*

1781 Genevans storm municipal arsenal

1782 Betje Wolff and Aagje Deken publish *Sara Burgerhart*

1782 América Francès de Crèvecoeur and her brother are rescued from their burned out farmhouse

1782 St. John de Crèvecoeur publishes *Letters from an American Farmer*

1782 British evacuate five thousand blacks from Charleston

1782 Black Loyalists sail to Nova Scotia

1782 Joel and Ruth Barlow are married

1782 Revolution in Geneva

1782 Jacques-Pierre Brissot writes *The Philadelphian in Geneva*

1783 Nancy Shippen Livingston leaves her husband

1783 Black Loyalists arrive in Nova Scotia

1784 Elkanah Watson returns to New York

1784 Thomas Jefferson arrives in Paris

1784 St. John de Crèvecoeur is reunited with his children in Boston

1785 Benjamin Franklin returns to Philadelphia

1785 Louis Otto is reassigned to Philadelphia as French chargé d'affaires

1785 William Short meets the duchesse de la Rochefoucauld

1786 Dutch Patriots take control of large cities in the United Provinces

1787 Belgian Estates protest against Austrian emperor Joseph II's reforms

1787 Charles Lambert d'Outrepont publishes *Consideration on the Constitution*

1787 Gerrit Paape flees United Provinces

1787 Quobna Ottabah Cugoano publishes his attack on the slave trade

1787 Sierra Leone settlers leave London

1787 Society Instituted for Effecting Abolition of the Slave Trade in London is organized

1787 Prussians crush Dutch Patriot Revolution, allowing return of Willem V

1788 Anne d'Yve writes *To the Nation* in Brussels

1788 Marquis de Condorcet writes *Letters of a Citizen of the United States*

1788 Mary Wollstonecraft joins the staff of the *Analytical Review*

1788 Mary Wollstonecraft publishes *Mary*

1788 Jacques-Pierre Brissot travels through America

1788 Abolitionists petition British Parliament

1788 Founding of Society of the Friends of the Blacks in Paris

1788 Joel Barlow travels to Paris

1789 Revolution in Geneva

1789 Olaudah Equiano publishes *The Interesting Narrative*

1789 Granville Town burned to the ground

1789 Jacobin society organized in Paris

1789 Brabant Revolution and defeat of the Austrian army

1789 Vincent Ogé addresses abolitionists in Paris

1789 Nancy Shippen Livingston unsuccessfully petitions for divorce

1789 French Estates General is convened in Versailles; organization of the National Assembly

1789 Storming of the Bastille

1789 *Declaration of the Rights of Man* decreed in France

1789 Thomas Clarkson visits Paris

1789 Thomas Jefferson returns to America from Paris

1790 Louis Otto and América Francès de Crèvecoeur marry

1790 Dutch revolutionary Etta Palm d'Aelders joins Cercle Social in Paris

1790 Helen Maria Williams travels to Paris

1790 Helen Maria Williams publishes first volume of memoirs

1790 Vincent Ogé leads revolt in Saint-Domingue

1790 *Léopard* seized by delegates from Saint Marc to sail for France

1791 Anna Maria Falconbridge and her husband arrive in Sierra Leone

1791 Brissot publishes journal of his American travels

1791 New Polish constitution

1791 Republican Club meets in Paris

1791 Thomas Paine publishes *Rights of Man*

1791 Society of the Friends of the Constitution organizes in Warsaw

1791 Free citizens of color in French colonies are granted citizenship

1791 French king attempts to flee, is caught at border at Varennes and returned to Paris

1791 Champs de Mars massacre in Paris

1791 Slave insurrection in Saint-Domingue

1791 John Frederick, son of Temne ruler, travels to London

1791 John Clarkson arrives in Nova Scotia to recruit settlers for Sierra Leone

1792 Louis and Fanny Otto leave for France

1792 Mary Wollstonecraft publishes *Vindication of the Rights of Woman*

1792 Fifteen ships sail from Nova Scotia to Sierra Leone

1792 London Corresponding Society is organized

1792 William Short is named minister resident in The Hague

1792 France declares war on Austria

1792 Russians invade Poland

1792 Prussia declares war on France

1792 Commissioners Léger Félicité Sonthonax, Jean Antoine Ailhaud, and Étienne Polverel go to Saint-Domingue

1792 Crowds storm the Tuileries and French monarchy is overthrown

1792 Royalists take Guadeloupe

1792 Genevan citizens are called to arms as French armies camp outside their gates

1792 French defeat Prussians at Valmy

1792 Republic is declared in France

1792 Joel Barlow and John Frost address National Convention

1792 French Decree offers aid to neighbors fighting tyranny

1792 Scottish Convention

1792 Mary Wollstonecraft leaves England for France

1793 French king is executed

1793 Prussians invade Poland

1793 Ruth Barlow comes to Paris to join her husband

1793 French Committee of Public Safety created

1793 Insurrection in Guadeloupe

1793 French Constitution is accepted by National Constitution

1793 Sonthonax frees slaves in Saint-Domingue in the North Province

1793 Boston King and David George travel to England from Sierra Leone

1794 Anna Falconbridge publishes her narrative

1794 William Jackson is sent by the French to Ireland

1794 Tricolor delegation travels from Saint-Domingue to France

1794 French abolish slavery

1794 British capture Martinique and Guadeloupe

1794 Victor Hugues arrives in Guadeloupe

1794 French assault on Freetown

1794 Polish Revolution led by Kościuszko, crushed by Russians and Prussians

1794 French invade the United Provinces

1795 Declaration of Batavian Republic; Willem V retreats to England

1795 Treaty of Basel

1795 Belgian provinces are annexed to France

1796 Boston King publishes his journal

1796 Wolfe Tone arrives in Paris

1796 Louis and Fanny Otto and St. John de Crèvecoeur move to farm near Meaux

1796 Mary Hays publishes *Memoirs of Emma Courtney*

1796 Joel Barlow goes on mission to Algeria

1796 Napoléon Bonaparte assumes command of Army of Italy

1796 Wolfe Tone joins General Lazare Hoche to invade Ireland

1797 Thaddeus Kościuszko released from Russian prison

1797 Creation of Cispadane Republic

1797 Creation of Cisalpine Republic

1797 Toussaint Louverture orders Sonthonax back to France

1797 Thaddeus Kościuszko returns to America

1797 Fructidor Coup

1797 Peace of Campo Formio

1798 William Godwin publishes *Maria* by Mary Wollstonecraft

1798 Mary Hays publishes *Appeal to the Men of Great Britain in behalf of Women*

1798 Lieve van Ollefen publishes *The Revolutionary Household*

1798 Louis Otto is posted to Berlin

1798 Roman Republic is established

1798 Helvetic Republic is established

1798 Thaddeus Kościuszko returns to Paris

1798 General Humbert sails with Army of Ireland

1798 Victor Hugues is removed from Guadeloupe

1799 Parthenopean Republic established

1799   Austria declares War of the Second Coalition

1799   Prairial coup in Paris

1800   Louis and Fanny Otto posted to London

1800   Maroons from Jamaica suppress Freetown uprising

1802   Thomas Paine returns to America

1802   LeClerc to Saint-Domingue

1803   Louverture to French prison

1804   Declaration of Independence of Haiti

Notes on Sources

This book could be read as an extended essay on sources. It focuses on how historians use documents, but not necessarily on how or where we find them. Sometimes we stumble by pure luck on a pamphlet or memoir that opens whole new perspectives, but more often our work involves following the thread of clues from one text to find another and another. What follows are some of my sources, which I hope will serve as introductory clues for readers interested in further exploration.

Almost all of the survey histories of Atlantic Revolution focus on the Americas and/or France. Among the entries on this expanding list, see: Manuela Albertone and Antonio De Francesco, eds., *Rethinking the Atlantic World: Europe and America in the Age of Democratic Revolutions* (New York: Palgrave Macmillan, 2009); Suzanne Desan, Lynn Hunt, and William Max Nelson, eds., *The French Revolution in Global Perspective* (Ithaca, N.Y.: Cornell University Press, 2013); Marcel Dorigny, *L'atlantique* (Paris: Presses Universitaires de France, 2001); Susan Dunn, *Sister Revolutions: French Lightning, American Light* (New York: Faber and Faber, 1999); Bernard Fay, *L'esprit révolutionnaire en France et aux États-Unis à la fin du XVIIIe siècle* (Paris: Champion, 1925); Claude Fohlen, *La Révolution américain et l'Europe* (Paris: Éditions du Centre national de la recherche scientifique, 1979); Jack Fruchtman Jr., *Atlantic Cousins: Benjamin Franklin and His Visionary Friends* (New York: Thunder's Mouth, 2005); Patrice Higonnet, *Sister Republics: The Origins of the French and American Republicanism* (Cambridge: Harvard University Press, 1988); Mark Hulliung, *Citizens and Citoyens: Republicans and Liberals in America and France* (Cambridge: Harvard University Press, 2002); Wim Klooster, *Revolutions in the Atlantic World* (New York: New York University Press, 2009); Lloyd Kramer, *Nationalism in Europe and America: Politics, Cultures, and Identities since 1775* (Chapel Hill: University of North Carolina Press, 2011); and David Parker, ed., *Revolutions and the Revolutionary Tradition in the West, 1560–1991* (New York: Routledge, 2000); Pierre Serna, Antonino De Francesco, and Judith A. Miller, eds., *Republics at War, 1776–1840* (New York: Palgrave Macmillan, 2013); and Pierre Serna, ed. *Républiques soeurs: Le Directoire et la Révolution atlantique* (Rennes: Presses Universitaires de Rennes, 2009). David Armitage and Sanjay Subrahmanyan, eds., *Age of Revolutions in Global Context, c. 1760–1840* (New York: Palgrave Macmillan, 2010); Thomas Benjamin, *The Atlantic World: Europeans, Africans, Indians and Their Shared History, 1400–1900* (New York: Cambridge University Press, 2009); and David Patrick Geggus, ed., *The Impact of the Haitian Revolution in the Atlantic World* (Columbia: University of South Carolina Press, 2001), have focused on other regions in their anthologies. On the Iberian Atlantic before 1804 see, among others, Jeremy Adelman, *Sovereignty and Revolution in the Iberian Atlantic* (Princeton: Princeton University Press, 2006); and Jane Landes, *Atlantic Creoles in the Age of Revolutions* (Cambridge: Harvard University Press, 2010). A few historians of Atlantic Revolution have followed the lead of Jacques Godechot, *La pensée révolutionnaire en France et en Europe* (Paris: Armand Colin, 1964), and of R. R. Palmer's two-volume *Age of the Democratic Revolution: A Political History of Europe and America, 1760–1800* (Princeton: Princeton University Press, 1959, 1964) in discussing a broader range of revolutions: Harriet B. Applewhite and Darline G. Levy, eds., *Women and Politics in the Age of Democratic Revolution* (Ann Arbor: University of Michigan Press, 1990); Bernard Bailyn, *Atlantic History: Concept and Contours* (Cambridge: Harvard University Press, 2005); Jonathan Israel, *Democratic Enlightenment: Philosophy, Revolution, and Human Rights, 1750–1790* (New York: Oxford University Press, 2011); Annie Jourdan, *La Révolution, une exception française?* (Paris: Flammarion, 2004), and *La Révolution Française et l'Europe. XXe exposition du Conseil de l'Europe* (Paris: Éditions de la Reunion des musées nationaux, 1989).

Dutch historians published pioneering work on individual revolutionary travelers, for example, Jacques Baartmans, *Hollandse wijsgeren in Brabant en Vlanderen: Geschriften van Noord-Nederlandse Patriotten in de Oostenrijkse Nederlanden, 1787–1792* (Nijmegen: Uitgeverij Vantilt, 2001); M. N. Bisselink and A. Doedens, eds., *Jan Bernd Bicker: een Patriot in Ballingschap 1787–1795* (Amsterdam: VU Boekhandel, 1983); Emillie Fijnje-Luzac, *Myne beslommerde Boedel. Brieven in Ballingschap 1787–1788*, ed. Jacques J. M. Baartmans (Nijmegen: Vantilt, 2003); Willem Frijhoff and Rudolf Dekker, eds., *Le Voyage revolutionnaire* (Hilversum: Verloren, 1991); Joost Roosendaal, *Bataaven. Nederlandse Vluchtelingen in Frankrijk 1787–1795* (Nijmegen: Vantilt, 2003); Wayne Te Brake, ed., *Carel de Vos Van Steenwijk. Een grand tour naar de nieuwe republiek: Journaal van een Reis door Amerika, 1783–84* (Hilversum: Verloren, 1999); and Madeleine van Strien-Chardonneau, *Le voyage de Hollande: récits de voyageurs français dans les Provinces Unies 1748–1795* (Oxford: Voltaire Foundation, 1994). Other studies of travelers at the end of the eighteenth century include Linda Colley, *The Ordeal of Elizabeth Marsh: A Woman in World History* (New York: Anchor, 2007); Brian Dolan, *Ladies of the Grand Tour* (London: Flamingo, 2002); Maya Jasanoff, *Liberty's Exiles: American Loyalists in the Revolutionary World* (New York: Knopf, 2011); and Rebecca J. Scott and Jean M. Hébrard, *Freedom Papers: An Atlantic Odyssey in the Age of Emancipation* (Cambridge: Harvard University Press, 2012).

Pamphlets from the American Revolution can be found at the Library of Congress, and many are also available online. The Koninklijke Bibliotheek in The Hague has digitized many of the more important eighteenth-century Dutch pamphlets. Genevan or Belgian documents can be consulted in the Bibliothèque de Genève, Geneva, the Bibliothèque Royale/Koninklijke Bibliotheek in Brussels, and university library collections in Geneva, Leiden, and Leuven. The classic guide to American pamphlets and their ideas is still Bernard Bailyn, *The Ideological Origins of the American Revolution* (Cambridge: Harvard University Press, 1992). On Belgian pamphlets see Stijn van Rossem, *Revolutie op de koper Plaat* (Louvain: Peeters, 2012).

Biographies of Thomas Paine and studies of his *Common Sense* are riddled with conflicting interpretations. I relied above all on Jack Fruchtman Jr., *Thomas Paine: Apostle of Freedom* (New York: Four Walls Eight Windows, 1994); Jill Lepore, "A World of Paine," in *Revolutionary Founders: Rebels, Radicals, and Reformers in the Making of the Nation*, ed. Alfred F. Young, Gary B. Nash, and Ray Raphael (New York: Knopf, 2011), 87–96; Simon P. Newman and Peter S. Onuf, eds., *Paine and Jefferson in the Age of Revolutions* (Charlottesville: University of Virginia Press, 2013); and Sophia Rosenfeld, *Common Sense: A Political History* (Cambridge: Harvard University Press, 2011). On the circulation of ideas in America, see Trish Loughran, *The Republic in Print: Print Culture in the Age of U.S. Nation Building, 1770–1870* (New York: Columbia University Press, 2007), and beyond, David Armitage, *The Declaration of Independence: A Global History* (Cambridge: Harvard University Press, 2007).

The central collections of documents on the Genevan, Dutch Patriot, and Brabant revolutions are the Archives d'État de Genève, the Nationale Archieven in The Hague, and the Archives royales de Belgique/Algemeen Rijsarchief in Brussels. On the Genevan Revolution of 1782, see Eric Golay, *Quand le peuple devient roi* (Geneva: Slatkine, 2001); Marc Lerner, *A Laboratory of Liberty: The Transformation of Political Culture in Republican Switzerland, 1750–1780* (London: Brill, 2011); *Révolutions genevoises 1782–1798* (Geneva: Maison Tavel, 1989); and Richard Whatmore, *Against War and Empire: Geneva, Britain, and France in the Eighteenth Century* (New Haven: Yale University Press, 2012). A plethora of histories of the Dutch Patriot Revolution appeared around its bicentennial, and others have been published more recently. See especially Pieter Geyl, *De Patriotten Beweging, 1780–1787* (Amsterdam: Van Kampen, 1947); Margaret C. Jacob and Wijnand W. Mijnhardt, eds., *The Dutch Republic in the Eighteenth Century: Decline, Enlightenment, and Revolution* (Ithaca, N.Y.: Cornell University Press, 1992); Joost Rosendaal, *De Nederlandse Revolutie. Vrijheid, Volk, en Vaderland, 1783–1799* (Nijmegen: Vantilt, 2005); Simon Schama, *Patriots and Liberators* (New York: Knopf, 1977); Jan Willem Schulte Nordholt, *The Dutch Republic and American Independence* (Chapel Hill: University of North Carolina Press, 1982); and Wayne Ph. te Brake, *Regents and Rebels: The Revolutionary World of an Eighteenth-Century Dutch City* (New York: Blackwell, 1989). For secondary literature on the Brabant Revolution, see Brecht Deseure, *Onhoudbaar Verleden. Geschiedenis als Politiek Instrument tijdens de franse Periode in België* (Louvain: Universitaire Pers Leuven, 2014); J. Koll, *Die belgische Nation: Patriotismus und Nationalbewusstsein in den Südlichen Niederlanden im späten 18. Jahrhundert* (Münster: Waxmann, 2003); Janet Polasky, *Revolution in Brussels, 1787–1793* (Brussels: Académie Royale de Belgique, 1986); and Suzanne Tassier, *Les démocrates belges de 1789. Etude sur le Vonckisme et la Révolution Brabançonne* (Brussels: Maurice Lamertin, 1930).

Some late-eighteenth-century travel journals have been published, but many more have not. Elkanah Watson's journals are available in the State Library of New York in Albany. An edited version was published: Elkanah Watson, *Men and Times of The Revolution: Memoirs of Elkanah Watson including his Journals of Travels in Europe and America from the Year 1777 to 1842*, ed. Winslow C. Watson (New York: Dana, 1856). Several French travelers published their journals, including François Barbé-Marbois, *Our Revolutionary Forefathers: the Letters of Francois, Marquis de Barbé-Marbois during his Residence in the United States as Secretary of the French Legation 1779–1785*, ed. Eugene P. Chase (New York: Duffield, 1929); Philip Mazzei, *Recherches historiques et politiques sur les Etats Unis de l'Amérique Septrionale* (Paris: Chez Froulie, 1788). Saint John de Crèvecoeur and Jacques Brissot's journals, available in English, are now classic texts: J. Hector St. John de Crèvecoeur, *Letters from an American Farmer* (1782; Oxford: Oxford University Press, 1997), and the extensively edited J. P. Brissot, *New Travels in the United States*, ed. Pierre de Jacques (Cambridge: Harvard University Press, 1964). Most of Saint John de Crèvecoeur's papers are in the Library of Congress.

Journals written from the perspective of outsiders provide unique insights into the French Revolution. Étienne Dumont's journals are available in an evolving set of editions: Étienne Dumont, *Letters, containing an account of the late revolution in France, and observations on the constitution, laws, manners, and institutions of the English; written during the author's residence at Paris, Versailles, and London, in the years 1789 and 1790* (London: J. Johnson, 1792); and Étienne Dumont, *The Great Frenchman and the little Genevese. Translated from Étienne Dumont's Souvenir sur Mirabeau*, ed. Elizabeth Seymour (London: Duckworth, 1904). Helen Maria

Williams, *Letters from France*, has been reprinted: Helen Maria Williams, *Letters Written in France 1790* (1790; Oxford: Woodstock, 1989); and Helen Maria Williams, *Letters Written in France in the Summer 1790, to a Friend in England; Containing Various Anecdotes Relative to the French Revolution*, ed. Neil Fraistat and Susan S. Lanser (Peterborough, Ont.: Broadview, 2001). One of the best guides to the vibrant community of expatriates is Philip Ziesche, *Cosmopolitan Patriots: Americans in Paris in the Age of Revolution* (Charlottesville: University of Virginia Press, 2010).

On the "autobiographical turn" of freed slaves, see James Sidbury, *Becoming African in America* (New York: Oxford University Press, 2007). In addition to the well-known journals of Equiano and Cuguoano—Olaudah Equiano, *The Interesting Narrative and Other Writings*, ed. Vincent Carretta (1789; New York: Penguin, 2003); and Ottobah Cugoano, *Thoughts and Sentiments on the Evil and Wicked Traffic of the Slavery and Commerce of the Human Species*, ed. Vincent Carretta (1787; New York: Penguin, 1999)—the collection edited by Vincent Carretta, *Unchained Voices: An Anthology of Black Voices in the English Speaking World of the Eighteenth Century* (Lexington: University of Kentucky Press, 2003), provides an excellent introduction and guide to additional sources. Several historians have told the story of the migration of the black loyalists, including Christopher X. Byrd, *Captives and Voyageurs: Black Migrants across the Eighteenth-Century British Atlantic World* (Baton Rouge: Louisiana State University Press, 2008); Cassandra Pybus, *Epic Journeys of Freedom: Runaway Slaves of the American Revolution and Their Global Quest for Liberty* (Boston: Beacon, 2006); and Simon Schama, *Rough Crossings: Britain, the Slaves, and the American Revolution* (New York: HarperCollins, 2006).

Studies of slaves, the black poor in London, and English abolitionists are many, including Stephen Braidwood, *Black Poor and White Philanthropists: London's Blacks and the Foundation of the Sierra Leone Settlement, 1786–1791* (Liverpool: Liverpool University Press, 1994); Christopher Brown, *Moral Capital: Foundations of British Abolitionism* (Chapel Hill: University of North Carolina Press, 2006); David Brion Davis, *The Problem of Slavery in the Age of Revolution, 1770–1823* (Oxford: Oxford University Press, 1999); Seymour Drescher, *Abolition: A History of Slavery and Antislavery* (Cambridge: Cambridge University Press, 2009); Adam Hochschild, *Bury the Chains: Prophets and Rebels in the Fight to Free an Empire's Slaves* (Boston: Houghton Mifflin, 2005); Claire Midgley, *Women against Slavery: The British Campaigns, 1780–1870* (London: Routledge, 1992); and Kathryn Kish Sklar and James Brewer Stewart, eds., *Women's Rights and Transatlantic Antislavery in the Era of Emancipation* (New Haven: Yale University Press, 2007). Thomas Clarkson, *The History of the Rise, Progress, and Accomplishment of the Abolition of the Slave-Trade by the British Parliament* (London: Longman, Hurst, Rees, and Orme, 1808); and Prince Hoare, ed.,

Memoirs of Granville Sharp, Esq. (London: Henry Colburn, 1820), are the classic narratives of eighteenth-century English abolitionism. On the French, see the invaluable multivolume *La Révolution française et l'abolition de l'esclavage* (Paris: Éditions d'histoire sociale, 1968); and Marcel Dorigny and Bernard Gainot, *La Société des Amis des Noirs 1788–1799* (Paris: Éditions Unesco, 1998).

There are two editions of Anna Falconbridge's journal: Deirdre Coleman, ed., *Maiden Voyages and Infant Colonies: Two Women's Travel Narratives of the 1790s* (London: Leicester University Press, 1999); and Anna Maria Falconbridge, *Narrative of Two Voyages to the River Sierra Leone during the Years 1791–1792–1793. An Account of the Slave Trade on the Coast of Africa*, ed. Christopher Fyfe (1793; Liverpool: Liverpool University Press, 2000). Also on the settlers in Sierra Leone, see Deirdre Coleman, *Romantic Colonization and British Anti-Slavery* (Cambridge: Cambridge University Press, 2005); and Christopher Fyfe, ed., *Our Children Free and Happy: Letters from Black Settlers in Africa in the 1790s* (Edinburgh: Edinburgh University Press, 1991). On Sierra Leone, see Ismail Rashid, "Escape, Revolt, and Marronage in Eighteenth and Nineteenth Century Sierra Leone Hinterland," *Canadian Journal of African Studies/Revue Canadienne des Études Africaines* 34 (2000): 656–83; and Bruce Mouser, "Rebellion, Marronage and Jihad: Strategies of Resistance to Slavery on the Sierra Leone Coast, c. 1763–1796," *Journal of African History* 48 (2007): 27–44.

On the press in the French Revolution, see, among others, Jack Censer, *Prelude to Power: The Parisian Radical Press, 1789–1791* (Baltimore: Johns Hopkins University Press, 1976); Jacques Godechot, *La presse française sous la révolution et l'empire. Histoire générale de la presse française* (Paris: Presses Universitaires de France, 1969); and Jeremy Popkin, *Revolutionary News: The Press in France, 1789–1799* (Durham: Duke University Press, 1990). On clubs in the French Revolution, see Alphonse Aulard, *La société des Jacobins. Recueil de documents pour l'histoire du Club des Jacobins de Paris* (Paris: Librairie Jouaust, 1889–97); Jean Boutier, Philippe Boutry, and Serge Bonin, *Atlas de la Révolution française*, vol. 6, *Les sociétés politiques* (Paris: Éditions de l'École des Hautes Études en Sciences Sociales, 1992); Patrice Higonnet, *Goodness beyond Virtue: Jacobins during the French Revolution* (Cambridge: Harvard University Press, 1998); Gary Kates, *The Cercle Social, the Girondins, and the French Revolution* (Princeton: Princeton University Press, 1985); Michael L. Kennedy, *The Jacobin Clubs in the French Revolution: The First Years* (Princeton: Princeton University Press, 1982); and Albert Mathiez, *Le Club des Cordeliers pendant la crise de Varennes et le massacre du Champ de Mars* (Paris: Librairie Aneienne H. Champion, 1910).

The papers of the English clubs can be found in the Treasurer Solicitor's papers at the National Archives in Kew; the Place Additional Manuscripts in the British Library, London; and the multivolume *Political Writings of the 1790's*, ed. Gregory Claeys (London: William Pickering, 1995). On the Polish Jacobins, see

J. Grossbart, "La presse polonaise et la révolution française," *Annales historiques de la Révolution française*, 14 (1937); Bogusław Lésnodorski, *Les Jacobins polonais* (Paris: Société des études robespierristes, 1965); and *Constitution and Reform in Eighteenth-Century Poland*, ed. Samuel Fiszman (Bloomington: Indiana University Press, 1997).

Archival documentation of Caribbean rumors can be found in Aix-en-Provence, in the Archives d'Outre Mer, and in the Colonial Office Records at the National Archives. Histories of this period in the British West Indies in the eighteenth century include Michael Craton, *Testing the Chains: Resistance to Slavery in the British West Indies* (Ithaca, N.Y.: Cornell University Press, 1982); Julius Scott's unpublished dissertation, "The Common Wind: Currents of Afro-American Communication in the Era of the Haitian Revolution"; and Andrew Jackson O'Shaughnessy, *An Empire Divided: The American Revolution and the British Caribbean* (Philadelphia: University of Pennsylvania Press, 2000). On Saint-Domingue see, among others, Yves Bénot, *La république française et la fin des colonies: Essai* (Paris: Éditions La Découverte, 1989); Marcel Dorigny, ed., *Les abolitions de l'esclavage de L. F. Sonthonax à V. Schoelcher, 1793, 1794, 1848* (Paris: Presses Universitaires de Vincennes, 1995); Laurent Dubois, *Avengers of the New World: The Story of the Haitian Revolution* (Cambridge: Harvard University Press, 2004); Carolyn Fick, *The Making of Haiti: The Saint Domingue Revolution from Below* (Knoxville: University of Tennessee Press, 1990); John D. Garrigus, *Before Haiti: Race and Citizenship in French Saint-Domingue* (New York: Palgrave, 2006); *A Turbulent Time: The French Revolution and the Greater Caribbean*, ed. David Barry Gaspar and David Patrick Geggus (Bloomington: Indiana University Press, 1997); Malick Ghachem, *The Old Regime and the Haitian Revolution* (Cambridge: Cambridge University Press, 2012); Jeremy Popkin, *You Are All Free: The Haitian Revolution and the Abolition of Slavery* (Cambridge: Cambridge University Press, 2010); and Ashli White, *Encountering Revolution: Haiti and the Making of the Early Republic* (Baltimore: Johns Hopkins University Press, 2010). On Guadeloupe, see Laurent Dubois, *A Colony of Citizens* (Chapel Hill: University of North Carolina Press, 2004); Anne Pérotin-Dumon, *Être patriote sous les tropiques: la Guadeloupe, la colonisation et la Révolution* (Basse-terre, Guadeloupe: Société d'histoire de la Guadeloupe, 1985). On Latin America in this early period, see among others François Xavier Guerra, *Modernidad E independencies, Ensayos sobre la revoluciones hispánicas* (Madrid: Editorial Mapfre, 1992); Lyman L. Johnson, *Workshop of Revolution: Plebian Buenos Aires and the Atlantic World, 1776–1810* (Durham: Duke University Press, 2011); Claudia Rosas Lauro, ed., *El Miedo en el Perú. Siglos XVI al XX* (Lima: Pontificia Universidadad Católica del Perú, 2005); and Gabriel Paquette, *Imperial Portugal in the Age of Atlantic Revolutions: The Luso-Brazilian World, c. 1770–1850* (Cambridge: Cambridge University Press, 2013).

Studies of novelists, and in particular women writers, at the end of the eighteenth century have concentrated on America, England, or France. See, among many, April Alliston, *Virtue's Faults: Correspondences in Eighteenth-Century British and French Women's Fiction* (Stanford: Stanford University Press, 1996); Sarah Knott, *Sensibility and the American Revolution* (Chapel Hill: University of North Carolina Press, 2009); Carla Hesse, *The Other Enlightenment: How French Women Became Modern* (Princeton: Princeton University Press, 2001); Ruth Perry, *Novel Relations: The Transformation of Kinship in English Literature and Culture, 1748–1818* (Cambridge: Cambridge University Press, 2004); Joan Hinde Stewart, *Gynographs: French Novels by Women of the Late Eighteenth Century* (Lincoln: University of Nebraska Press, 1993); and Nicola J. Watson, *Revolution and the Form of the British Novel, 1790–1825: Intercepted Letters, Interrupted Seductions* (Oxford: Clarendon, 1994). Biographies of individual writers are numerous, as are edited editions of the novels.

Few works on eighteenth-century letter writing cross the Atlantic. A noteworthy exception is Sarah M. S. Pearsall, *Atlantic Families: Lives and Letters in the Later Eighteenth Century* (Oxford: Oxford University Press, 2008). On sentimentality in America, see Eve Tavor Bannet, *Empire of Letters: Letter Manuals and Transatlantic Correspondence, 1680–1820* (Cambridge: Cambridge University Press, 2005); Konstantin Dierks, *In My Power: Letter Writing and Communication in Early America* (Philadelphia: University of Pennsylvania Press, 2009); Sarah Knott, *Sensibility and the American Revolution* (Chapel Hill: University of North Carolina Press, 2009); and Rosemarie Zagarri, *Revolutionary Backlash: Women and Politics in the Early American Republic* (Philadelphia: University of Pennsylvania Press, 2007). On France, among others, see Suzanne Desan, *The Family on Trial in Revolutionary France* (Berkeley: University of California Press, 2004); Dena Goodman, *Becoming a Woman in the Age of Letters* (Ithaca, N.Y.: Cornell University Press, 2009; Carla Hesse, *The Other Enlightenment: How French Women Became Modern* (Princeton: Princeton University Press, 2001); Lynn Hunt, *The Family Romance of the French Revolution* (Berkeley: University of California Press, 1992); and Lindsay A. H. Parker, *Writing the Revolution: A French Woman's History in Letters* (New York: Oxford University Press, 2013).

Shippen and Otto's letters of courtship were excerpted and edited by Ethel Ames, *Nancy Shippen, Her Journal Book: The International Romance of a Young Lady of Fashion of Colonial Philadelphia with Letters to Her and about Her* (1935; New York: Benjamin Blom, 1968), while a typewritten copy is preserved at the Historical Society of Pennsylvania, and Shippen family papers are at the Library of Congress. The Barlows' letters are at the Houghton Library at Harvard University. For William Short and the duchesse de la Rochefoucauld, I have relied on *Lettres de la duchesse de La Rochefoucauld à William Short. Texte inédit*, ed. Doina Pasca Harsanyi (Paris: Mercure de France, 2001). William Short's papers are at the

Library of Congress. The story of the missing Otto-Crèvecoeur correspondence and its discovery in Acquisitions Extraordinaires 135 and 188, Archives du Ministère des Affaires Étrangères, Paris, is outlined in the introduction.

Most French revolutionary decrees and much of the correspondence can be consulted in the Archives des Affaires Étrangères in Paris in the Correspondance Politique and Mémoires et Documents. See also, among many histories of the French revolutionary wars, Marc Belissa, *Fraternité universelle et intérêt national (1713–1795)* (Paris: Éditions Kimé, 1998); David Bell, *The First Total War: Napoleon's Europe and the Birth of Warfare as We Know It* (Boston: Houghton Mifflin, 2007); Albert Sorel, *L'Europe et la Révolution française* (Paris: E. Plon, 1887); and Michel Vovelle, *Les Républiques-soeurs sous le regard de la Grande Nation 1795–1803* (Paris: L'Harmattan, 2000).

The literature on eighteenth-century cosmopolitanism and patriotism is large and contentious. Some representative works are Marc Belissa and Bernard Cottret, *Cosmopolitismes, Patriotismes, Europe et Amériques, 1773–1802* (Rennes: Perséides, 2005); Marc Belissa, *Fraternité universel et intérêt national (1913–1795)* (Paris: Éditions Kimé, 1998); David Avrom Bell, *Cult of the Nation in France* (Cambridge: Harvard University Press, 2001); Seyla Benhabib, *Another Cosmopolitanism* (New York: Oxford University Press, 2006); Seth Cotlar, *Tom Paine's America: The Rise and Fall of Transatlantic Radicalism in the Early Republic* (Charlottesville: University of Virginia Press, 2011); Suzanne Desan, "Foreigners, Cosmopolitanism, and French Revolutionary Universalism," in *The French Revolution in Global Perspective*, ed. Suzanne Desan, Lynn Hunt, and William Max Nelson (Ithaca, N.Y.: Cornell University Press, 2013), 86–100; Margaret C. Jacob, *Strangers Nowhere in the World: The Rise of Cosmopolitanism in Early Modern Europe* (Philadelphia: University of Pennsylvania Press, 2006); Martha Nussbaum, *The Love of Country: Debating the Limits of Patriotism* (Boston: Beacon, 1996); Jonathan Rée, "Cosmopolitanism and the Experience of Nationality," in *Cosmopolitics. Thinking and Feeling beyond the Nation*, ed. Pheng Cheah and Bruce Robbins (Minneapolis: University of Minnesota Press, 1998); Sophia Rosenfield, "Citizens of Nowhere in Particular: Cosmopolitanism, Writing, and Political Engagement in Eighteenth-Century Europe," *National Identities* 4, no. 1 (2002): 25–43; and Thomas J. Schlereth, *The Cosmopolitan Ideal in Enlightenment Thought: Its Form and Function in the Ideas of Franklin, Hume, and Voltaire, 1694–1790* (Notre Dame: University of Notre Dame Press, 1977).

Notes

INTRODUCTION

1. Elkanah Watson, *Men and Times of The Revolution: Memoirs of Elkanah Watson including his Journals of Travels in Europe and America from the Year 1777 to 1842*, ed. Winslow C. Watson (New York: Dana, 1856), 159, 33, 271.

2. Settlers' petition in *Our Children Free and Happy: Letters from Black Settlers in Africa in the 1790's*, ed. C. Fyfe (Edinburgh: Edinburgh University Press, 1991), 36.

3. Gerrit Paape cited by Joost Rosendaal, "'Parce que j'aime la liberté, je retourne en France,' Les réfugiés bataves en voyage," in *Le voyage révolutionnaire*, ed. W. Frijhoff and R. Dekker (Hilversum: Verloren, 1991), 37; and Gerrit Paape, *Mijne vrolijke Wijsgeerte in mijne Ballingschap*, ed. Peter Altena (1792; Hilversum: Verloren, 1996).

4. Thomas Paine to George Washington, 16 October 1789, in *The Papers of George Washington: Presidential Series*, ed. Dorothy Twohig (Charlottesville: University Press of Virginia, 1987), 4: 198.

5. "Comme nous étions et ce que nous avons fait," *Écrits politiques*, 23: 236–94, Archives générales du Royaume, Brussels.

6. On continuities and ruptures see Malick W. Ghachem, *The Old Regime and the Haitian Revolution* (Cambridge: Cambridge University Press, 2012).

7. On entangled revolutions see Eliga Gould, "Entangled Histories, Entangled Worlds: The English-Speaking Atlantic as a Spanish Periphery," *American Historical Review* 112, no. 3 (2007): 764–86.

8. Jacques-Pierre Brissot, "Discours sur un Projet de décret relatif à la révolte des noirs" (30 October 1791), vol. 8, *La révolution française et l'abolition de l'esclavage* (Paris: Éditions d'histoire sociale, 1968).

9. Nicolas de Condorcet, "Éloge de Franklin," cited by Durand Echeverria, *Mirage in the West: A History of the French Image of American Society to 1815* (Princeton: Princeton University Press, 1957), 406–7.

10. *"Mercure Flandrico-Latino-Gallico-Belgique,"* *Révolution belge*, vol. 19, Bibliothèque Royale/Koniklijke Bibliotheek, Brussels.

11. Denis Diderot, *Encyclopédie, ou dictionnaire raisonné des sciences, des arts, et des métiers*, in Lynn Hunt, *The French Revolution and Human Rights: A Brief Documentary History* (Boston: Bedford/St. Martin's, 1996), 37.

12. Marquis de Lafayette, 19 April 1777, in *Lafayette in the Age of the American Revolution: Selected Letters and Papers, 1776–1790*, ed. Stanley Idzerda (Ithaca, N.Y.: Cornell University Press, 1977), 1: 27.

13. Louis Sebastien Mercier, *L'An 2440*, ed. Alain Pons (1771; Paris: Adel, Bibliothèque des Utopies, 1977), 313.

14. Betje Wolff, *Holland in 't jaar MMCCCCXL* (1777; Rotterdam: Manteau Marginaal, 1978).

15. Gerrit Paape, *De Bataafsche Republiek, zo als zij behoord te zijn, en zo als zij weezen kan: of revolutionaire droom in 1798, wegens toekomstige gebeurtinissen tot 1998*, cited by Willem Frijhoff, "La société idéale des patriotes bataves," in *Le Voyage revolutionnaire*, ed. Willem Frijhoff and Rudolf Dekker (Hilversum: Verloren 1991), 141. See also Peter Altena, *Gerrit Paape (1752–1803): Levens en Werken* (Nijmegen: UItgeverij Vantilt, 2012).

16. Louis Sebastien Mercier cited by Bronislaw Baczko, *Lumières de l'utopie* (Paris: Payot, 1978), 40.

17. Marquis de Condorcet cited by Raymond Trousson, Preface to Louis Sebastien Mercier, *L'An Deux Mille Quatre Cent Quarante* (1779; Geneva: Slatkine Reprints, 1979), xiii.

18. John Adams to Thomas Jefferson, 1815, quoted by Bernard Bailyn, *The Ideological Origins of the American Revolution* (Cambridge: Harvard University Press, 1992), 1.

19. Historian Paul Hazard described the late eighteenth century as a time when "no one stayed in one place"; cited by Madeleine van Strien-Chardonneau, *Le voyage de Hollande: Récits de voyageurs français dans les Provinces Unies 1748–1795* (Oxford: Voltaire Foundation, 1994), 1.

20. Bernard Bailyn, *Atlantic History: Concept and Contours* (Cambridge: Harvard University Press, 2005), 61.

21. Olaudah Equiano, *The Interesting Narrative and Other Writings*, ed. Vincent Carretta (1789; New York: Penguin, 2003), 171.

22. Helen Maria Williams cited by Lionel D. Woodward, *Une anglaise amie de la révolution française: Helene Maria Williams et ses amis* (Paris: H. Champion, 1930), 34.

23. Diderot, "Cosmopolite, ou Cosmopolitan," in *Encyclopédie*, 19: 600, as cited by Thomas J. Schlereth, *The Cosmopolitan Ideal in Enlightenment Thought: Its Form and Function in the Ideas of Franklin, Hume, and Voltaire, 1694–1790* (Notre Dame: University of Notre Dame Press, 1977), 47. See also Margaret C. Jacob, *Strangers*

Nowhere in the World: The Rise of Cosmopolitanism in Early Modern Europe (Philadelphia: University of Pennsylvania Press, 2006).

24. Kurt Kersten, *Ein Europäischer Revolutionär: Georg Forster, 1754–1794* (Berlin: A. Seehof, 1921), 71. On shifting claims to citizenship, see Rebecca J. Scott and Jean M. Hébrard, *Freedom Papers: An Atlantic Odyssey in the Age of Emancipation* (Cambridge: Harvard University Press, 2012).

25. See Amanda Anderson, *The Way We Argue Now: A Study in the Cultures of Theory* (Princeton: Princeton University Press, 2006), esp. chapter 3, "Cosmopolitanism, Universalism, and the Divided Legacies of Modernity."

26. See Marc Belissa and Bernard Cottret, *Cosmopolitismes, Patriotismes, Europe et Amériques, 1763–1802* (Paris: Les Perséides, 2005). As an example of the literature, see *Les bigarures d'un citoyen de Genève à ses Conseils républicains, dediés aux Américains* (Philadelphia: L'Imprimerie du Conseil Général, 1776).

27. William Cobbett, *Farewell to America*, in *Life and Adventures of Peter Porcupine with other Records of his Early Career in England & America*, ed. G. D. H. Cole (Port Washington, N.Y.: Kennikat, 1927), 125.

28. William Cobbett cited by Raymond Williams, *Cobbett* (New York: Oxford University Press, 1983), 8.

29. Jean-Paul Marat, *Appel à la nation* (1790).

30. British historian John Brewer has called this broader debate "an alternative structure of politics"; cited by Nicolaas C. F. Van Sas, "The Patriot Revolution: New Perspectives," in *The Dutch Republic in the Eighteenth Century: Decline, Enlightenment, and Revolution*, ed. Margaret C. Jacob and Wijnand W. Mijnhardt (Ithaca, N.Y.: Cornell University Press, 1992), 115.

31. Abraham Bishop, "Rights of Black Men," in Tim Matthewson, "Abraham Bishop, 'The Rights of Black Men,' and the American Reaction to the Haitian Revolution," *Journal of Negro History* 67 (1982): 153.

32. Watson, *Men and Times of The Revolution*, 159, 33, 271. Moving through what sociologist Paul Gilroy describes as "the shifting spaces in between the fixed places they connected," itinerants saw things differently than did those who stayed at home; Gilroy, *The Black Atlantic: Modernity and Double Consciousness* (Cambridge: Harvard University Press, 1993), 16–17.

33. "Adresse des nouveaux citoyens," 3 March 1793, C 7A 46, Archives d'Outre Mer, Aix-en-Provence.

34. In his *Letters from a Citizen of New-Heaven* (*Lettres d'un bourgeois de New-Heaven*), the marquis de Condorcet asked Americans why they excluded women from owning property and holding public office in their new republic.

35. The terms come from Laurent Dubois, *Avengers of the New World: The Story of the Haitian Revolution* (Cambridge: Harvard University Press, 2004), 6.

36. Historians making the case for a more expansive definition of the time period include, among many, Jeremy Adelman, *Sovereignty and Revolution in the Iberian*

Atlantic (Princeton: Princeton University Press, 2006); François-Xavier Gabriel Guerra, *Modernidad e Independencias, Ensayos sobre las revoluciones hispánica* (Madrid: Editorial Mapfre, 1992); Jane Landers, *Atlantic Creoles in the Age of Revolutions* (Cambridge: Harvard University Press, 2010); Claudia Rosa Lauro, ed., *El Miedo en el Perù. Siglos XVI al XX* (Lima: Pontificia Universidad Católica del Perú, 2005); and Gabriel Paquette, *Imperial Portugal in the Age of Atlantic Revolutions: The Luso-Brazilian World, c. 1770–1850* (Cambridge: Cambridge University Press, 2013).

37. The most frequently read documents, those left by the most famous of the travelers, can now be found online. Endnotes indicate the path to find them. At the other extreme, a few of the documents, hidden away at the end of the eighteenth century by reluctant revolutionaries, were discovered in the possession of nineteenth-century ancestors and cited in obscure histories, only to disappear again completely over the course of the last hundred years. They have been read, cited, and returned to their folios in provincial archives.

38. Emily Pierpont Delesdernier, *Fannie St. John: A Romantic Incident of the American Revolution* (New York: Hurd and Houghton, 1874), vi.

CHAPTER 1. "THE CAUSE OF ALL MANKIND" IN REVOLUTIONARY PAMPHLETS

1. J. D. Candaux, "La Révolution genevoise de 1782: Un état de la question," in *Études sur le XVIIIe siècle, L'Europe et les révolutions (1779–1800)* 8 (1980): 84.

2. Thomas Paine, "Common Sense to the Public on Mr. Deane's Affair," *Pennsylvania Packet*, 31 December 1778, in Thomas Paine, *The Writings of Thomas Paine*, ed. Moncure Daniel Conway (New York: G. P. Putnam's Sons, 1894), 1: 409.

3. Thomas Paine, *Common Sense*, in Thomas Paine, *Collected Writings*, ed. Eric Foner (New York: Library Classics of the United States, 1995), 12.

4. Anne Thérèse Philippine d'Yve, *À la nation*, 10 November 1788, Goethals 210, Archives générales du Royaume/Rijksarchief, Brussels.

5. Camille Desmoulins, *Révolutions de France et de Brabant* (1789).

6. John Adams, *Thoughts on Government*, ed. George A. Peek (Indianapolis: Hackett, 2002), 82; John Adams, *The Works of John Adams, Second President of the United States: Autobiography*, ed. Charles Francis Adams (Boston: Charles C. Little and James Brown, 1850), 2: 507.

7. Benjamin Rush cited by Scott Liell, *46 Pages: Thomas Paine, Common Sense, and the Turning Point to American Independence* (Philadelphia: Running Press, 2003), 57.

8. Thomas Paine cited by Jack Fruchtman Jr., *Thomas Paine: Apostle of Freedom* (New York: Four Walls Eight Windows, 1994), 44.

9. Ibid., 77. Trish Loughran argues that the actual number of copies printed and sold was much less. Historians have too readily believed Paine's exaggerated figures, she charges. Trish Loughran, *The Republic in Print: Print Culture in the Age of U.S. Nation Building, 1770–1870* (New York: Columbia University Press, 2007).

10. Benjamin Rush cited by Gary Nash, *The Unknown American Revolution, The Unruly Birth of Democracy, and the Struggle to Create America* (New York: Penguin, 2005), 189.

11. Josiah Bartlett, 13 January 1776, cited by Liell, *46 Pages*, 88.

12. Samuel Ward, 19 February 1776, cited by Liell, *46 Pages*, 89.

13. John Penn to James Warren cited by Harvey J. Kaye, *Thomas Paine and the Promise of America* (New York: Hill and Wang, 2005), 51.

14. Paine, *Common Sense*, 5, 10, 17. On the power of Paine's prose, see Jill Lepore, "A World of Paine," in *Revolutionary Founders: Rebels, Radicals, and Reformers in the Making of the Nation*, ed. Alfred F. Young, Gary B. Nash, and Ray Raphael (New York: Knopf, 2011), 87–96.

15. Paine, *Common Sense*, 25, 48, 28, 52, 14.

16. James Chalmers, *Plain Truth: Addressed to the Inhabitants of America, containing Remarks on a late Pamphlet intitled Common Sense: wherein are Shewn, that the scheme of Independence is ruinous, delusive and impracticable*, 2nd ed. (London: J. Almon, 1776), Gould Library, Carleton College. I am grateful to Professor Clifford Clark for calling the document housed in the rare books collection to my attention.

17. John Cartwright to Edmund Burke, in *The Life and Correspondence of Major Cartwright*, ed. F. D. Cartwright (London: Henry Colburn 1826), 53.

18. John Cartwright, *American Independence. The Interest and Glory of Great Britain. A new Edition* (London: H. S. Woodfall, 1775), 7.

19. Richard Price, *Observations on the Nature of Civil Liberty*, in *Cambridge Texts in the History of Political Thought*, ed. D. O. Thomas, http://www.constitution.org/price/price_x.htm.

20. Richard Price cited by David Oswald Thomas, *Richard Price and America (1723–91)* (Aberystwyth: Thomas, 1975), 11. Price replied that he hoped to be remembered by the Americans "as a zealous friend to liberty who is anxiously attentive to the great struggle in which they are engag'd." Richard Price to Arthur Lee, 18 January 1779.

21. Richard Price, *Aanmerkingen over den aart der burgerlijke Vrijheid enz*, trans. Joan van der Capellen (Leiden: L. Herding, 1776). Van der Capellen also served as a conduit, sending other pamphlets to Price in what developed into a regular correspondence.

22. Johan Derk van der Capellen tot den Pol, *Advis door Jonkheer Johan Derk van der Capellen tot den Pol, over het verzoek van zyne Majesteit den koning van Groot Brittannien, raakende het leenen der Schotsche Brigade, op den 16 December 1775, ter Staats-vergadering van Overyssel uitgebragt, en in de Notulen dier Provincie geinsereerd* (n.p., n.d.). Van der Capellen's pamphlet had originally been delivered as an address to the Estates of the eastern province of Overijssel protesting Willem V's promise of his "Scots Brigade" to King George for use in subduing the Americans. Why, he asked, would the Dutch, who had fought their own revolution for independence in the seventeenth century, align themselves against the Americans?

23. Jonathan Trumbull to Joan Derk van der Capellen, 17 June 1777, Collectie Fagel 1.10.29, 1463, Algemeen Rijksarchief, The Hague.

24. Joan Derk van der Capellen to Jonathan Trumbull, Zwolle, 7 December 1778, in *Brieven van en aan Joan Derck van der Capellen tot den Pol*, ed. W. J. de Beaufort (Utrecht: Kemink en zoon, 1879), 85. Van der Capellen meanwhile struggled to secure his "rightful" place in the knighthood of Overijssel. He had been removed after his condemnation of Willem V.

25. Joan Derk van der Capellen to William Livingston, in de Beaufort, *Brieven*, 91.

26. William Livingston to van der Capellen, Trenton, 30 November 1778, in de Beaufort, *Brieven*, 67; and Jonathan Trumbull to Joan van der Capellen, Lebanon, 17 June 1797, Collectie Fagel 1463, Algemeen Rijksarchief, The Hague.

27. John Adams to Joan Derk van der Capellen, Amsterdam, 22 October 1780, in de Beaufort, *Brieven*, 200; and John Adams to Robert Livingston, The Hague, 4 September 1782, Papers of Charles Guillaume Fréderic Dumas, Library of Congress.

28. Edmund Burke cited by David Armitage, *The Declaration of Independence: A Global History* (Cambridge: Harvard University Press, 2007), 87.

29. Jacques-Pierre Brissot, *Mémoires*, cited by Eloise Ellery, *Brissot de Warville: A Study in the History of the French Revolution* (New York: Houghton Mifflin, 1915), 11.

30. [J.-P. Brissot de Warville], *Le Philadelphien à Genève ou Lettres d'un Américain sur la dernière révolution de Genève: sa constitution nouvelle, l'émigration en Irlande, &c. pouvant servir de tableau politique de Genève jusqu'en 1784* (Dublin, 1783), 47.

31. Ibid., 152.

32. J.-P. Brissot, *New Travels in the United States*, ed. Pierre de Jacques (Cambridge: Harvard University Press, 1964), 78.

33. [Brissot], *Le Philadelphien*, 40, 43.

34. Jacques-Antoine du Roveray, *Très humble et très-respectueuse représentation*, cited by Richard Whatmore, *Against War and Empire: Geneva, Britain, and France in the Eighteenth Century* (New Haven: Yale University Press, 2012), 156.

35. V.T.O.S., *Lettre d'un Philosophe François à un Citoyen de Genève (26 April 1782)*, in *Écrits politiques faits & imprimés à Genève en 1781*, 315 39, Bibliothèque de Genève, Geneva.

36. [Brissot], *Le Philadelphien*, 65.

37. [Isaac Cornuaud and Jacques Mallet du Pan], *Relation de la conjuration contre le gouvernement et le Majesté de Genève, qui a éclaté le 8 avril, 1782* (Geneva, 1782).

38. Jacques Mallet du Pan, *Memoirs and Correspondence of Mallet du Pan Illustrative of the History of the French Revolution*, ed. A. Sayous (London: Richard Bentley, 1852), 1: 7.

39. *Un natif isolé à ses concitoyens, les natifs partisans des aristocrates*, in *Écrits politiques faits & imprimés à Genève en 1781*, Gf 567 218, Bibliothèque de Genève, Geneva.

40. Micheli du Crest, Conseiler d'État de la Ville et République de Genève, 2 May 1782, cited by Édouard Chapuisat, *La prise d'armes de 1782 à Genève* (Geneva: A. Jullien, 1932).

41. [Brissot], *Le Philadelphien*, 47, 51.

42. Jean de Roget, *Lettres de Jean Roget, 1753–1783*, ed. F.-F. Roget (Geneva: Georg, 1911), 211–12.

43. *Dernière déclaration des Genevois remise aux seigneurs sindics, le mardi 2 juillet 1782 à deux heures, après minuit par eux envoyée le même matin aux trois Généraux*," 2480a, in Émile Rivoire, "Bibliographie historique de Genève au XVIII siècle," in *Mémoires et documents publies par la société d'histoire et d'archéologie de Genève*, 26–27 (Geneva and Paris, 1897).

44. [Brissot], *Le Philadelphien*, 54, 47. See J. Bénétruy, *L'atelier de Mirabeau. Quatre proscrits génevois dans la tourmente révolutionnaire* (Paris: A. et J. Picard, 1962), 38–39.

45. Mercy Otis Warren, *History of the Rise, Progress, and Termination of the American Revolution* (Boston: Edward Larkin, 1805), vol. 3, chapter 22. On Warren's history, see Rosemarie Zagarri, *A Woman's Dilemma: Mercy Otis Warren and the American Revolution* (Wheeling, Ill.: Harland Davidson, 1995).

46. *Précis historique de la dernière révolution de Genève, et en particulier de la réforme que le souverain de cette république a faite dans les conseils inférieurs* (Geneva, 1782), GF 315 39, Bibliothèque de Genève, Geneva.

47. *Relation d'un voyage fait aux Indes orientales*, GF 567218, Bibliothèque de Genève, Geneva.

48. Joan Derk van der Capellen tot den Pol cited by Craig Harline, *Pamphlets, Printing, and Political Culture in the Early Dutch Republic* (Dordrecht: Martinus Nijhoff, 1987), 23. The impact of the Genevan defeat in the United Provinces can be seen in the debates waged in Cérisier's radical newspaper, the *Politique hollandois*, and the conservative *Courrier du Bas-Rhin*.

49. Benjamin Franklin to Charles Dumas, 1 August 1781, in Hella S. Haasse, *Schaduwbeeld of het geheim van Appeltern. Kroniek van een leven* (Amsterdam: Em. Querido's Uitgeverij, 1989), 347.

50. Peter Ochs to Iselin, 8 September 1776, in *Korrespondenz des Peter Ochs*, ed. Gustav Steine (Basel: Verslag von Henning Opperman, 1927), 1: 86.

51. John Paul Jones for Anna Jacoba Dumas, cited by Jan Willem Shulte Nordholt, *The Dutch Republic and American Independence*, trans. Herbert H. Rowen (Chapel Hill: University of North Carolina Press, 1982), 75. See also Friedrich Edler, *The Dutch Republic and the American Revolution* (Baltimore: Johns Hopkins University Press, 1911,), 62–69.

52. Franklin assured van der Capellen that "our virgin state is a jolly one & though at present not very rich, will in time be a great fortune to any suitor." Benjamin Franklin to Joan van der Capellen, 22 September 1778, Collectie Fagel 1464, Nationaal Archief, The Hague.

53. Joan van der Capellen, *An Address to the People of the Netherlands on the Present alarming and most Dangerous Situation of the Republick of Holland: showing the true motives of the most unpardonable delays of the executive power in putting republick into a proper state of Defence and the Advantages of an Alliance with Holland, France and America. Translated from the Dutch Original* (London: J. Stockdale, 1782), 137, 37, 40, 137. See also John Sterk, "The Pamphlet That Woke a Nation," M.A. thesis, University of Victoria, 2004.

54. Adriaan Kluit cited by Harline, *Pamphlets, Printing, and Political Culture*, 23.

55. Abigail Adams to John Adams, 23 April 1781, cited by G. C. Gibbs, "The Dutch Revolt and the American Revolution," in *Royal and Republican Sovereignty in Early Modern Europe: Essays in Memory of Ragnhild Hatton*, ed. Robert Oresko, G. C. Gibbs, and H. M. Scott (Cambridge: Cambridge University Press, 1997), 617.

56. John Adams, *Memorial to their High Mightinesses, the States General of the United Provinces of the Low Countries*, in *The Works of John Adams, Second President of the United States*, ed. Charles Francis Adams (Boston: Little, Brown, 1852), 7: 400.

57. Cited by Simon Schama, *Patriots and Liberators* (New York: Knopf, 1977), 95. See also Stephan Klein and Joost Rosendaal, "Democratie in Context. Nieuwe Perspectieve op het Leids Ontwerp (1785)," *De Achttiende Eeuw* 26 (1994): 71–100.

58. *Lettre sur l'invasion des Provinces-Unies à M. Le comte de Mirabeau et sa réponse, publiées par la Commission que les Patriotes Hollandois ont établie à Bruxelles* (Brussels: 1787).

59. Mirabeau, *Aux Bataves. Sur le Stathoudérat* (London, 1788), 4, 5, 71, 70. Authorship was not always straightforward at the end of the eighteenth century. The pamphlet was actually written by Brissot and others in Mirabeau's workshop. See Whatmore, *Against War and Empire*, 225.

60. Van der Capellen tot den Pol, *Advis door Jonkheer Johan Derk van der Capellen tot den Pol*, 2.

61. John Adams to John Trumbull, 13 February 1776, cited by Joseph J. Ellis, *American Creation: Triumphs and Tragedies at the Founding of the Republic* (New York: Knopf, 2007), 44.

62. Charles Lambert d'Outrepont, *Considérations sur la Constitution des Duchés de Brabant et Limbourg* (May 13, 1787), *Révolution belge*, vol. 35, pamphlet 13, Bibliothèque Royale/Koninklijke Bibliotheek, Brussels.

63. George Talker, *Quelques réflexions politcopratiques, ou adieux à Bruxelles*, Acquisitions récentes 4/13, Archives génerales du Royaume/Rijksarchief, Brussels.

64. d'Outrepont, *Considérations sur la Constitution*.

65. Jan Bicker cited by M. N. Bisselink and A. Doedens, eds., *Jan Bernd Bicker: een Patriot in Ballingschap 1787–1795* (Amsterdam: VU Boekhandel, 1983), 40. See also Emillie Fijnje-Luzac, *Myne beslommerde Boedel. Brieven in Ballingschap 1787–1788*, ed. Jacques J. M. Baartmans (Nijmegen: Vantilt, 2003). Gerrit Paape was getting a shave at the barber in Brussels when he learned of the Belgians' plans to attack

the Austrians. The barber announced that Paape was his last client before he left to join the revolution; Peter Altena, *Gerrit Paape, 1752–1803. Levens en werken* (Nijmegen: Universiteit Nijmegen, 2011), 268.

66. *Trompette anti-autrichienne*, in *Revolution belge*, vol. 162, pamphlet 20, Bibliothèque Royale/Koninklijke Bibliotheek, Brussels.

67. *Stormklok ofte rechtveerdigen Roep om Hulp*, in *Revolution belge*, vol. 114, pamphlet 10, Bibliothèque Royale/Koninklijke Bibliotheek, Brussels; Liasse 611, Archives de la Ville de Bruxelles/Archief van de Stad Brussel, Brussels; Abbé de Feller, 17 September 1787, ms. 21142, Bibliothèque Royale/Koninklijke Bibliotheek, Brussels; and *Représentation des États*, 22 October 1787, Liasse 610, Archives de la Ville de Bruxelles/Archief van de Stad Brussel, Brussels.

68. Stijn van Rossem, *Politieke Prenten tijdens de Brabantse Omwenteling (1787–1792)*, Verhandeling aangeboden tot het behalen van de graad van licenciaat in de Geschiedenis, Katholieke Universiteit Leuven, 2000, fig. 11.1 (2); and Stijn van Rossem, *Revolutie op de Koper Plaat. Repertorium van politieke Prenten tijdens de Brabantse Omwenteling* (Louvain: Peeters, 2012).

69. See Jan Roegiers, "De Gedaantewisseling van het zuidnederlands Ultramontanisme, 1750–1830," *De Kruistocht tegen het Liberalisme*, ed. Emiel Lamberts (Louvain: Universitaire pers Leuven, 1984).

70. *Trompette anti-autrichienne*, in *Revolution belge*, vol. 162, pamphlet 20, Bibliothèque Royale/Koninklijke Bibliotheek, Brussels.

71. Henri van der Noot, *Mémoire sur les droits du peuple brabançon*, 24 April 1787, in *Révolution belge*, vol. 35, pamphlet 4, Bibliothèque Royale/Koninklijke Bibliotheek, Brussels.

72. "Peuple Belgique/cour tyranique/faisons comme l'Amérique." Madame de Bellem, Préliminaires de la Révolution, 1787–1790, États Belgiques Unis 1, Archives Générales du Royaume/Algemene Rijksarchief, Brussels.

73. Anne Thérèse Philippine d'Yve, *À la nation*, 10 November 1788, Goethals 210, Archives générales du Royaume/Rijksarchief, Brussels.

74. *Précis historique sur les anciennes Belges*, Bibliothèque 813/2, Archives de la Ville de Bruxelles/Archief van de stad Brussel, Brussels. On women in the Brabant Revolution, see Janet Polasky, "Women in Revolutionary Brussels: 'The Source of Our Greatest Strength,'" in *Women and Politics in the Age of Democratic Revolution*, ed. Darline Levy and Harriet Applewhite (Ann Arbor: University of Michigan Press, 1989), 147–62.

75. Ms. 19648, Bibliothèque Royale/Koninklijke Bibliotheek, Brussels; and *Précis historique de la Révolution des États Unis de l'Amérique, précédé de l'histoire de ces provinces jusqu'à l'époque de la Révolution et suivi du Manifeste ou de l'Acte de l'Indépendance des treize États Unis* (Ghent: P. F. de Goesin, 1789).

76. *Les Auteurs secrets de la Révolution présente*, in *Révolution helge*, vol. 48, Bibliothèque Royale/Koninklijke Bibliotheek, Brussels.

77. *Mémoire justificatif en faveur de Ph. Secrétan; Citoyen de Lausanne en Suisse* (Brussels, 1790), Bibliothèque Royale/Koninklijke Bibliotheek, Brussels.

78. *Manifeste du peuple brabançon,* in *Révolution belge,* vol. 72, pamphlet 12, Bibliothèque Royale/Koninklijke Bibliotheek, Brussels. In contrast to the American Declaration of Independence, triumphantly displayed at the U.S. National Archives, the original *Manifeste du Peuple Brabançon* was almost passed over at auction even though it was offered for less than one thousand euros. Representatives of the Archives générales du Royaume/Algemeen Rijksarchief were finally persuaded to acquire the *Manifeste.* Thanks to the late Jan Roegiers, former librarian, archivist, and professor of history at Katholieke Universiteit Leuven, for sharing this story with me.

79. *Mercure Flandrico-Latino-Gallico-Belgique,* in *Révolution belge,* vol. 19, Bibliothèque Royale/Koninklijke Bibliotheek, Brussels.

80. Abbé de Feller, *Journal historique et littéraire,* 1 December 1789, États Belgiques Unis 181, Archives générales du Royaume/Rijksarchief, Brussels.

81. *Journal général de l'Europe* 152 (19 December 1789): 321.

82. *Projet d'adresse à présenter à l'illustre assemblée des états de Brabant par plusieurs citoyens de tout rang & de tout état* (Brussels, 1790).

83. *Reflexions politiques et historiques sur la République des Provinces Belgiques Unies et sur les troubles qui ont filli étoufer dans sa naissance* (Liège, 1790).

84. *Relation d'un député de la lune qui avoit été envoyé dans la Belgique pour y prendre des informations relatives à la Révolution qui s'y opéroit & aux effets qu'y avoient produits les troupes Lunaires qui y étoient descendues* (Brussels, 1790), *Révolution belge,* vol. 51, pamphlet 23, Bibliothèque Royale/Koninklijke Bibliotheek, Brussels.

85. Price, *Observations on Civil Liberty.*

86. Charles Lambert d'Outrepont, "Qu'allons nous devenir?" *Révolution Belge,* vol. 46, pamphlet 2, Bibliothèque Royale/Koninklijke Bibliotheek, Brussels.

87. Jean-Baptiste Mailhe, *Discours sur la Grandeur et l'importance de la révolution dans l'Amérique septentrional* (Toulouse, 1784), 38.

88. Benjamin Franklin to Samuel Cooper, 1 May 1777, as cited by Thomas J. Schlereth, *The Cosmopolitan Ideal in Enlightenment Thought: Its Form and Function in the Ideas of Franklin, Hume, and Voltaire, 1694–1790* (Notre Dame: University of Notre Dame Press, 1977), 106.

89. Richard Price to Benjamin Franklin cited by Thomas, *Richard Price and America,* 39.

90. *Reflexions d'un cosmopolite demeurant à Bruxelles en janvier mdccxc* (Brussels, 1790).

91. Paine, *Common Sense,* 53, 52.

92. Condorcet, *On the Influence of the American Revolution on Europe* (1786), in *Condorcet: Selected Writing,* ed. Keith Baker (Indianapolis: Bobbs Merrill, 1976), 76.

93. Submitted in response to a question posed by the Abbé Raynal, Condorcet's *Letters of a Citizen of the United States to a Frenchman on Present Affairs by Mr. Le M***

de C** was republished two years later in French by a friend of Thomas Jefferson's, the Tuscan merchant Filippo Mazzei, *Lettres d'un Citoyen des États Unis à Un Français sur les Affaires Présentes, par Mr. Le M** de C**** (Philadelphia, 1788). See also Durand Echeverria, "Cordorcet's *The Influence of the American Revolution on Europe,*" *William and Mary Quarterly* 25 (1968): 85–108.

94. Guillaume Raynal, *L'histoire philosophique et politique des établissemens du commerce des Européens dans les deux Indes,* vol. 9 (Paris: Berry, 1781), 284; and Guillaume-Thomas Raynal, *Révolution de l'Amérique* (London: L. Davis, 1781), 12–13, 78.

95. Thomas Paine, *A Letter Addressed to the Abbé Raynal on the Affairs of North America. In which the Mistakes in the Abbé's Account of the Revolution are Corrected and Cleared Up* (London: J. Ridgway, 1792); and [Guillaume-Thomas Raynal], *The Sentiments of a Foreigner on the Disputes of Great Britain with America* (Philadelphia: James Humphreys, junior, 1775), 16.

96. Thomas Paine, *Remarques sur les erreurs de l'Histoire philosophique et politique de Mr. Guillaume Thomas Raynal,* trans. A. M. Cérisier (Amsterdam: A. Crajenschot, 1783).

97. Cited by Craig Nelson, *Thomas Paine: Enlightenment, Revolution, and the Birth of Modern Nations* (New York: Viking, 2006), 163. See also Frank Smith, *Thomas Paine, Liberator* (New York: Frederick Stokes, 1938), 100; and Jack Fruchtman Jr., "Thomas Paine's Early Radicalism," in *Paine and Jefferson in the Age of Revolutions,* ed. Simon P. Newman and Peter S. Onuf (Charlottesville: University of Virginia Press, 2013), 60–64.

98. Richard Price to Benjamin Franklin cited by Thomas, *Richard Price and America,* 39.

99. Desmoulins, *Révolutions de France et de Brabant,* 3: 131.

100. Paine, *Letter Addressed to the Abbé Raynal on the Affairs of North America.*

101. Peter Ochs, 9 October 1789, *Korrespondenz des Peter Ochs 1752–1821,* 1: 218.

CHAPTER 2. JOURNALS RELATING "A SHARE IN TWO REVOLUTIONS"

1. Étienne Dumont to Samuel Romilly cited by J. Bénétruy, *L'atelier de Mirabeau. Quatre proscrits génevois dans la tourmente révolutionnaire* (Paris: A. et J. Picard, 1962), 187.

2. Madeleine Van Strien-Chardonneau, *Le voyage de Hollande: récits de voyageurs français dans les Provinces-Unies 1748–1795* (Oxford: Voltaire Foundation, 1994), 183.

3. Count Leopold Berchtold (1789) discussed by Justin Stagl, *A History of Curiosity: The Theory of Travel, 1550–1800* (Australia: Harwood Academic, 1995), 223–25.

4. Elkanah Watson, *A Tour in Holland in 1784 by an American* (Worcester, Mass.: Isaiah Thomas, 1790), 25.

5. Ralph Griffiths cited by Charles L. Batten Jr., *Pleasurable Instruction: Form and Convention in Eighteenth-Century Travel Literature* (Berkeley: University of California Press, 1978), 1.

6. Guillaume-Thomas Raynal, ed., *Histoire philosophique et politique, des établissemens & du commerce des Européens dans les deux Indes* (Amsterdam, 1770).

7. Georg Förster, *Voyage philosophique et pittoresque* (Paris: F. Buisson, 1794), 1: 286. Published originally as *Ansichten vom Niederrhein, von Brabant, Flandern, Holland, England und Frankreich im April, Mai und Junius 1790* (Berlin: Voss, 1794).

8. Elkanah Watson, *Men and Times of The Revolution. Memoirs of Elkanah Watson including his Journals of Travels in Europe and America from the Year 1777 to 1842*, ed. Winslow C. Watson (New York: Dana, 1856), 32 and 271.

9. Elkanah Watson, "Travels in France 1779 & 1780," GB 12579, box 1, vol. 3, New York State Library, Albany.

10. Ibid.

11. Watson, *Men and Times of The Revolution*, 96.

12. Watson, "Travels in France 1779 & 1780."

13. François Barbé-Marbois, *Our Revolutionary Forefathers: The Letters of François, Marquis de Barbé-Marbois during his Residence in the United States as Secretary of the French Legation 1779–1785*, ed. Eugene P. Chase (New York: Duffield, 1929), 54.

14. Watson, "Travels in France 1779 & 1780."

15. Ibid.

16. Watson, *Men and Times of The Revolution*, 103, 79; and Elkanah Watson, Journal A, 1758–1781, GB 12579, box 2, folio 2, New York State Library, Albany.

17. Watson, Journal A.

18. Watson, *Men and Times of The Revolution*, 95, 115, 158.

19. Elkanah Watson to John Adams, 10 March 1780; and John Adams to Elkanah Watson, and Elkanah Watson to John Adams, 4 May 1780, in Watson, "Travels in France 1779 & 1780."

20. Watson, *Men and Times of The Revolution*, 159, 126, 169.

21. Ibid., 127. Watson's account was possibly colored in hindsight by subsequent hostile press coverage of Paine's travels in France.

22. Thomas Paine cited by Jack Fruchtman Jr., *Thomas Paine: Apostle of Freedom* (New York: Four Walls Eight Windows, 1994), 133.

23. Watson, *Men and Times of The Revolution*, 32.

24. John Adams to Abigail Adams cited by Jan Willem Shulte Nordholt, *The Dutch Republic and American Independence*, trans. Herbert H. Rowe (Chapel Hill: University of North Carolina Press, 1982), 226.

25. Watson, *Men and Times of The Revolution*, 267, 268.

26. Watson, *A Tour in Holland*, 49.

27. Jacques-Pierre de Brissot and Étienne de Clavière, *De la France et des États Unis, ou de l'importance de la révolution de l'Amérique pour le bonheur de la France, des rapports de ce Royaume et des États-Unis, des avantages réciproques qu'ils peuvent retirer de leurs liaisons de commerce, et enfin de la situation actuelle des États Unis* (1787; Paris: Éditions du CTHS, 1996), xxxi.

28. J. Hector Saint John de Crèvecoeur, *Letters from an American Farmer* (1782; Oxford: Oxford University Press, 1997), 45.

29. Procès-Verbaux de la Société Gallo-Américaine, Séance du 9 janvier 1787, in J.-P. Brissot, *Correspondance et papiers*, ed. Cl. Perroud (Paris: Librairie Alphonse Picard, n.d.), 108.

30. J.-P. Brissot, *New Travels in the United States*, ed. Pierre de Jacques (Cambridge: Harvard University Press, 1964), 78, 84.

31. Ibid., 19, 21.

32. Ibid., 84, 21.

33. Ibid., 145.

34. The Quakers could do little to reassure him about an end to slavery in America, leaving Brissot to propose sending American blacks back to Africa; ibid., 222.

35. Barbé-Marbois, *Our Revolutionary Forefathers*, 48.

36. Carel de Vos Van Steenwijk, *Een grand Tour naar de nieuwe Republiek: Journaal van een Reis door Amerika, 1783–84*, ed. Wayne te Brake (Hilversum: Verloren, 1999), 113.

37. Philip Mazzei, *Recherches historiques et politiques sur les États Unis de l'Amérique Septentrionale* (Paris: Chez Froulie, 1788), 4: 127.

38. Crèvecoeur, *Letters from an American Farmer*, 154.

39. Barbé-Marbois, *Our Revolutionary Forefathers*, 78.

40. Brissot, *New Travels in the United States*, 6.

41. Étienne Dumont, *The Great Frenchman and the little Genevese. Translated from Étienne Dumont's Souvenir sur Mirabeau*, ed. Elizabeth Seymour (London: Duckworth, 1904), 19.

42. Étienne Dumont to Samuel Romilly cited by Bénétruy, *L'atelier de Mirabeau*, 187. On Dumont's role in the workshop, see also Jefferson P. Seth, *Firm Heart and Capacious Mind: The Life and Friends of Étienne Dumont* (Lanham, Md.: University Press of America, 1997), 57–80; and Richard Whatmore, *Against War and Empire: Geneva, Britain, and France in the Eighteenth Century* (New Haven: Yale University Press, 2012), 228–43.

43. Dumont, *The Great Frenchman*, 7.

44. Ibid., 21.

45. Étienne Dumont, Versailles, 18 June 1789, *Letters, containing an account of the late revolution in France, and observations on the constitution, laws, manners, and institutions of the English; written during the author's residence at Paris, Versailles, and London, in the years 1789 and 1790* (London: J. Johnson, 1792), 15.

46. Ibid., Versailles, 26 June 1789, 90, and 18 June 1789, 53.

47. Ibid., Versailles, 24 July 1789, 153.

48. Ibid., Versailles, 24 July 1789, 122.

49. Dumont, *The Great Frenchman*, 85.

50. Jean Baptiste Salle cited by David Andress, *1789: The Threshold of the Modern Age* (New York: Farrar, Straus and Giroux, 2008), 332.

51. Étienne Dumont cited by Seth, *Firm Heart and Capacious Mind*, 53.

52. Dumont, *The Great Frenchman*, 3.

53. On the reception of English constitutional ideas on the Continent, see Whatmore, *Against War and Empire*.

54. Étienne Dumont to Samuel Romilly, Versailles, 13 November 1793, in Samuel Romilly, *Memoirs of the Life of Sir Samuel Romilly, Written by Himself; with a Selection from his Correspondence* (London: John Murray, 1840), 2: 31–32.

55. Dumont, *The Great Frenchman*, xviii.

56. Dumont, Paris, 15 August 1789, *Letters*, 225. Richard Whatmore, "Étienne Dumont, the British Constitution, and the French Revolution," *Historical Journal* 30 (2007): 23–47.

57. *Letters, containing an account of the late revolution in France.*

58. J. L. Duval, Preface to Dumont, *The Great Frenchman*, xix.

59. Helen Maria Williams, *Letters Written in France 1790* (1790, Oxford: Woodstock, 1989), 5. On Williams's response to the festival, see the editors' introduction to Helen Maria Williams, *Letters Written in France in the Summer 1790, to a Friend in England; Containing Various Anecdotes Relative to the French Revolution*, ed. Neil Fraistat and Susan S. Lanser (Peterborough, Ont.: Broadview, 2001).

60. Helen Maria Williams cited by Woodward, *Une anglaise amie de la révolution française*, 34.

61. Williams, *Letters Written in France*, 37.

62. Ibid., 50.

63. Helen Maria Williams, *Letters from France* (London: G. G. J. and J. Robinson, 1792), 2: 52, 76.

64. Williams, *Letters Written in France*, 48–49.

65. Ibid., 91.

66. Elizabeth Montagu cited by Brian Dolan, *Ladies of the Grand Tour* (London: HarperCollins, 2002), 277.

67. Mary Wollstonecraft to Everina Wollstonecraft, Paris, 24 December 1792, cited by Ray Adams, "Helen Maria Williams and the French Revolution," in *Wordsworth and Coleridge: Studies in Honor of George Mclean Harper*, ed. Earl Leslie Griggs (Princeton: Princeton University Press, 1939), 92.

68. [Laetitia Matilda Hawkins,] *Letters on the Female Mind, Its Powers and Pursuits, Addressed to Miss H. M. Williams, with Particular Reference to Her Letters from France* (London: Hookham and Carpenter, 1793), 1: 128, 6–8; 2: 90.

69. Williams cited by Woodward, *Une anglaise amie de la révolution française*, 46.

70. Helen Maria Williams cited by Gary Kelly, *Women, Writing, and Revolution* (Oxford: Clarendon, 1993), 36; and Helen Maria Williams, *Nouveau voyage en Suisse* (Paris: Charles Pougens, 1798), 18.

71. Williams cited by Woodward, *Une anglaise amie de la révolution française*, 45.

72. Anna Seward cited by Adams, "Helen Maria Williams and the French Revolution," 104.

73. Williams, *Letters Written in France*, 82.

74. Williams, *Letters from France*, 2: 103.

75. Helen Maria Williams cited by Chris Jones, "Helen Maria Williams and Radical Sensibility," *Prose Studies* 12 (May 1989): 13.

76. Brissot, *New Travels in the United States*, 20.

77. Thomas Paine to George Washington, London, 16 October 1789, in Thomas Paine, *Collected Writings* (New York: Library Classics of the United States, 1995), 370.

78. Thomas Paine to George Washington, London, 1 May 1790, ibid., 374.

79. Thomas Jefferson to Richard Price, Paris, 8 January 1789, *The Letters of Thomas Jefferson 1743–1826*, http://www.let.rug.nl/usa/presidents/thomas-jefferson/letters-of-thomas-jefferson/.

80. Edward Thornton cited by Gordon S. Wood, "The Radicalism of Thomas Jefferson and Thomas Paine," in *Paine and Jefferson in the Age of Revolutions*, ed. Simon P. Newman and Peter S. Onuf (Charlottesville: University of Virginia Press, 2013), 14.

81. Gouverneur Morris to the Comte de Moustier, 23 February 1789, cited by Philip Ziesche, *Cosmopolitan Patriots: Americans in Paris in the Age of Revolution* (Charlottesville: University of Virginia Press, 2010), 20.

82. William Short to Thomas Jefferson, 29 June 1791, cited by ibid., 47.

83. Gouverneur Morris to William Short, 29 November 1790, cited ibid., 44.

84. Roger G. Kennedy, *Orders from France: The Americans and the French in a Revolutionary World, 1780–1820* (Philadelphia: University of Pennsylvania Press, 1990), 88.

CHAPTER 3. THE REVOLUTIONARY NARRATIVES OF BLACK "CITIZENS OF THE WORLD"

1. Carl Wadström and August Nordenskiold, *Plan for a Free Community upon the Coast of Africa, under the Protection of Great Britain, but intirely independent of all European Laws and Governments* (London: R. Hindmarsh, 1789).

2. See James Sidbury, *Becoming African in America* (New York: Oxford University Press, 2007), 39.

3. Olaudah Equiano, *The Interesting Narrative and Other Writings*, ed. Vincent Carretta (1789; New York: Penguin, 2003), 71. On reception, see David Richardson,

"Through a Looking Glass: Olaudah Equiano and African Experiences of the British Atlantic Slave Trade," in *Black Experience and the Empire*, ed. Philip D. Morgan and Sean Hawkins (Oxford: Oxford University Press, 2004), 58–85.

4. Anna Falconbridge, Bance Island, 10 February 1791, in *Maiden Voyages and Infant Colonies: Two Women's Travel Narratives of the 1790s*, ed. Deirdre Coleman (London: Leicester University Press, 1999), 65. Anna Falconbridge's published journal, *Narrative of Two Voyages to the River Sierra Leone*, was one of very few books about Africa written by a woman before 1850. For another modern edition see Anna Maria Falconbridge, *Narrative of Two Voyages to the River Sierra Leone During the Years 1791–1792–1793. An Account of the Slave Trade on the Coast of Africa*, ed. Christopher Fyfe (1793; Liverpool: Liverpool University Press, 2000).

5. John Clarkson, "Diary of Lieutenant Clarkson R.N.," *Sierra Leone Studies* 8 (March 1927): 1–114.

6. On imperialism and abolition see Deidre Coleman, *Romantic Colonization and British Anti-Slavery* (Cambridge: Cambridge University Press, 2005), 5; Christopher L. Brown, "Envisioning an Empire without Slavery, 1772–1834," in Morgan and Hawkins, *Black Experience and the Empire*, 111–40; and Cassandra Pybus, "'A Less Favourable Specimen': The Abolitionist Response to Self-Emancipated Slaves in Sierra Leone, 1793–1808," *Parliamentary History* 26, Supplement (2007): 97–112.

7. "Understanding the foundations of abolitionism, then, means understanding human choices," historian Christopher Brown explains as he advocates looking to sources other than Clarkson's journal because it is so intimately tied to Clarkson's personal cause; Christopher Brown, *Moral Capital: Foundations of British Abolitionism* (Chapel Hill: University of North Carolina Press, 2006), 20.

8. See Ismail Rashid, "Escape, Revolt, and Marronage in Eighteenth and Nineteenth Century Sierra Leone Hinterland," *Canadian Journal of African Studies/Revue Canadienne des Études Africaines* 34 (2000): 656–83; and Bruce Mouser, "Rebellion, Marronage, and Jihad: Strategies of Resistance to Slavery on the Sierra Leone Coast, c. 1763–1796," *Journal of African History* 48 (2007): 27–44. Their history, too, is based on the testimony of travelers.

9. Equiano, *Interesting Narrative*, 221, 77.

10. Ibid., 31

11. Equiano to the Rev. Mr. Raymund Harris, *Public Advertiser*, 28 April 1788, ibid., 137.

12. Ibid., 36.

13. Vincent Carretta, "Olaudah Equiano or Gustavus Vassa? New Light on an Eighteenth-Century Question of Identity," *Slavery and Abolition* 20 (1999): 95–105; Vincent Carretta, *Equiano the African: Biography of a Self-Made Man* (Athens: University of Georgia Press, 2005); Paul Lovejoy, "Autobiography and Memory: Gustavus Vassa, alias Olaudah Equiano, the African," *Slavery and Abolition* 27 (2006): 317–47; and Vincent Carretta, "Response to Paul Lovejoy's 'Autobiography

and Memory: Gustavus Vassa, alias Olaudah Equiano, the African," *Slavery and Abolition* 28 (2007): 115–19. I will draw upon the narrative as an account of his life, because that is how it was read in the eighteenth century.

14. Douglas R. Egerton, *Death or Liberty: African Americans and Revolutionary America* (Oxford: Oxford University Press, 2009), 15–16; James Sidbury, *Becoming African in America: Race and Nation in the Early Black Atlantic* (New York: Oxford University Press, 2007); and James H. Sweet, "Mistaken Identities? Olaudah Equiano, Domingos Alvares, and the Methodological Challenges of Studying the African Diaspora," *American Historical Review* 114 (2009): 279–306. Egerton cautions: "After all he remained a man of color in an Atlantic world dominated by slavery. . . . In the end, Equiano's mysterious story serves as a reminder of the unreliability of the words of Africans and African Americans filtered through the pens of whites."

15. Equiano, *Interesting Narrative*, 31.

16. Ottobah Cugoano, *Thoughts and Sentiments on the Evil and Wicked Traffic of the Slavery and Commerce of the Human Species*, ed. Vincent Carretta (1787; New York: Penguin, 1999).

17. Equiano, *Interesting Narrative*, 55, 61.

18. Ibid., 138.

19. Ibid., 137, 138; and Carretta, *Equiano the African*, xiii.

20. Olaudah Equiano to Parliament, London, 14 May 1792, in Equiano, *Interesting Narrative*, 7. See also Brown, *Moral Capital*, 5.

21. Cugoano, *Thoughts and Sentiments*, 66.

22. Equiano, *Interesting Narrative*, 233.

23. Ibid., 164.

24. Ibid., 193.

25. Boston King, "Memoirs of the Life of Boston King, a Black Preacher. Written by Himself, during his residence at Kingswood School," in *The Life of Boston King*, ed. Ruth Holmes Whitehead and Carmelita A. M. Robertson (Halifax: Nimbus, 2003), 351.

26. Ibid., 15, 16–17.

27. David George cited by Kathleen Tudor, "David George: Black Loyalist," *Nova Scotia Historical Review* 3, no. 1 (1983): 72.

28. King, "Memoirs," 21, 20.

29. Anthony Kirk-Greene, "David George, the Nova Scotia Experience," *Sierra Leone Studies* 14 (December 1960): 98.

30. "Petition to Governor Parr" cited by Maya Jasanoff, *Liberty's Exiles: American Loyalists in the Revolutionary World* (New York: Knopf, 2011), 280.

31. King, "Memoirs," 22, 23, 24.

32. David George, "An Account of the Life of Mr. David George, from Sierra Leone in Africa," in *Unchained Voices: An Anthology of Black Authors in the*

English-Speaking World of the 18th Century, ed. Vincent Carretta (Lexington: University of Kentucky Press, 1996), 337.

33. Jacob Bailey cited by Ellen Wilson, *The Loyal Blacks* (New York: Putnam, 1976), 120.

34. George, "Account of the Life," 339.

35. Thomas Clarkson, *The History of the Rise, Progress, and Accomplishment of the Abolition of the Slave-Trade by the British Parliament* (London: Longman, Hurst, Rees, and Orme, 1808), 2: 286.

36. Granville Sharp, *Memoirs of Granville Sharp, Esq.*, ed. Prince Hoare (London: Henry Colburn, 1820), 114.

37. Granville Sharp cited by Brown, *Moral Capital*, 164.

38. Sharp, *Memoirs*, 121.

39. "At a Committee of the Society, instituted in 1787, for effecting the Abolition of the Slave Trade," British Library. On the Quaker network of communications that spanned the Atlantic, see David Bryon Davis, *The Problem of Slavery in the Age of Revolution, 1770–1823* (Oxford: Oxford University Press, 1999).

40. Clarkson, *Rise, Progress, and Accomplishment*, 2: 23.

41. Cited by Claire Midgley, *Women against Slavery: The British Campaigns, 1780–1870* (London: Routledge, 1992), 22.

42. Cited by Seymour Drescher, "Women's Mobilization in the Era of Slave Emancipation: Some Anglo-French Comparisons," in *Women's Rights and Transatlantic Antislavery in the Era of Emancipation*, ed. Kathryn Kish Sklar and James Brewer Stewart (New Haven: Yale University Press, 2007), 100.

43. "At a Committee of the Society."

44. Clarkson, *Rise, Progress, and Accomplishment*, 1: 267.

45. Ibid., 1: 555.

46. *Discours sur la nécessité d'établir à Paris une Société pour concourir, avec celle de Londres, à l'abolition de la traite & de l'esclavage des Nègres* (Paris, 1788), British Library, London.

47. C. B. Wadström, *Additions aux règlements de la Société des Amis des Noirs*, in *La Révolution française et l'abolition de l'esclavage* (Paris: Éditions d'histoire sociale, 1968), vol. 7.

48. Marcel Dorigny, "Mirabeau et la Société des amis des noirs: Quelles voies pour l'abolition de l'esclavage," in *Les abolitions de l'esclavage de L. F. Sonthonax à V. Schoelcher, 1793, 1794, 1848* (Paris: Presses Universitaires de Vincennes, 1995), 154.

49. Société des Amis des Noirs, "Seconde Adresse à l'Assemblée Nationale, par la Société des Amis des Noirs, établie à Paris," in *La Révolution française et l'abolition de l'esclavage*, 7: 2.

50. Étienne Clavière, *Adresse de la Société des Amis des Noirs à l'Assemblée Nationale, à toutes les Villes de Commerce* . . . (Paris: Desenne, 1791), in *La Révolution française et l'abolition de l'esclavage*, vol. 9.

51. Étienne Dumont, *Letters, containing an account of the late revolution in France, and observations on the constitution, laws, manners, and institutions of the English; written during the author's residence at Paris, Versailles, and London, in the years 1789 and 1790. Translated from the German of Henry Frederic Groenvelt.* London, 1792, Eighteenth Century Collections Online, Gale Group, 32.

52. Thomas Jefferson to Brissot, 1788, in J.-P. Brissot, *Correspondance et papiers,* ed. Cl. Perroud (Paris: Librairie Alphonse Picard, n.d.), 165–66.

53. Clarkson, *Rise, Progress, and Accomplishment,* 2: 122.

54. Cited by Robert Forster, "The French Revolution, People of Color and Slavery," in *The Global Ramifications of the French Revolution,* ed. Joseph Klaits and Michael H. Haltzel (Cambridge: Cambridge University Press, 1994), 90. See also *Découverte d'une conspiration contre les intérêts de la France"* (1790), British Library, London. On the threat international connections posed to the abolition movement, see J. R. Oldfield, *Transtlantic Abolitionism in the Age of Revolution: An International History of Antislavery, c. 1787–1820* (Cambridge: Cambridge University Press, 2013).

55. Clarkson, *Rise, Progress, and Accomplishment,* 2: 125.

56. Ibid., 2: 132, 131. See also Appendix, Charles Mackenzie, *Notes on Haiti* (1830; New York: Frank Cass, 1971), 2: 246–59.

57. Ogé's wealth and transatlantic connections have made it difficult for historians to categorize him; he seems at the time to have moved with ease in white society. John D. Garrigus, "'Thy coming Fame, Ogé! Is Sure': New Evidence on Ogé's 1790 Revolt and the Beginnings of the Haitian Revolution," in *Assumed Identities. The Meanings of Race in the Atlantic World,* ed. John D. Garrigus and Christopher Morris (College Station: Texas A and M Press, 2010), 19–45.

58. *Il est encore des Aristocrates ou réponse à l'infâme auteur d'un écrit intitulé: Découverte d'une conspiration contre les intérêts de la France* (1790), British Library, London; and Clavière, *Adresse de la Société des Amis des Noirs.*

59. Vincent Ogé cited by Clarkson, *Rise, Progress, and Accomplishment,* 2: 149–50.

60. Thomas Clarkson, 15 August 1828, in Mackenzie, *Notes on Haiti,* 2: 251.

61. See Garrigus, "'Thy Coming Fame,'" 31–33; and Jeremy Popkin, *Facing Racial Revolution: Eyewitness Accounts of the Haitian Insurrection* (Chicago: University of Chicago Press, 2007), 43–48.

62. Louis François-René Verneuil, in Popkin, *Facing Racial Revolution,* 43–48.

63. See Garrigus, "'Thy Coming Fame,'" 33–34.

64. Joseph Antonio Vrizar to Porlier, Santo Domingo, 25 November 1790, AGI, Santo Domingo, leg 1027 cited by Julius Scott, "The Common Wind: Currents of Afro-American Communication in the Era of the Haitian Revolution," Ph.D. diss., Duke University, 1986, 180.

65. Adam Williamson to Lord Grenville, 4 July 1791, C.O. 137/89, Public Records Office cited by Scott, "The Common Wind," 181.

66. Leading antislavery activists in France, including Helen Maria Williams, John Hurford Stone, Carl Wadström, and the Abbé Gregoire, discussed projects with French foreign minister, Charles Talleyrand, for colonial expansion in Africa and the Near East, but these went nowhere. See Marcel Dorigny and Bernard Gainot, *La Société des Amis des Noirs, 1788–1799* (Paris: Éditions Unesco, 1998).

67. On the British uncertainty and imperialism, see Linda Colley, *Britons: Forging the Nation, 1707–1837* (New Haven: Yale University Press, 1992); and Jasanoff, *Liberty's Exiles*. On the conflicting motives involved in the colonization of Sierra Leone, see Isaac Land and Andrew M. Schochet, "New Approaches to the Founding of the Sierra Leone Colony, 1768–1808," *Journal of Colonialism and Colonial History* 9, no. 3 (2008).

68. Lamin Sahhen, *Abolitionists Abroad: American Blacks and the Making of Modern West Africa* (Cambridge: Harvard University Press, 1999), 26. See also Christopher X. Byrd, *Captives and Voyageurs: Black Migrants across the Eighteenth-Century British Atlantic World* (Baton Rouge: Louisiana State University Press, 2008).

69. Henry Smeathman, *Substance of a Plan of a Settlement, to be Made near Sierra Leone, on the Grain Coast of Africa, Intended More Particularly for the Service and Happy Establishment of Blacks and People of Colour to be Shipped as Freemen . . . ,"* cited by Brown, *Moral Capital*, 315. On race as a determining factor in the Sierra Leone settlement schemes see Emma Christopher, "A 'Disgrace to the very Colour': Perceptions of Blackness and Whiteness in the Founding of Sierra Leone and Botany Bay," *Journal of Colonialism and Colonial History* 9, no. 3 (2008). On the plethora of schemes for resettlement see Deidre Coleman, "Afterword: Rough Crossings to New Beginnings," *Journal of Colonialism and Colonial History* 9, no. 3 (2008); and Coleman, *Romantic Colonization and British Anti-Slavery*.

70. George Cumberland cited by Stephen J. Braidwood, *Black Poor and White Philanthropists: London's Blacks and the Foundation of the Sierra Leone Settlement, 1786–1791* (Liverpool: Liverpool University Press, 1994), 7.

71. Granville Sharp, 19 October 1788, Clarkson Papers, Reel 1.

72. Ibid. Here was colonization understood, historian Deidre Coleman suggests, as Michel Foucault saw it: "a leap of the imagination as well as a leap in geographical space and time"; Coleman, *Romantic Colonization and British Anti-Slavery*, 2, 109.

73. Clarkson, *Rise, Progress, and Accomplishment*, 1: 488.

74. Wadström and Nordenskiold, *Plan for a Free Community upon the Coast of Africa*, xiv, 60.

75. Gretchen Holbrook Gerzina, *Black London: Life before Emancipation* (New Brunswick, N.J.: Rutgers University Press, 1995), 145–46.

76. Granville Sharp to Dr. J. Sharp, 31 October 1787, cited by Sharp, *Memoirs*, 2: 83.

77. *Substance of a Report of the Court of Directors, (19 October 1791) Sierra Leone Company* (London, 1792). On the free trade of Freetown, see Philip Misevich, "The Sierra Leone Hinterland and the Provisioning of Early Freetown, 1792–1803," in *Journal of Colonialism and Colonial History* 9, no. 3 (2003).

78. Henry Thornton to Thomas Clarkson, 14 September 1792, cited by Coleman, *Romantic Colonization*, 115.

79. Anna Maria Falconbridge, London, 5 January 1791, *Narrative of Two Voyages to the River Sierra Leone During the Years 1791–1792–1793*, 11. See also Deirdre Coleman, "Sierra Leone, Slavery, and Sexual Politics: Anna Maria Falconbridge and the 'Swarthy Daughter' of Late 18th Century Abolitionism," in *Women's Writing* 2, no. 1 (1995): 12.

80. Falconbridge, Granville Town, 13 May 1791, *Narrative*, 43.

81. Falconbridge, Bance Island, 10 February 1791, *Narrative*, 18. See also Coleman, *Maiden Voyages and Infant Colonies*, 24–25.

82. Falconbridge, London, 30 September 1791, *Narrative*, 69.

83. Petition cited by Wilson, *The Loyal Blacks*, 180.

84. James Walker, *Black Loyalists* (London: Africana, 1976), 95.

85. Henry Clinton cited by Jasanoff, *Liberty's Exiles*, 287.

86. William Wilberforce cited ibid., 289.

87. John Clarkson, 19 October 1791, in *Clarkson's Mission to America, 1791–1792*, ed. Charles Bruce Ferguson (Halifax: Public Archives of Nova Scotia, 1971), 45.

88. See Byrd, *Captives and Voyageurs*.

89. John Clarkson, 19 October 1791, in Ferguson, *Clarkson's Mission to America*, 43, 45.

90. Carl Wadström, *An Essay on Colonialization, Particularly Applied to the Western Coast of Africa* (London: Darton and Harvey, 1794).

91. Anna Falconbridge, Freetown, 24 January 1793, *Narrative*, 111.

92. John Clarkson, cited by Ellen Gibson Wilson, *John Clarkson and the African Adventure* (London: Macmillan, 1980), 95.

93. Anna Falconbridge, Freetown, 1 July 1792, *Narrative*, 82.

94. Johnson Asiegbu, *Slavery and the Politics of Liberation, 1787–1861* (London: Longman, 1969), 13.

95. Anna Falconbridge, Freetown, 10 April 1792, *Narrative*, 74.

96. John Clarkson, *Journal*, cited by Cassandra Pybus, *Epic Journeys of Freedom: Runaway Slaves of the American Revolution and Their Global Quest for Liberty* (Boston: Beacon, 2006), 170.

97. Directors, Sierra Leone Company, cited by Carl Wadström, *An Essay on Colonization, Particularly Applied to the Western Coast of Africa* (London: Darton and Harvery, 1794), 43.

98. Petition, 25 June 1792, cited by Wilson, *John Clarkson*, 97.

99. John Clarkson cited ibid., 79.

100. On the vote for women see Schama, *Rough Crossings*, 374. On the layout of Freetown see Pybus, *Epic Journeys of Freedom*, 183.

101. John Clarkson to Isaac Dubois, 1 July 1793, Clarkson Papers, Add MS 41263, British Library, cited by Pybus, *Epic Journeys of Freedom*, 177.

102. Zachary Macaulay, 1 October 1793, in Zachary Macaulay, *Zachary Macaulay and the Development of the Sierra Leone Company, 1793–94. Journal*, ed. Suzanne Schwarz (Leipzig: Institut für Afrikanistik, Universität Leipzig, 2000), 67.

103. Ibid., 17 September 1793, in *Journal*, 62.

104. Zachary Macaulay, *Journal, 1793–1799*, microfilm, Abolition and Emancipation, Papers of Zachary Macaulay, part 1, reel 2.

105. Ibid., *Journal, 1793–1799*, microfilm, part 1, reel 6. See also Kevin G. Lowther, *The African American Odyssey of John Kizell: A South Carolina Slave Returns to Fight the Slave Trade in His African Homeland* (Charleston: University of South Carolina Press, 2011), 136.

106. King, "Memoirs," 33.

107. Ibid.; and David George to Messrs. Grigg and Rodway, Free Town, 19 April 1796, in Carretta, *Unchained Voices*, 346.

108. Falconbridge, "Preface," *Narrative*, 10; and Falconbridge, Freetown, 1 July 1792, *Narrative*, 83.

109. Ibid., London, October 1793, 135. Over Clarkson's protests, her husband, Isaac Dubois, was ultimately dismissed, faulted by the company for siding with the Nova Scotians in their demands and for traveling aboard a slave ship.

110. Ibid., "Preface," 10.

111. Wadström, *Essay*, cited by Christopher Fyfe, "Editor's Comment," Falconbridge, *Narrative*, 164.

112. John Clarkson, 30 August 1792, "Diary of Lieutenant Clarkson R.N," *Sierra Leone Studies* 8 (1927): 31.

113. Cato Perkins and Isaac Anderson, London, 26 October 1993, in *Our Children Free and Happy: Letters from Black Settlers in Africa in the 1790s*, ed. Christopher Fyfe (Edinburgh: Edinburgh University Press, 1991), 38.

114. Luke Jordan and Isaac Anderson, Freetown, 28 June 1794, ibid., 42–43.

115. Luke Jordan et al., Sierra Leone, 19 November 1794, ibid., 44.

116. Zachary Macaulay, *Journal of Zachary Macaulay*, 8 September 1794, in *Life and Letters of Zachary Macaulay*, ed. Viscountess Knutsford (London: Edward Arnold, 1900), 63.

117. Sierra Leone Company, *Substance of Report of the Sierra Leone Company to the General Court of Proprietors on Thursday the 27th of May, 1794* (London: James Phillips, 1794), 65.

118. John Clarkson to the Marquis de Lafayette, 2 July 1792, cited by Coleman, *Romantic Colonization*, 127.

119. Jasanoff, *Liberty's Exiles*, 301; and Simon Schama, *Rough Crossings: Britain, the Slaves, and the American Revolution* (New York: HarperCollins, 2006), 380–83.

120. Macaulay, *Journal*, 28 September 1794, 66.

121. For more on Mary Perth, see Cassandra Pybus, "'One Militant Saint': The Much Traveled Life of Mary Perth," *Journal of Colonialism and Colonial History* 9, no. 3 (2008).

122. Moses Wilkinson, Luke Jordan, Jn Jordan, Rubin Simmons, America Tolbert, Isaac Anderson, Stephen Peters, Jas. Hutcherson, Luke Jordan, and "A great many More the Paper wont afford" to John Clarkson, Sierra Leone, 19 November 1794, in Fyfe, *Our Children*, 43.

123. Sharp, *Memoirs*, 372; and Henri Grégoire, *Notice sur la Sierra-Leona, et sur une colomnie répandice à son sujet contre le gouvernement français* (Paris, 1794).

124. Marcel Dorigny, "Intégration républicaine des colonies et projets de colonisation de l'Afrique: Civiliser pour émanciper?" in *Grégoire et la cause des Noirs (1789–1831). Combats et projets*, ed. Yves Bénot and Marcel Dorigny (Paris: Société française d'histoire d'outre-mer, 2000), 103; and Alyssa Goldstein Sepinwall, *The Abbé Grégoire and the French Revolution: The Making of Modern Universalism* (Berkeley: University of California Press, 2005), 154.

125. Macaulay, *Journal*, 26 August, 30 September, 2 October 1797, as cited by Pybus, " 'A Less Favourable Specimen,' " 106–7.

126. See Egerton, *Death or Liberty*, 219.

127. Bruce L. Mouser, "The 1805 Forékariah Conference: A Case of Political Intrigue, Economic Advantage, Network Building," *History in Africa* 25 (1998): 226.

128. Thomas Ludlam cited by Schama, *Rough Crossings*, 393.

129. George Ross cited by Mavis C. Campbell, ed., *Back to Africa: George Ross and the Maroons: From Nova Scotia to Sierra Leone* (Trenton, N.J.: Africa World, 1993), 17.

130. R. C. Dallas, *The History of the Maroons, from their Origin to the Establishment of their Chief Tribe at Sierra Leone* (London, 1803), 2: 285, cited by Srinivas Aravamudan, *Tropicopolitans: Colonialism and Agency, 1688–1804* (Durham: Duke University Press, 1999), 267.

131. Ross, *Back to Africa*, 17.

132. Wilberforce cited by Schama, *Rough Crossings*, 390.

CHAPTER 4. THE PRESS AND CLUBS

1. *Les Révolutions de Paris* 73 (1790): 401–6, in Jack R. Censer and Lynn Hunt, *Liberty, Equality, Fraternity: Exploring the French Revolution* (University Park: Pennsylvania State University Press, 2001), 69.

2. Jean-Jacques Rousseau, *The Social Contract* (1762; New York: Penguin, 1968), 140.

3. Johann Nikolas Bischoff cited by Eckhart Hellmath and Wolfgang Piereth, "German 1760–1815," in *Press, Politics, and the Public Sphere in Europe and North America, 1760–1820*, ed. Hannah Barker and Simon Burrows (Cambridge: Cambridge University Press, 2002), 70.

4. Historian John Brewer coined the phrase "an alternative structure of politics" to delineate this new political space that opened at the end of the eighteenth century. John Brewer cited by Nicolaas C. F. Van Sas, "The Patriot Revolution: New

Perspectives," in *The Dutch Republic in the Eighteenth Century: Decline, Enlightenment, and Revolution*, ed. Margaret C. Jacob and Wijnand W. Mijnhardt (Ithaca, N.Y.: Cornell University Press, 1992), 115.

5. Duc de Choiseul cited by Hugh Gough, *The Newspaper Press in the French Revolution* (Chicago: Dorsey, 1988), 4–5.

6. John Adams to Robert Livingston, The Hague, 4 September 1782, in the Papers of Charles Guillaume Frederic Dumas, Library of Congress; and "A Harvard Student" quoted by Stephen Botein, "'Meer Mechanics' and an Open Press: The Business and Political Strategies of Colonial American Printers," *Perspectives in American History* 9 (1975): 158.

7. John Adams to Robert R. Livingston, 16 May 1782, in *The Adams Papers*, ed. Gregg L. Lint (Cambridge: Harvard University Press, 2006), 13: 48.

8. Antoine Cérisier to John Adams, 15 April 1781, cited by Jeremy D. Popkin, "From Dutch Republican to French Monarchist: Antoine-Marie Cérisier and the Age of Revolution," in *Tijdschrift voor Geschiedenis* 102 (1989): 534.

9. *Le Politique hollandois*, 12 February 1781, 1: 1.

10. *Le Patriote français*, 1 April 1789, cited by J. Gilchrist and W. J. Murray, eds., *The Press in the French Revolution: A Selection of Documents from the Press of the Revolution for the Years 1789–1794* (New York: St. Martin's, 1971), 46.

11. Comte de Mirabeau, *Première lettre du comte de Mirabeau à ses commettants*, 1, cited by Gough, *The Newspaper Press in the French Revolution*, 22.

12. J. F. Bertaud, "Histoire de la presse et révolution," *Annales historiques de la Révolution française* 285 (1991): 283.

13. Gérard Walter, *La Révolution française vue par ses journaux* (Paris: Tardy, 1948), 8.

14. Bertaud, "Histoire de la presse et révolution," 287.

15. Antoine de Rivarol, *Journal politique national* 1, 6, cited by Walter, *La Révolution française vue par ses journaux*, 28.

16. *Révolutions de Paris*, 2–8 August 1789, 1.

17. Antoine de Rivarol, *Journal politique national*, ed. Willy de Spons (Paris: Editions du Rocher, 1989), 71.

18. *L'Ami du Peuple*, 7 May 1791, cited by Jack Censer, *Prelude to Power: The Parisian Radical Press, 1789–1791* (Baltimore: Johns Hopkins University Press, 1976), 39.

19. *Révolutions de Paris*, 18–25 July 1789, 2.

20. *Pennsylvania Mercury*, 3 December 1789, 478: 2, America's Historical Newspapers, www.infoweb.newsbank.com.

21. Marat, *L'Ami du Peuple*, 23 September 1789, 116.

22. Michael L. Kennedy, *The Jacobin Clubs in the French Revolution: The First Years* (Princeton: Princeton University Press, 1982), 56.

23. Ibid., 59.

24. Cited by Patrice Higonnet, *Goodness beyond Virtue: Jacobins during the French Revolution* (Cambridge: Harvard University Press, 1998), 211.

25. Camille Desmoulins cited by Kennedy, *Jacobin Clubs in the French Revolution*, 14.

26. Cited by Jean Boutier, Philippe Boutry, and Serge Bonin, *Atlas de la Révolution française*, vol. 6, *Les sociétés politiques* (Paris: Éditions de l'École ds Hautes Études en Sciences Sociales, 1992), 9.

27. Higonnet, *Goodness beyond Virtue*, 211.

28. Cited by Boutier, Boutry, and Bonin, *Atlas de la Révolution française*, 6: 44.

29. "Organisation intérieure de la société des Jacobins," in Alphonse Aulard, *La société des Jacobins. Recueil de documents pour l'histoire du Club des Jacobins de Paris* (Paris: Librairie Jouaust, 1889–97), 1: xxix.

30. Boutier, Boutry, and Bonin, *Atlas de la Révolution française*, 6: 9.

31. Étienne Dumont, *Souvenirs sur Mirabeau et sur les deux premières assemblées législatives* (Paris: Charles Gosselin, 1832), 100.

32. Anacharsis Cloots, 18 March 1790, "Motion," in *La Société des Jacobins. Recueil de documents pour l'histoire du club des Jacobins de Paris*, ed. F.-A Aulard (Paris: Librairie Jouaust, 1889), 1: 41.

33. Maximilien Robespierre cited by Higonnet, *Goodness beyond Virtue*, 252.

34. Cited by Simon Schama, *Citizens: A Chronicle of the French Revolution* (New York: Knopf, 1989), 529.

35. Etta Palm d'Aelders, "Adresse des citoyens françaises à l'Assemblée nationale," in *Women in Revolutionary Paris, 1789–1795*, ed. Darline Levy, Harriet Applewhite, and Mary Johnson (Urbana: University of Illinois Press, 1979), 75.

36. Etta Palm d'Aelders, *Adresse des citoyens françaises à l'Assemblée nationale*, ibid., 75–76.

37. Etta Palm d'Aelders, *Lettre d'une amie de la vérité*, 23 March 1791, ibid., 71. See also Gary Kates, *The Cercle Social, the Girondins, and the French Revolution* (Princeton: Princeton University Press, 1985).

38. Madame Roland cited by Albert Mathiez, *Le Club des Cordeliers pendant la crise de Varennes et le massacre du Champ de Mars* (Paris: Librairie Aneienne H. Champion, 1910), ii.

39. Thomas Paine, *Aux étrangers sur la révolution françoise*; and Thomas Paine, *Suite des observations sur le memoire du roi*, both in *Le républicain. Aux origines de la République* (Paris: Courier de Provence, 1791). Dumont had tried to dissuade Chastellet from acting without approval from the National Assembly, and refused to translate the address for Paine.

40. "Pétition de la Société des Amis des Droits de l'homme et du citoyen aux Représentants de la Nation," in Mathiez, *Le Club des Cordeliers*, 33.

41. François Robert cited by Hugh Gough, *The Newspaper Press in the French Revolution* (Chicago: Dorsey, 1988), 112.

42. Cited by H. Hardenberg, *Etta Palm, een hollandse Parisienne, 1743–1799* (Assen: Van Gorcum, 1962), 87.

43. Etta Palm d'Aelders, cited by Judith Vega, "Feminist Republicanism: Etta Palm d'Aelders on Justice, Virtue and Men," *History of European Ideas* 10 (1989): 344. On the "republic of brothers," see Lynn Hunt, *The Family Romance of the French Revolution* (Berkeley: University of California Press, 1993).

44. "Règlement de la Société des citoyennes républicaines révolutionnaires de Paris," in Levy, Applewhite, and Johnson, *Women in Revolutionary Paris*, 161.

45. Minutes of the Jacobin Society, 16 September 1793, ibid., 182–85.

46. *Procès-verbal, Revolutionary Republican Women*, ibid., 209–12.

47. The club-based politics that "the Revolution created in France overnight," social theorist Jürgen Habermas explains, had evolved in England over the course of a century. Jürgen Habermas, *The Structural Transformation of the Public Sphere: An Inquiry into a Category of Bourgeois Society* (Cambridge: MIT Press, 1991), 69–70.

48. *Political Tracts of the Society for Constitutional Information* (London: W. Richardson, 1783), British Library, London.

49. Sheffield Society for Constitutional Information, 14 March 1792, in Treasurer Solicitor's papers, 11/962, National Archives, London.

50. Thomas Hardy, *Memoirs of Thomas Hardy* (London: James Ridgeway, 1832), 13.

51. John Horne Tooke, Treasurer Solicitor's papers, 11/951, National Archives, London.

52. Vassa the African to Thomas Hardy, 28 May 1792, Treasurer Solicitor's papers, 24/12, National Archives, London.

53. Calling cards in Treasurer Solicitor's papers, 11/951, National Archives, London; Society for Constitutional Information, 25 May 1792, Treasurer Solicitor's papers, 11/962, National Archives, London.

54. Society for Constitutional Information, 25 May 1792, Treasurer Solicitor's papers, 11/962, National Archives, London.

55. Edmund Burke cited by Thomas Hardy, *A Short History of the London Corresponding Society*, Place Additional Manuscripts 27814, British Library, London.

56. *New York Journal*, 4 January 1792, cited by Seth Cotlar, *Tom Paine's America: The Rise and Fall of Transatlantic Radicalism in the Early Republic* (Charlottesville: University of Virginia Press, 2011), 73.

57. Cited by Ian Dyck, "Thomas Paine: World Citizen in the Age of Nationalism," in *Thomas Paine: In Search of the Common Good*, ed. Joyce Chumbley and Leo Zonneveld (Nottingham: Spokesman, 2009), 34.

58. London Corresponding Society cited by Jack Fruchtman Jr., "Two Doubting Thomases: The British Progressive Enlightenment and the French Revolution," in *Radicalism and Revolution in Britain, 1775–1848: Essays in Honour of Malcolm*

I. Thomas, ed. Michael T. Davis (New York: St. Martin's, 2000), 35; and Stuart Andrews, *The British Periodical Press and the French Revolution, 1789–1799* (New York: Palgrave, 2000), 47.

59. Treasurer Solicitor's papers, 24/10, National Archives, London.

60. Joel Barlow, *Advice to the Privileged Orders in the Several States of Europe, Resulting from the Necessity and Propriety of a General Revolution in the Principle of Government* (London: J. Johnson, 1793–95), 107.

61. Richard Buel Jr., *Joel Barlow: American Citizen in a Revolutionary World* (Baltimore: Johns Hopkins University Press, 2011), 148.

62. Address from the Revolution Society in London, November 5, 1792, Treasurer Solicitor's papers, 24/3/117, National Archives, London.

63. Mr. Groves, 21 May 1794, Treasurer Solicitor's papers, 11/954, National Archives, London.

64. Mr. Groves, 13 February 1794, Treasurer Solicitor's papers, 11/952, National Archives, London.

65. Thomas Cooper, *A Reply to Mr. Burke's Invective against Mr. Cooper, and Mr. Watt in the House of Commons* (London: J. Johnson, 1792).

66. *A Defense of the Constitution of England against the libels that have lately published on it; particularly in Paine's pamphlet on the Rights of Man* (Dublin, 1791) in *Political Writings of the 1790's*, ed. Gregory Claeys (London: William Pickering, 1995), vol. 5.

67. Hardy, *Memoirs*, 21.

68. Joel Barlow cited by Yvon Bizardel, *The First Expatriates: Americans in Paris during the French Revoution*, trans. June P. Wilson and Cornelia Higginson (New York: Holt, Rinehart and Winston, 1975), 143. See also Joel Barlow and John Frost, Treasurer Solicitor's papers, 24/3/117, National Archives, London.

69. Pétition, Treasurer Solicitor's papers 11/951, National Archives, London.

70. Edward Royle and James Walvin, *English Radicals and Reformers, 1760–1848* (Brighton: Harvester, 1982), 65.

71. Thomas Hardy to John Horne Tooke, 15 September 1792, Treasurer Solicitor's papers, 11/951, National Archives, London.

72. Petition, Nottingham, Treasurer Solicitor's papers, 11/951, National Archives, London.

73. London Corresponding Society, 8 July 1793, Tracts of the London Corresponding Society, British Library, London.

74. Minutes of the London Corresponding Society, 24 October 1793, Place 27814, British Library, London.

75. *Regalus*, 3 June 1793, Treasurer Solicitor's papers, 11/951, National Archives, London.

76. John Thelwell, Universal Society of the Friends of the People, Treasurer Solicitor's papers, 24/3/08, National Archives, London.

77. *Revolutions without Bloodshed: or Reformation preferable to Revolt* (1794), Treasurer Solicitor's papers, 24/3/153, National Archives, London.

78. William Fox, *On Jacobinism* (1794).

79. Cited by Royle and Walvin, *English Radicals and Reformers*, 71.

80. King Stanislas to Filippo Mazzei, 22 September 1790, Warsaw, in *Philip Mazzei: Selected Writings and Correspondence*, ed. Margherita Marchione (Prato: Cassa di Risparmi e Depositi di Prato, 1983), 2: 431.

81. *St. James Chronicle*, 2 January 1790, 1.

82. Bogusław Leśnodorski, *Les Jacobins polonais* (Paris: Société des études robespierristes, 1965), 60–62.

83. Stanisław Małachowski cited by Zofia Libiszowska, "The Impact of the American Constitution on Polish Political Opinion in the Late Eighteenth Century," in *Constitution and Reform in Eighteenth-Century Poland*, ed. Samuel Fiszman (Bloomington: Indiana University Press, 1997), 233.

84. King Stanislas to Filippo Mazzei, 11 June 1791, cited by Jerzy Kowecki, "The Kościuszko Insurrection," in Fiszman, *Constitution and Reform*, 499.

85. *Gazeta Warsawska*, January 1791, cited by J. Grossbart, "La presse polonaise et la révolution française," *Annales historiques de la Révolution française* 14 (1937): 144.

86. Kennedy, *Jacobin Clubs in the French Revolution*, 228. The Parisian Société de 1789 had proposed the publication of many of the king's speeches, but Stanislas refused out of fear that they could be misinterpreted in France; King Stanislas to Filippo Mazzei, 29 September 1790, Warsaw, in Marchione, *Philip Mazzei*, 2: 438.

87. Filippo Mazzei to King Stanislas, 23 May 1791, Paris, ibid., 2: 553.

88. Anacharsis Cloots, *L'Orateur du genre humain à la nation polonaise*, in *Écrits revolutionnaires, 1790–1794*, ed. Michèle Duval (Paris: Éditions Champ Libre, 1979), 186.

89. Joel Barlow to King Stanislas, 22 March 1791, Paris, cited by Richard Butterwick, *Poland's Last King and English Culture: Stanisław August Poniatowski, 1732–1798* (Oxford: Clarendon, 1998), 141.

90. *Pennsylvania Gazette*, 18 August 1790.

91. "Interview between the Emperor and the King of Prussia," *Public Advertiser*, 2 September 1791.

92. *Gazeta Narodowa i Obca*, 1 January 1791, cited by Grossbart, "La presse polonaise," 146.

93. Leśnodorski, *Les Jacobins polonais*, 7.

94. Hiacynthe Malachowski to Bucholz cited ibid., 11.

95. *Public Advertiser*, 13 August 1792.

96. Hugo Kollataj, [Ignacy Potocki, Franciszek K. Dmochowski], *O ustanowieniu I upadku Konstytucji polskiej 3 Maja 1791 roku*, cited by Kowecki, "The Kościuszko Insurrection," 499.

97. Pierre Lebrun cited by William Fiddian Reddaway, *The Cambridge History of Poland* (Cambridge: Cambridge University Press, 1971) 2: 150.

98. *Act of Insurrection*, in Miecislaus Haimon, *Kościuszko: Leader and Exile* (New York: Polish Institute of Arts and Sciences in America, 1946), 131.

99. Kościuszko cited by Leśnodorski, *Les Jacobins polonais*, 89.

100. Catherine II to Marshal Suvorov, cited by R. R. Palmer, *Age of the Democratic Revolution: A Political History of Europe and America, 1760–1800* (Princeton: Princeton University Press, 1964), 2: 155.

101. J. Pawlekowski, *Journal*, 71, cited by Leśnodorski, *Les Jacobins polonais*, 168.

102. W. Kalinka cited ibid., 168.

103. *De Omwenteling in Polen onder den Burger-Generaal. Thaddaeus Kosciuszko, Vercierd met het welgelijkend portrait van dien onstervellijken Vrijheids-Vriend* (Amsterdam), Universiteitsbibliotheek, Leiden.

104. *Nouvelles politiques*, 21 May 1794, cited by Higonnet, *Goodness without Virtue*, 179.

105. *Annales politiques civiles et littéraires*, 3: 349.

106. *Révolutions de France et de Brabant*, 3: 131.

107. Ibid., 1: 27, 3: 131.

108. *Courrier de l'Europe*, 29 (7 January 1791): 14.

109. André Chénier, *Le Journal de Paris*, 26 February 1792, in Gilcrest and Murray, *The Press in the French Revolution*, 175–77.

110. *La Politique Hollandois*, 5 November 1781, 1.

111. Joel Barlow, *Advice to the Privileged Orders* (1792), cited by Cotlar, *Tom Paine's America*, 41.

112. *Cocarde nationale* cited by J. F. Bertaud, "Histoire de la presse et revolution," *Annales historiques de la révolution française* 285 (1991): 285.

113. London Corresponding Society cited by Ian Dyck, "Thomas Paine: World Citizen in the Age of Nationalism," in *Thomas Paine: In Search of the Common Good*, ed. Joyce Chumbley and Leo Zonneveld (Nottingham: Spokesman, 2009), 34.

114. Marat, *L'Ami du Peuple*, 23 September 1789, 116.

115. Edmund Burke, 28 December 1792, cited by Boyd Hilton, *A Mad, Bad, and Dangerous People? England, 1783–1846* (Oxford: Clarendon, 2006), 62.

116. Republican Society of South Carolina, Charleston, *Declaration of the Friends of Liberty and National Justice*, 13 July 1793, cited by Philip Foner, *The Democratic Republican Societies, 1790–1800* (Westport, Conn.: Greenwood, 1976), 379.

117. William Cooper, Massachusetts Constitutional Society, Boston, 13 January 1794, Evans Early American Imprints.

CHAPTER 5. RUMORS OF FREEDOM IN THE CARIBBEAN

1. Unsigned letter, Saint Lucia, 22 October 1789, C 10 C 5, Archives d'Outre Mer, Aix-en-Provence.

2. George Pinckard, *Notes on the West Indies* (London, 1816), 1: 229, cited by Julius Sherrard Scott III, "The Common Wind: Currents of Afro-American Communication in the Era of the Haitian Revolution," Ph.D. diss., Duke University, 1986, 129.

3. César Henri de la Lucerne cited by Julius S. Scott, "'Negroes in Foreign Bottoms': Sailors, Slaves, and Communication," in *Origins of the Black Atlantic*, ed. Laurent Dubois and Julius S. Scott (New York: Routledge, 2010), 72.

4. Robin Blackburn, *The Overthrow of Colonial Slavery, 1770–1848* (New York: Verso, 1988), 163.

5. "Notes sur la situation," 20 October 1792, CC 9A 16, Archives d'Outre Mer, Aix-en-Provence.

6. Sue Peabody, "Négresse, Mulâtresse, Citoyenne: Gender and Emancipation in the French Caribbean, 1650–1848," in *Gender and Slave Emancipation in the Atlantic World*, ed. Pamela Scully and Diana Paton (Durham: Duke University Press, 2005), 61.

7. James Eyma cited by Anne Pérotin-Dumon, "Les Jacobins des Antilles ou l'esprit de liberté dans les Iles du Vent," *Revue d'histoire moderne et contemporaine* 35 (1988): 284.

8. Nicolas-Robert Cocherel, "Observations sur la demande des mulâtres," AD XVIIIc 118, no. 13, Archives Nationales, Paris, cited by Florence Gauthier, "Comment la nouvelle de l'insurrection des esclaves de Saint Domingue fut-elle reçue en France," in *L'insurrection des esclaves de Saint-Domingue*, ed. Laennec Hurbon (Paris: Editions Karthala, 2000), 19.

9. Georges Danton cited by Laurent Dubois, "'The Price of Liberty': Victor Hugues and the Administration of Freedom in Guadeloupe, 1794–1798," *William and Mary Quarterly* 56 (1999): 379.

10. Malick Ghachem, *The Old Regime and the Haitian Revolution* (Cambridge: Cambridge University Press, 2012), 273–76; and Wim Klooster, "Le décret d'émancipation imaginaire: Monarchisme et esclavage en Amérique du Nord et dans la Caraïbe au temps des revolutions," *Annales historiques de la révolution française* 1 (2011): 111–28. On royalism in the Iberian Atlantic, see Jane Landers, *Atlantic Creoles in the Age of Revolutions* (Cambridge: Harvard University Press, 2010); and Gabriel Paquette, *Imperial Portugal in the Age of Atlantic Revolutions: The Luso-Brazilian World, c. 1770–1850* (Cambridge: Cambridge University Press, 2013).

11. Yves Benot, *La Guyane sous la Révolution française* (Paris: Ibis Rouge Éditions, 1997).

12. Unsigned Letter, Saint Lucia, 14 October 1790, C 10 C 5, Archives d'Outre Mer, Aix-en-Provence; and Report, 6 September 1790, C 10 C 5, Saint Lucia, Archives d'Outre Mer, Aix-en-Provence.

13. Michael Craton, *Testing the Chains: Resistance to Slavery in the British West Indies* (Ithaca, N.Y.: Cornell University Press, 1982), 175.

14. Governor Keith to Lord Germaine, 6 August 1776, cited by Richard B. Sheridan, "The Jamaican Slave Insurrection Scare of 1776 and the American Revolution," *Journal of Negro History* 61, no. 3 (1976): 298.

15. General John Grizell to General Palmer, 19 July 1776, cited ibid., 296.

16. Andrew Jackson O'Shaughnessy, *An Empire Divided: The American Revolution and the British Caribbean* (Philadelphia: University of Pennsylvania Press, 2000), 56; and W. J. Gardner, *A History of Jamaica: From Its Discovery by Christopher Columbus to the Year 1872* (London: Frank Cass, 1971), 144.

17. Five hundred fifty Trelawney Maroons were sent to Halifax in 1796, a measure intended by the Jamaican Assembly "to dispose of the body of people who had given them so much uneasiness." From there they sailed to Sierra Leone and put down the insurrection of the black residents of Freetown. R. C. Dallas, *The History of the Maroons, from their Origin to the Establishment of their Chief Tribe at Sierra Leone* (London: T. N. Longman and O. Rees, 1803), 2: 196.

18. Dr. John Lindsay to Dr. William Robertson, 6 August 1776, St. Jago de la Vega, Jamaica, cited by Sheridan, "Jamaican Slave Insurrection Scare," 301.

19. Rev. John Lindsay cited by Craton, *Testing the Chains*, 172.

20. Selwyn H. H. Carrington, "The American Revolution and the British West Indies' Economy," *Journal of Interdisciplinary History* 17 (1987): 827.

21. Lord Effingham to Henry Dundas, 17 September 1791, Colonial Office Records 137/89, National Archives, cited by Scott, "The Common Wind," 143.

22. John Whittaker to J. L. Winn, 11 January 1792, Colonial Office Records 137/90, National Archives, cited ibid., 19–20.

23. Luckey, "Examinations of sundry Slaves in the Parish of St. Ann Jamaica respecting an intention to revolt," 31 December 1791, 11 January 1792, and the examinations of Duke and Glamorgan, "Examinations of sundry Slaves in the Parish of Trelawny Jamaica," 5 January 1792, Colonial Office Records 137/90, National Archives, cited ibid., 19.

24. Report of Robert Parker in "Minutes of the proceedings of the Committee of Secrecy and Safety in the Parish of St. James's, Jamaica," Colonial Office Records 137/90, National Archives, London, cited ibid., 20.

25. On the black loyalists in Jamaica, see Maya Jasanoff, *Liberty's Exiles: American Loyalists in the Revolutionary World* (New York: Knopf, 2011), especially chapter 8. On support for the king among slaves and creoles, see also Landers, *Atlantic Creoles in the Age of Revolutions*, 235.

26. Clarke to Sydney, 22 April 1788, Colonial Office Papers 137/87, National Archives, London, cited by Scott, "The Common Wind," 131.

27. Dallas, *History of the Maroons*, 1: 167. On those harsh conditions see Vincent Brown, *The Reaper's Garden: Death and Power in the World of Atlantic Slavery* (Cambridge: Harvard University Press, 2008).

28. Williamson to Dundas, 6 November 1791, C.O. 137/89 cited by Scott, "The Common Wind," 211.

29. Cited by David Geggus, "The Enigma of Jamaica in the 1790s: New Light on the Causes of Slave Rebellions," *William and Mary Quarterly* 44 (1987): 277.

30. The causes of the Second Maroon War had more to do with the shortage of land and grievances related to the treaty with the British than with the French Revolution. Even if French agents did not directly instigate the rebellion, as colonial officials suspected, rumors in Jamaica among slaves as well as the Maroons that in France "all are Citizens and upon a footing" may have contributed. Historian Michael Craton concludes that by the time the messages of revolution reached the British islands, they were so convoluted and confused that they did little to inspire insurrection; Craton, *Testing the Chains*, 213.

31. *Savanna-la Mar Gazette*, 9 September 1788, cited by Scott, "The Common Wind," 159.

32. Yves Benot, "La chaine des insurrections d'esclaves aux Caraïbes," in *Les abolitions de l'esclavage 1793, 1794, 1848, de L. F. Sonthonax à V. Schoelcher*, ed. Marcel Dorigny (Vincennes: Presses Universitaires de Vincennes, 1995), 179–86.

33. [Felix Carteau], *Soirées bermudiennes, ou entretiens sur les événemens qui ont opéré la ruine de la partie française de l'isle Saint-Domingue* (Bordeaux, 1802), 75–78, cited by Scott, "The Common Wind," 170.

34. Baron de Wimpffen, *Saint Domingue à la veille de la Révolution*, ed. Albert Savinne (Paris: Louis Michaud, 1911), 19.

35. The largest of the Antilles after Cuba, in 1777 Saint-Domingue was split between Spain and France; the French territory was divided into Northern, Southern, and Western provinces, separated by mountain ranges. Until 1787, when slaves carved a stairway up the mountains, travel between the two major cities, Le Cap in the Northern Province and Port au Prince in the Western Province, was possible only by sea.

36. Wimpffen, *Saint Domingue*, 28.

37. John Garrigus contrasts this biological definition of race in Saint-Domingue with the social categories that continued to define race in Jamaica. There, Raimond would have been considered part of the slaveowning elite. John D. Garrigus, *Before Haiti: Race and Citizenship in French Saint-Domingue* (New York: Palgrave, 2006). See also Ghachem, *The Old Regime and the Haitian Revolution*, 239–43.

38. "Lettre des députés de Saint Domingue à messieurs les rédacteurs du Journal de Paris" (1789), discussed by Malick W. Ghachem, "The Coming of the Haitian Revolution 1789–1791," work paper no. 01–05, International Seminar on the History of the Atlantic World, 1500–1800, Harvard University.

39. Ghachem, *The Old Regime and the French Revolution*, 205.

40. M. le comte de Peiner, 10 August 1789, C 9A 163, Archives d'Outre Mer, Aix-en-Provence.

41. Vincent, Port au Prince, 3 July 1789, C 9A 162, Archives d'Outre Mer, Aix-en-Provence.

42. Vincent and Durant, 14 August 1789, C 9A 162, Archives d'Outre Mer, Aix-en-Provence.

43. Nouvelles de Saint Domingue, D/XXV/115, Archives Nationales, Paris; Carolyn E. Fick, *The Making of Haiti: The Saint Domingue Revolution from Below* (Knoxville: University of Tennessee Press, 1990), 82–84; Laurent Dubois, *Avengers of the New World: The Story of the Haitian Revolution* (Cambridge: Harvard University Press, 2004), 86–88; and Blanche Maurel, *Saint Domingue et la Revolution francaise* (Paris: Presses Universitaires de France 1943).

44. Maximilien Robespierre cited by Carolyn E. Fick, "The French Revolution in Saint Domingue," in *A Turbulent Time: The French Revolution and the Greater Caribbean*, ed. David Barry Gaspar and David Patrick Geggus (Bloomington: Indiana University Press, 1997), 58–59. On Robespierre's position that the free people of color already enjoyed the rights of active citizens under the terms of the Code Noir, see Ghachem, *The Old Regime and the French Revolution*, 245.

45. Camille Desmoulins cited by Benot, *La Guyane sous la Révolution française*, 76.

46. Benot, "Chaine des insurrections," 180. Rumors coming from all different directions, in the words of historian Julius Scott, "intertwined and reinforced one another" in Saint-Domingue; Scott, "The Common Wind," 193. On the king's role in mitigating torture based on provisions of the Code Noir, see Ghachem, *The Old Regime and the Haitian Revolution*, especially chapter 5.

47. According to Carolyn Fick, insurrection in the south of the island "originated in a rumor the slaves believed to be true, expected to be implemented, and for which they were determined to risk their lives"; Fick, "The French Revolution in Saint Domingue," 63.

48. Boukman Dutty cited by Carolyn E. Fick, "The Saint Domingue Slave Insurrection of 1791: A Socio-Political and Cultural Analysis," *Journal of Caribbean History* 25 (1991): 4. On the ceremony see Robin Law, "La cérémonie du Bois Caïman et le 'pacte de sang' dahoméen," in Hurbon, *L'insurrection des esclaves de Saint-Domingue*, 131–48; and David Geggus, "La cérémonie du Bois Caïmen," ibid., 149–70. The timing of the insurrection is not certain. Different sources contradict one another.

49. No contemporary sources mention this ceremony, now popularly celebrated as the beginning of the insurrection of 1791. The historian David Geggus believes the details of the ceremony have been embellished with poetic license by generations of historians, beginning with the imagination of Moreau de Saint Méry; Geggus, "La cérémonie du Bois Caïmen," 163.

50. Accounts of the insurrection are many, including Fick, "The Saint Domingue Slave Insurrection of 1791"; Fick, *The Making of Haiti*, 91–117; Dubois, *Avengers of the New World*, 91–114; and Hurbon, *L'insurrection des esclaves de Saint-Domingue*.

51. "A letter from James Perkins Esq, resident at Cape François 9 Sept 1791," in the *Boston, Independent Chronicle and universal Advertiser*, 20 October 1791, cited by Fick, "The Saint Domingue Slave Insurrection of 1791," 8. For a study of fear, see Mariselle Meléndez, "Fear as a Political Construct: Imagining the Revolution and the Nation in Peruvian Newspapers, 1791–1824," in *Liberty! Égalité! Independencia! Print Culture, Enlightenment, and Revolution in the Americas, 1776–1838* (Worcester, Mass.: American Antiquarian Society, 2007), 41–56.

52. See John K. Thornton, "African Soldiers in the Haitian Revolution," in Dubois and Scott, *Origins of the Black Atlantic*, 195–213; John Thornton, "African Soldiers in the Haitian Revolution," *Journal of Caribbean History* 25 (1991): 59–80; and John Thornton, " 'I am the Subject of the King of Kongo': African Political Ideology and the Haitian Revolution," *Journal of World History* 4 (1993): 181–214.

53. Cited by Dubois, *Avengers of the New World*, 94.

54. Deposition, Le Cap 27 Sept 1791, AN DXXV 78 722. AA 183, French National Archives, cited by Fick, "The Saint Domingue Slave Insurrection of 1791," 18.

55. Cited by Dubois, *Avengers of the New World*, 96.

56. "La Révolution de Saint Domingue," cited by Jeremy Popkin, *You Are All Free: The Haitian Revolution and the Abolition of Slavery* (Cambridge: Cambridge University Press, 2010), 75.

57. Michael Duffy, "The French Revolution and British Attitudes to the West Indian Colonies," in Gaspar and Geggus, *A Turbulent Time*, 82–83.

58. "Indeed, the fear of slave uprisings was as contagious as was the lure to invest in more slaves," historian Jeremy Adelman writes; Adelman, *Sovereignty and Revolution in the Iberian Atlantic* (Princeton: Princeton University Press, 2006), 84. See also Peter Blanchard, *Under the Flags of Freedom: Slave Soldiers and the Wars of Independence in Spanish South America* (Pittsburgh: University of Pittsburgh Press, 2008), 10; François Xavier Guerra, *Modernidad E independencies, Ensayos sobre la revoluciones hispánicas* (Madrid: Ediotrial Mapfre, 1992), 38; Lyman L. Johnson, *Workshop of Revolution: Plebian Buenos Aires and the Atlantic World, 1776–1810* (Durham: Duke University Press, 2011), 151, 154–58; Landers, *Atlantic Creoles in the Age of Revolutions*, 51; Claudia Rosas Lauro, "El Miedo a la revolución. Rumores y temores desatados por la Revolución Francesa en el Perú," in *El Miedo en el Perú. Siglos XVI al XX*, ed. Claudia Rosas Lauro (Lima: Pontificia Universidadad Católica del Perú, 2005), 139–66; and Gabriel Paquettte, *Imperial Portugal in the Age of Atlantic Revolution* (Cambridge: Cambridge University Press, 2013), 104.

59. Aline Helg, *Liberty and Equality in Caribbean Colombia, 1770–1835* (Chapel Hill: University of North Carolina Press, 2004), 118.

60. AHU, DA, Caisa 157, doc. 53 cited by Adelman, *Sovereignty and Revolution*, 91.

61. Jacques-Pierre Brissot, "Discours sur un projet de décret relatif à la révolte des noirs," 30 October 1791, 2.

62. *Philadelphia General Advertiser*, 10–11 October 1791, cited by Dubois, *Avengers of the New World*, 105.

63. See David Geggus, "Print Culture and the Haitian Revolution: The Written and the Spoken Word," *Liberty! Égalité! Independencia!* 79–96; and David Geggus, "Slave Resistance and Emancipation: The Case of Saint-Domingue," in *Who Abolished Slavery: Slave Revolts and Abolitionism, A Debate with João Pedro Marques*, ed. Seymour Drescher and Pieter C. Emmer (New York: Berghahn, 2010): 112–19.

64. M. L. E. Moreau de Saint Méry, *Considérations présentées aux vrais amis du repos et du bonheur de la France, a l'occasion de nouveaux mouvemens de quelques soi-disant Amis des Noirs* (Paris: L'Imprimerie Nationale, 1791).

65. Jean-Paul Marat cited by Dubois, *Avengers of the New World*, 129.

66. Olympe de Gouges cited ibid., 129. See also Gregory S. Brown, "The Self-Fashionings of Olympe de Gouges, 1784–1789," *Eighteenth-Century Studies* 34 (2001): 383–40.

67. Governor Blanchelande cited by Dubois, *Avengers of the New World*, 139.

68. Blanchelande, 23 January 1792, C9A 166, Archives d'Outre Mer, Aix-en-Provence; and Blanchelande, 25 January 1792, C 9A 166, Archives d'Outre Mer, Aix-en-Provence.

69. Corréspondance d'Assemblées provinciales. Les commerçants et colons de St. Domingue ci devant à Nantes, CC 9A 6, Archives d'Outre Mer, Aix-en-Provence.

70. Cited by Dubois, *Avengers of the New World*, 105.

71. Cited ibid., 130.

72. Anne Pérotin-Dumon, "Free Coloreds and Slaves in Revolutionary Guadeloupe," in *The Lesser Antilles in the Age of European Expansion*, ed. Robert Paquette and Stanley Engerman (Gainesville: University of Florida Press, 1996), 259–60.

73. Baron de Clugny, 20 July 1790, C 7A 44, number 36, Archives d'Outre Mer, Aix-en-Provence.

74. Cited by Anne Pérotin-Dumon, "The Emergence of Politics among Free-Coloureds and Slaves in Revolutionary Guadeloupe," *Journal of Caribbean History* 25 (1991): 115.

75. Baron de Clugny, 30 November 1790, C 7A 44, number 47, Archives d'Outre Mer, Aix-en-Provence.

76. Baron de Clugny, 3 June 1791, C 7A 45, Archives d'Outre Mer, Aix-en-Provence.

77. "Relation des événements qui se sont passés de l'insurrection de la compagnie," Point à Pitre, CC 9A 16, Archives d'Outre Mer, Aix-en-Provence.

78. Jean-Baptiste Lacrosse cited by Anne Pérotin-Dumon, *Être patriote sous les tropiques: la Guadeloupe, la colonisation et la Révolution* (Basse-terre, Guadeloupe: Société d'histoire de la Guadeloupe, 1985), 169.

79. "Adresse des nouveaux citoyens," 3 March 1793, C 7A 46, Archives d'Outre Mer, Aix-en-Provence.

80. Lacrosse, Capitaine de Vaisseaux de la Republique Française, Commandant la Frigate La Felicité, "Le Dernier Moyen de Conciliation entre la Mère Patrie et les Colonies revoltées," C 10 C 6, Archives d'Outre Mer, Aix-en-Provence.

81. Pierre-Claude Gerlain, "Mémoire sur la Guadeloupe," cited by Anne Pérotin-Dumon, "Les Jacobins des Antilles ou l'esprit de liberté dans les Iles du Vent," *Revue d'histoire moderne et contemporaine* 35 (1988): 286.

82. Historian Laurent Dubois documents the "links between plantations of different regions and between slaves and free [that] provided the channels through which plans, ideas, and rumors could travel"; Laurent Dubois, *A Colony of Citizens: Revolution and Slave Emancipation in the French Caribbean, 1787–1804* (Chapel Hill, University of North Carolina Press, 2004), 134.

83. *General Advertiser* (Philadelphia), 31 May 1793, cited ibid., 130.

84. "Rapport du comité," 8 May 1793, in AN D XXV, 129, 1008, nos. 7–13, cited ibid., 134; and Pérotin-Dumon, "Emergence of Politics," 118.

85. "Extrait des régistres de la Société des amis de la République française," 5 February 1794, AN, AD VII, 21 C, no. 45, cited by Dubois, *A Colony of Citizens*, 150.

86. Report of the Sainte-Anne municipal bureau on August 26, AN DXXV/121, 959, Archives Nationales, Paris, cited by Pérotin-Dumon, "Emergence of Politics," 123.

87. Cited by Pérotin-Dumon, "Free Coloreds and Slaves in Revolutionary Guadeloupe," 272.

88. Deputé de la Guadeloupe, C 7A 49, 122, Archives d'Outre Mer, Aix-en-Provence. French military officials specified alarms to be raised in case of attack—two shots from the cannon followed by the raising of a red flag—to prevent the myriad of false alarms from inciting unrest. Only official couriers, or dragons, were authorized to carry the message from one part of the island to another.

89. Victor Hugues to Comité du Salut public, 10 December 1794, C 7A, 47, 37, in Archives d'Outre Mer cited by Dubois, *A Colony of Citizens*, 211.

90. Victor Hugues, "Arrête," C 7A 48, 41, Archives d'Outre Mer, Aix-en-Provence.

91. Victor Hugues, "Bref détail de ce qui s'est passé à Marie Galante," C 7A 48, 235, Archives d'Outre Mer, Aix-en-Provence.

92. "Les Commissaires Délégués aux Ministre de la Marine et des Colonies," 9 August 1796, ANSOM C7A 49, 43–45 cited by Dubois, " 'The Price of Liberty,' " 387.

93. Blanchelande to MM. Les commissaires civiles avant leur arrivée, 15 September 1792, CC 9A 6, Archives d'Outre Mer, Aix-en-Provence.

94. *The Charibbean Register, or Ancient and Original Dominica Gazette*, 26 March 1791 in C.O. 71/20, National Archives, cited by Scott, "The Common Wind," 200.

95. "Mémoire du Roy pour servir d'instruction aux Polverel, Sonthonax, et Ailhard," D XXV 4, Archives Nationales de France, Paris.

96. On the efforts by whites to discredit the commissioners see Ashli White, *Encountering Revolution: Haiti and the Making of the Early Republic* (Baltimore: Johns Hopkins University Press, 2010), 99–100.

97. Jean-Antoine Ailhaud, Étienne Polverel, and Léger Félicité Sonthonax, 25 August 1792, D XXV 4, Archives Nationales de France, Paris.

98. Jean-Antoine Ailhaud, Étienne Polverel, and Léger Félicité Sonthonax, 23 August 1792, D XXV 4, Archives Nationales de France, Paris.

99. "Lettre de la Paroisse d'Ouananminthe à l'Assemblée du Cap," 27 August 1790 in *Nouvelles de Saint Domingue*, 1, D XXV 115, Archives Nationales de France, Paris.

100. Rapport de Guadeloupe, C 7A 47, Archives d'Outre Mer, Aix-en-Provence; see also CC 9A 16, Archives d'Outre Mer, Aix-en-Provence.

101. Léger Félicité Sonthonax cited by Dubois, *Avengers of the New World*, 154.

102. "Détail des événements qui se sont passés au Cap dans les journées des 20, 21, 22 et 23 juin 1793," cited by Popkin, *You Are All Free*, 185.

103. Declaration of Lefebvre, Brest, 26 mess. II cited ibid., 193.

104. *My Odyssey*, cited ibid., 203.

105. Étienne Polverel and Léger Félicité Sonthonax cited by Dubois, *Avengers of the New World*, 159.

106. Jeremy Popkin defines the offer as "a turning point in the struggle over slavery." This was no military expedient, Popkin argues, contrasting the commissioner's proclamation of freedom for soldiers to Lord Dunmore's offer to slaves on patriots' plantations in America; Popkin, *You Are All Free*, 213.

107. "Historic Narrative," cited ibid., 221. See Popkin for a detailed narrative and analysis of the events of 20 and 21 June 1793.

108. François Laplace, *Histoire des desastres de Saint-Domingue*, cited ibid., 242.

109. J. Garnier cited by Florence Gaulthier, "Le rôle de la députation de Saint-Domingue dans l'abolition de l'esclavage," in Dorigny, *Les abolitions de l'esclavage*, 203.

110. Bramante Lazzary cited by Dubois, *Avengers of the New World*, 163.

111. *Archives parlementaires* cited ibid., 170.

112. Geggus, "Slave Resistance and Emancipation," 113. The insurrections in Saint-Domingue, the largest slave rebellion in the Americas, constituted a necessary, if not a sufficient cause of the abolition of slavery, historian David Geggus argues. Legal historian Malick Ghachem understands the events of 1793–94 as part of a

longer process of transforming the Code Noir; Ghachem, *The Old Regime and the Haitian Revolution*, 255–57.

113. Abbé Grégoire cited by Popkin, *You Are All Free*, 365.

114. Toussaint Louverture cited by Dubois, *Avengers of the New World*, 182. See also Srinivas Aravamudan, *Tropicopolitans: Colonialism and Agency, 1688–1804* (Durham: Duke University Press, 1990).

115. Cited by Geggus, "Print Culture and the Haitian Revolution," 85.

116. General Victor Collot, 23 May 1792, C 7A 46, 233, Archives d'Outre Mer, Aix-en-Provence.

117. "Extrait de la dépêche de l'Assemblée Coloniale de Sainte-Lucie le Fidèle, à la Convention Nationale, du 9 Juillet 1793, l'an 21ème de la Republique Française," C 10 C 6, Archives d'Outre Mer, Aix-en-Provence.

118. The idea of reading against the grain comes from Laurent Dubois, *Avengers of the New World*, 6.

119. Ada Ferrer, "Talk about Haiti: The Archive and the Atlantic's Revolution," in *Tree of Liberty: Cultural Legacies of the Haitian Revolution in the Atlantic World*, ed. Doris L. Garraway (Charlottesville: University of Virginia Press, 2008), 30. On revolts in Cuba in the 1790s, see David Patrick Geggus, "Slave Resistance in the Spanish Caribbean in the Mid–1790s," in Gaspar and Geggus, *A Turbulent Time*, 131–55.

120. Sue Peabody, "A Dangerous Zeal: Catholic Missions to Slaves in the French Antilles, 1635–1800," *French Historical Studies* 25 (2002): 89.

121. Jorge Biassou and Captain General Joaquín, cited by Landers, *Atlantic Creoles in the Age of Revolutions*, 78–81.

122. C 7A 47, 35, Archives d'Outre Mer, Aix-en-Provence.

123. General Victor Collot, C 7A 46, 8, Archives d'Outre Mer, Aix-en-Provence.

124. Sonthonax cited by Dubois, *Avengers of the New World*, 207.

125. General Collot, C 7A 46, Archives d'Outre Mer, Aix-en-Provence. Collot went on to explore the Illinois and Louisiana territories, seeking economic opportunities before being arrested by the Spanish in New Orleans in 1796.

126. Leonora Sansay, *The Secret History; or, The Horrors of St. Domingo in a Series of Letters Written by a Lady at Cape Francois, to Colonel Burr, Late Vice-President of the United States, Principally during the Command of General Rochambeau* (Philadelphia: Bradford and Inskeep, 1808), 3, Early American Imprints, series 2, no. 15201.

127. Ibid., 34.

CHAPTER 6. THE REVOLUTIONARY HOUSEHOLD
IN FICTION

1. Jean-Jacques Rousseau, *Émile, or On Education* (1762; New York: Basic, 1979), 358. See Susan Moller Okin, *Women in Western Political Thought* (Princeton: Princeton University Press, 1979), 116–18.

2. Rousseau, *Émile*, 365. Annie Smart argues that Rousseau's ideal wife was a thinking being, a civic mother. That interpretation lends itself more readily to his adoption by all of the novelists considered in this chapter; Annie K. Smart, *Citoyennes: Women and the Ideal of Citizenship in Eighteenth-Century France* (Newark: University of Delaware Press, 2011).

3. Mary Wollstonecraft, *Maria, or The Wrongs of Woman*, in *Mary and Maria, Matilda*, ed. Janet Todd (1798: London: Penguin Classics, 1992), 59.

4. Ibid., 59. Nicola Watson explains that sentimental novels "typically dramatized subjectivity as fragmentary, passionate to the point of irrationality and peculiarly unfitted to do more than sympathize with, and occasionally relieve, local distress." Nicola J. Watson, *Revolution and the Form of the British Novel, 1790–1825: Intercepted Letters, Interrupted Seductions* (Oxford: Clarendon Press, 1994), 24.

5. Countess Flahaut, *Adéle de Senange ou Lettres de Lord Sydenham en Deux Volumes* (London: Debrett, 1794), i.

6. Lynn Hunt, *The Family Romance of the French Revolution* (Berkeley: University of California Press, 1992).

7. Sarah Knott, *Sensibility and the American Revolution* (Chapel Hill: University of North Carolina Press, 2009), 12.

8. Hunt, *The Family Romance*, 4.

9. Knott, *Sensibility and the American Revolution*, 21.

10. Carla Hesse, *The Other Enlightenment: How French Women Became Modern* (Princeton: Princeton University Press, 2001), 147. For a discussion of American novels in this context, see Cathy N. Davidson, *Revolution and the Word: The Rise of the Novel in America* (New York: Oxford University Press, 1986).

11. Mary Wollstonecraft cited by Barbara Taylor, *Mary Wollstonecraft and the Feminist Imagination* (Cambridge: Cambridge University Press, 2003), 148.

12. Mary Hays, *Letters and Essays, Moral, and Miscellaneous* (London: T. Knott, 1793), 17.

13. Lieve van Ollefen, *Het riete Kluisje van mejuffrouw Elizabeth Wolff* (Amsterdam: Elwe, 1784), 7.

14. Karin Westerink, "Het Interieur van het Kluisje van Betje Wolff in Beverwijk (1782–1788)," in *O Laage Hut! Meer grootsch dan vorstelyke Hoven. Het Kluisje van Betje Wolff en Aagje Deken in Beverwijk* (Beverwijk: De Stichting tot Behoud van het Tuinshuisje van de Dames Betje Wolff en Aagje Deken te Beverwijk, nd).

15. Eve Tavor Bannet, *Empire of Letters: Letter Manuals and Transatlantic Correspondence, 1680–1820* (Cambridge: Cambridge University Press, 2001), 1.

16. Betje Wolff to Govert Jan van Rijswij, n.d., in Betje Wolff and Aagje Deken, *Briefwisseling van Betje Wolff en Aagje Deken*, ed. P. J. Buijnsters (Utrecht: HES Uitgevers, 1987) 2: 505.

17. Betje Wolff, *Proeve over de Opvoeding aan de Nederlandsche Moeders, door E. Bekker, wed. A Wolff* (Amsterdam: Johannes Allart, 1779), 3, vii, 32–33.

18. Betje Wolff cited by Marijke Meijer Drees, "Bekker, Elisabeth," Instituut voor Nederlands Geschiedenis, *Digitaal Vrouwenlexicon van Nederland,* http:/www.inghist.nl/Onderzoek/Projecten/DVN/lemmata/data/Bekker.

19. Betje Wolff to Maaraten Houttuyn cited by P. J. Buijnsters, *Wolff en Deken. Een Biografie* (Leiden: Martinus Nijhoff, 1984), 33.

20. Betje Wolff cited ibid., 71.

21. Sarah Knott has called it a "marriage rewritten in friendship's light." Usually this marriage of friends is described, as Knott does, in America. Visitors from Europe idealized the companionate marriage they imagined from travelers' glimpses into American homes; Knott, *Sensibility and the American Revolution,* 22.

22. Betje Wolff and Aagje Deken, *De Historie van Mejuffrouw Sara Burgerhart* (1782; Amsterdam: Wereldbibliotheek, 1905), 19.

23. See April Alliston, *Virtue's Faults: Correspondences in Eighteenth-Century British and French Women's Fiction* (Stanford: Stanford University Press, 1996), chapter 4, for a discussion of the spectral mother.

24. Wolff and Deken, *Sara Burgerhart,* 135, 74.

25. Ibid., 181, 115, 135.

26. Ibid., 290.

27. Ibid., 308.

28. Ibid., 345, 325.

29. Mary Wollstonecraft, *Vindication of the Rights of Woman, with Strictures on Moral and Political Subjects* (1792; New York: Norton, 1988), 10.

30. Mary Wollstonecraft, *Thoughts on the Education of Daughters with Reflections on Female Conduct in the more Important Duties of Life* (London: J. Johnson, 1787), 54.

31. Mary Wollstonecraft cited by Taylor, *Mary Wollstonecraft and the Feminist Imagination,* 1.

32. Mary Wollstonecraft, *Mary,* in Todd, *Mary and Maria, Matilda,* 17.

33. Ibid., 2, 33, 31.

34. Ibid., 49, 53; italics in original.

35. Mary Wollstonecraft cited by Mary A. Waters, " 'The First of a New Genus': Mary Wollstonecraft as a Literary Critic and Mentor to Mary Hays," *Eighteenth Century Studies* 37 (2004): 415.

36. Mary Hays to William Godwin, 11 May 1796, cited by Gina M. Luria, "Mary Hays's Letters and Manuscripts," in *Signs* 3 (1977): 528.

37. Mary Hays, *Memoirs of Emma Courtney* (1794; Oxford: Oxford University Press, 1996).

38. Ibid., 124, 161.

39. Ibid., 39.

40. Ibid., 4, 139, 117; italics in original. Initially, Hays's novel was well reviewed, especially by such liberal magazines as the *Analytical Review.* It was only later, after

the publication of Godwin's *Memoirs of the Author of a Vindication of the Rights of Woman* and the discrediting of Mary Wollstonecraft as the mother of an illegitimate child and the author of letters to her lover Gilbert Imlay, that critics attacked Hays's protagonist, Emma. Reverend Richard Polwhele caricatured her in his poem *The Unsex'd Females.*

41. Historian Michael Rapport describes "'cosmopolitanism' in the old sense" as "fitting chameleon-like into élite society across Europe"; Rapport, *Nationality and Citizenship in Revolutionary France: The Treatment of Foreigners, 1789–1799* (Oxford: Clarendon, 2000), 139.

42. Isabelle de Charrière cited in *Une Européenne. Isabelle de Charrière en son siècle. Actes du colloque de Neuchâtel, 11–13 novembre 1993*, ed. Doris Jakubec and Jean-Daniel Candaux (Hauterive-Neuchâtel: Gilles Attinger, 1994), 60.

43. Belle van Zuylen cited by W. H. de Beaufort, "De Meisjesjaren van Mevrouw de Charrière," *De Gids* 72 (1908): 112. See also Aimé Guedj, "Isabelle de Charrière et le sentiment national dans l'Europe des Lumières," in *Expansions, ruptures et continuités de l'idée européenne*, ed. Daniel Minary (Besançon: Les Belles Lettres, 1993), 69–109; and Margriet Lacy, "Belle van Zuylen—Isabelle de Charrière (1740–1805). Tradition and Defiance," *Canadian Journal of Netherlandic Studies—Revue canadienne d'études néerlandaises* 11, no. 2 (1990): 35.

44. Charles Emmanuel de Charrière to Mme. Charrière de Mex cited by William and Clara Sévery, *La vie de société dans le pays de Vaud à la fin du dix-huitième siècle* (Lausanne: Georges Bridel, 1911–12), 2: 103.

45. Isabelle de Charrière, *Lettres de Mistriss Henley publiées par son amie* (Geneva: 1784), 102.

46. Ibid., 104.

47. De Charrière turns Samuel Constant's novel *Le Mari sentimental ou le marriage comme il y en a quelques-uns* on its head "by giving voice not to the upright husband but to the restless wife, who is represented as the victim of her husband's very righteousness through a dissociation of 'right' (raison) from 'reason' (raison)"; Susan Sniader Lanser, *Fictions of Authority: Women Writers and Narrative Voice* (Ithaca, N.Y.: Cornell University Press, 1992), 144.

48. Isabelle de Charrière, *Lettres écrites de Lausanne*, cited by Joan Hinde Stewart, *Gynographs: French Novels by Women of the Late Eighteenth Century* (Lincoln: University of Nebraska Press, 1993), 112–13.

49. Wollstonecraft, *Maria*, 68, 121.

50. Ibid., 145, 114.

51. Their fictive but realistic protagonists struggled valiantly within what literary critic Ruth Perry identifies as "the refracted reality" of their societies; Ruth Perry, *Novel Relations: The Transformation of Kinship in English Literature and Culture, 1748–1818* (Cambridge: Cambridge University Press, 2004), 314.

52. Wollstonecraft, *Maria*, 68, 61, 115, 64, 93, 83.

53. Betje Wolff to Jan Everhard Grave, 13 October 1776, cited by Wies Roosenchoon, *Leven & Werk van Betje Wolff & Aagje Deken* (Beemester: Historisch Genootschap J. A. Leeghwater, 1986), 25. That Wolff and Deken alone of the novelists not only imagine a happy household but create one for themselves suggests, as Susan Lanser advises, "that we scrutinize what passes for the heteronormative to see where it might already carry the seeds of its own resistance or critique"; Susan Lanser, "Of Closed Doors and Open Hatches: Heternormative Plots in Eighteenth-Century (Women's) Studies," *Eighteenth Century: Theory and Interpretation (ECTI)* 53 (2012): 283.

54. Mary Wollstonecraft to Gilbert Imlay, 31 December 1793, in *Memoirs of Mary Wollstonecraft*, ed. William Godwin (London: Constable, 1927), xlv.

55. Ibid., 65.

56. Wollstonecraft, *Vindication of the Rights of Woman*, 118.

57. Ibid., 140.

58. Ibid., 21.

59. Mary Wollstonecraft, *Thoughts on the Education of Daughters* (1787; Bristol: Thoemmes, 1995), 99–100. Wollstonecraft is not alone in making this argument. Catharine Macaulay had argued against the training of girls "to lisp with their tongues, to totter in their walk, and to counterfeit more weakness and sickness than they really have, in order to attract the notice of the male"; Macaulay, *Letters on Education* (1790), cited by Lyndall Gordon, *Vindication: A Life of Mary Wollstonecraft* (New York: Harper Perennial, 2005), 151.

60. Hays, *Memoirs of Emma Courtney*, 90.

61. Cited by Eleanor Ty, Introduction, to Hays, *Memoirs of Emma Courtney*, xxxvii.

62. Mary Wollstonecraft cited by Taylor, *Mary Wollstonecraft*, 2.

63. Mary Wollstonecraft cited ibid., 195.

64. Isabelle de Charrière to Mlle. Hardy, 26 September 1794, cited by Hesse, *The Other Enlightenment*, 129.

65. Margriet Bruijn Lacy, "Noblesse Oblige: Belle van Zuylen and Social Responsability," in *The Great Emporium: The Low Countries as a Cultural Crossroads in the Renaissance and the Eighteenth Century*, ed. C. C. Barfoot and R. Todd (Amsterdam: Rodopi, 1992), 252.

66. Mary Wollstonecraft to Imlay cited by Taylor, *Mary Wollstonecraft*, 195.

67. Mary Wollstonecraft, Introduction to "Letters on the French Nation," in *Posthumous Works by the Author of a Vindication of the Rights of Woman in Four Volumes* (London: J. Johnson, 1798), 4: 43

68. Aagje Deken and Betje Wolff to Chr. A. Nissen and Magdalena Nissen-Greeger, in Betje Wolff and Aagje Deken, *Briefwisseling van Betje Wolff en Aagje Deken*, ed. P. J. Buijnsters (Utrecht: HES Uitgevers, 1987), 2: 562. See also Myriam Everard, " 'Twee dames hollandoises' in Trevoux. De politieke ballingschap van

Elisabeth Wolff en Agatha Deken, 1788–1797," *De Achttiende Eeuw* 38 (2006): 147–67.

69. Aagje Deken en Betje Wolff to Chr. A. Nissen and Magdalena Nissen-Greeger, in Wolff and Deken, *Briefwisseling*, 2: 562.

70. Liewe Van Ollefen, *Het revolutionaire Huishouden* (Amsterdam: Cornelius Romyn, 1798). Van Ollefen's fellow Dutchman Gerritt Paape, back from his years of exile in France, also envisioned a family of equal partners in his play *De Bataafsche Republiek, zo als zij behoord te zijn, en zo als zij weezen kan: of Revolutionnaire Droom in 1798 wegens toekomstige Gebeurtenissen tot 1998. Vrolyk en Ernstig* (Amsterdam: V.d. Burg, Craijenschot, 1798).

CHAPTER 7. CORRESPONDENCE BETWEEN A "VIRTUOUS SPOUSE, CHARMING FRIEND!"

1. Dena Goodman, *Becoming a Woman in the Age of Letters* (Ithaca, N.Y.: Cornell University Press, 2009).

2. Konstantin Dierks, *In My Power: Letter Writing and Communication in Early America* (Philadelphia: University of Pennsylvania Press, 2009).

3. Comtesse de Damas to St. John de Crèvecoeur, 28 January [1788?], Crèvecoeur papers, Library of Congress.

4. See Diercks, *In My Power*, especially chapter 3.

5. Louis Otto to Nancy Shippen, reel 3, Shippen Family Papers, Library of Congress.

6. Joel Barlow to Ruth Barlow, 9 March 1790, Paris, AM MS 1448 (181), Houghton Library, Harvard University. Historian Sarah Pearsall calls these claims on sentiment "the coercive language of affection"; Pearsall, " 'After All These Revolutions': Epistolary Identities in an Atlantic World, 1760/1815," Ph.D. diss., Harvard University, 2001, 94.

7. *The Complete Letter-Writer*, 11th ed. (1767), 333, cited by Pearsall, " 'After All These Revolutions,' " 45.

8. See Sarah Knott, *Sensibility and the American Revolution* (Chapel Hill: University of North Carolina Press, 2009).

9. Sarah M. S. Pearsall, *Atlantic Families: Lives and Letters in the Later Eighteenth Century* (Oxford: Oxford University Press, 2008).

10. For this wider definition of politics, see Rosemarie Zagarri, *Revolutionary Backlash: Women and Politics in the Early American Republic* (Philadelphia: University of Pennsylvania Press, 2007).

11. François Barbé-Marbois in *Our Revolutionary Forefathers: The Letters of François, Marquis de Barbé-Marbois during his Residence in the United States as Secretary of the French Legation 1779–1785*, ed. Eugene P. Chase (New York: Duffield, 1929), 92.

12. "I was assured that such an extreme and intimate familiarity did not detract from the innocence of the virgin," Barbé-Marbois wrote in his journal.

Barbé-Marbois noted that mothers soon forbade the practice with French officers, who apparently did not respect the innocence of their daughters. Ibid., 103.

13. Ibid., 65.

14. Ibid., 78.

15. Marquis de Chastellux, *Travels in North America in the Years 1780, 1781, and 1782* (1787; New York: New York Times and Arno Press, 1968).

16. Martha Bland to Frances Bland Tucker cited by Ethel Armes, *Nancy Shippen, Her Journal Book: The International Romance of a Young Lady of Fashion of Colonial Philadelphia with Letters to her and about her* (1935; New York: Benjamin Blom, 1968), 102.

17. Barbé-Marbois cited by Chase, *Our Revolutionary Forefathers*, 162.

18. Based on Shippen's journal, Sarah Knott uses the name Anne. I had come to know her as Nancy from her correspondence. See Knott, *Sensibility and the American Revolution*.

19. "A Female Education," *New York Magazine*, September 1794, 590, cited by Jan Lewis, "The Republican Wife," *William and Mary Quarterly* 3rd ser. 44 (1987): 702.

20. Alice Shippen to Nancy Shippen, reel 3, Shippen Family Papers, Library of Congress. On female education in the early republic, see Mary Kelley, *Learning to Stand and Speak: Women, Education, and Public Life in America's Republic* (Chapel Hill: University of North Carolina Press, 2006).

21. Louis Otto cited by Armes, *Nancy Shippen*, 82.

22. Louis Otto to Nancy Shippen, reel 3, Shippen Family Papers, Library of Congress.

23. Louis Otto cited by Armes, *Nancy Shippen*, 85.

24. Louis Otto to Nancy Shippen, reel 3, Shippen Family Papers, Library of Congress.

25. Ibid.

26. Henry Beekman Livingston to Nancy Shippen cited by Armes, *Nancy Shippen*, 19.

27. Louis Otto to Nancy Shippen, cited ibid., 96–97.

28. William Shippen to Thomas Lee Shippen, Philadelphia, 27 January 1781, cited ibid., 101.

29. Louis Otto to Nancy Shippen cited ibid., 104.

30. Louis Otto cited ibid., 80.

31. Louis Otto to Nancy Shippen, Tuesday evening, reel 3, Shippen Family Papers, Library of Congress.

32. Louis Otto to Nancy Shippen, reel 3, Shippen Family Papers, Library of Congress.

33. Louis Otto to Nancy Shippen, Tuesday evening, reel 3, Shippen Family Papers, Library of Congress.

34. Louis Otto to Nancy Shippen, 10 May, reel 2, Shippen Family Papers, Library of Congress.

35. Ibid.

36. Louis Otto to Nancy Shippen, reel 3, Shippen Family Papers, Library of Congress.

37. Frances Brooke, *The History of Emily Montague* (London: J Dodsley, 1769). I am grateful to Laurel Ulrich for passing along this passage found by Elaine Crane.

38. Thomas Shippen to Nancy Shippen, Philadelphia, 24 July 1781, reel 4, Shippen Family Papers, Library of Congress.

39. Nancy Shippen, Journal, reel 2, Shippen Family Papers, Library of Congress.

40. Knott, *Sensibility and the American Revolution*, 134–35. This moment in American history has been described by historian Sarah Knott as "between the apex of imperial crisis and the moment just before the public articulation of the American sentimental project"; ibid., 113.

41. Margaret Livingston to Nancy Shippen, 29 October 1792, reel 3, Shippen Family Papers, Library of Congress. On Henry Livingston's liaisons and the "staggering number of bastard Livingston babies of a variety of hues, religious persuasions and social classes," see Clare Brandt, *An American Aristocracy: The Livingstons* (New York: Doubleday, 1986), 139.

42. Nancy Shippen to Margaret Livingston, 1783, Philadelphia, reel 3, Shippen Family Papers, Library of Congress.

43. Nancy Shippen to Margaret Livingston, September 1794, reel 4, Shippen Family Papers, Library of Congress.

44. Margaret Livingston to Nancy Shippen, reel 3, Shippen Family Papers, Library of Congress.

45. Nancy Shippen to Peggy Livingston, reel 4, Shippen Family Papers, Library of Congress.

46. Nancy Shippen, Journal, 6 September 1785, in Armes, *Nancy Shippen*, 233.

47. Nancy Shippen, "A Journal," ibid., 140–41.

48. Louis Otto to Nancy Shippen, 26 August [1789], cited ibid., 259.

49. Nancy Shippen cited ibid., 130.

50. Nancy Shippen, Journal, 11 May 1783, cited by Sarah Knott, *Sensibility and the American Revolution*, 136.

51. Nancy Shippen, Journal, reel 2, Shippen Family Papers, Library of Congress.

52. Brooke, *Emily Montague*, Letter 116. Elaine Crane has traced the letters from Adams and Shippen and the novel. On the meaning of the Declaration for Adams, see Woody Holton, "The Battle against Patriarchy that Abigail Adams Won," in *Revolutionary Founders: Rebels, Radicals, and Reformers in the Making of the Nation*, ed. Alfred F. Young, Gary B. Nash, and Ray Raphael (New York: Knopf, 2011): 273–88.

53. Nancy Shippen, Journal, 19 May 1783, in Armes, *Nancy Shippen*, 146.

54. Louis Otto to Ministre des Affaires Étrangères, New York, 19 May 1787, cited by Peter Hill, *French Perceptions of the Early American Republic, 1783–1793* (Philadelphia: American Philosophical Society, 1988), 11.

55. Manasseh Cutler cited by Julia Post Mitchell, *St. Jean de Crèvecoeur* (New York: Columbia University Press, 1916), 280.

56. Her daughter, Eliza Otto, lived and was raised by Louis Otto. She traveled to France with Louis Otto and his second wife, América Francès (St. John) Otto, and grew up alongside their daughter, Sophie.

57. Louis Otto to Nancy Shippen, cited by Armes, *Nancy Shippen*, 257.

58. Ethel Armes, her biographer, writes, "The end of Nancy's long death-in-life came in the summer of 1841. For the greater part of forty years she had been immersed in hopeless melancholy. . . . She took a morbid interest in composing epitaphs and hymns and in writing long confused letters of condolence, which are chiefly accounts of her dreams of the dead. Her daughter lived after her for twenty-three years. . . . Peggy too became a religious fanatic. . . . Peggy Livingston was literally buried alive. She who was the accomplished daughter of one of the first families of the United States, the most historic figure among American children in the days of the nation's making—the pet of President Washington, of her uncle Chancellor Livingston, of her great-uncle, Richard Henry Lee, and of other statesmen of the First Congress—this gifted child strangely, terribly dropped from sight"; Armes, *Nancy Shippen*, 300–301.

59. Joel Barlow to Ruth Barlow, 4 June 1792, Paris, AM MS 1448 (192), Houghton Library, Harvard University.

60. Ruth Barlow to Joel Barlow, 18 January 1796, Paris, AM MS 1448 (545), Houghton Library, Harvard University.

61. Ruth Barlow to Joel Barlow, 30 Nivôse (20 January) 1796, Paris, AM MS 1448 (551), Houghton Library, Harvard University.

62. Ruth Barlow to Joel Barlow, 18 January 1796, Paris, AM MS 1448 (545), Houghton Library, Harvard University.

63. Elizabeth Whitman to Joel Barlow cited by James Woodress, *A Yankee's Odyssey* (Philadelphia: Lippincott, 1958), 63.

64. Elizabeth Whitman to Joel Barlow, 29 March 1779, cited by Richard Buel Jr., *Joel Barlow: American Citizen in a Revolutionary World* (Baltimore: Johns Hopkins University Press, 2011), 32.

65. Joel Barlow to Ruth Barlow, 6 April 1779, New Haven, AM MS 1448 (108), Houghton Library, Harvard University.

66. Joel Barlow to Ruth Barlow, 17 April 1781, Hartford, AM MS 1448 (140), Houghton Library, Harvard University.

67. Joel Barlow to Michael Baldwin cited by Woodress, *A Yankee's Odyssey*, 69.

68. Joel Barlow to Ruth Barlow cited ibid., 77.

69. Joel Barlow to Ruth Barlow, 11 June 1784, Hartford, AM MS 1448 (176), Houghton Library, Harvard University.

70. William Duer, a former secretary of the treasury, had acquired the right to buy four million acres in Ohio, and expected to sell them to Frenchmen with savings to invest or a reason to leave France. Barlow was teamed up with the unscrupulous English promoter William Playfair.

71. Joel Barlow to Ruth Barlow, 1 January 1790, Paris, AM MS 1448 (178), Houghton Library, Harvard University.

72. The French minister, the comte de Moustier, blamed Crèvecoeur's idyllic depictions in *Letters from an American Farmer* for luring Frenchmen across the ocean in search of a fortune; Hill, *French Perceptions*, 161.

73. Historian Suzanne Desan characterizes the émigrés as "nervous aristocrats, restless youths with blocked careers, out-of-work servants, and artisans specializing in the luxury trades"; Desan, "Transatlantic Spaces of Revolution: The French Revolution, Sciotomanie, and American Lands," *Journal of Early Modern History* 12 (2008): 468.

74. Joel Barlow cited by Woodress, *A Yankee's Odyssey*, 101.

75. Joel Barlow to Ruth Barlow cited by Woodress, *A Yankee's Odyssey*, 104–5.

76. Ruth Barlow to Mary Woolsey, 3 October 1790, AM MS 1448 (650), Houghton Library, Harvard University.

77. Joel Barlow to Ruth Barlow, 9 Janaury 1796, Marseille, AM MS 1448 (229), Houghton Library, Harvard University.

78. Joel Barlow cited by Yvon Bizardel, *The First Expatriates: Americans in Paris during the French Revolution*, trans. June P. Wilson and Cornelia Higginson (New York: Holt, Rinehart and Winston, 1975), 143.

79. Charles Burr Todd, *Life and Letters of Joel Barlow, LLD, Poet, Statesman, Philosopher* (New York: Putnam, 1886).

80. Thomas Jefferson to Joel Barlow, cited by ibid., 89; and Ruth Barlow to Joel Barlow, 9 January 1793, London AM MS 1448 (539), Houghton Library, Harvard University.

81. Ruth Barlow to Joel Barlow, 28 January 1793, AM MS 1448 (540), Houghton Library, Harvard University.

82. Joel Barlow to Ruth Barlow, 16 January 1796, AM MS 1448 (236), Houghton Library, Harvard University.

83. Eight thousand dollars had been appropriated by Congress for a tribute to be paid to the dey in Algiers, in addition to twenty-seven thousand dollars' worth of carpets, jeweled snuffboxes, robes of state, and linen, extravagant even by the diplomatic standards of the Old World.

84. Joel Barlow to Ruth Barlow, 11 February 1796, AM MS 1448 (248), Houghton Library, Harvard University.

85. Joel Barlow to Ruth Barlow, 14 March 1796, AM MS 1448 (258), Houghton Library, Harvard University.

86. Joel Barlow to Ruth Barlow, 8 July 1796, Algiers, AM MS 1448 (271), Houghton Library, Harvard University.

87. Joel Barlow to Ruth Barlow, 3 April 1797, Algiers, AM MS 1448 (296), Houghton Library, Harvard University.

88. Ruth Barlow to Joel Barlow, 28 January 1793, London AM MS 1448 (540), Houghton Library, Harvard University.

89. "Character of a Good Husband," *Massachusetts Magazine*, March 1789, 177, cited by Lewis, "The Republican Wife," 696.

90. "On Matrimonial Felicity," *Gentleman and Lady's Magazine*, September 1784, 194; and "The Felicity of Matrimony," *Gentleman and Lady's Magazine*, August 1789, 375–76, both cited ibid., 706.

91. Ruth Barlow to Joel Barlow, 1 February 1793, London, AM MS 1448 (541), Houghton Library, Harvard University.

92. Joel Barlow to Ruth Barlow, 9 January 1796, Marseille, AM MS 1448 (229), Houghton Library, Harvard University.

93. Joel Barlow to Ruth Barlow, 2 January 1796, AM MS 1448 (232), Houghton Library, Harvard University.

94. Joel Barlow to Ruth Barlow, 13 January 1796, AM MS 1448 (233), Houghton Library, Harvard University.

95. Joel Barlow to Ruth Barlow, 15 January 1796, AM MS 1448 (235), Houghton Library, Harvard University.

96. Joel Barlow to Ruth Barlow, 21 Janaury 1796, AM MS 1448 (241), Houghton Library, Harvard University.

97. Joel Barlow to Ruth Barlow, 15 December 1792, Chambéry, AM MS 1448 (197), Houghton Library, Harvard University.

98. Joel Barlow to Ruth Barlow, 13 April 1796, Algiers, AM MS 1448 (261), Houghton Library, Harvard University.

99. Ruth Barlow to Joel Barlow, 9 April 1796, Paris, AM MS 1448 (554), Houghton Library, Harvard University.

100. Mary Wollstonecraft cited by Woodress, *A Yankee's Odyssey*, 127. Wollstonecraft hoped the Barlows would take her younger brother with them to America, but realized from Joel's letters, as did Ruth, that Joel was unlikely to abandon the French Revolution before it ended.

101. Mary Wollstonecraft to Everina Wollstonecraft, 14 September 1792, in Buel, *Joel Barlow*, 153.

102. Thomas Jefferson to Anne Bingham, Paris, 11 May 1788, cited by Edward Dumbauld, *Thomas Jefferson: American Tourist* (Norman: University of Oklahoma Press, 1946), 210.

103. Thomas Jefferson to Anne Bingham, 7 February 1787, *Papers of Thomas Jefferson*, ed. Julian P. Boyd (Princeton: Princeton University Press, 1955), 11: 392–93.

104. Anne Bingham to Thomas Jefferson, 1 June 1787, in Sarah Nicholas Randolph, *The Domestic Life of Thomas Jefferson* (New York: Harper, 1871), 98.

105. Thomas Jefferson to Bannister, 15 October 1785, *The Papers of Thomas Jefferson*, 5: 186–87, cited by George Green Shackelford, *Jefferson's Adoptive Son: The Life of William Short, 1759–1848* (Lexington: University Press of Kentucky, 1993), 111.

106. St. John de Crèvecoeur to Thomas Jefferson, 15 July 1784, *The Papers of Thomas Jefferson*, 8: 376–77, cited ibid., 20.

107. Thomas Jefferson expounded his views of the French Revolution in detailed letters to Thomas Paine, Richard Price, Abigail Adams, James Madison, and George Washington. See, among others, Dumbauld, *Thomas Jefferson*; Lloyd Kramer, *Paine and Jefferson on Liberty* (New York: Continuum, 1988); Conor Cruise O'Brien, *The Long Affair: Thomas Jefferson and the French Revolution* (Chicago: University of Chicago Press, 1996); and R. R. Palmer, "The Dubious Democrat: Thomas Jefferson in Bourbon France," *Political Science Quarterly* 72 (1957): 388–404.

108. Thomas Jefferson to William Short, 24 March 1789, *The Papers of Thomas Jefferson*, 14: 694–97.

109. William Short to Thomas Jefferson, 3 April 1789, *The Papers of Thomas Jefferson*, 25: 27–30, cited by Shackelford, *Jefferson's Adoptive Son*, 43.

110. Duchesse de la Rochefoucauld to William Short, 20 November 1794, *Lettres de la duchesse de La Rochefoucauld à William Short. Texte inédit*, ed. Doina Pasca Harsanyi (Paris: Mercure de France, 2001), 193.

111. Suzanne Desan, *The Family on Trial in Revolutionary France* (Berkeley: University of California Press, 2004), 48.

112. Duchesse de la Rochefoucauld to William Short, 1 October 1791, in Harsanyi, *Lettres de la duchesse de La Rochefoucauld à William Short*, 57.

113. Duchesse de la Rochefoucauld to William Short, 7 November 1791, ibid., 64.

114. Duchesse de la Rochefoucauld to William Short, 6 January 1791, ibid., 23.

115. William Short to Rutledge, 17 September 1792, Papers of William Short, cited by Shackelford, *Jefferson's Adoptive Son*, 61.

116. Thomas Jefferson to William Short, Philadelphia, 3 January 1793, Jefferson Papers, Library of Congress.

117. "He seems to have come from the backwoods of America and to have had little business with civilized people," the duchess complained of Monroe's moral scruples to Short; Duchesse de la Rochefoucauld to William Short, 14 December 1794, in Harsanyi, *Lettres de la duchesse de La Rochefoucauld à William Short*, 197.

118. William Short to Duchesse de la Rochefoucauld, 19 November 1794, ibid., 188.

119. Duchesse de la Rochefoucauld to William Short, 5 November 1791, ibid., 62.

120. Duchesse de la Rochefoucauld to William Short, 22 September 1791, ibid., 53.

121. William Short to duchesse de la Rochefoucauld, 30 September 1794, ibid., 184; and William Short to Jefferson, 6 August 1798, Papers of William Short, cited by Shackelford, *Jefferson's Adoptive Son*, 135.

122. As retold in tales handed down in the family, cannibalistic "Redskins" burned down the farm, but a family friend had saved the children and taken them to Boston, where Crèvecoeur entrusted them to the eminent teachers of the time to break the influence of the Indians. In the tale, elephants roamed the forests of America; Paul F. Mealy, *La Comtesse Pelet de la Lozère. Souvenirs 1793–1874* (Dijon: Imprimerie Victor Darantière, nd).

123. J. Hector St. John de Crèvecoeur, *Lettres d'un cultivateur américain écrites à Wm. S[et]on, Esqr. depuis l'année 1770, jusqu'en 1786. Greatly enlarged from the edition of 1784* (Paris: Cuchet, 1787), 3: 11.

124. Ibid., 3: 13.

125. "The Sassafras and the Vine," Crèvecoeur Papers, Library of Congress.

126. Comtesse de Damas to St. John de Crèvecoeur, 24 October [1787], in Crèvecoeur Papers, Manuscripts, Library of Congress.

127. Comtesse de Damas to St. John de Crèvecoeur, August 1789, in Crèvecoeur Papers, Manuscripts, Library of Congress.

128. Emily Pierpont Delesdernier, *Fannie St. John: A Romantic Incident of the American Revolution* (New York: Hurd and Houghton, 1874), 44.

129. Comtesse de Damas to St. John de Crèvecoeur, 24 October [1789], in Crèvecoeur Papers, Manuscripts, Library of Congress. Crèvecoeur had stayed, while in Paris, with the comtesse de Houdetot, the model for Rousseau's Julie.

130. Tardieu to St. John de Crèvecoeur, 7 October 1789, Danville, Crèvecoeur Papers, Manuscripts, Library of Congress.

131. Comtesse de Damas to St. John de Crèvecoeur, 24 October [1789], in Crèvecoeur Papers, Manuscripts, Library of Congress.

132. Louis Otto cited by Gay Wilson Allen and Roger Asselineau, *St. John de Crèvecoeur: The Life of an American Farmer* (New York: Viking, 1987), 92.

133. América Francès Otto to Louis Otto, Lesche, 30 Messidor, An 6 (18 July 1798), Acquisitions Extraordinaires 135, Archives du Ministère des Affaires Étrangères, Paris.

134. América Francès Otto to Louis Otto, Lesche, 16 Thermidor, An 6 (3 August 1798), Acquisitions Extraordinaires 135, Archives du Ministère des Affaires Étrangères, Paris.

135. América Francès Otto to Louis Otto, Lesche, 30 Brumaire, An 7 (20 November 1798), Acquisitions Extraordinaires 135, Archives du Ministère des Affaires Étrangères, Paris.

136. América Francès Otto to Louis Otto, Lesche, 17 Nivôse, An 7 (6 January 1799), Acquisitions Extraordinaires 135, Archives du Ministère des Affaires Étrangères, Paris.

137. *América Francès Otto* to *Louis Otto*, Lesche, 20 Germinal, An 7 (9 April 1799), Acquisitions Extraordinaires 135, Archives du Ministère des Affaires Étrangères, Paris.

138. *América Francès Otto* to *Louis Otto*, Lesche, 30 Messidor, An 6 (18 July 1798), Acquisitions Extraordinaires 135, Archives du Ministère des Affaires Étrangères, Paris.

139. *América Francès Otto* to *Louis Otto*, Lesche, 20 Brumaire, An 7 (10 November 1798), Acquisitions Extraordinaires 135, Archives du Ministère des Affaires Étrangères, Paris; and *América Francès Otto* to *Louis Otto*, Lesche, 30 Messidor, An 6 (18 July 1798), Acquisitions Extraordinaires 135, Archives du Ministère des Affaires Étrangères, Paris.

140. *América Francès Otto* to *Louis Otto*, Lesche, 20 Brumaire, An 7 (10 November 1798), Acquisitions Extraordinaires 135, Archives du Ministère des Affaires Étrangères, Paris.

141. Desan, *The Family on Trial in Revolutionary France*, 83.

142. *América Francès Otto* to *Louis Otto*, Lesche, 17 Nivôse, An 7 (6 January 1799), Acquisitions Extraordinaires 135, Archives du Ministère des Affaires Étrangères, Paris.

143. *Ally Crèvecoeur* to *Louis Otto*, Lesche, 16 Brumaire, An 7 (6 November 1798), Acquistions Extraordinaires 135, Archives du Ministère des Affaires Étrangères, Paris.

144. Letter to *Louis Otto*, Paris, 19 Thermidor, An 8 (7 August 1800), Acquisitions Extraordinaires 135, Archives du Ministère des Affaires Étrangères, Paris.

145. *Louis Otto* to his mother, 21 October 1803, Munich, in Raymonde Dunan, *L'Ambassadeur Otto de Mosloy, d'après des lettres inédites* (Paris: A. Pedone, 1955), 3.

146. "Une feuille volante," 18 January 1811, cited in Marcel Dunan, *Napoléon et l'Allemagne, Le système continental et les débuts du royaume de Bavière 1806–1810* (Paris: Plon, 1942), 455.

147. *Louis Otto* to *Fanny Otto*, 22 May [1795], Acquisitions Extraordinaires 188, Archives du Ministère des Affaires Étrangères, Paris. Otto turned down a diplomatic posting to the United States, citing his wife's health. In fact, his diplomatic career may have had more to do with his rejection of the post.

148. Stadion, 25 March 1807, cited in Dunan, *Napoléon et l'Allemagne*, 455.

149. *Louis Otto* to *América Francès Otto*, 29 June 1809, Munich, in Dunan, *L'Ambassadeur Otto de Mosloy*.

150. Mealy, *La Comtesse Pelet de la Lozère*.

151. Not so Otto's diplomatic career. In addition to his diplomatic correspondence and dispatches that are the subject of the next chapter, catalogued and filed in the Archives of the Ministry of Foreign Affairs in Paris, his grandson compiled a biography of Louis Otto in 1820. "When a man has occupied high posts in the service of his country, when he has represented it abroad and signed important treaties, his life

belongs to history," the grandson writes on the opening page. In contrast, América Francès de Crèvecoeur Otto has all but disappeared from the historical record.

152. Louis Otto, "Mémoire remise par le Sr. Otto," cited by Hill, *French Perceptions*, 162. Long before the French revolutionaries set out to remake the world on their own terms, historian Sarah Knott argues, social generation was an American project; Knott, *Sensibility and the American Revolution*.

153. Duke de la Rochefoucauld Liancourt cited by Armes, *Nancy Shippen*, 91.

CHAPTER 8. DECREES "IN THE NAME OF THE FRENCH REPUBLIC"

1. François Lanthenas cited by Yves Benot, *La Révolution française et la fin des colonies 1789–1794* (Paris: La Découverte, 1987), 197.

2. Nicolas de Condorcet cited by Michel Vovelle, *Les Républiques-soeurs sous le regard de la Grande Nation 1795–1803* (Paris: L'Harmattan, 2000), 13. See also Marc Belissa, "Du droit des gens à la guerre de conquête (Septembre 92–Vendémiaire an IV), in *Révolution et république: l'exception française: Actes du colloque de Paris I Sorbonne, 21–26 septembre 1992*, ed. Michel Vovelle (Paris: Kimé, 1994), 457–66.

3. Maximilien Robespierre, 2 January 1792, cited by Annie Jourdan, *La Révolution, une exception française?* (Paris: Flammarion, 2004), 220.

4. Joachim Heinrich Campe cited by Simon Schama, *Citizens* (New York: Vintage, 1990), 513.

5. The National Assembly had debated at length, in May 1790, who in revolutionary France had the right to declare war and peace. Constantin-François Volney claimed power for legislators to "deliberate for the universe and in the universe," resolving "that the National Assembly considers the entire human race as forming but a single and same society, whose object is the peace and happiness of each and all of its members"; Volney cited by David Bell, *The First Total War, Napoleon's Europe, and the Birth of Warfare as We Know It* (Boston: Houghton Mifflin, 2007), 103–4.

6. Bartolomeo Boccardi, 23 December 1794, Paris, Correspondance politique Genes 164, Archives des Affaires Étrangères, Paris; and d'Ange-Marie Eymar, January 1794, Mémoires et Documents, Italie 12, Archives des Affaires Étrangères, Paris.

7. Barthélemy Joubert to Garrau cited by Bell, *The First Total War*, 1: 45.

8. Eighty percent of French consuls kept the posts they had held under the Old Regime into the revolution. Stéphane Bégaud, Marc Belissa, and Joseph Visser, *Aux origines d'une alliance improbable: le réseau consulaire français aux États-Unis, 1776–1815* (Paris: Direction des Archives, Ministère des affaires étrangères: 2005), 29. See also Anne Mezin, *Les consuls de France au siècle des Lumières 1715–1792* (Paris: Ministère des Affaires Étrangères, 1997).

9. Charles Dumouriez to François Barthélemy, 27 March 1792, in *Papiers de Barthélemy*, ed. Jean Kaulek (Paris: Felix Alcan, 1886), 57.

10. François Barthélemy cited by Marc Peter, *Genève et la Révolution. Les Comités provisoires, 28 decembre 1792–13 avril 1794* (Geneva: Albert Kundig, 1921), 16; and François Barthélemy to Pierre Lebrun, 11 September 1792, Baden, in Kaulek, *Papiers de Barthélemy*, 1: 286.

11. Wolfgang von Goethe cited by Owen Connelly, *The Wars of the French Revolution and Napoleon, 1792–1815* (New York: Routledge, 2006), 31.

12. Charles Dumouriez, *Moniteur* 14 (1 November 1792): 367.

13. Charles Dumouriez, *Moniteur* 14 (21 November 1792): 21.

14. Alexandre Balza, *Moniteur* 14 (28 November 1792): 580. See Janet Polasky, *Revolution in Brussels, 1787–1793* (Brussels: Académie Royale de Belgique, 1986).

15. Charles Dumouriez to Jean Nicolas Pache, 6 December 1792, in A. Chuquet, *Lettres de 1792* (Paris: H. Champion, 1911).

16. Alexandre Balza and J. J. Torfs cited by Suzanne Tassier, *Histoire de la Belgique sous l'occupation française en 1792 et 1793* (Brussels: Falk, 1934), 136–37.

17. Charles Dumouriez, *Mémoires* (London: C. and G. Kearsley, 1794), 1: 89. The general subsequently suffered a defeat at the Battle of Neerwinden in the United Provinces in March 1793 and defected to the Austrians. He spent the next decade wandering through Europe, spawning intrigue, before he settled in England to advise the government in its war against Bonaparte.

18. P. J. Cambon, *Moniteur* 14 (18 December 1792): 759.

19. "Les Français aux Belges et les Belges aux Français," *Écrits politiques*, vol. 157, 173–74, Archives générales du Royaume/Algemeen Rijksarchief, Brussels.

20. Lettre de SMJ au Corps helvétiques, 19 September 1792, Registres du Conseil 300, Archives d'État de Genève, Geneva; and De Rochemont and the Conseil des Deux Cents, 21 September 1792, Registres du Conseil 300, Archives d'État de Genève, Geneva.

21. Anne-Pierre Montesquiou to Premier syndic de Geneva, Carouge, 10 October 1792, in Kaulek, *Papiers de Barthélemy*, 1: 337.

22. Anne-Pierre Montesquiou, 6 November 1792, in Albert Sorel, *L'Europe et la Révolution française* (Paris: E. Plon, 1887), 3: 125.

23. Convention, 8 November 1792, ibid, 3: 197.

24. Pierre Lebrun to Châteauneuf, 8 October 1792, Paris, in Kaulek, *Papiers de Barthélemy*, 1: 326.

25. Pierre Lebrun, 7 December 1792, cited by Eric Golay, *Quand le peuple devint roi* (Geneva: Slatkine, 2001), 91.

26. Merlin de Thionville, 8 January 1794, Paris, in Joseph Hansen, *Quellen zur Geschichte des Rheinlandes im Zeitalter der französischen Revolution* (Bonn: Peter Hanstein Verslagsbuchhandlung, 1931–38), 3: 7–8.

27. Einnahme der Stadt Trier durch die Französische Armee, 8 August 1794, Trier, ibid., 3: 173–75.

28. Proklamation der Zentralverwaltung des bestezten Gebiets zwischen Maaas und Roer an ihre Mitbürger, 4 November 1794, ibid., 3: 286–87.

29. Der Volksrepräsentant Gillet bei der Sambre und Maasarmee an den Magistrat der Stadt Köln, 10 October 1794, Cologne, ibid., 3: 259.

30. Bürgermeister J. N. Dumont an den Volksrepräsentanten Frécine, 17 January 1795; and Der Rat der Stadt Köln an den Nationalkonvent in Paris, 18 January 1795, ibid., 3: 354-58.

31. Der Volkspräsentant Bourbotte, 1 September 1794, Trier, ibid., 3: 213.

32. Abbé Sieyès, Traité de Paix, An 3, Mémoires et Documents, Allemagne 117, Archives des Affaires Étrangères, Paris.

33. Denkschrift von A. J. Dorsch uber die Länder am linken Rehinufer, in Hansen, *Quellen zur Geschichte des Rheinlandes im Zeitalter der franzosischen Revolution*, 3: 557.

34. *Moniteur* 21, 324: 433-34, cited by Marc Belissa, *Fraternité universelle et intérêt national (1713-1795)* (Paris: Éditions Kimé, 1998), 410.

35. Directory cited by Sorel, *L'Europe et la Révolution française*, 5: 70.

36. Napoléon Bonaparte cited ibid.

37. Napoléon Bonaparte cited ibid., 5: 76.

38. Delacroix cited ibid., 5: 74.

39. Lettres et instructions du Directoire executif relatives aux operations diplomatiques et militaires depuis le 23 prairial au 4 jusqu'au 28 thermidor, Mémoires et Documents, Italie 12, Archives des Affaires Étrangères, Paris.

40. Delacroix cited by Vovelle, *Républiques-soeurs*, 31; and Citizen Miot, 26 prairial, an 4, Florence, Mémoires et Documents, Italie 12, Archives des Affaires Étrangères, Paris.

41. Extrait du dépeche du C. Miot, Mémoires et Documents, Italie 12, Archives des Affaires Étrangères, Paris.

42. Axel von Fersen, *Dagbok*, cited by R. R. Palmer, *Age of the Democratic Revolution: A Political History of Europe and America, 1760-1800* (Princeton: Princeton University Press, 1964), 2: 331.

43. Die Mittelkommission to General Augereau in Strasbourg, 18 October 1797, Bonn, in Hansen, *Quellen zur Geschichte des Rheinlandes im Zeitalter der franzosischen Revolution*, 4: 229.

44. Der Kommissär to the Mittelkommission in Bonn, 13 August 1797, ibid., 3: 1112.

45. A. G. F. Rebmann cited by Marita Gilli, "La République de Mayence et les mouvements en rhénanie à la suite de l'occupation française," in *La Révolution française vue des deux côtés du Rhin/textes rassemblés*, ed. Andre Dabezies (Aix-en-Provence: Université de Provence, Aix-Marseille 1, 1990), 27.

46. Cited by Palmer, *Age of the Democratic Revolution*, 2: 440.

47. Leonard McNally cited by Nancy J. Curtin, *The United Irishmen: Popular Politics in Ulster and Dublin, 1791-1798* (Oxford: Clarendon, 1994), 180. See also Ultán Gillen, "Constructing Democratic Thought in Ireland in the Age of

Revolution, 1775–1800," in *Re-imagining Democracy in the Age of Revolutions: America, France, Britain, Ireland, 1750–1850*, ed. Joanna Innes and Mark Philp (Oxford: Oxford University Press, 2013), 149–61.

48. Rowan traveled to the United States as private secretary to the governor of South Carolina. He complained of his rough passage home, which found "my raccoon dead, my bear washed overboard, and my opossum lost in the cable tier"; Archibald Hamilton Rowan, *The Autobiography of Archibald Hamilton Rowan, Esq.* (Dublin: Thomas Tegg, 1840), 35, 191.

49. A.D.S.M I Mi 62/157/2095 cited by Marianne Elliott, *Partners in Revolution: The United Irishmen and France* (New Haven: Yale University Press, 1982), 155–56.

50. Napoléon Bonaparte to Charles Talleyrand cited by Thomas Pakenham, *The Year of Liberty: The Story of the Great Irish Rebellion of 1798* (London: Hodder and Stoughton, 1969), 29.

51. Earl Camden cited by Elliott, *Partners in Revolution*, 216.

52. Cited by Pakenham, *Year of Liberty*, 296, 299.

53. Cited ibid., 332.

54. To historian Marianne Elliott, the French invasions of Ireland definitively demonstrated that revolutionary France was less "the dispassionate saviour of popular tradition" than "a pragmatic European power fighting a bitter war at home and abroad"; Elliott, "The Role of Ireland in French War Strategy, 1796–1798," in *Ireland and the French Revolution*, ed. Hugh Gough and David Dickson (Dublin: Irish Academic Press, 1990), 220.

55. Sorel, *L'Europe et la Révolution française*, 5: 318. See also Theda Skocpol and Meyer Kestenbaum, "Mars Unshackled: The French Revolution in World Historical Perspective," in *The French Revolution and the Birth of Modernity*, ed. Ferenc Fehér (Berkeley: California University Press, 1990).

56. François Barthélemy to François Deforgues, 27 July 1793, Baden, in Kaulek, *Papiers de Barthélemy*, 2: 396.

57. Bacher to François Deforgues, 22 September 1793, Basel, ibid., 3: 76.

58. François Barthélemy, Baden, 3 November 1792, Correspondance politique Suisse 430, 18082, Archives du Ministère des Affaires Étrangères, Paris.

59. Brillat Savarin to Sam Hopkins, 1798, in "Unpublished Letters Written in English by Brillat Savarin and Benjamin Constant," *Modern Language Notes* 45, no. 1 (January 1930): 4.

60. Frédéric-César de La Harpe, 9 March 1798, in *Correspondance de Frédéric-César De la Harpe sous la République helvétique*, ed. J. C. Biaudet and M. C. Jéquier (Neuchâtel: Baconnière, 1982–1985), 2: 61.

61. Ibid.; and Frédéric-César de La Harpe to Talleyrand, 15 April 1798, ibid., 2: 285.

62. Frédéric-César de La Harpe to Reubell, 6 July 1798, ibid., 2: 468.

63. Frédéric-César de La Harpe to Corps législatif helvétique, 9 July 1798; and Frédéric-César de La Harpe to Reubell, 6 July 1798, ibid., 2: 475.

64. Registres du Conseil 313, Archives d'État de Genève, Geneva.

65. Sauter, cited by A. Rufer, *La Suisse et la Révolution française* (Paris: Société des études robespierristes, 1973), 104.

66. Napoléon Bonaparte cited by J.-R, Suratteau, "Ochs, Pierre," in *Dictionnaire historique de la révolution française*, ed. Albert Soboul (Paris: Presses Universitaires de France, 1989), 795.

67. Henry Dundas cited by David Geggus, "The Enigma of Jamaica in the 1790s: New Light on the Causes of Slave Rebellions," *William and Mary Quarterly* 44 (1987): 279.

68. "Discours préliminaire de la constitution de Saint Domingue," in Joseph Élysée-Ferry, *Journal des opérations militaires de l'armée à Saint-Domingue*, ed. Jacques Dussart (Paris: Éditions de Paris, 2006), 245.

69. Louverture did not bother to wait for Bonaparte's approval before he promulgated the new constitution, in what Srinivas Aravamudan calls "an exceptional coda to the eighteenth century"; Aravamudan, *Tropicopolitans: Colonialism and Agency, 1688–1804* (Durham: Duke University Press, 1990), 23. See also C. L. R. James, *The Black Jacobins: Toussaint Louverture and the San Domingo Revolution* (New York: Dial, 1938).

70. Bonaparte, Premier Consul de la République Française, to Citoyen Toussaint Louverture, général en chef de l'armée de Saint Domingue, 27 Brumaire, An 10 (16 November 1801), in Élysée-Ferry, *Journal des opérations militaires*, 257.

71. General Leclerc to General Christophe, 3 February 1802, in *Lettres du Général Leclerc, commandant en chef de l'armée de Saint-Domingue en 1802*, ed. Paul Roussier (Paris: Société de l'histoire des colonies françaises et Librairie Ernest Leroux, 1937), 61.

72. Bonaparte, "Proclamation. Les Consuls de la République aux habitants de Saint Domingue," 17 Brumaire, An 10 (8 November 1801), ibid., 63.

73. General Christophe cited by Carolyn E. Fick, *The Making of Haiti: The Saint Domingue Revolution from Below* (Knoxville: University of Tennessee Press, 1990), 216.

74. General Leclerc, 25 August 1802, cited ibid., 226.

75. General Leclerc to Bonaparte, 6 August 1802, in *Lettres du Général Leclerc*, 202.

76. See Ashli White, *Encountering Revolution: Haiti and the Making of the Early Republic* (Baltimore: Johns Hopkins University Press, 2010), 164–65.

CHAPTER 9. REVOLUTIONARIES BETWEEN NATIONS

1. Benjamin Franklin to David Hartley, Philadelphia, 4 December 1789, in Richard N. Rosenfeld, *American Aurora: A Democratic-Republican Returns; The Suppressed History of Our Nation's Beginnings and the Heroic Newspaper That Tried to Report It* (New York: St. Martin's Griffin, 1997), 496.

2. Thomas Jefferson to Thomas Paine, Paris, 11 July 1789, *The Writings of Thomas Jefferson*, ed. Albert Ellery Bergh (Washington, D.C.: Thomas Jefferson Memorial Association, 1903), 7: 405.

3. *Gazette of the United States*, 29 July 1789, cited by Beatrice Hyslop, "The American Press and the French Revolution of 1789," *Proceedings of the American Philosophical Society* 104, no. 1 (1960): 65.

4. "Mr Robespierre's Speech on the National Assembly of France," *Pennsylvania Mercury* 478 (December 3, 1789): 2.

5. Alexander Hamilton to George Washington, 14 April 1794, cited by Lloyd Kramer, "The French Revolution and the Creation of American Political Culture," in *The Global Ramifications of the French Revolution*, ed. Joseph Klaints and Michael H. Haltzel (Cambridge: Cambridge University Press, 1994), 31.

6. *Gazette of the United States*, 16 January 1793, cited by Rachel Hope Cleves, *The Reign of Terror in America: Visions of Violence from Anti-Jacobinism to Antislavery* (Cambridge: Cambridge University Press, 2009), 80. See also Seth Cotlar, *Tom Paine's America: The Rise and Fall of Transatlantic Radicalism in the Early Republic* (Charlottesville: University of Virginia Press, 2011).

7. L. E. Moreau de Saint Méry, "Rapport du Voyage aux États Unis," F3 123, Archives d'Outre Mer, Aix-en-Provence.

8. *Porcupine's Gazette*, 12 March 1798, cited by Carol Sue Humphrey, *The Press of the Young Republic, 1783–1833* (Westport, Conn.: Greenwood, 1996), 59.

9. Thomas Paine, *Common Sense* in *Thomas Paine: Collected Writings*, ed. Eric Foner (New York: Library of America, 1995), 36.

10. William Cobbett, cited by David Wilson, *William Cobbett, Peter Porcupine in America: Pamphlets on Republicanism and Revolution* (Ithaca, N.Y.: Cornell University Press, 1994), 3; and William Cobbett cited by Cotlar, *Tom Paine's America*, 101.

11. Thomas Paine, *Letters to the Citizens of the United States Upon his arrival from France* (Washington City: Duane, 1802). Paine laid the blame for the rise of partisan politics in America on "the clamours of anonymous scribblers" and "the fury of newspaper writers" who incited public opinion. Rather than applauding the freedom of the press, he placed his faith directly in the "large body of people who attend quietly to their farms, or follow their several occupations"; Thomas Paine, *Aurora*, 831 (19 November 1792): 2.

12. *The Herald: A Gazette for the Country*, 266 (12 December 1796): 3; and "From the Virginia Gazette," *The Republican*, Baltimore, 17 November 1802, 1.

13. Louis-Guillaume Otto, Comte de Mosloy, *Considérations sur la conduite du gouvernement américain envers la France depuis le commencement de la Révolution jusqu'en 1797* (Princeton: Princeton University Press, 1945), 23. These stories were picked up and reported up and down the East Coast. Paine, living in an apartment in the house of Nicolas Bonneville, a radical French journalist, rarely went out, preferring to receive guests including the Polish revolutionary, Thaddeus Kościuszko, the

Marquis de Lafayette, and Joel Barlow. He still did not speak French, so his contacts with French revolutionaries were limited. He did dine with Louis Sebastien Mercier, the author of the legendary utopian novel *L'An 2440*.

14. James Perhouse to John Perhouse, cited by Cotlar, *Tom Paine's America*, 1. Cotlar points to the irony "that two years after America had supposedly witnessed its democratic revolution with the election of 1800, the man who had spent his life articulating and popularizing some of the Atlantic world's most democratic principles had a hard time finding a drink in a town full of sailors"; ibid., 3. Many historians attribute his cold reception to his religious irreverence, while others point to the more radical politics of *The Rights of Man*. On Paine's homelessness, see Gordon S. Wood, "The Radicalism of Thomas Jefferson and Thomas Paine Considered," in *Paine and Jefferson in the Age of Revolutions*, ed. Simon P. Newman and Peter S. Onuf (Charlottesville: University of Virginia Press, 2013), 13–25.

15. Cited by Jack Fruchtman Jr., *The Political Philosophy of Thomas Paine* (Baltimore: Johns Hopkins University Press, 2009), 153.

16. Thomas Paine to George Washington in *The Political and Miscellaneous Works of Thomas Paine* (London: R. Carlile, 1819), 2:16. Paine accused Washington of having abandoned his principles. Joel Barlow added a private poem entitled, "Thomas Paine's direction to the Sculptor who should make the statue of Washington"; Jack Fruchtman Jr., *Thomas Paine: Apostle of Freedom* (New York: Four Walls Eight Windows, 1994), 318.

17. Cited by James Pula, *Thaddeus Kościosko: The Purest Son of Liberty* (New York: Hippocrene, 1999), 240.

18. *The Diary*, 21 August 1797, 1723; and *Aurora General Advertiser*, 19 August 1791, 3.

19. *New Jersey Journal*, 27 September 1797, 3. See also Della Durahadda, "Address to Kosciusko, Late Commander in Chief of the Armies of Poland, and Defender of the Rights of Man," in *The Bee*, New London, Conn., 20 September 1797, 4.

20. Cited by Pula, *Thaddeus Kościosko*, 240–41.

21. *Porcupine's Gazette*, 8 November 1798, 2. As if in response to the charge, Kościuszko directed in his will that his estate be used to set Thomas Jefferson's slaves free.

22. *Aurora General Advertiser*, 20 June 1798, in Rosenfeld, *American Aurora*, 159.

23. Anacharsis Cloots, in *Écrits révolutionnaires 1790–1794*, ed. Michéle Duval (Paris: Éditions Champ Libre, 1979), 458.

24. Anacharsis Cloots cited by Michael Rapport, *Nationality and Citizenship in Revolutionary France: The Treatment of Foreigners, 1789–1799* (Oxford: Oxford University Press, 2000), 2.

25. Among others, see Peter Sahlins, *Unnaturally French* (Ithaca, N.Y.: Cornell University Press, 2004).

26. Elkanah Watson, April 1780, *Journal A, 1758–1781*, GB 12579, box 2, folio 2, New York State Archives, Albany.

27. Joel Barlow, John Trumbull, David Humphreys, and Lemuel Hopkins, *The Anarchiad*, discussed in David Waldstreicher, *In the Midst of Perpetual Fetes: The Making of American Nationalism, 1776–1820* (Chapel Hill: Omohundro Institute of Early American History and Culture, 1996), 59–61.

28. Washington Irving, "Rip Van Winkle," http://www.bartleby.com/195/4.html.

29. Martin Luther King Jr., "Remaining Awake through a Great Revolution," Martin Luther King, Jr., Research and Education Institute, http://mlk-kpp01. stanford.edu/index.php/kingpapers/article/remaining_awake_through_a_great_ revolution/.

30. Naimbanna, *The Black Prince, A True Story: Being An Account of the Life and Death of Naimbanna, an African King's Son, who arrived in England in the year 1791, and set sail on his return in June* (Philadelphia: Benjamin Johnson, 1813), 6.

31. Ibid., 12.

32. Zachary Macaulay, 18 July 1793, *Journal, 1793–1799*, Papers of Zachary Macaulay, Microfilm, Abolition & Emancipation. Zachary Macaulay, the hated British overseer of Sierra Leone, published a narration of his trip after the death of "the Black Prince" to convince readers that the English had not poisoned him. In his will, reprinted in Macaulay's journal, John Frederick allegedly avowed his faith in the Sierra Leone Company and his opposition to the slave trade. His Temne family claimed, to the contrary, that on a paper found in his pocket book, John Frederick declared his faith that the Lord would deliver him from the "wickedness" and "filthy" oaths of the English ship's crew transporting him back to his homeland.

33. Noah Webster cited by Cotlar, *Tom Paine's America*, 101.

34. See Sophie Wahnich, *L'impossible citoyen. L'étranger dans le discours de la Révolution Française* (Paris: Albin Michel, 1997), 339.

35. Richard Price, *A Discourse on the Love of our Country* (London: R. Cadell, 1790). See also Mark Philp, "Revolutionaries in Paris," in Newman and Onuf, *Paine and Jefferson*, 137.

36. Miliscent, *Le Creuset*, 21 September 1791, cited in Yves Benot, *La Révolution française et la fin des colonies 1789–1794* (Paris: La Découverte, 1987), 196.

37. Thomas Paine, *Letter Addressed to the Abbe Raynal on the Affairs of North America: in which the mistakes of the abbe's account of the Revolution of America are corrected and cleared up* (London: J. Ridgeway, 1792).

38. Thomas Paine, *Maritime Compact* (1800), cited by Bernard Vincent, "From Social to International Peace: The Realistic Utopias of Thomas Paine," in *Thomas Paine: In Search of the Common Good*, ed. Joyce Chumbley and Leo Zonneveld (Nottingham: Spokesman, 2009), 66.

39. See Marc Belissa, *Fraternité universel et intérêt national (1913–1795)* (Paris: Éditions Kimé, 1998).

40. *Independent Gazetteer*, 5 January 1793, cited by Cotlar, *Tom Paine's America*, 50–51.

41. Immanuel Kant, *Idee zu einer allgemeinen Geschichte in welbügerlicher Absicht* (1784), cited by Jonathan Rée, "Cosmopolitanism and the Experience of Nationality," in *Cosmopolitics: Thinking and Feeling beyond the Nation*, ed. Pheng Cheah and Bruce Robbins (Minneapolis: University of Minnesota Press, 1998), 78. See also Seyla Benhabib, *Another Cosmpolitanism* (Oxford: Oxford University Press, 2006), 147–53.

42. Philipp Ziesche makes a convincing argument for the coherence and mutual dependence of nationalism and cosmopolitanism; Ziesche, *Cosmopolitan Patriots: Americans in Paris in the Age of Revolution* (Charlottesville: University of Virginia Press, 2010).

43. Peter Ochs cited by R. R. Palmer, *Age of the Democratic Revolution: A Political History of Europe and America, 1760–1800* (Princeton: Princeton University Press, 1959), 1: 364.

44. Amanda Anderson affiliates cosmopolitanism with "a vivid spectrum of diverse dialectics of detachment, displacement and affiliation." It simultaneously evokes the local and the global and is ever shifting; Anderson, *The Way We Argue Now: A Study in the Cultures of Theory* (Princeton: Princeton University Press, 2006), 78–79.

45. Mary Wollstonecraft, *Letters during a short residence in Sweden, Norway, and Denmark* (London: J. Johnson, 1796), letter 12.

46. Wollstonecraft, *Letters during a short residence in Sweden, Norway, and Denmark*, letter 12.

Acknowledgments

Revolutions without Borders marks the culmination of forty years of research and reflection on Atlantic revolution. Ever since I was an undergraduate sifting through boxes of handwritten letters in the Public Records Office linking the London Corresponding Society to French revolutionaries, I have wondered why historians would divide a transnational revolutionary movement into self-contained national stories. Two historians in particular encouraged me to continue as a historian to ask comparative questions. This book is dedicated to them, my undergraduate and graduate thesis advisers. Professor Carl Weiner at Carleton College and the late Professor Gordon Wright at Stanford University, both French historians, encouraged my forays into realms neither of them studied. They taught me that learning is a collegial, collaborative project. In courses on the French Revolution, May–June 1968, and on Marxism taught on both sides of the Atlantic, but also over spaghetti dinners and games of Risk, Carl Weiner taught me to ask questions and to seek connections. Together with his wife, Ruth, he has never ceased being my adviser. In graduate school, Gordon Wright's own wide-ranging scholarship inspired me to follow my curiosity about the Brabant Revolution in the neighboring Belgian provinces. As important as the model of his judicious, ever-balanced, and eloquent analysis, the generous humanity of his and Louise's mentoring and the meticulous care of his line editing are still with me in every page that I write.

The two volumes of R. R. Palmer's *Age of Democratic Revolutions* that defined the modern field of Atlantic history lived on the shelf of my

Stanford library carrel throughout graduate school. I am grateful to Professor Palmer, who unexpectedly emerged as my first defender, championing my challenge to his interpretation of the Brabant Revolution, and launching my first article on Atlantic Revolution into print in the *Journal of Modern History*. Publishers and colleagues, years later, suggested that I write a sequel to Palmer, including women and people of color, and ranging south to Africa and the Caribbean. Daunting as that task appeared, I also quickly realized that it would not have answered my questions about how revolutionary ideas traveled.

It was my students who showed me how to engage friends and neighbors asking about obscure eighteenth-century revolutionaries who dreamed of worlds never realized. A freshman general education seminar populated by future engineers got so involved in the Rare Books and Manuscripts department of the Boston Public Library handling original pamphlets and letters, some in French from Saint-Domingue, that they almost missed the train back to Durham. They reminded me of the excitement of the documents.

The revolutionaries I encountered in the archives ignored borders. Each set of documents led to another repository. Archivists and librarians in Albany, Amsterdam, Aix-en-Provence, Boston, Brussels, Cambridge, Massachusetts, Geneva, The Hague, Leiden, London, Louvain, Paris, Warsaw, and Washington, D.C., were more helpful than I had any reason to expect, especially as I was usually working under tight time constraints and eager to follow the trails they suggested that might lead to other sets of correspondence or decrees or pamphlets. In particular, Barbara Bair at the Library of Congress and Gregoire Eldin at the Archives du Ministère des Affaires Étrangères went above and beyond. I am also grateful to the Interlibrary Loan staff at the University of New Hampshire, who procured everything they could so I could also stay at home and work at my own desk, too.

Each of the nine chapters of this book not only took me to a different set of sources but exposed new questions and methodologies. I have been more reliant than is customary on the counsel and draft reading of other scholars. The readers who commented on individual chapters are so numerous that I am certain to forget some, but all deserve acknowledgment not only for saving me from errors but for steering me in directions I had not planned to take. I am extremely grateful to them all, including Nadine Berenguier, Jeff Bolster, the late Charles Clark, Alex Cronheim, Suzanne Desan, Marcela Echeverri, Bronwen Everill, Malick Ghachem, Dena Goodman, Lynn Hunt, Annie Jourdan, Sarah Knott, Mallory Murrell, Jeremy Popkin, Mary Rhiel, the late Jan Roegiers, David Troyansky, Laurel Ulrich, Carl Weiner, Ashli White, Serena Zabin, and an anonymous reader for Yale. Jeff Bolster not only read but reread, and then read again. Other scholars provided crucial advice at critical moments: Bernard Bailyn, David Bell, Jack Censer, William Chew, Natalie Davis, Rudolf Dekker, Ellen Fitzpatrick, Eliga Gould, Craig Harline, Bill Harris, Maya Jasanoff, Lloyd Kramer, Margriet Lacy, Jane Landers, Susan Lanser, Marc Lerner, Sarah Pearsall, Cassandra Pybus, Rebecca Scott, Henk te Velde, Lotte van de Pol, Nik van Sas, Judith Vega, Richard Whatmore, Ashli White, and Els Witte. In the Alternative History Annex on the third floor of the Horton Social Science Center, colleagues Jeff Bolster, Bill Harris, and Julia Rodriguez have shared every step on this book's path. Thanks to them and all of my colleagues in the UNH history department.

I have presented various chapters in varied venues and appreciate the questions and advice from fellow historians, students, scholars, and active retirees at the Flemish Royal Academy, Carleton College, the Durham Active Retirement Association, Katholieke Universiteit Leuven, Harvard University, the Graduate Center of the City College of New York, the University of Kansas, Ohio State University, and the University of Michigan. I have tried out tentative formulations of chapters at French Historical Studies, the Western Society for French Historical Studies, the Consortium on the Revolutionary Era, the William and Mary Quarterly–EMSI workshop, the Dunfey Conference on Networks in the Atlantic World, the American Historical Association, the Berkshire Conference, the Goethe Institute Conference on Liberalism, and the American Association of Netherlandic Studies. Special mention should go not only to the faculty seminar of the UNH history department, which over the years has defined the essence of collegiality, but to UNH students, from freshmen seminars to graduate colloquia, who have been assigned chapters and responded with invaluable insights and the occasional typo alert. The lively, insightful exchange of the Carleton History Department faculty seminar a few years ago reminded me why I started down this path.

Jeanette Hopkins helped me to frame my project with her probing questions. Fellowships from the National Endowment for the Humanities and the Flemish Royal Academy allowed me to finish my research and start writing. My fellow fellows in residence at VLAC, the Center for Scholarship in the Arts and Sciences directed by Professor Marc de Mey in the heart of Brussels, shared drafts, but also beers, dinners, coffees, and dish towels. The Reverend Lauren Smith's thoughtful sermon interweaving Martin Luther King and Rip van Winkle sparked the conclusion to my last chapter. Critical computer assistance from the Liberal Arts computer gurus, especially Dee Ann Dumas and Stormy Gleason, helped me all along the way, and averted disaster when my hard drive crashed two weeks before I had promised to submit the manuscript to Yale. Without them and the office staff in the history department, Jeanne Mitchell, Susan Kilday, Laura Simard, and Lara Demerest, I would never have finished this book. Deans Marilyn Hoskin and Ken Fuld have been incredibly supportive, as have my chairs, Jan Golinski and Eliga Gould. My neighbor and friend Debbie Needleman provided crucial assistance in locating illustrations and securing rights. At Yale University Press, Christopher Rogers's enthusiasm and understanding of my project has meant more to me than he could know. Not every author has the luxury of looking forward to e-mails from her editor. I also appreciate the wonderful team working at Yale, who have made the production of this book a pleasure, including Eva Skewes, once a UNH student; Erica Hanson, thoughtful, efficient, and able answerer of all questions; and Dan Heaton, a meticulous copyeditor with a sense of humor. Finally, I am once again grateful to Bill Nelson for realizing my sketchy ideas in his maps, and then tolerating multiple revisions. Thanks to David Lyons for timely indexing.

As every author acknowledges, it is family and friends who keep us going, on what is invariably a long slog, with conversations, walks, swims, kayak expeditions, bike rides, and cups of tea. Mary Beth Rhiel and Laurel Ulrich have talked me over hurdles along the way as we walked Portsmouth and Cambridge. Friends in Leuven—the late Jan Roegiers, Robert Brusten, Hedwig Schwalle, Melvyn Collier, Rita Schepers, Jeroen Nilis, Anton Barten, Herman and Monique van der Wee, Els Roeykens, and Eric Min—have once again housed me, provided access to libraries, and conversed late into the night over truly wonderful dinners.

My son, David Lyons, could have a second career as a writer, if he ever tires of his day job as a lawyer. His editing, his sense of the bigger picture, and the example of his perseverance made this a better book. My daughter Marta, an academic in her own right, has lent not only her ear through many a phone conversation but also her compassion and intelligence. My husband, Bill, witnessed this project from its beginnings in the Public Record Office in 1972 to its conclusion, and has tolerated all of the eighteenth-century revolutionaries who for the past decade not only have filled our house but came along on all of our vacations.

Index

abolitionism: boycotts, 87; British, 81, 86, 110, 112; Caribbean insurrection and, 92, 146, 149, 151, 155, 157, 159; fear of, 146, 149, 151, 155–57, 159, 165, 169; French, 88–89, 92, 149, 168; gradualism, 163; imperialism and, 76, 77, 92–93, 99, 105; as international movement, 86–90, 92, 94, 157; narratives on, 79; petitions in support of, 87, 167, 279; political connections, 58, 75, 128–29; religion and, 77, 86–87, 100; Swedish, 94

Act of Mediation of *1738*, 27

Act of Targowica, 131

Adams, Abigail, ix, 34, 207

Adams, John, ix, 7, 19, 34, 54–55, 112–13

Adams, John Quincy, 9, 59, 197–98

Aelders, Etta Palm d', ix, 120, 122, 277

Africa, idyllic picture of, 79–80; resettlement schemes in, 75, 92–110; and slave trade, 75

Aitken, Robert, 18, 20

American Revolution: and Brabant Revolution, 42; Burke on, 26; *Common Sense*, 22–23; contradiction of slavery, 58–60; disillusionment with, 266–67; and the Dutch Revolution, 25, 34; exceptionalism of, 26, 44, 50, 274; and exodus of slaves, 75–76, 83–84, 99–100; and French Revolution, 121; and Genevan Revolution, 30–31; as revolutionary model, 18, 44–46, 73,

103, 121, 126–27, 236; revolutionary travelers role in, 266–67, 277–78; transatlantic impact of, 26, 264–65. *See also* United States

Anderson, Isaac, 106, 109

Anglican Church, 86, 100–101, 104

Anglo-Dutch war, Fourth, 33, 278

Annis, John, 81

Arab Spring, 12

aristocracy: and despotism, 136, 231, 234; French, 58, 192, 219, 223; plunder by revolutionary armies, 243, 244–45

Armes, Ethel, 338*n*58

armies, imperial: counterrevolutionary activity, 41, 91–92, 108–9, 132–34, 136; intervention in Belgian provinces, 38, 41–43; threat to small republics, 36

Atlantic as world's highway, 273–74

Austria, 18–19, 37–38, 41, 42

Austrian Netherlands. *See* Belgian provinces

Bance Island, 96–97

Baptist Church, 83, 85, 104

Barbé-Marbois, François de, xi, 58–60, 149, 197–99, 277

Barlow, Joel, xii; and arrest of Paine, 213; courtship, 209–10, 335*n*6; diplomatic travels of, 213–14, 270; marriage to Ruth Barlow, 210; relocation to Altona, 213–14; return to America, 270; revolutionary activity of, xi, 212–13

Barlow, Ruth, xi, 68, 209–16, 270